CAHENA

WARRIOR QUEEN

Dov Silverman

Cahena: Warrior Queen
Dov Silverman

To find out more about Dov Silverman, visit dov-silverman.com

Published by The Writers of the Apocalypse
117 N Carbon Street, PMB 208
Marion, IL 62959
www.apocalypsewriters.com

ISBN: 978-1-944322-88-5

ALL RIGHTS RESERVED. This book contains material protected under International and Federal Copyright Laws and Treaties. Any unauthorized reprint or use of this material is prohibited. No part of this book may be reproduced or transmitted in any form or by any means, electronic or mechanical, including photocopying, recording, or by any information storage and retrieval system without express written permission from the author / publisher.

Cover and format by Katrina Joyner:
http://ebookcovers4u.wordpress.com

CAHENA:

WARRIOR

QUEEN

CHAPTER 1

THE MISSION

JERUSALEM'S HOLY TEMPLE, 67 CE

Rabbi Yochanan ben Zakkai ordered one of his scribes, "Bring Eliezer Ha-Cohen to me."

"You mean Shimi?"

"Why do you call him that?"

"It is short for Shim-Shon: Samson. That's who he looks like."

"He's more intelligent and pious than that backsliding breaker of oaths. Tell him to meet me at the gate of the Money Exchangers."

The scribe found Shimi Ha-Cohen squatting before a group of young people on the outskirts of the vegetable market, speaking in his calm modulated voice, "If it is written in the Torah that something is forbidden, it indicates we Jews were doing it."

"You mean we worshipped idols?" A boy asked.

"Of course. Didn't our high priest, Aaron, brother of Moses make a golden calf?" Without turning around to see the scribe, Shimi Ha-Cohen said. "Rabbi Yochanan calls me to meet him at the Money Exchange."

The scribe stood mouth agape, for he had not announced his presence or the message. He stared up at the giant before him. When the average man was five feet two inches, Shimi Ha-Cohen stood six feet five inches. He was broader than most men by half, and blessed with an extraordinary powerful physique. His labor was not physical, but he liked to run every day before the Morning Prayers. He would circle the Temple compound twice, bathe in the Mikva ritual pool, enter the Temple and recite the Shakrit prayers. He then assigned work to other priests and himself was given tasks as a Cohen Tzaddik—the second highest ranking of priest—for the daily sacrifices.

Shimi Ha Cohen went to meet the Rabbi. On his way, he unobtrusively slipped behind the money exchangers with their tables, scales, weights and measures. He watched from the shadow of the Temple wall as pilgrims from all over the Roman Empire came to exchange their coins for those acceptable in the Temple. Every day the rates of exchange were written on a black slate by the gate. Shimi checked this official chart on his daily run. The problem arose with pilgrims from small villages who had no teachers, and could neither read, nor write, nor do their sums.

Such a group approached an exchange table near Shimi, where they spoke Hebrew and Babylonian with the Exchanger. He smiled, joked, moved around stacks of shiny Temple coins on the table quoting a lower price for the exchange of Babylonian Darios, Siglios and ancient Drachmas from their families in Fallujah, Iraq. The Pilgrims sensed something wrong. They gathered their coins and were about to leave when the Exchanger signaled. A group of five ruffians forced the pilgrims back to the table.

Shimi stepped forward, grabbed the money changer by the scruff of the neck and the seat of his pants, lifted and whirled him over his head then threw him against the stone wall of the old city. Everyone else within sight froze in shock. In a calm, even tone he addressed the men from Fallujah, quoting the advertised rate of exchange —and adding ten percent in their favor for their troubles.

By the time he had completed the exchange, the money lender regained consciousness, staggered to his feet and shouted to the ruffians, "Get my money or you don't get paid!"

The five toughs tried to vault the table to attack Shimi, but were stopped in mid-leap. The heel of the High Priest's left hand crushed the nose of one man, Shimi's right fist broke the jaw of a second man, and the sound of broken bones stopped the other three. They grabbed their injured fellows and scuttled away.

"I have chosen well," said Rabbi Yochanan ben Zakkai, who had seen the whole incident.

The renowned Rabbi smiled, and his light blue eyes danced under a high brow and balding head. He adjusted the conical hat identifying him as a member of the Sanhedrin, and motioned for Shimi to follow. People fell back in respect.

"You wish me to go on an extended journey," Shimi commented as they walked away.

"I've warned you about revealing your gift of second sight. You could be accused of sorcery or witchcraft."

"I don't try; it just happens," Shimi said. "I just know things. I don't know how I know them or why. Do you think it is prophecy?"

"We don't need another prophet," said the Rabbi. "Anyone can predict problems for Israel. Vespasian has been named the new commander of the Roman Legions in Israel."

"I too foresee very difficult times ahead."

"Keep your visions to yourself. I want you to leave Jerusalem."

"I know."

"Quiet! If you interrupt again, I'll tweak your

large ear through the market place. You are going to Bosor, Ramoth and Golan."

"The three Sanctuary cities east of the Jordan. May I take my family?"

"Don't you know the answer?"

"Yes."

"Then why did you ask?"

"To show respect."

"Ah, so. You will adjudicate those who seek sanctuary for unintentional manslaughter as opposed to those who committed murder. Murderers will not be punished in the city, but set outside the walls. If the families of the dead wish, they may take retribution."

"Why did you choose me?"

"I didn't and I wouldn't. The Sanhedrin did. Your scholarly achievements, intelligence and common sense are even greater than your strength. All of those will be required to reach your destinations and fulfill your duties."

"Do you think my visions of the future are corruptive?"

"I hope you can resist the temptations of your revelations."

"How long do you estimate I and my family will be gone?"

"Three to five years. You will gather witnesses, ascertain their integrity, in some cases have to visit the site of the alleged crime. And please don't throw anyone else against the wall."

"You wish me to make a good impression."

"You always make an impression."

"Will I have the power to excommunicate corrupt judges?"

"Are you saying that some of our Rabbis are dishonest?"

"If there is a law against it, then it must exist."

"If you find corruption and can't correct it, send the offender to us. The Sanhedrin will decide."

The Rabbi raised both his hands, Shimi lowered his head, and Rabbi Yochanan ben Zakkai pronounced, "May the Lord bless you and keep you. May He shine his countenance upon you. May you and your children's children walk all your days in the paths of righteousness for His name's sake. Amen.'"

Shimi visited the temple treasurer, who had him sign for a purse of gold drachmas to cover living and travel expenses for his wife and five sons. He sold his house near the Temple Mount for a tidy sum, bade his parents farewell and departed. Forbidden by Roman law to carry sword or dagger, Shimi walked with a shepherd's crook the size of a small tree. His priestly robes were bound at the waist by a braided rope, with a stone the size of an apple woven into the end. He wielded these weapons when necessary.

Even when traveling in an official caravan with professional guards, life on the road could be dangerous. It was one of the reasons Vespasian now commanded Judea. The other was that Emperor Nero had proclaimed himself a god. He had ordered his statue placed in the Holy of Holies, in the Temple, for the Jews to worship, and all Rome knew the Jews would fight. Vespasian was chosen because of his victories in Britain and Gaul. Nero also saw his general as contender for the Curule Chair, and Jerusalem was two thousand miles from Rome. The Jews would distract Vespasian.

For three years the General remained occupied with the Jewish revolt. He was a persistent but patient man. His troops probed here and there avoiding major confrontations. He allowed the Jews to argue, then fight, then kill each other over whether to oppose the Roman Legions or sue for peace. The Zealots won. It was war. On the ninth of the month of Av in the year 70 C. E, the Roman legions broke into the Temple and slaughtered everyone. They looted, burned, then tore down the Judaism's most holy edifice.

Rabbi Yochanan ben Zakkai made a secret agreement with Vespasian prior to the Temple's destruction. He told the Roman General that one of his high priests had a vision of Vespasian being crowned emperor. He predicted Nero's death and Vespasian's installation, and Shimi Ha-Cohen's prediction came to pass. The General allowed the rabbi and several students to found a school in the town of Yavneh, a coastal town twelve miles south of the port of Jaffa.

The Jews were devastated by the destruction of the Temple. Survivors went into exile where, like sheep, they followed whoever led. Most went to Babylon, Iraq. Many just scattered, feeling that God had abandoned them. Some believed God had lost his power, and they turned to local Pagan gods. Others believed they were being punished, and became more religious.

Droves of Jews fled across the Jordan River into Africa, where often they were welcomed by local kings or tribal chieftains. Most Jews knew how to read and write. Beleaguered by Christians to accept Christ, Jews were encouraged by Pagans to teach reading, writing and arithmetic. These transplanted Jews practiced and preached the laws of Moses. But preaching was a two way street, and Pagans preached to them. The Pagans saw the advantages of Judaism but rejected three major stipulations: painful male circumcision, loss of a day's work once a week by keeping the Sabbath, and the laws of kosher food. The Jews found Pagan gods less restrictive, more forgiving and easily adaptable. Through time and inter-marriage, Jews were equally influenced by Pagans and Christians, as they were by fellow Jews.

The sun and moon shone day and night for five hundred and forty-two years on the descendants of Shimi Ha-Cohen, the priestly line being conferred from father to son. There was never another like Shimi. Stories were told of his judgments in Israel, his feats of strength, and ability to see the future. He remained on the African side of the Jordan River with his family, and his offspring were welcomed into wandering Bedouin tribes. They moved with the Bedouin, Berbers, Tuaregs and nomads of the desert, teaching reading, writing, and arithmetic, and continuing their religion as outlined in correspondence with Rabbi Yochanan ben Zakkai and his disciples in Yavneh.

After almost five and a half centuries, neither the illustrious Rabbi nor Shimi would have recognized many of the religious observance of those Jews and Nomads who called themselves the Sons of Abraham. They worshipped Yahweh, the one and superior God, the Virgin Mary and a host of Pagan deities. Portions of the Torah were read aloud on market days in the Suks. Because of the Jews many Pagan tribes became literate in Hebrew, Latin and Berber.

In the year 612 CE, on September 8th at six in the evening on the plains of the Maghreb in North Africa, the Sabbath was about to begin.

There came a high-pitched scream from the midwife's tent. It was a breech birth. The baby was so large that the mother hemorrhaged and died. Fear gripped the midwife. She did not bring the child to its father; knowing the intense love he had for his wife, she feared he might kill the child. Instead, she entered the tent of Moshe ben Shimi Ha-Cohen, who was about to inaugurate the Sabbath. He looked at the midwife standing empty-handed and obviously distraught, and asked quietly, "Did they both die?"

"Only one," the woman almost whispered.

"Which?"

"Miriam, your wife."

The rabbi gave a long sigh. "Bring the lad."

"You have a very large daughter."

Moshe twitched in recognition. "My wife knew it was a girl, and knew the birth would kill her. Miriam Ha-Cohen was renowned for her piety, learning, and visions of the future."

"Had she told me in time," the midwife said, "I could have aborted the child and saved her."

The rabbi shook his head. "My wife saw signs of this baby being special. This child will lead the Sons of Abraham to glory. Bring her. The sun is going down. My daughter will celebrate the Sabbath with her father."

Moshe Ha-Cohen blessed the wine, dipped his pinky into it and placed it on the lips of the child. The baby sucked greedily and cried for more. Her father recited the benediction over the show-bread, blessed the child and asked, "How will she be fed?"

"I can try a goat."

"What about the woman who gave birth this morning?"

"Her child was still-born."

"She must have milk."

"I'll see.'"

The midwife was gone before Moshe could ask her why she hadn't thought of it first. She hurried across the sparse grass to the visitor's tent and had a nervous coughing fit. The woman she approached came from a small Berber tribe, and had been found wandering in the desert. The still-born child was grotesquely deformed and quickly buried. The midwife had learned this and more while helping with the ordeal of the still-birth, and no one else knew.

The mother's milk was needed. The newborn baby of Moshe ben Shimi Ha-Cohen was the largest child she had ever seen, and survival in normal births was tenuous enough. The baby required mother's milk to live. The midwife paused outside the visitor's tent, took a deep breath, pushed aside the flap and entered—pulling out her curved, razor-sharp dagger. The bereaved mother was a small figure wrapped in a blanket, sitting in the center of the tent, leaning over a fire-pan as if trying to draw heat from it. She looked up. Her skin was almost white, and her large dark eyes were sunken with dark circles under them. She was twenty years old but appeared fifty. Her voice sounded older. "Put away that pig sticker," she gestured toward the knife. "You need my milk for the child."

The midwife drew a deep breath. "I swear by the gods Yahweh, Isis and Baal, I will cut your throat if you ever reveal you were sent to die in the desert for witchcraft."

"How do you know I am not a benevolent witch?" The woman dropped the blanket from her shoulders and patted her hunched back. "This is the mark of good luck. It was tribal politics that doomed me, people fighting over power, not my predictions or magic."

"Whatever it was, that is the past. Will you suckle the headman's child? Will you care for her as her own mother would?"

"I swear by all the gods to obligate myself, body and soul, as if this is my own daughter whom I lost. I will teach her of the Free People."

"Teach her magic and I'll cut your heart out." The midwife brandished the knife.

"Bring the child."

"Moshe ben Shimi is leader of this tribe. Don't order me or anyone else. We are the Free People." The midwife sheathed her dagger, stepped closer and said. "You are a slave."'

"I too am Berber."

The midwife slapped the woman so hard she fell over sideways. "You are what I say you are!"

She stalked from the tent and returned with the baby. The hunchback undid the swaddling and presented her swollen left breast to the child. The moment the Witch of the Maghreb suckled the infant, the child stopped crying and gave the most beatific smile to the wizened face.

"How shall I call her?"

"She has no name until the seventh day from her mother's death," the midwife said. "It is the custom of the Sons of Abraham. Call her, Child.

There will be a celebration, and she will be named."

The Witch of the Maghreb undid her shawl and presented her second breast. 'Child' drained it quickly, and fell asleep.

Prior to the naming-ceremony, Ozeret—the witch of the Maghreb—spoke again to the midwife. They entered Moshe Ha-Cohen's tent together.

"Listen to what this wretch has to tell you," the midwife snapped. "After hearing, if you agree, I will cut her heart out."'

"That would be a bad omen on this festive occasion," Moshe noted.

Ozeret the hunchback bowed and said, "I have sworn to dedicate my life to your daughter. She is special."

"My wife foresaw that."

"And I foresee great things in her life."

"What is it you want to tell me?"

"I was sent out into the desert to die because I am a witch."

"I know," Moshe said, "But you are the only one with mother's milk."

"But now there are at least three women in the visiting tribes with milk," the midwife cut in.

"But this one saved my daughter's life."

"She has a request," the midwife grumbled.

"Let her speak."

"What name have you chosen?'" Ozeret asked.

"Miriam, for her mother."

"For your daughter's safety, call her Miriam—but in your heart, name her Dihya."

"What have you foreseen?" Moshe asked.

"Satan will know her as Miriam. To work his evil he must know her true name. The name Dihya must remain secret, never spoken aloud by anyone, including Dihya."

"Will she have a good marriage?"

"She will not marry her intended. So it is foretold, but your daughter will be the greatest Berber who ever lived."

Flutes tambourines and drums sounded outside the tent. Ozeret carried the child, and followed Moshe and the midwife from the tent.

Miriam Ha-Cohen was buried in a hole dug into the ground, lined with rocks. Her body had been washed in the Hebrew tradition, then painted with ochre in the Berber tradition. Placed in the fetal position, she was lowered to the bottom of the hole facing Jerusalem. Moshe Ha-Cohen, priest and tribal chieftain, said Hebrew, Christian, and Berber Prayers.

There were two visiting tribal delegations led by Selim, the tribal chieftain. Selim was accompanied by a Roman Centurion from the city of New Carthage. All filed dutifully past the grave, dropping a stone onto the body to prevent wild animals from digging up the grave, until the hole was filled.

Moshe Ha-Cohen called, "Ozeret," and she handed the child to him. He placed it on the fresh turned earth of the grave and said the simple Kaddish for the dead: "*Y'hay shmai rahba mvorak l'olam l'olamai olamaiyah, yitbarak.* May your great name be blessed forever and ever, Amen."

The centurion and the chieftain of the visiting tribes took their places next to Moshe. The centurion said, "In the name of the Roman Empire and the Emperor Heracles, we bless this child about to be named. We approve of the marriage arrangements to be announced. The emperor's gift is a free education to your new daughter when you believe she is capable of learning. Her expenses in New Carthage will be assumed by the state." The centurion handed a scroll to Moshe who tucked it in his belt.

Then Moshe clasped both hands of the other chieftain, and they stepped on either side of the grave looking down at the child. Moshe ben Shimi Ha-Cohen spoke, "I pledge this daughter of mine in marriage to your son, future King of the Helawi, and the combining of our tribes under your son's leadership as King of the mountain Berbers."

The chieftain motioned his son forward. "My son Ali is fifteen. When your daughter reaches that age she will become his wife. My son will take my place as leader, and I will prepare for them two thrones. My son will be King and your daughter Queen of the Amazigh Berbers."

The festivities lasted seven days. The departure of the visiting tribesmen was celebrated with true joy, for they were a rough group, haughty in their attitude to the Jrawa tribe and everyone else. They ate as if food was something they hadn't known for years. The joke in the tents of the Jrawa was that four of the visitors were caught each eating one leg of a live camel, and they hadn't removed the hair. These ruffians brought little food, but barrels of cheap Roman wine and animal bladders full of beer—and they drank it as if they had hollow legs.

"Will you now name your daughter?" The centurion asked.

Moshe ha-Cohen raised the child to the sun and intoned, "I enter my daughter into a covenant with God." He recited in Hebrew, Berber, and Latin blessings for the baby's wellbeing. "Please God, bless this child. I name Miriam Cahena for her mother, may her eternal soul be free in the Garden of Eden with the righteous of Israel and all peoples. Bless my daughter that she may study Torah and be a light unto her people by the performance of good deeds." He then whispered in his heart, "I truly name my daughter Dihya. Protect her from satanic influence and evil advisors."

Her father wished Miriam to be a student of the Hebrew Law and lead her tribe and people, for Berber women had the same rights as men, and in marriage even more power. Berber society was matriarchal; women had the right to marry who they desired and divorce without cause. Some were known to replace husbands once a year. Women farmed, did blacksmithing and animal husbandry, fought beside their men as warriors, sat as judges in territorial disputes, and cases of theft, robbery, and murder.

Miriam/Dihya Cahena's education began at the first opportunity Ozeret had. It wasn't Torah.

She took the child from the festivities to her tent, tied the flaps closed, and performed her own ceremony initiating the newborn into the ancient, secret, league of magicians and soothsayers. The ritual was brief. It consisted of undressing the child, submerging her in water, passing her quickly through fire, pricking the palm of her right hand, mixing the blood with ashes from the fire and several drops of honey, then putting it on Miriam's lips. The child's little pink tongue tasted, then swallowed.

To be discovered would mean death for Ozeret. She pledged the child in the names of Moses, the Virgin Mary, Jesus, the Sun and the Moon, and the wizened hunchback vowed to teach all her skills to this special child. She then pulled from her pocket the ear of a goat that had been slaughtered for the feast. She undid the tent flap, went outside, and with her back to the tent she threw the ear over the tent and said, "Oh gods on high and below, bless this child. Please watch over my daughter's soul, and I will watch over this future queen of the Berbers."

Growing up in the Atlas Mountains was an experience of wonder and discovery. Berbers were the Free People; they wandered where and when they wanted. Ozeret taught this to Cahena. She also taught that Berbers, like most nomads, followed their sheep, goats, camels and horses to the seasonal grazing grounds. The child smiled and said, "Daddy follows the horses."' The child was phenomenal in growth, intelligence, and physical coordination. She was also beautiful.

By chance her father discovered her ability as a natural healer. She was only three months old when she placed her little hands on her father's elbow, which was covered by a thick gray rash. He felt the warmth of her hands and a blissful pain that caused him to moan. His baby daughter withdrew her hands, and the gray hard crust crumpled like ashes onto the carpet. The skin was red but soon lost its angry color, and was smooth with no sign of inflammation. He promptly summoned Ozeret.

"I told you she is special."

"She will be a healer?"

"Much a more than that. Your daughter will learn to control people by thought, influence the weather, and see the future."

"These things are against Mosaic Law. Are you teaching her magic?"

"Never!" Ozeret lied. "She is naturally gifted. Your name is Moshe *ben Shimi*."

"Yes, Shimi was my father's name," Moshe admitted, squirming a bit.

"It is a famous name. They tell stories about the strength and wisdom of Shimi the Great, some hundreds of years ago. They say he foretold the future."

"He was a special person, and a student of Rabbi Yochanan ben Zakkai."

"Your daughter is also special. I believe she inherited Shimi's soul."

"That's witchcraft! I should beat you."

"You won't."

"Why won't I?"

'You hit me, and the neighbors will scold you for scattering garbage." Ozeret grinned.

"Leave!" Moshe ben Shimi chuckled. "Teach my daughter something about Judaism."

The little that Ozeret knew about Jews she never imparted to Miriam Cahena. The girl was taught Hebrew and Torah by her father, who was the most learned in these subjects.

At the age of nine Miriam was as tall as her father and most men in the tribe. Her skin was light and creamy, with the Caucasian features of the Amazigh of the mountains. Her eyes were large, wide-set, provocatively slanted, and either piercing gray or unfathomable opaque, depending on her mood. Her hair was thick, long, and ebony-black with a slender feather of a silver streak from over the right eye to behind her ear. People believed this was the mark of an oracle, but no one spoke of it openly. Twice Moshe cut the silver hair away, but it grew back. He tried to have her wear a turban, but she refused. From infancy the child knew what she wanted in food, dress, or actions, and would fight anyone—including Ozeret—to get her way. When she smiled those around her smiled. She beamed and people unconsciously responded. She was a natural leader and center of attention by virtue of her aura.

CHAPTER 2

REVELATIONS

NINE YEARS LATER:

Ozeret questioned Moshe ben Shimi about the newly arrived centurion from Carthage. He decided to inform everyone. He invited the village chiefs and opened his tent to all.

The tribe had moved down to the foothills of the Atlas Mountains for the winter. The weather was warm, dry and sunny, and the evenings cool with a refreshing breeze. Moshe ben Shimi's tent was lit by torches. Tent flaps were rolled up and people sat outside on the grass.

"The centurion," said Moshe, "Is the representative of Emperor Heracles in Constantinople."

"Is it true he also gave you a pouch of drachmas in addition to the scroll of education for your daughter?" A woman asked.

"Yes. One hundred gold pieces. I bought two racing camels so we can compete in the spring roundup."

Everyone agreed the two racing camels was a good idea. They disliked those sons of jackals from the other tribes who ate them out of house and home. "Forgive us, Moshe Ben Shimi, but your daughter will be marrying into a tribe of unlearned, pigs." The crowd murmured agreement. "Why was the Roman so generous?" another woman asked.

"He arranged the marriage, and is trying to form a confederation of nomad tribes in the Maghreb."

"Against who?"

"The Muslims."'

"What does Constantinople want from us?"

"That is why I summoned you. Since the fall of the Western Empire in Italy, a hundred and fifty years ago, Romans in Constantinople stand alone against the Gothic barbarians from the west and the Arabs from the east."

"But Arabia and the Muslims are closer by land to Constantinople than through the Maghreb and the sea."

'Muhammad's followers tried that and failed,' Moshe explained. "They had to go through Iraq, Iran and Syria, over three mountain ranges— and then fight Romans, their Christian allies, and Pagans, the whole length of Turkey to reach Constantinople. They laid siege to the city, but it was useless. Their lines of supply and communication were unsustainable. They retreated."

"It appears that the Muslims are going in the opposite direction, invading Algeria to reach Constantinople."

"You are correct," Moshe answered.

"Are they in that group of Arab thinkers who believe the world is round?" a man asked. The people laughed and made jokes about standing upside-down and the water emptying out of the seas.

Moshe unrolled a large Roman map of the middle-east, Africa and Europe. Two boys held the zebra-skin map aloft, and Moshe used his Toledo steel saber as a pointer. "By going west from the Arabian Desert, the Muslims enter Egypt where they pick up more volunteers for their religious crusade in Libya. Except for the Tuaregs and other desert tribes, Moslems control the cities. They will be hosted along the way and enlist more recruits for their holy war against Christianity."

"Where in the hell are they going?" a woman warrior-chief demanded.

"Tangiers."

"I've been there," the woman said. "If all us Berbers pissed at once, we could wash that town into the Mediterranean Sea."

The crowd applauded and Moshe waited for quiet. "When the Muslims retreated from Constantinople, they immediately made a plan to attack again, this time by sea. They have set up shipyards in the port of Tangier. They commissioned the Italians in Sicily to build a fleet of fighting ships, to escort the troop and supply ships to Thrace, then patrol and control the Mediterranean, Tyrrhenian, Adriatic, Ionian and Aegean Seas."

The crowd was hushed by the enormity and commitment of such a plan.

A girl asked, "Where is Thrace?"

'In Bulgaria, less than a half mile across the water from Constantinople. The people there were converted to Islam. Encouraged by General Khalid ibn Al Walid, they are preparing for this invasion. All trade to and from the Mediterranean, Aegean and Black Seas will be controlled by the Muslims. The Arab lines of communication and supply will be secured. The Silk Road and all trade from China will end in Gaza. The Arabs will strangle Christian Constantinople and control the entire Middle East with easy access to Europe."

"Maybe we should join them," a chieftain said. "The Romans must have some idea of what's going on."'

"That is who informed me," Moshe said.

"The Emperor in Constantinople wants us to oppose the invasion of the Maghreb by the Islamic forces."

"You mean cut them off from Tangiers?"

"Yes. We in return will receive monetary rewards from the Romans—plus slaves, lands and booty captured from the Muslims. We will obtain preferred shipping prices in the seven seas. We will also control and collect all import and export taxes from the Maghreb to the sea."

"What do the Muslims offer?" another man asked.

"I don't know enough about them," Moshe said. "Muhammad began preaching only a few years ago. I have invited the storyteller and Berber historian Abu Abak. He will explain Islam."

The people muttered, excited. They knew of Abu Abak as the most famous storyteller in the Maghreb. "When will he arrive?' several voices asked.

"November."

"This year?"

"With God's help."

Abu Abak wandered into camp two weeks later.

He was greeted with honey, bread, and salt in the tent of Moshe ben Shimi, who sent messengers to other tribes about the lectures on

Islam. It was an unusual winter gathering. Tribes were designated special areas to camp because of blood-feuds. Everyone had to swear not to steal, maim, or incite during the gathering. The most problematic tribe was the Helawi, into which Moshe's daughter Miriam would marry. Moshe didn't care for his daughter's future father in-law, and managed to avoid him.

Abu Abak had Moshe appoint men and women with powerful voices to stand thirty meters apart in the crowd and repeat his words so all could hear. To have such a gifted orator was an unexpected and pleasurable distraction for the tribes in winter quarters. There were four thousand men and women seated in a semicircle on the ground in front of a raised platform. Torches lit the area. Moshe led Abu Abak onto the stage. He was greeted by cheers from the men and high pitched undulating exhortations from the women.

Abu Abak was tall for a Berber, thin, fifty years old, and his dark piercing eyes were always darting to emphasize a point or evoke an answer. His voice sounded as if it came from his toes through mahogany-lined lungs. It reverberated with a resonance of truth. He could modulate his speech to the sound of a soft flowing stream, or boom it out like a clap of thunder. The people settled back to listen.

"I usually begin by saying, 'Give me a silver coin, and I will spin you a golden story'. I then speak about djinn and genies. But tonight your leader, Moshe ben Shimi Ha-Cohen, requests I tell you about a man.

"I may appear a little down in the mouth. On my entrance into this camp, a little puppy ran out to greet me. I petted it and it appeared thirsty, so I gave it some wine. The little dog lapped the bowl dry, looked up with a glow in his eyes, his pink tongue curled and tail wagging. Suddenly the glow left the eyes, the tail stopped wagging, the mouth closed and the dog began running in circles around my camel. He stopped, and rolled over on his back with four feet in the air, stiff as a board. '

The audience sighed and many said, "He died! Poor dog."

"No," boomed Abu Abak. "He ran out of wine."

It was the kind of humor Berbers prized. They laughed at themselves for being taken in.

The storyteller of the Maghreb then said, "Muhammad is the name of the man I will speak of. He claims to be the last and most important prophet of Allah, the one and only god. Forty-two years ago in Medina, Muhammad was born—a pagan like us. His father died before his birth. His mother was frightened by the predictions of a witch, that her child was consecrated to Satan. His mother gave him to be raised by a wet nurse named Amina bint Wahab. Believing the baby was possessed by demons, Amina returned Muhammad to his mother—who died two years later. He was taken in by his grandfather for two years—and the grandfather died. All the deaths were premature, but natural. His uncle Abu Talib took the child. He raised and educated the boy. Muhammad shows no signs of superior skills or intelligence. He was trained by his uncle to be a merchant. The uncle arranged a marriage of convenience for Muhammad with a distant cousin. She is forty-two: a wealthy, twice-divorced woman with two sons and a daughter. Muhammad is twenty-five years old. Initially, the couple is not well suited. She is wealthy, so he remains subservient—and resentful."

"Why didn't she divorce him?" A woman shouted.

"The people of Medina and Mecca are not free like Berbers and Tuaregs. Women in the cities do as men tell them."

"Don't try that in the Maghreb."

"That is why I am a lonely bachelor. To continue the story, in the year 610, Muhammad receives his first revelation."

Someone shouted, "They have revelations

and messiahs every week in Jerusalem."

"These Jesus freaks are a pain in the ass," another replied.

"And may you Jews be infected with lice of the crotch, with arms too short to scratch."

"Son of a donkey! I piss on the rocks you pray to!"

Abu Abak covered his ears and waited for silence. From the dark outside the camp a jackal barked, a hyena laughed, and the crowd quieted. The storyteller of the Maghreb continued. "There is much consternation about Muhammad's revelations and dreams. The sections are known as the Satanic Verses. They refer to dreams Muhammad had, in which an angel told him to worship three Pagan goddesses: Ellāt, Uzza, and Manāt."

"I have two of those statues," a man called out. Others expressed familiarity with these goddesses. Abu Abak ignored them and continued.

"The Meccans were pleased that this crazy prophet finally recognized their gods. The Muslims were upset, thinking Muhammad could be another irrational prophet: first he proclaims one god, then several more. But Muhammad later revealed that the angel Gabriel visited him and explained. The angel who taught him to worship idols was actually Satan. Muhammad took up his ministry in earnest and recanted. He preached that these particular verses were Satanic. He was to study them and understand the devious methods and forms the devil can take."

"So our goddesses are devils?" a woman growled.

"A year ago Muhammad was preparing to go to bed. He claims to have been taken by the angel Gabriel from Medina to Jerusalem in one night."

"That's a hell of a distance in so short a time," another woman said. "He must have grown wings on his feet."

'Not on his feet," Abu Abak answered. "There were wings on his horse. It was a remarkable animal called Buraq."

"Did the horse tell Muhammad his name?" a chieftain asked.

"No, the angel Gabriel did. Gabriel had to help Muhammad mount this magnificent steed. '

"No horse could make it to Jerusalem in one night," someone said, and others murmured their agreement.

"His was an enchanted horse sent by God," Abu Abak replied. "He was large, pure white, with wings sprouting from his hindquarters. One step, and he traveled as far as the human eye can see."

"You said it was nighttime," a man challenged. "Can both horse and man see in the dark?"

"Some of my stories are from my imagination. Tonight, at the request of your tribal leader, I am telling you about a man who believes he spoke with God and traveled to the seven heavens, where he was instructed by the prophets Abraham, Isaac, Jacob, Moses and Jesus. God then dictated the Holy teachings to him which he is to teach to the world."

"Why did God choose him?"

"I don't know and Muhammad doesn't either. The Angel Gabriel did test him. He offered the prophet a jug of wine, one of milk and one of water. Muhammad drank the milk. He passed the test. Thus all wines or intoxicating beverages are forbidden to Muslims."

"That settles it!" one man shouted. "I'll keep my wine, and the Prophet can keep his religion."

"What happened in the heavens?" people asked. "Where did he land in Jerusalem?"

"Both are very good questions. I will save them for tomorrow night."

The storyteller of the Maghreb accepted a goblet of wine from Moshe ben Shimi, and bowed to the audience. The Amazigh responded with cheers and rattling of sabers in appreciation.

The tribesmen retired to their campsites for the evening meal. Abu Abak was hosted in Moshe ben Shimi's tent, along with tribal elders and Selim, chieftain of the Helawis, the future father-in-law of his daughter Miriam.

The sides of the main tent were rolled up. Men and women sat on carpets. Wild shouts emanated from the dark, and five horsemen and women galloped full speed out of the dark toward the tent. They reined in their horses at the tent, and the horses reared back on their haunches in a cloud of dust, and pawed the air. The people applauded. The riders dismounted and joined the guests. Music came from out of the dark: drums, tambourines, flutes, lutes and voices raised in song of the Amazigh Berbers. The musicians followed by prostitutes formed a semi-circle and serenaded the gathering. Prostitution was considered as respectable a profession as any other. They were looked on as desirable wives, and most married before the age of eighteen.

Moshe ben Shimi addressed his guests, "Tonight we are blessed with the presence of the Storyteller of the Maghreb, Abu Abak." He bowed to the older man. "Sir, on behalf of all those who attended your most informative and interesting talk, I thank you. My people thank you. On behalf of all the tribes here tonight we bid you long life and pleasant dreams."

Abu Abak looked up at Moshe ben Shimi. "I thank you for your expression of appreciation, but my stomach is empty and howling for food." The crowd roared its approval.

Moshe ben Shimi clapped twice and from four sides of the large tent entered boys and girls carrying platters of couscous, followed by tajine—a meat stew with vegetables—that was plucked from the tray with the right hand, rolled in the couscous and deposited in the mouth. This was followed by *pastille,* a traditional meat pie and bread. Then small trays of *bouchiar,* a thin wafer, and *boucher,* a light pancake, both soaked in butter and honey. Moshe ben Shimi invited the various chieftains to address the people. He saved the most honored positions for his future son-in-law and father in-law. When the fifteen year old stood it was clear he was nervous. He kept looking at his father as if asking permission for what he was about to say. His voice was weak and his face and stance indicated he'd rather be somewhere else. The best part of his hesitant speech was its brevity. His father boomed out the name of his tribe: "We the Helawi are the bravest warriors, have the fastest horses and strongest camels in the Maghreb!" And he elaborated from there.

Abu Abak leaned over and whispered to Moshe ben Shimi, "The man is so full of himself his eyes are brown."

"What has that got to do with the color of his eyes?"

"He's full of shit up to here." Abu Abak pointed to his eyebrows.

Moshe almost fell off his cushion laughing. His future father-in-law looked down and said, "What I just stated was fact. It wasn't funny!"

"Excuse me," Moshe said. "Your presentation interested everyone. Nowhere else could we have received such a deep explanation of the glorious history of the Helawi tribe. To close the talks for the evening, I call upon our honored guest the storyteller of the Maghreb." The people sighed in relief that Moshe had cut his future father-in-law short.

Abu Abak stood and said, "I fear our host has deprived our last speaker from making known a very important historical fact: how the Helawi tribe got its name.

The Helawi chieftain beamed at the storyteller, "It has always been a mystery to me. Please enlighten us."

"In days long past," Abu Abak began, "Your tribe was a group of aimless wanderers like the Bedouin of today. Your people weren't so numerous or powerful as they are today. Larger tribes forced them from oasis to oasis further into the Sahara desert where temperatures bake thornbushes dry. But one thing your tribe was always proud of was who they were. They proclaimed it from sand dune to sand dune... At least that is what the other tribes thought they were saying: 'We are the Helawi.' In fact, they were asking, 'Where the hell are we?' The other tribes named you. You are still lost amongst the Amazigh Berbers."

A hushed silence like that before a sand storm embraced the audience. Then a woman broke out laughing. Others joined her. The laughter became so infectious and ribald people held their sides or each other to prevent themselves from rolling on the carpets. They laughed so hard tears rolled down their weathered cheeks.

The Helawi chieftain attempted to maintain his dignity in the face of such an insult. His son said, "Father your face is turning purple." The chieftain looked at his tribesmen in the tent. They sat stiff and stony faced. He could walk out. This would mean retreat in the eyes of all Berber warriors. Or he could join the laughter. He was intelligent enough to know if he chose the former it would break the marital arrangements for his son. He needed the alliance with the Jrawa tribe of Moshe ben Shimi to cement the relationship with Roman Constantinople. He threw back his head and laughed. He slapped Moshe ben Shimi on the shoulder and bowed to the storyteller. The Helawi tribesmen took the cue from their chieftain and laughed.

Moshe was keen enough to recognize their faces were laughing but their eyes burned with hate.

That night Abu Abak slept in Moshe ben Shimi's tent, and six of Moshe's finest warriors stood guard through the night. There was a distinct possibility of a Helawi tribesman attempting to satisfy the public insult to his people.

The night passed peacefully. Moshe's spies reported no unusual activity in the Helawi camp. And the second evening Moshe had the musicians and prostitutes arrive early to alleviate any tension. The atmosphere was convivial when Abu Abak began to speak. The audience settled in as his rich, deep-throated voice reached those at the edge of the tent.

"I am often asked what I do when not telling stories. The answer is, I collect them—from people like you. Every human being has at least one story worth repeating. And so it was after a good night's rest and breakfast shared with Selim and his son, leaders of the Helawi tribe, I strolled from Moshe ben Shimi's tent and struck up a conversation with an old camel herder. We were talking about our camels, how well trained they were, what food would get the most speed over the longest distance, when he said: 'My camel can go 110 Roman miles on one refill at the oasis.' Now every child knows a camel can only carry 100 liters of water. And every camel on this good earth only gets one mile to the liter. I told him so. He answered, 'It's all in the way the camel drinks the water.'

"'What do you mean?' say I. 'You bring the animal to the oasis and he drinks. That's it!'

"'You've got to brick him,' says he.

"'What does that mean?' I ask.

"The old fellow reached into his saddle bag and pulled out two bricks. He said, 'You sneak up behind the camel while he's drinking. When he's about to take his last gulp, you slam the bricks together on the camels balls. Whoosh! The animal inhales ten extra liters!'

"'Doesn't that hurt?' I asked?

"He replied: 'Not if you keep your fingers out of the way'"

The crowds roared with laughter. A chant arose from the guests, and the musicians and singers joined in. Belly dancers gyrated among the guests who sang:

"Abu Abak, Abu Abak, Abu Abak, his fame is well earned.

Abu Abak, Abu Abak, his stories will be learned.

Abu Abak, Abu Abak, Abu Abak.

His stories will be told by the fire.

Legions of Amazigh they will inspire.

Abu Abak, Abu Abak, Abu Abak."

The storyteller bowed in acknowledgement. "Friends and fellow tribesmen," he said, "Yesterday evening I told you Muhammad made the trip from Medina to the Temple Mount in Jerusalem. From there he went to heaven. All in one night."

"Where did you learn this?" a warrior asked.

"From the Muslims' holy book, the Quran, Chapter 17 verse 1. *Glory to Allah who did take his servant for a journey by night from the sacred Mosque (the Ka'ba in Mecca) to the farthest Mosque, in Jerusalem. He is the One who hearest and seeth all.'* Your question is a good one. For this is the only thing in the entire Quran written about this momentous journey. The remainder of what you hear comes from the Hadith. '

'What is that?'

"Hadith means report. The way Muslims refer to it, they are reports by friends, relatives and companions of Muhammad relating to his visions."

"Was what you are telling us a dream, vision, or an actual trip?"

"I don't know. It is not written in the Quran that Muhammad went to heaven. That trip is described by others in the Hadith."

"You say he went to the furthest mosque in Jerusalem. But there is no mosque. There is not even a temple of the Jews. The Romans burnt it to the ground."

"Which mosque did he leave from in Mecca?" asked another woman.

"The Ka'ba."

"But that's our shrine, to Elah-ga-Baal. It's pagan!"

"The Prophet wants to throw out all pagan images and idols. He wants it dedicated it to Allah."

"I'll cut that Muslim's head off and shit down his neck!"

"Several attempted to do it. His god protects him."

"He never had a big balls Berber come after his ass.'"

"Tell us about his trip to heaven. What did he see? Who did he meet?"

"The mosque in the Hadith refers to the holy site in Jerusalem where once stood King Solomon's temple. The word mosque doesn't refer to a building; it means a place of prostration to God. Muhammad tethered his horse Buraq there and prayed to God. Muhammad's journey was in two stages. The first, called *Isra,* his ride from Mecca to Jerusalem. The second, called *Mi'raj,* his trip to heaven. You all recognize the Arabic word meaning, to ascend. Those who speak Latin will recognize 'mirage' as a Roman word, meaning mirror– or a trick the eyes play on one in the desert, when you see reflected in the air an oasis or city that isn't there. Much has been said and written about Muhammad's MI'raj. For Muslims his journey to heavens is more than an act of faith; it is a fact. His detractors say he was smoking too much hashish."

"Get on with the story."

"A cup of wine first," Moshe said, and signaled the young people who poured wine from goat skins for the guests.

Abu Abak refilled his cup, drained it and continued his recitation. "Muhammad's trip to Paradise is not mentioned in the Quran. It is called the seven *samaawat* (تاوامس), traditionally meaning heaven, derived from the Hebrew word *shamayim* (םימש). Allah created the *samaawat, the heavens*—sun, moon, stars and so on. He completed them as seven firmaments in two days, and he assigned to each heaven its duty. 'And he adorned the lower heaven with lights, and provided it with guards. Such is the Decree of the Exalted in Might, Full of

Knowledge, that ye may know Allah has power over all things, and that Allah comprehends all things. See you not how Allah has created the seven heavens one above another.'[1]

"Each of the seven heavens is described as being composed of a different material, and Islamic prophets are resident in each. The first heaven is made of silver, and is the home of Adam and Eve, as well as the angels of each star. The second heaven is made of gold, and is the home of John the Baptist and Jesus. The third heaven is made of pearls or other dazzling stones; Joseph and Azrael are resident there. The fourth heaven is made of white gold, or platinum; Enoch and the Angel of Tears reside there. The fifth heaven is made of silver again; Aaron and the Avenging Angel hold court there. The sixth heaven is composed of garnets and rubies; Moses can be found here. The seventh heaven is composed of divine light incomprehensible to mortals. Abraham is a resident of the seventh heaven.

"But what is heaven like?

"Ahaa!" Abu Abak said, and put his wine-cup aside. "The descriptions of paradise are mentioned in the Qur'an and Hadiths. Paradise is

---

[1] "Quran 71:15 (Yusuf Ali) Seven Heavens: From Wikipedia, the free encyclopedia, abridged

described as surrounded by eight principal gates, each level generally being divided into a hundred degrees. The highest level is known as *firdaws,* sometimes called Eden. It will be entered first by Muhammad, then those who lived in poverty, and then the most pious. Entrants will be greeted by angels with salutations of peace.

"'They shall enter gardens of perpetual bliss and angels shall enter unto them from every gate with greeting: "Peace unto you for that ye persevered in patience! Now how excellent is the final home!"[2]

"The Islamic texts describe life for its immortal inhabitants as: one that is happy—without hurt, sorrow, fear or shame—where every wish is fulfilled. Traditions relate that inhabitants will be of the same age, and of the same standing. Their life is one of bliss, and includes wearing sumptuous robes, bracelets, and perfumes as they partake in exquisite banquets served in priceless vessels by immortal youths, as they recline on couches inlaid with gold or precious stones. They will eat delicious food and drink, and every bowl will have a new taste. They will take eructation which will digest the food and there will be perfumed sweating for the diges-

---

[2] Qur'an, sura 13 (al-Ra'd), ayat 23-24'

tion of water. Inhabitants will rejoice in the company of their parents, spouses, and children—provided they were admitted to paradise—conversing and recalling the past.

"Other foods mentioned include meat and aromatic wine, which is non-intoxicating and brings joy to those who drink. The dwellings for inhabitants will be pleasant, with lofty gardens, shady valleys, fountains scented with camphor or ginger, rivers of water, milk, honey and *Sharabun Tahoora* (pure drink), with trees bearing delicious fruits of all seasons.

"One day in paradise is considered equal to a thousand years on earth. Palaces are made from bricks of gold, silver, and pearls, among other things. Traditions also note the presence of horses and camels of 'dazzling whiteness', along with other creatures. Large trees are described, mountains made of musk, between which rivers flow in valleys of pearls and rubies.

"The names of four rivers are *Saihan (Syr Darya), Jaihan (Amu Darya), Furat (Euphrates) and Nil (Nile). Salsabil i*s the name of a spring that is the source of the rivers of Rahma—mercy — and Al-Kawthar—abundance. Sidrat al-Muntaha is a Lote tree that marks the end of the seventh heaven, the boundary where no creation can pass.

"In spite of the goodly dwellings given to the

inhabitants of paradise, the approval of God and closeness to him is considered greater. According to the Qur'an, God will bring the elect near to his throne *('arsh),* a day on which 'some faces shall be shining in contemplating their Lord.' The vision of God is regarded as the greatest of all rewards, surpassing all other joys." [3]

"I understand the men receive seventy-two beautiful virgins?" a man asked.

'What about us women?" a warrior-chieftainess asked. "Do we get seventy-two well-endowed young men?"

"According to the Holy teachings," Abu Abak said, "Women are chattel. They can be bought, sold, divorced or abandoned as the man sees fit."

"We'll have none of that shit around here," the female warrior sneered.

"Speak for yourself," a man said. "It sounds right to me. How do I get the virgins?"

"You've got to die a Muslim, fighting for Islam," the storyteller said.

"How do I get into Islam?"

"Belief in just one God, Allah."

"That's it? I can get seventy-two virgins for

---

[3] Seven Heavens: From Wikipedia, the free encyclopedia. Descriptions of Paradise abridged.

just believing in one god?"

"No, that gets you into Islam. There are eight entrances to heaven."

"You mean I must be dead before I get the girls?"

"And," Abu Abak held up four fingers of each hand, saying, "You must also fulfill the criteria to enter one of the eight gates to Paradise. Those who believe in the Qur'an, and those who follow the Jewish scriptures, and the Christians and the Sabians— 'any who believe in Allah and work righteousness, shall have their reward with their Lord; on them shall be no fear, nor shall they grieve.'"

"If they accept the Jews, why did they kill all the Jewish men, women, and children in Medina?" a woman chieftain demanded. "We are part Jewish. Would they have killed us?"

"Probably," Abu Abak said. "Muhammad has a temper. At first he accepted the Jews and Christians as believers in one god. He was prepared to teach them Allah's new way, and expected them to flock to Islam. They politely told him to shove it up his camel's arse. Muhammad got angry. That is where the world of Islam—*Dar el Islam*—and *Dar el HaRab*—the world of war, are revealed. Either you swear to Allah alone as your god, or you die. That is why he killed the Jews. Most Christians converted."

"I don't care how I die: Jew, Christian or Pagan. How do I get the virgins?"

"The eight doors to heaven are only open to those Muslims who are...

"1. *Bāb al-Ṣalāh*: punctual in prayer.

"2. *Bāb al-Jihād*: took part in jihad.

"3. *Bāb al-Ṣadaqah*: gave charity.

"4. *Bāb al-Rayyān*: who fasted (*siyam*).

"5. *Bāb al-Ḥajj*: participate in the annual pilgrimage to Ka'ba in Mecca.

"6. *Bāb al-Kāẓimīn al-Ghayẓ wa-al-'Āfīn 'an al-Nās*: withheld their anger and forgave others.

"7. *Bāb al-Aymān*: by virtue of their faith are saved from reckoning and chastisement.

"8. *Bāb al-Dhikr*: For those who showed zeal in remembering God. [4]

"Being punctual in prayers originally meant praying fifty times a day."

"That's a lot of praying! I wouldn't have time

---

[4] Seven Heavens: From Wikipedia, the free encyclopedia. Descriptions of Paradise abridged.

for all those virgins."

"You'd be dead," Abu Abak said. "But on his return journey through the heavens, Muhammad met Moses, who advised him to ask Allah to reduce the times of prayer. They bargained down to five times a day. It is called *Salat*. So:

"•*Salat al-fajr:* prayer before sunrise,

"•*Salat al-zuhr*: midday,

"•*Salat al-'asr:* in the afternoon,

"•*Salat al-maghrib*: just after sunset, and—

"•*Salat al-'isha*: between sunset and midnight."

"That's still a lot of praying."

"That's what you must do to get the virgins."

"What does it mean, you go directly to heaven if you die in jihad?"

"It refers to a holy war. If you die in a war against the infidels you go straight to heaven."

"And get the women?"

"Yes."

"Who are these infidels?"

"You. Or your neighbors. Or anyone who is not Muslim."

"Does that mean if I become a Muslim and kill myself I go to heaven, drink, feast and fornicate?"

"I'll send you to hell myself," the woman chieftain said. "Shut up and listen to the man."

"Muhammad answered that question," said Abu Abak. "'Did ye think that ye would enter Heaven without Allah testing?' The Qur'an also asserts that those who reject the Prophet of God are damned in the afterlife to hell."

"No virgins in hell?"

"Rarer than a rose growing out a camel's ear. Did I ever tell you the story about the Pagan who died and went to heaven?" The storyteller of the Maghreb waited for his audience to settle in. "This well-to-do merchant died and arrived at the gates of heaven. There he met an angel who was keeper of the gate. 'What must I do to enter heaven?' the merchant asked.

"'Nothing,' the angel replied. 'You are judged by your actions during your life on earth. You may enter. Try it out for a week and then make your decision. '

"'You mean I get a choice?'

"'Yes.'

"'Between heaven and what else?'

"'Hell.'

"'Who wants to go to hell?'

"'You'd be surprised. You can also try that for a week and then make a decision. '

"A week later the merchant returns to the gate and asks the angel if he could try a week down in hell.

"'With pleasure,' the angel replied. In a flash the merchant was standing before a great wooden door. From the other side he heard the soft whisper of many voices repeating over and over, 'Don't make a wave. Don't make a wave.' He tried to reason what could be on the other side of the door. Satan bowed to the man and pointed to the iron door ring. The merchant took hold of the ring and pulled. The door opened. He was struck by music so loud it almost knocked him down. Men and women were drinking, dancing, fornicating and performing weird sexual acts. Food was in abundance and for the taking. He smiled at Satan and jumped into the melee.

"A week later he appeared before the Angelic gatekeeper, who asked, 'Have you decided?'

"'Without a doubt, heaven is the most tranquil place I have ever known,' the merchant said. 'But in hell it is one continuous party. I had a wonderful time. I've decided on hell.'

"'Your decision is for eternity.'

"'I hope so.'

"The angel waved his hand and the merchant was standing before Satan and the door. Once again he heard the repeated dirge from the other side of the door, 'Don't make a wave. Don't make a wave.' The merchant bowed to Satan and asked, 'May I enter?'

"Satan smiled and he pulled the iron door ring. The massive door swung open on a vast room stretching to the horizon. It was filled with people standing in a sea of piss, shit and corruption up to their lower lip saying, 'Don't make a wave. '

"'May the gods have mercy!' the merchant shouted. This is not what I found before!'

"Satan grinned and said, 'That was for the tourists.'

"'It's not fair!' the merchant screamed. 'I have to spend eternity here!'

"It's not so bad now. ' A pitiful voice cried. 'Wait until Satan comes by in his sailboat!'"

It took the audience five minutes to stop laughing and begin singing a drinking song in honor of the Storyteller of the Maghreb.

> "Here's to your health Abu Abak
>
> "May your life be as old as the sacred Ka'ba rock.
>
> "Here's to your health through thick and thin.
>
> "The wineskins are empty so fill them again."

Abu Abak raised his hand for attention and

said, "More or less I have told you about Muhammad and Islam. However there is another man you should be aware of. He is called the Sword of Allah."

"Khalid ibn Al Walid," the warriors shouted. "He's a great Pagan general."

"No longer Pagan," Abu Abak said. "He is now a companion of Muhammad and devout Muslim."

"How can that be?" the warriors demanded. "Khalid defeated the Muslim army in the battle of Uhud. He even wounded Muhammad."

"Khalid wasn't the commander of the Pagan army," the storyteller replied. "He was in charge of the cavalry. His tribe from Mecca was more numerous, but the Muslims more spirited. They wished to die in *jihad,* and had defeated a larger number of Pagans in battle before."

"They wanted the virgins," a warrior called out.

"What they got was defeat. They did not adhere to the Prophet's battle plan. Muhammad placed his smaller force on the plain facing the larger Pagan army. To the right rear of the formation was a hillock on which the prophet placed his archers. They were instructed to cover the Muslim army's right flank and rear. The commander of the army was given specific orders not to move from under the archer's protection. The battle began. The Muslims fought with such ferocity the Pagans began to retreat. The Muslims followed and started looting the Pagan camp. They left the protection of the archers. The archers wanted to loot and joined them.

"Khalid, the Pagan general saw this. He led his cavalry to attack the Muslim army in the rear. The archers were too far away to help. Fear, then panic spread among the Muslims. They broke and ran. Khalid recognized the Muslim's panic. He personally led a picked group of fighters to capture Muhammad. He succeeded in wounding the prophet. When the Muslim army heard, they thought god abandoned them and fled.

"In this battle, Khalid's older brother was captured by the Muslims. It took Khalid some time to pay the ransom and free his brother. On the return journey his brother spoke of Muhammad and the one god of Islam. Khalid was impressed. He always felt there had to be one superior god. He didn't realize how deeply Muhammad influenced his brother while in captivity. The brother left during the night on the fastest camel and returned to become a devout Muslim. This influenced Khalid to learn more about Islam. His studies were interrupted when his Pagan army of ten thousand men, six hundred horses and a camel corps were ordered to lay siege to Medina. Muhammad had three thousand fighting men. He prepared the city for battle. They brought in all the crops and livestock they could. They stored water and fouled the wells outside the city. Every tree and shrub within a five mile radius was cut down or pulled out by the roots. All unharvested crops were burnt in the fields. Muhammad ordered a deep, wide trench dug in front of the city. The trench ran from the mountains on the right to the mountains on the left. Behind the trench were the high city walls. Enemy foot soldiers would have to somehow cross the trench while under attack by archers, slingers and ballistae. The enormous trench rendered Khalid's cavalry useless. The weather helped the prophet. The cold winter winds of January and February made life miserable for the besieging army. Twenty-seven days later the Pagans packed their tents and abandoned the battle of the Trench.

"Khalid ibn Walid used the siege time to study Islamic writings. Through spies, and his brother, he arranged a meeting with the Prophet. It was agreed he and the prophet would rendezvous in a tent outside the walls of Medina, but on the inside of the trench. His older brother greeted him at the tent entrance and introduced Khalid to the prophet.

"This is enough for tonight. We shall meet again tomorrow when I will complete the tale of How Khalid Ibn Al-Walid Embraced Islam."

"Tell us another joke so that we may laugh ourselves to sleep," A warrior pleaded.

"I have no more puns. But there is a Muslim anecdote. You may recall that a Muslim is allowed four wives?"

"And he can divorce them when and where he wants," A male warrior called out.

A female chieftain replied, "Be quiet, twerp, or I'll divorce your head from your shoulders."

"My lady..." Abu Abak responded.

"I'm no lady. I am a chieftain of the Amazigh Berbers."

'Be that as it may. This young wealthy Muslim had four wives, each more beautiful than the next. His father was dying and called his first son to his bedside. 'Son' he said, 'there are two family heirlooms, one for you and one for your brother. As the elder, you have a choice.' 'Thank you, Father. I wish to have the hour glass.' 'I prefer you choose the Toledo Sword.' 'Father the hour glass once belonged to the prophet himself. I can use it to call people to pray.' 'My son, what happens when you one day you return early with your caravan and find one of your beautiful wives in bed with another man? Are you going to show him the hour glass and tell him it's time for prayer?"

CHAPTER 3

CAHENA

"Why did you request we dine alone?" Moshe ben Shimi asked.

Abu Abak stroked his goatee and said, "I'm, a storyteller. My stories come from the people whose tribes I visit. I've heard whispers about Cahena."

"My daughter?"

"Yes."

"What do they say?"

"She is a healer, can read peoples thoughts and tell the future. She can make things appear and disappear with the snap of her fingers."

"Do they call her a witch?"

"I never heard that word mentioned. They say she is as strong as a grown man—and taller than most."

"You saw her."

'When?'

"The last two evenings, she brought you the wine."

"She has a silver streak in her hair?"

"That's my daughter."

"I can't believe she is only nine."

"She is also intelligent beyond her years. Give her a tool and she masters it. Musical instruments the same. She composes music and writes words."

"At age nine?"

"No. She started at six. Her language skills are even more impressive. She speaks Arabic, Berber, and Latin. Since the Romans in Constantinople instituted Greek as the official language, she is one of the few in our tribe who is fluent in that language."

"Can she read and write?"

"She even learned hieroglyphics from an Egyptian."

"Does she realize how special she is?"

"She accepts her gifts as normal. Yet she is not haughty."

"You must be proud to have such a daughter."

"Sometimes I wonder if she is my daughter. Her mother had foresight; she could tell the future. My father's namesake, Shimi Ha Cohen, five hundred years ago, had some of her attributes. He was a high priest and judge in the Sanhedrin at the holy temple in Jerusalem. She talks to animals. The elders elected my nine-year-old to be in charge of our camel herd. The animals listen to her."

"Did you ever hear her speak with a camel?"

'Of course not. She does it with thought, not words. I watched her scold the largest animal in our herd, and I swear the camel began to cry."

"Moshe ben Shimi, you have a problem."

"I am hoping to solve it by sending her to New Carthage three years early, to be educated."

"It sounds as if she will educate the Romans."

"Would you like to meet her?"

"Absolutely!"

"We will go to her tent. There is something I wish to show you."

The two men made their way to what was a strange building. It looked more like a Mongolian Yurt or South African Ronda Val than a Berber tent. It was round, and the thatched roof was tied down with a tent-cover of animal skins. To enter, the two men passed through a vestibule protruding from the building. Boots were left at the entrance. Moshe ben Shimi held aside the interior flap for Abu Abak. The warmth and smell of a green forest greeted him, accompanied by a cacophony of bird-calls and whistles.

A young girl stood in the center of a menagerie of birds. She was stripped to the waist, her petulant little breasts glistening with perspiration. She placed the forefinger and ring finger of her right hand to her lips and whistled. There was silence. All the birds in the Yurt fastened their eyes on her. "I've been expecting you," she said. "Will you have some tea?"

"Yes," her father said.

"And you, Master Storyteller, will you have oolong or yasmin?"

"How could you know we were about to visit you?"

Al Cahena answered with an indulgent smile and said, "I recommend the yasmin."

"Yes, of course. But where do all these birds come from?"

"The Maghreb."

"How did you catch them?"

"They come to me."

"How did you transport them from the plains into the mountains?"

"They flew."

"By themselves, and returned to you?"

Al Cahena giggled like any other girl of nine. "How else would they get here?" She pointed up to the smoke hole in the roof. "They are free to come and go as they like." At that moment the sound of flapping wings overhead announced a brown spotted falcon. It flew to a perch on a trapeze suspended from the ceiling.

Cahena opened her mouth and emitted a high screech from the back of her throat. The hawk fluttered his wings looked right and left then flew out the smoke hole and was gone.

"What just happened?" Abu Abak asked.

'He knows this place is not for him. He remains outside with the hawks, eagles, and other birds of prey. That one is special. He actually captures small birds and stores them alive until he's ready to eat."

Abu Abak scratched his head, tugged his beard, and said, "I cannot believe I am having this conversation with a nine person—Please excuse me. I meant to say a nine-year-old person."

"At least you call me a person. Most refer to me as a child. If I were born in China I would be ten years old. They consider time in the womb as another year."

"And what a difference a year makes."

"Have you ever seen carrier pigeons?"

"I heard the Romans use them."

"I am trying to train my hawks and falcons to bring down pigeons."

"Why?"

"We will one day fight the Romans."

"How do you know?"

"I just know." Her stance and tone were petulant.

For fear she might stop talking, Abu Abak asked, "May I see your homing pigeons?"

"I keep them outside. They are very dirty birds."

Behind the Yurt was a large cage made of split bamboo. There were nesting places for the birds and straw on the floor. Cahena made a deep throated sound, opened the cage door and plucked a bird from the flock. "This is Marta. She is my fastest flyer."

"But you can only send her back from the field to this cage? You couldn't send a message to me on the caravan trail or another village."

"I've been told it is possible. I haven't tried it yet. Would you like to help?"

"What must I do?"

"I'll give you several birds when you leave camp. Your caravan will average about twenty miles a day. You release one every day for five days. When the bird arrives, I won't feed it. It should return to you where it has been fed before."

"Will you use Marta?"

"She'll make the last and longest flight of a hundred miles."

"How long will that take?"

"Three and a half hours, depending on the wind direction."

"I'll gladly do it." Abu Abak said. "Now let us

have that tea you promised."

In the Yurt the storyteller helped identify two birds for Cahena: the Maghreb Lark and the African Desert Warbler. She immediately wrote the names and their description on a scroll of parchment. "Do you always describe the birds?" Abu Abak asked.

"How else will future generations learn? I also draw pictures of them."

"Your father has been silent. He should be proud to have a daughter such as you."

"He is. But my father is also sad. He is going to send me away to the Roman school in New Carthage."

"It doesn't make it any easier when your own daughter knows in advance what you are going to say," ben Shimi sighed.

"Do you always know what people are thinking?" Abu Abak asked.

"No. It just comes to me, or does not. I am learning how to concentrate on people's thoughts. I can do it with some animals. When I was holding Marta she told me she was hungry."

"Why didn't you feed her?"

"She's always hungry. I use food to train them, and that is why I think the pigeons will fly back to your caravan if I don't give them food. They will remember where they were last fed."

Cahena poured tea and said, "With respect, I must tell you that your last story to the tribes, about the hour-glass, was old. You told that five years go."

"Impossible," the old man snorted. "I am very careful not to do that." Cahena bowed her head and remained silent. The storyteller said, "The people laughed."

"Out of respect for you.'"

"You would have been only four years old."

"My daughter is correct," ben Shimi noted. "I too remember the story."

"If she was as respectful as she said, she would have remained silent. You did."

"Sir," Cahena said, "Please don't take it to heart. I wish to give you an original story in place of that one."

"Teach the teacher, eh? Go ahead. Tell me this story."

Cahena put aside her tea-cup and said, "The father came home from a long journey on the caravan trail with a dazzling pure white camel.

"'No doubt it is the most beautiful beast,' his wife said, 'But it appears too small to carry a load over a long distance. '

"'It has another quality which makes it far more valuable,' said the husband. "The animal always reacts to anyone who lies.'

"'Does that really work?' the wife asked.

"'It did when I bought it. '

"'Good! You'll have a chance to try it on your son. He's coming now, three hours late. I have chores for him to do. '

"The father sat his son in the middle of the tent and brought in the camel. 'Son, this camel knows who lies and who tells the truth. Where were you?'

"'Father, I was collecting firewood for the blind widow. '

"The camel waddled over and kicked the boy off his chair.

"'Son, I warned you to tell the truth. Where were you?'

"'Learning Greek with Jamal the saddlemaker.'

"The camel walloped him again.

"'I told you to be honest, as I am,' said the father.

"The camel turned and knocked the father against the tent wall.

"The mother broke out laughing, and pointed at her husband. 'The boy takes after you', she said. 'He's your son.'

"The camel knocked her through the tent door."

Abu Abak laughed into his tea-cup, spraying father and daughter. He stood to help dry each of them and apologize, but ended up hugging

Cahena. He said, "I would like to be considered your godfather."

"It would be my fondest wish."

"Then, with your father's permission, let it be so."

Abu Abak and Cahena spent the following day with the pigeons. That evening was the last of his talks on Islam. Cahena had an unsettling premonition about the gathering. She asked Ozeret to help her understand it, but to no avail. Cahena told her father and Abu Abak. They were busy and offered no help.

The stage was lit by torches. The audience sat in the dark with a few torches so people did not step on each other. A new tribe had entered the encampment. Cahena's future father-in-law, Selim, complained bitterly about them to Moshe ben Shimi. Moshe listened and replied, "I have no authority to disallow them. They are ancient members of the Maghreb Berbers with all rights to participate."

"We have a blood-feud with them," Selim said.

"Everyone in this camp agreed to put the blood-feuds aside. This is the last night. I will see they are first to leave in the morning."

Abu Abak began the evening with the story about the truth-telling camel. It was well received. He winked at Cahena as she poured his wine. The storyteller of the Maghreb began.

"The following was imparted to me by Adil Salahi, in the Hijri calendar year of 1438, How the Muslim General Khalid Ibn Al-Walid embraced Islam. Khalid was a division commander of the Pagan forces after the Battle of Uhud, where he personally defeated the Muslims and wounded Muhammad. His conversion to Islam was a long process. He claims that the development began when he started to reflect on his past attitude during events of great importance.

"He said, 'I fought all those battles against Muhammad. Every time I felt that all my efforts were to no avail. I was certain that Muhammad would eventually be the winner. When the Prophet came and encamped at Al-Hudaybiyah, I commanded a detachment of horsemen from among the idolaters until we met the Prophet and his companions at Asafan. I drew close to provoke him. He and his companions prayed in front of us. We thought of attacking them, but we refrained. He must have realized what we were thinking of when the next prayer was due. He therefore, led his companions in what is known as 'the prayers of fear'. Half of his men formed two lines across the valley floor and prostrated themselves before us in prayer. When finished they moved to the rear and the second half moved forward and prayed with the prophet. When these men arose their faces gleamed and they radiated the certainty that Allah is god and Muhammad his greatest prophet. It affected us profoundly and we realized that he was immune from our attack. We withdrew.

"'When the terms of the peace agreement of Al-Hudaybiyah were eventually negotiated and the Prophet and his companions went home, I started thinking about what might come next and what was in store for us. I thought hard: Where should I go? Should I join Negus? But then I remembered that he had already become a follower of Muhammad and that Muhammad's companions were safe under his protection. Should I go and join Heraclius the Roman? That would have made me a Christian convert. That prospect did not appeal to me. Should I emigrate or should I stay where I was, waiting for something to happen?'

"This state of confusion was not to be easily resolved for Khalid. He did not wish to emigrate to where he would have had to prove his worth. If he stayed in Mecca, he knew for certain that the eventual triumph of Islam was only a matter of time. His confusion, however, clouded his vision and he could not see that the right course of action was to look at Islam objectively. Weeks and months passed and he could not make up his mind. When a year was over, Prophet Muhammad and his companions came to Mecca for their compensatory Umrah. Khalid did not wish to look at the Muslims. He went into the mountains and stayed until the Prophet and his companions departed.

"'When he went back home, he found a letter left him by his brother, who had been a Muslim for some time. The letter read as follows:

"'In the name of God, the Merciful, the Beneficent. I am infinitely amazed at the fact that you continue to turn away from Islam when you are as intelligent as I know you to be. No one can be so blind to the truth of Islam. God's Messenger asked me about you, and said: 'Where is Khalid?' I said to him: 'God will bring him to us.' He said: 'A man of his caliber cannot remain ignorant of Islam. If he would use his intelligence and his experience for the Muslims against the idolaters, he would benefit from it a great deal. We would certainly give him precedence over others.' It is high time, brother, for you to make amends for the great benefits you have missed.'

"When Khalid read his brother's letter, he felt as if a curtain which had blurred his vision for a long time was removed. He was pleased at the fact that the Prophet himself inquired about him. He felt a strong desire to become a Muslim. That night he dreamt that he was in a narrow strip of land in a barren desert and he was walking on and on until he came into an open, green, limitless field. It did not take him long to make up his mind that the right course for him was to become a Muslim. He decided to join the Prophet at Medina.

"He felt that he needed a companion to go with him. He discreetly asked several close friends, 'Do you not see that Muhammad is gaining the upper hand against both the Arabs and the non-Arabs? It is certainly expedient for us to join him and share in whatever success he may achieve.' These men all had suffered losses of family members. They replied to Khalid: 'If all the Arabs followed Muhammad and I was the only one left, I would still not join him.'

"The reply was consistent, and he was about to give up when he met Uthman ibn Talhah, whose father, uncle, and his four brothers were all killed at the battle of Uhud. Khalid hesitated, expecting a similar reply. Eventually, he probed Uthman, speaking first about the fact that the Muslims continued to gain strength. He then said: 'I compare our position to that of a fox in a hole. If you pour a bucket of water down into the hole, you can be certain that the fox will come out.' Then Khalid proposed to Uthman that they join the Prophet in Medina. Uthman responded positively, and the two agreed to start their journey after midnight. They continued their trip together until they arrived at Al-Haddah, where they met Amr ibn Al-Aas. He said to them: 'Welcome. Where are you heading?' Realizing that they all had the same purpose, the three of them moved together until they arrived on the outskirts of Medina, where they stopped to change clothes. Khalid's report is as follows:

"'God's Messenger (peace be upon him) was informed of our arrival, and he was pleased. I went ahead to meet the Prophet. On the way I was met by my brother, who said to me: "Be quick. God's Messenger has been informed of your arrival and he is pleased. He is waiting for you." We then moved faster until we saw him at a distance, smiling. He wore his smile until I reached him and greeted him as God's Prophet and Messenger. He replied to my greeting with a face beaming with pleasure.

"'I said: 'I declare that there is no deity but God, and that you are God's Messenger.' He said: 'Come forward.' When I drew nearer, he said to me: 'I praise God for guiding you to Islam. I have always been aware that you are endowed with great intelligence, and I have always hoped that your intelligence will lead you only to what is right and beneficial.' I said to him: 'Messenger of God, I am thinking of those battles at which I was fighting against the side of the truth. I request you to pray to God to forgive me.'

"'He said: 'When you embrace Islam, all your past sins are forgiven." I said: "Messenger of God, please pray for me." He said: "My Lord, forgive Khalid ibn Al-Walid every effort he exerted to turn people away from Your path." Uthman and Amr then pledged their allegiance to the Prophet.'[5]

Abu Abak stopped speaking, and there was a hushed silence. It was suddenly broken by an unearthly human scream. A man stood in the middle of the audience waving his arms and pointing down to a man who appeared to have fallen asleep. He was slumped forward over his crossed legs. "It is Ahmed the mute!" someone shouted.

"See what he is pointing at," Moshe ben Shimi ordered.

Several men examined the man slumped over and said, "He's got a Helawi 'Toothpick' stuck up his left kidney into his heart." People in

---

[5] How Khalid Ibn Al-Waleed Embraced Islam. From Wikipedia, the free encyclopedia, abridged

the audience began shifting closer to their tribesmen in case a fight ensued.

"Bring the body and Ahmed the Mute to this stage, so we may examine both." Moshe ordered.

"How will you handle this?" Abu Abak asked.

Moshe summoned his daughter and pointed to the body. "Can you do anything?"

Without hesitation Cahena touched the man's face, put her cheek on his nostrils, and said, "I cannot raise the dead."

In a hushed whisper Moshe asked his daughter to question Ahmed the mute. "Find out what he knows."

"How can you question a mute?" Abu Abak asked.

"I'll need his mother," Cahena said. "Come, you'll see."

"Have you done this before with Ahmed?" the storyteller asked.

"His mother understands his sign language. Last year I began hearing his thoughts. He can actually answer his mother in sign language, but I don't understand that. He cannot express thoughts about colors, or sounds, or topics that they have no hand signs for."

"Is he bright?"

"Not particularly, but he is extremely strong. He can knock a camel down with one punch. He helps me care for the herds. ...Ah, here is his mother."

A short older woman with a blanket hooded over her head entered the Yurt. She kissed Cahena's hand, then asked her son in hand signals, "What did you do?"

His reaction was immediate. His right hand slashed in front of his body, indicating 'Nothing'. He then pointed to his eye and then the ground, and made an underhanded gesture as if stabbing a man from behind.

"Even I can interpret that," Abu Abak said.

Cahena pointed to her eye, then to Ahmed's, and spoke to the mother. "Ask him if he knows the man."

Ahmed's head nodded vigorously up and down.

Moshe ben Shimi entered the Yurt. "Father," said Cahena, "Ahmed can identify the killer."

"That presents a problem."

"Why so?" Abu Abak asked.

"First learn which tribe the killer is from."

The mother signed, Ahmed replied, and his mother faced Moshe saying, "The Helawi."

"I suspected as much," Moshe said. "The problem is, Ahmed must face the accused and say to his face, 'This is the man who killed so-and-so.'"

"My son cannot speak."

"There is the Test of Truth." Moshe then ordered, "Bring the Helawi Chieftain here."

Selim entered the tent, his hand on his sword.

Moshe did not mince words. "One of your tribe stands accused of murder."

"I understand the accuser is a deaf mute," Selim answered. "According to the Amazigh Berber, he must speak the accusation to the man's face."

"Line up all your male warriors before this Yurt. We will identify the man first."'

"Is that an order?" Selim demanded.

"It is," Moshe replied. "You are in the Jrawa tribal camp. You took an oath on behalf of your tribe about blood-feuds."

Selim's eyes rolled back into his head, then focused on Moshe ben Shimi. "Technically you are correct, but as your future father-in-law, I claim that I and my tribe should be shown more respect."

"Understood. Please assemble your fighting men in front of this Yurt."

Two hundred and fifty men lined up in five rows before Cahena's Yurt. In the tent Moshe ben Shimi had Selim, two of his chieftains, Abu Abak, Ahmed the deaf mute and his mother watch Cahena go into a trance. She was seated on pillows facing Ahmed. They had done this before, but never with witnesses. Cahena had sent all the birds from the Yurt, and it was quiet. She rocked back and forth humming to herself.

Her eyes closed and she stopped humming. She entered Ahmed's thoughts and the man became physically relaxed. His arms hung loose at his side. His mouth opened and saliva dripped out. Cahena could see his thoughts roll by in slow, parallel streams. She had to find the one related to the murder...

It was dark. She recognized the torch lights. She saw a man seated in the audience lean forward, place his left hand over the man's mouth in front of him, and ram the long thin-bladed knife up through the left kidney to open the man's heart. She saw the killer's face! His eyes were filled with hatred. He pulled away and disappeared into the crowd.

Cahena opened her eyes and said, "Father, I saw who did it."

"Can you identify him?"

"Yes."

"Are you condoning witchcraft?" the Helawi chieftain demanded.

"Never use that word to my daughter," Moshe growled. "You and I will accompany her to inspect your tribesmen. If she identifies a person, she will say nothing but scratch her nose. She will continue until the end. Then two of your chieftains will escort Ahmed to examine your men. If he selects the wrong man, his testimony is invalid."

"And if he selects the right one?" Selim challenged.

"We'll cross that bridge when we come to it."

Escorted by her father and Selim, nine-year-old Cahena walked past the angry Helawi warriors without the least sign of fear. In the middle of the third row, she scratched her nose in front of a lean warrior with a hawk nose that had been broken. She continued to the end and stepped aside, flanked by her father and the Helawi chieftain.

Ahmed appeared from the Yurt, accompanied by two chieftains. He passed up and down the lines until, in the center of the third line, he reached out at the man with the misshapen nose and tapped the man on the shoulder.

Moshe ben Shimi turned to Selim. "Do you accept your warrior's guilt?"

"I do not, and you know why. The accuser must declare the guilt of the accused to his face. Your man cannot speak."

"Then we'll have your man stand the Test of Truth."

"That is your privilege, but what is good for the accused must be equally good for his accuser."

"Meaning what?"

"The mute must also stand the Test of Truth."

"He doesn't understand."

"Then his accusations are invalid."

At that moment the Chief of the tribe of the murdered man entered the argument. "Moshe ben Shimi, this may be your tribal land, but guests of Berbers have certain rights. I exercise my right, as the representative of the dead man's family and clan, to have both accuser and accused be tested according to our law."

Moshe ben Shimi felt trapped. To his knowledge, neither Ahmed nor Cahena ever witnessed such a testing. He ordered the storyteller to take Cahena, Ahmed, and his mother back to the yurt and explain to them what would soon take place.

"Can you tell Ahmed what I am about to tell you?" Abu Abak asked.

"No," Cahena said. "I have only learned to witness his thoughts. I cannot speak to them."

"Can his mother relay to him what I tell you about the testing?"

"Speak to me. The mother will listen and try to interpret."

Abu Abak faced the three and began. The

mother interpreted for Ahmed in sign language as best she could.

"In cases where the identity of the killer is in question, the accused must first go through a series of oath swearings. That is now taking place in your father's tent. If he gulps or coughs at the wrong time it could cost him his life, but I and your father suspect that Selim, your future father-in-law, has prepared the man so he will not falter."

"What then?" Cahena asked.

"The Test of Truth. Hot water, cold water, a hot iron, or the sword."

Ahmed's mother began to weep as she interpreted the meanings of these things to her son.

"How are they used?" Cahena asked.

"A stone is dropped into boiling cauldron of water. The accused and the accuser must retrieve the stone from the bottom. His injured arm is then bandaged. After three days the bandages are removed. If there are signs of healing, the man has told the truth. Infection indicates guilt. It is similar with the hot iron. He must grip it and place it on the ground at his feet. The wound is bound as it was with the water, and the results determined in three days. The most immediate results are obtained by the cold water and sword. In the former, the accused is bound hand and foot and thrown into a body of water. If he sinks, he is guilty and dies right there. The trial by sword entails a sword being brought to white hot temperature. Then passed over the tongue of both accused and accuser. The one who is unscarred is the truth teller."

"Does it work?" Cahena asked.

"It works," Abu Abak said. "And the reason I think it works is that the truth teller's mouth is full of saliva. His tongue is wet. The liar's mouth and tongue are dry."

"Who chooses which method?"

"The accused. There is nothing to do but wait."

Time for the evening meal passed and still no decision came from Moshe ben Shimi's tent. People crowded outside in expectation. At nine in the evening the tent flaps opened and Selim, the chieftain of the offended tribe and Moshe ben Shimi came out to address the people. Moshe announced, "The trial will take place tomorrow morning. Trial by sword. May the gods render justice."

Cahena returned to her Yurt. Ahmed was playing with the birds. Cahena explained to the mother. Ahmed seemed unconcerned about the test. When questioned his mother said, "My son knows what he said is true. He will prove it tomorrow."

Cahena believed Ahmed, but her sleep was restless thinking of the white-hot blade sliding down his tongue. Would he shy away at sight of the glowing blade? He'd be judged guilty for doing so.

Morning came, and Ahmed helped Cahena feed the birds and clean the pigeon cage. They returned from caring for the camels to find Abu Abak in the yurt stirring a dark black brew over the fire. The aroma was tantalizing to both Ahmed and Cahena. "What is that?" she asked.

"Ethiopians call this kaffa. It grows wild in their forests. It's a bean. The Ethiopian soldiers use it to keep up their strength on long marches. *Bunna* in Amharic, they chew the bean. I roast it over a fire then grind it with a stone and boil it in water. The invigorating properties were discovered by a shepherd. His sheep and goats started jumping and running around after eating the beans from the kaffa tree. He tried a few beans and was elated. He told his wife and the rest is history. Have some Kaffa." He passed over two cups. Ahmed's mother entered the tent, but refused the black brew. She was distraught.

Cahena pronounced, "The taste is bitter, but the kaffa filled my spine and gives me strength. It wakes up the muscles."

"Some people chew a piece of sugar cane while drinking it," Abu Abak said.

There was the sound of people entering the vestibule, then the inside door burst open. Two men entered and dragged Ahmed from the Yurt. Mother, storyteller and Cahena followed. All the tribes were gathered around the platform used by Abu Abak. On it stood Moshe ben Shimi, Selim, and the Chieftain of the aggrieved tribe. A man stood off to the side, working a goat-skin bellows into a fire with a long straight sword buried in the red-hot coals. Moshe pointed to Ahmed and said, "You will be first."

Held by two powerful men, Ahmed was brought forward. Moshe said to the mother, "Tell him to extend his tongue as far as he can and not to move."'

The mother translated this in sign language and was then pushed out of the way as the man withdrew the sword from the coals. It was glowing pale orange in the bright light of morning. He approached Ahmed whose tongue was extended. In one steady motion the man brought down the flat of the sword blade on Ahmed's tongue. Those on the stage could hear the sizzle and sputter. Ahmed never flinched or blinked. The sword was replaced in the coals and the bellows reworked. The people saw the accused tense and strain at the men holding his arms. Sweat broke out on his face and ran into his beard. The sword was withdrawn from the fire and held aloft for the people to see its color. The accused struggled as the sword came closer. He was ordered to stick out his tongue.

"I did it!" He screamed. "I did it!" He collapsed.

Selim, his chieftain, spat in the man's face.

Abu Abak nodded toward Selim and whispered to Cahena, "That was for show. Selim's man would never kill without permission. Now your father will pronounce the death-sentence."

Moshe ben Shimi addressed the crowd. "Most of us in the Jrawa tribe adhere to a loose form of Jewish Law. The Talmud defines four methods of imposing the death penalty: by fire, beheading, stoning or strangulation. The first three mutilate the body and the Holy Torah says, Man is made in God's image. Therefore I order strangulation. We will have to build another platform to implement the sentence. After the strangulation there will be a Sulka, a ceremony of reconciliation to render any blood-feud invalid. The Jrawa will host the Sulka."

Cahena tugged on Abu Abak's robe. "You handed Ahmed something before the test?"

"A piece of Elm bark. It thickens the mucous in the mouth."

"Don't you trust religious rites?"

'No. And neither does Muhammad. He often speaks common sense. but is brutal with those who disagree. Tell me, how do they implement the death penalties in your tribe?"

Nine-year-old Cahena sucked on her thumb but answered as an adult. 'We adhere to the Jewish traditions. We don't burn and we don't cut heads off, except our enemies'"

"That leaves stoning and hanging."

"We don't stone like the Arabs. They surround the person and throw rocks until they are dead. I once saw a woman buried in sand until only her head was showing, and then she was stoned to death."

"I have witnessed that," the old man said. "How do you Jrawa do it?'

"For stoning, the Talmud dictates the guilty one be brought to a cliff at least thirty feet high. Boulders and large rocks are placed below. The person either jumps or is pushed. If they don't die from the fall they are stoned from above. Burning is not in a fire. It requires that molten metal be poured down the throat of guilty one."

"Oh, what joy that must bring to the onlookers."'

"My father banned its use because the victim struggled so hard, some of the molten metal disfigured him and burned the men trying to control him."

"The second platform your father ordered built: is that the scaffold for hanging?"

"We do not hang. We strangle."

"Who does that?"

"Seven men from the aggrieved tribe, and seven from guilty tribe."

"Fourteen men to strangle one man?"

"It prevents the murderer's family from declaring a feud with any one of the executioners."

"How is it done?"

"You will see this evening. Come, let's exercise the pigeons."

On the way to the pigeon cage they passed men and women using camels to haul dead trees and freshly chopped timber from the stream beds and forest. There was a festive air in the Jrawa camp. On the outskirts, men and women set up a slaughterhouse, while children herded sheep and goats to them. Giant pots of water for couscous were set on tripods over fires. Other pots were filled to make vegetables for the couscous. Smaller fires were attended by men and women kneading dough for the luffa bread. The dough was rolled thin, tossed in the air, caught on the back of the hands and thrown onto an inverted Chinese wok. Quickly it was taken off, flipped over and replaced on the wok, then stacked up at the side. Other fires boiled cauldrons of hummus, some to be ground into a paste and thinned with fresh pressed olive oil, seasoned with herbs and served with pickled vegetables. The rest of the hummus would be served hot with the couscous.

Half of a dozen warriors stood guard over the Jrawa wine supply. Moshe ben Shimi had decreed no drinking until after the strangulation. Abu Abak stood aside while Cahena argued a group of her tribesmen out of raiding her pigeons for the feast. She took out her favorite, Marta and stuffed her into a small knitted sleeve. The bird peeked out, and Cahena said, "This is how you will carry them on your journey. When you stop for the day, you feed them for five minutes in the cage I will give you. Then let them fly. They should have an hour of exercise. Feed them again when they return. Only five minutes. Clean the cage of all food and droppings. I will send someone with you to perform these chores. The pigeons will react when you do not give them food and fly here to me. When I don't give them food they should return to your cage."

The smells of sizzling meat, spices, and fresh hot bread permeated the hillside. Seven sullen Helawi warriors mounted the newly built stage. Seven warriors of the aggrieved tribe stood only ten feet away on the original stage. Moshe ben Shimi supervised a single strand of hemp rope, the thickness of a man's wrist, to be stretched across both stages and sag down in the middle between the platforms.

"Bring the condemned man!" Moshe ordered.

The man was escorted by two warriors. He had a placid but puzzled look about him. "He was more upset before the burning sword-blade than he is now before he dies," Abu Abak observed.

"My father had Ozeret make a calming drug."

"He appears serene."

The two men escorted the condemned man to the center of the ground between the two stages, standing him alongside the rope. He remained docile as they looped the roped over his head and around his throat. Moshe signaled the fourteen men. They picked up the ends of the rope. 'If you pull hard and hold it until I shout to let go," he called, "There will be less pain on the guilty. Pull!"

The two groups of men strained. The rope tightened and the victim was lifted into the air, his feet kicking. His face turned white, red, blue, and then black. His mouth opened and his tongue protruded. His body shuddered, and his legs jerked. Moshe continued a silent count to himself, then shouted, "Release!" The body crumpled to the earth between the platforms.

There was silence, and Moshe ben Shimi announced, "Justice is served. Let all who are witness bear no grudge, and let us celebrate Berber integrity, justice, and unity."

At the direction of Selim their chieftain, Helawi tribesmen recovered the body and took it away for burial.

"It is my opinion," Abu Abak said, "That your future father-in-law will never forget or forgive this evening."

Most people made for the wine skins, then to the cooking fires. An hour after the festivities began, the Helawi returned from their burial ceremony. They were a grim and sullen lot. Moshe felt the mood dampen, and called on the musicians and singers to entertain.

At about midnight the wine ran out, and it was the Helawi chieftain Selim who saved the day; he ordered all his tribe's wine brought to the Sulka. That made it a much more joyous occasion, and he was toasted and lauded in song, poems, and witty ditties. He and his men joined in. The smoke of fires left unattended for hours drifted over the camp.

The sun arose on bodies of men, women, and children strewn all over the ground. "It's a land of the dead," Abu Abak said to Cahena, "But these are dead drunk. I thought to leave today, but even the camels are drunk. There aren't five people in this entire encampment who can see or walk straight."

"When you do leave," Cahena asked. "Would my godfather take Ozeret with you?"

"I thought your father would want her to accompany you to New Carthage."

"He doesn't trust her. He thinks she's a witch and influences me."

"Does she?"

"When I allow it."

"But I am not going to New Carthage."

"She will caravan-hop to that city, and meet me there."

"Are you excited about going to school?"

"I never saw a large city. I understand they have a thing they call 'streets'."

"A Roman innovation. They lay out the plots in large grids, then number the streets in consecutive order. Then they number the houses on these streets."

"Why?"

"Before they had streets, people built their houses right next to one another. People had to walk with their animals over the roofs of other people's houses to reach their homes. In the middle of the streets there are channels to garbage and human waste. The numbering also makes it easier to collect taxes." The old storyteller pointed at Cahena. "You will have to cover up your breasts."

"Why?"

"Romans do not go around half naked."

"Berber women are proud of our beauty."

"You're still a child."

Cahena touched her tiny breasts. "These will grow."

"I am certain they will. But if you don't cover yourself you may not get much older. Roman soldiers are a rough lot. Chances are they would be grabbing your breasts or raping you in the street."

"I'd cut off their balls."

"And within an hour the Roman magistrate would flog and crucify you. Attack a Roman and you die. Break Roman law and you suffer."

"How far is New Carthage?"

"From the Atlas mountains, about a thousand miles."

"I've never been more than fifty miles from here."

"Then you have never seen the Mediterranean Sea."

"I heard about it."

"Ah," the old storyteller sighed. "To be young again, and with your intelligence, to witness what you will on your trip to the second most populated city in the world."

"Which is the first?"

"Alexandria in Egypt has over a million people."

"A million?!"

"Do you know what a million is?"

"I know the word– a thousand thousand—but can't conceive the number, in people or things."

"If you were to start counting now, you would die of old age before you reached a million."

"How can they all live together?"

"That is the Roman genius. No one can explain. You must witness it."

CHAPTER 4

CARAVANS

Abu Abak's caravan left two days late. It took that long to sober up the travelers and cameleers, round up donkeys, sheep, goats and professional guards. They packed the animals and the caravan master assigned positions. It was a medium sized caravan: twenty camels, fifty men, four with horses to guard along the trail. Everyone walked but the children, the elderly, and the caravan master. He rode a large grey mare. Camels were loaded with rugs, dried fruits, handiwork and salt to be traded in the bazaars along the way. Cahena's father provided a slave to exercise and train the pigeons.

The first two birds arrived. There was no third. A fourth flew in from a hostel fifty miles away. It carried a message from Abu Abak warning of tribesmen using hunting falcons. Cahena starved the pigeons that arrived, and of five two returned to the caravan along the trail. Upon receiving this information, Cahena stopped all flights unless the pigeons were trained in one place for a week or more. She judged they did not have enough time to orient themselves to return to the caravan.

Marta made a two hundred mile flight from the caravan and then returned. She carried a message from Abu Abak. Blight had devastated the plum harvest in one of the major fruit growing areas. The dried plums from the mountains brought a higher price than expected. Pecans and almonds were in abundance but salted pistachio nuts from Iran brought higher prices.

The swiftness of this information was recognized and appreciated by merchants and warriors. They soon took an interest in Cahena's pigeons for other purposes than eating them. They helped her trap rock pigeons by spreading bread crumbs on the ground and resting a loose noose over the crumbs with its end tied to a rock. The shuffling pigeons eventually trapped their clawed toes in the noose and were then subjected to a training period before flying with the flock. Small caravans leaving the mountains were now communicating by carrier pigeon from along the caravan trails of the Maghreb.

The swiftness of communication and the ability to read and write was not lost on the tribesmen. They asked Moshe to set up a school so they could learn to read and write.

One of the pigeons brought a message which told of a raid by bandits. It was thwarted by a Roman patrol that had been tracking them. The Byzantine commander said: "They are coming your way, at least two hundred fighters."

Moshe ben Shimi contacted the three remaining tribes in the area and suggested a mutual defense force, and the tribes agreed.

The meeting was held in the Jrawa council tent. At the rear of the tent was a large high-backed chair covered with a leopard skin. On either side of Moshe ben Shimi sat two tribal chieftains. One stood and said, "We must have a leader to fight these bandits. We three tribes agree that Moshe ben Shimi of the Jrawa shall lead us. He showed his intelligence in previous battles, his political wisdom with his intended father-in-law of the Helawi, and his ability to bring the Berber together by using the storyteller of the Maghreb."

It was then that Cahena first appreciated her father's foresight. The tribal Chieftain confirmed it when he said, "We proclaim Moshe ben Shimi our sharif. His word is law. He holds the right of life or death, trial and punishment including execution."

Cahena had been puzzled by her father's lavish hosting of the tribes for the storyteller, but now she understood. It was his way of showing leadership. The oncoming bandits and pigeons were a coincidence; he took advantage of these to emphasize his abilities and be elected sharif of the four tribes. Suddenly her marriage to the future Helawi chief made sense. Through her, Moshe ben Shimi would become sharif of three more tribes. Sharif of seven tribes meant he would lead the largest contingent of Berbers in North Africa. This would put him in line for leadership of all Berbers in the Maghreb. From the Nile River in Egypt to the Atlantic Ocean in Morocco, his word would be law to Berbers, Tuaregs and their vassals— more than a million and a half people.

This was a revelation of religious proportions. She decided to make an idol of her father and place it in front of her other idols.

When she returned from the clay pit with a blob of the damp, pliable material she was informed that her father required her immediately.

In his tent were chieftains and senior warriors from all four tribes. With a motion of his hand her father indicated she was to sit behind the leopard-covered chair which he occupied. In this way she was out of sight in the adult gathering, but she listened.

"We are here to devise a plan of action," her father said.

"Against the marauders heading this way!" one of the young warriors said.

"They number two hundred. We can stop them in any one of the passes they must traverse to reach our camps, but they will retreat and find another way through. They will plunder and kill our people, steal our slaves, burn and rape throughout the Maghreb."

Cahena sensed that her father had larger plans, and she listened.

"We won't be able to contain all of them," he said.

"Then we kill all of them," a woman chieftain replied.

"How?" one of the older chieftains asked.

"Our four tribes can field twice as many warriors."

"And we would take twice as many casualties. These are professional fighters coming for us. They have no families, children or homes to protect. We haven't had mounted training sessions for years. Yes, we know how to fight as individuals but not as a group. I understand these bastards are mounted."

"What's there to know?" the young chieftain asked. "Get on your horse, throw your javelin, and draw your sword. Cut the fool's head off."

"Bravery is to be admired," the older chief replied. "Stupidity will get your balls cut off and shoved down your throat."

Moshe ben Shimi intervened before a fight erupted. "There is a time for the young chief's actions. We must find the place to maneuver our enemy so they can do the least harm. Then cut his heart out and make him eat it." Moshe beckoned the younger chief. "They are coming from the northwest. They must pass through your territory. Where would be the most advantageous place to trap and wipe them out?"

The young man forgot his anger and pondered the territory in his mind's eye. "Satan's Saddle," he proclaimed.

"The youngster is right," the older chief said. "Overlooking that narrow pass are steep cliffs on both sides. The bandits wouldn't be able to maneuver their horses. If we occupied the high ground we could pick them off with arrows, slings and javelins. They'd have to retreat"

"No retreat for them," Moshe said. "I want to kill them all."

"Satan's Saddle is the place," the young chieftain said. "At its narrowest part there is little protection from above, and no water for two miles. But how do we get them to take that route, then get behind them and block their retreat? The only way to enter that wadi is from several miles behind. That area is open for their horses, and we would be sighted by their rear guard."

"You will make a good leader," the older chieftain admitted. "The ambush place you've chosen is perfect. Now I will explain an old Berber trick. We lure them into that canyon by leaving the trail of a wealthy caravan for them to follow and attack. Your men will build an avalanche to cut off their retreat. I will build a wall at the head of the canyon defended from above and below to prevent a breakthrough. We will sit on the heights and kill them at our leisure."

"How will we know where and when—and if—they enter that wadi?" the younger chieftain asked.

Cahena tugged on the leopard skin and her father listened to her whisper. "Tell them my pigeons can make the flight in less than an hour. Send me with spies, and we will warn you.'"

Moshe ben Shimi presented this proposal to the warriors.

It was discussed, then agreed, but only after Cahena explained she was the only one who could direct and fly the pigeons—which was untrue. She wanted with all her heart to be a part of this great adventure.

It was agreed, and within the hour five Jrawa warriors—three men, two women, and Cahena with six caged pigeons—were led by the young chieftain from the encampment to Satan's Saddle.

They rode at a steady trot in single file over the foothills of the Atlas Mountains. They ate bread and drank in the saddle.

Then began the steep ascent to Satan's Saddle. The moon silhouetted the monumental rock formation with its curved shape that looked like a camel's saddle. They moved at a slow but steady pace for two hours on the slippery shale.

The stars appeared brighter than Cahena had ever seen before. The Chieftain explained to her that it was the purity and dryness of the air that allowed one to see further in the higher areas. She fell asleep in the saddle, and was held in place by the young chieftain walking his horse alongside hers. She awoke at noon, when he helped her down and told her they would sleep until evening. They had already passed Satan's Saddle and were on the route overlooking the pass that hopefully the oncoming bandits would take.

Just before evening, a thousand feet below, a group of horsemen and cameleers entered the wadi from the south, readily identified as the older chieftain's tribe. They rode further into the canyon, then abruptly turned about and set six horsemen in a row trailing woolen blankets by rope from their horses, eliminating their incoming trail. The remaining animals and men lined up, as if in a caravan leaving trail marks. The young chieftain explained that they were leaving tracks to lure the bandits into Satan's Saddle in hopes of raiding an unsuspecting caravan. He and the others surveyed the area and picked a spot to cause an avalanche.

When the location was agreed upon, he left two men to direct the tribesmen who would arrive to build the avalanche trap. He and Cahena pressed on until one of his outriders signaled them to stop. Leaving the horses behind, they crept up to the canyon rim and peered below at an army of men, horses, camels and donkeys, plus a small herd of sheep and goats for food. It was then Cahena realized the young chieftain couldn't count more than his fingers and toes. "How much is two hundred"' he asked.

She tried to explain ten times the fingers and toes, but she couldn't get the idea across. In frustration he asked, "Can you count them?"

It took time but in the end she said, "Three hundred and twenty fighting men. I didn't count the slaves."

"There are more than we expected."

"And more than my father planned for."

"How long will it take your pigeon to tell

him?"

"The pigeons don't talk. I write a message tie it to the bird's leg and my father will read it within an hour."

"Who taught you to read and write?"

"The sharif."

"Do you think your father will teach me?"

"He does mostly what I ask. He loves me."

"How do you know when someone loves you?"

Cahena thought for a moment. "I'm not sure. You just feel it."

"Is it when they do whatever you ask of them?"

"No. We have slaves for that. Sometimes it is what they don't do."

"I never had a conversation with a nine-year-old. Is that your true age?"

"Yes. I am tall for my age."

"And you are going to be even more beautiful."

"How do you know?"

"I may not read or count, but for beautiful women I am an expert."

"What is this expert's name?"

"Aksil of the Amazigh Berber, Chieftain of the Chawia Tribe."

"Aksil means Leopard, like the skin on the sharif's chair."

"If we don't send that message my skin will be covering your father's chair."

Cahena sent two different birds, released several minutes apart.

The pigeons arrived. Immediately Moshe realized the danger. The bandits must have picked up more recruits on the way, as well as the horses and camels. Three hundred and twenty men would mean a caravan stretched out along the road at least two miles. There would be far too many to fit into the gorge and be blocked by the avalanche behind. The rear guard of the raiders would escape.

He pondered the problem and called in his scouts, who detailed the lay of the land for him above Satan's canyon. He dispatched several scouts on the swiftest horses, two horses to a man, to warn Aksil. He had sent all but fifty of his best warriors with the older Chieftain to block the oncoming bandits. Now he ordered these fifty to prepare for inspection, with their weapons and two horses per man, with enough food and water for five days. He prepared his own kit and ordered two horses to be saddled. When he finished packing he brought his gear outside and placed it on one horse. The other horse he mounted and faced his warriors.

He explained the problem and the need to

send support Aksil and his men. "Our scouts are on the way to warn Aksil. I doubt they will be in time, but they will leave a marked path for us to follow to Satan's Saddle. I am ordering every man to ride his first horse into the ground. There will be not stops, rests or helping the injured. I will lead, but if any of you can pass me I order you to do so. Senior warriors, check your men: two horses, saddled, and cinched with water and food. *Takoba*: one meter long straight sword. *Allagh*: two meter long lance. *Agher*: one fifty meter high shield. *Tagheda*: small sharp javelin. *Taganze*: leather covered-wooden bow. *Amur*: arrows. *Sheru*: long dagger. *Tellak*: short dagger strapped to the left forearm. *Alakkud*: riding crop. When we complete this journey your riding crop should be beaten to a stub."

Moshe ben Shimi pointed to the North Star and shouted, "Forward!"

He led them at a trot out of the camp, then into a half gallop until the horses were warmed up, then into a race for Satan's Saddle.

The pace slowed as they climbed the slopes of the Atlas Mountains. Men dismounted and with one hand held the horses' tails to help them up the slope. The trail narrowed. Injured animals had their throats slit and were pushed off the trail. Injured men were left where they fell. There was cursing but little conversation as they followed Sharif Moshe to what they now called the Devil's Playground.

Aksil left four of his men to observe and report the progress of the bandits. He and Cahena returned to the place on the sloping cliffs where the avalanche was being prepared. Fifty men and women warriors worked stripped to the waist, carrying stones and rocks to a point where they had arranged several logs held in place by stout ropes overhanging the canyon below. Behind the logs was piled rubble from the mountain. Aksil took off his leather jacket and shirt to join the men. Cahena observed his physique and enjoyed it.

An hour later one of his scouts reported, "They have taken the bait. The bandits are entering this wadi at a fast pace, thinking they are about to capture a caravan."

Aksil sent a messenger to the old chieftain at the head of the wadi. When he arrived there was already a six foot stone wall across the narrowest part of the canyon. Warriors were climbing the slopes. Those already in position prepared stones, rocks and boulders. Horses were herded into a blind canyon not far from the ambush point. A few camels with bogus loads were left standing before the ambush wall tended by two men imitating the rear of a caravan. The old chief listened to the report of Aksil's scout, and like Moshe ben Shimi he immediately recognized the danger.

"The bandits' caravan will never fit into our trap," He said. "They are at least one third more numerous than we thought." He took the messenger by the shoulders and said. "Fly back there like Muhammad on his winged horse and tell Chieftain Aksil to cause the avalanche now. Throw rocks at those below, but save your javelins and arrows for the fight to come. The rear guard of the bandits not caught in our trap will make for the waterhole two miles back. They will use it as a rallying point. Aksil must stop them at all costs. We haven't enough food, water or men to wait them out. Go now!"

"Can I tell Aksil you will send reinforcements?"

"Not until I see what kind of fight we have here. The sharif is on his way with some fifty warriors. I will try and divert them to help you. Now go!"

The old chief chose his best scout to meet Moshe and send the sharif to reinforce Aksil at the water hole. In the wadi bandit scouts approached the bend in the wadi where they would see the camels and the wall.

The bandit scouts were experienced. They

kept to the sides of the canyon to avoid detection. Their horses and clothing blended into the gray rocky background of the steep canyon walls. They stopped and recognized the camels and handlers as the rear of a caravan. The stone wall was an anomaly. It didn't belong there. They charged forward followed by armed riders to attack the cameleers. The two men tending the camels scrambled over the stone wall and disappeared. The main body of bandits came forward at a trot but stopped short of the wall. The old chieftain of the Amazigh Berbers signaled and a bare-chested woman warrior raised a large curled ram's horn to her lips and blew three long blasts that echoed through the canyon. From the slopes and up the walls on both sides. Berber warriors hurled stones and rocks. They dislodged boulders and rolled them down on the raiders. More bandits entered that part of the wadi. With little room to move the crowded bandits were struck or knocked over with their horses by stones, rocks and boulders. Cries of anger and pain from men and animals filled the Canyon. Those below sought shelter along the sides of the slopes and cliffs to little avail. The Berbers held the high ground on both sides of the canyon. The bandits used long shields captured from Tuaregs as protection against slingers and small stones. Their swords, spears and javelins were of no use. The few bowmen were unable to reach their attackers. Berber archers above sent their shafts whizzing down into the melee. The old Berber chieftain watched and waited. He looked for some semblance of order to be brought to those in his trap so he could either eliminate them or negotiate. Wounded horses, donkeys and several pack camels charged back and forth trampling their owners and other animals. The chaos below brought the bandit caravan to a halt. It took thirty minutes before the rear of the column closed up and stopped.

Back at the avalanche trap Aksil and Cahena peered over the cliffs edge. "Why do they stop?" She asked.

"Holy shit!" Aksil slapped his forehead. "Because they have more men than we thought, the caravan is too long. We can't trap all of them."

"Are you going to set loose the avalanche?"

Aksil slipped down and sat with his head in his hands. Cahena asked again but was gestured into silence. He looked over the ledge at the confusion as the caravan below scrunched together. Horsemen from the rear guard came trotting forward to determine the delay. Horsemen from the head of the column raced back.

The two groups met below.

"It's now or never." Aksil said.

He signaled four swordsmen who leapt over the ledge, down to the sides of the timber holding the stones and boulders. They wielded their broadswords against the ropes. One strand after another parted. The wood creaked, rocks and boulders shifted. Like an animal set free when the ropes gave way, trees and boulders burst from their restraint and sailed out from the cliff. Heavier boulders crashed down the canyon walls dislodging more boulders, rocks, crashing through overhangs gathering momentum and volume. The sound from above reached those below. Cahena watched the faces look up at the oncoming maelstrom. People ran, rode, and crawled to avoid the oncoming landslide. The massive volume of earth roared into the canyon, obliterating everything below. A dust cloud obscured the canyon.

Aksil gathered his warriors. There were forty-five. "It will be hours before we can see below," he said. "Only a hundred or so bandits were not caught in the trap. Their caravan was too long. Those in the trap will be taken care of by the sharif.

"We must stop the remainder from reaching water at the Cave of Esau. It is two miles back. The cave has an underground spring that leads into a large deep pool of water.

"It is distinguished by the date palms growing around it and large open pasture land in front. This bandit caravan must have been there last night. They will try to regroup there. We must stop them."

"What will stop the bandits from eventually climbing the rocks blocking the canyon?" Cahena asked.

"I am leaving five women archers to stop them. Use stones at first until you must use your arrows. When they are gone, join us at the Cave of Esau. You will remain with the archers."

"I can't use a bow."

"Throw stones, and mind the pigeons." Aksil leapt into the saddle and led his men at a gallop along the ledge of the canyon to Esau's Cave at the base of the mountain.

The scout sent by the old chieftain missed Moshe ben Shimi and his band. The scout expected them on the lower road to reinforce the old chieftain, but warned by Cahena's pigeon her father took the high road to support Aksil and his men.

Five hours after the landslide, the dust cleared enough to reveal the carnage below. Those in the path of the avalanche were buried and out of sight forever. On both sides of the blocked canyon were dead and wounded animals and men. The living moved around aimlessly. The rear guard of the bandits were not caught in the avalanche. They organized survivors. Wounded men and animals were left to fend for themselves. The healthy rounded up horses, donkeys and camels.

The woman chieftain above prevented her warriors from throwing stones and rocks, for the bandits were wasting time scavenging their own dead and wounded. They picked their own people clean of valuables, weapons, food and water. The bodies they left for the carrion bids circling overhead.

Those inside of the trap began exploring their way over the blocked pass. It was an impossible climb for animals. Men on all fours climbed the rubble.

The warriors above promptly threw stones at the climbers. Cahena joined them. Below, the bandits took cover under their large, sturdy shields. The shields stopped both rocks and arrows, but hampered the climbers. Their progress was painfully slow. A few people made it over the blocked pass. The women warriors above attempted to create minor landslides with little success. They prepared to join Aksil at the cave when short bursts of a ram's horn from behind brought into view the sharif and forty warriors. Moshe ben Shimi choked back a sob of joy upon seeing his daughter. He held her close but his first question was to the women. They detailed the situation. He looked at the chaos below on the inside of the trap. On the outside, bandits had formed a caravan and were moving back toward Esau's Cave.

"Mount up," Moshe ordered the women warriors. "Fall in with my archers. We must help Aksil defend the waterhole."

At the other end of the canyon the old chief looked up at the sun. It was now eight hours since the fight began. Hawks, eagles and buzzards circled in the clear blue sky, anxious to feast on the dead. There were few targets near the front of the ambush. Most tribesman moved along the cliffs and canyon walls deeper into the canyon throwing stones on those unprotected bandits in the center of the caravan. The old chief's patience was rewarded. Leaders of the bandits established a place protected by an overhang of rock. They built up a wall of stone for protection from, arrows, javelins and stones. There was little more they could do in defense.

Then what the old man had been waiting for occurred. A turban tied to a long sword was waved. With blasts from the ram's horn he stopped the missiles raining down on the trapped men. Silence in the canyon was broken by screams and moans of wounded men and animals. Three bandits came forward. The old chief left specific instructions to his dhieftains on what his plan was, and he insisted on meeting the enemy alone.

They were three hard-looking men. Their leader had a roughly healed scar from his hairline to his jaw. His dark eyes were disconcerting, as the scarred one looked north when the other moved back and forth. "Who am I speaking with?" the bandit chief demanded.

"Your executioner," The old chief said. "And don't tell me your name."

"If you are going to kill us, why come out and talk?"

"I have these grey hairs because I learned to listen. There is no chance you can break out of this ambush. You can eat your dead horses, camels and men, and probably drink their blood. But in the end you will die, either of thirst or my men's arrows. There is little wood for cooking, so you will eat the meat raw—and eventually with maggots."

"Old man, if we are going to die anyway we may as well take as many of you with us as possible. We are fighters, not shepherds or farmers."

"We Berbers may tend flocks and vineyards, but we can also fight." He motioned at the carnage around them.

"Before we die I will order my men to destroy all the animals," the bandit replied. "We have over 150 camels, three hundred horses and a herd of the fat-tailed sheep captured from the Tuaregs. I will destroy all the wealth we earned over the last year. Jewels and fifty thousand dinars to melt in the sand."

"Are you offering all these in return for your lives?" the old chief asked.

I ask that each man be allowed a horse, some food and ten dinars each. You keep the camels other animals and the wealth they carry. There are a hundred slaves."

"It is interesting bargaining with a dead man," the chief said. "Horses and animals will do you no good. They cannot make it over the landslide behind you. You must surrender your weapons."

"Never our weapons. That is who we are."

"And that is why you will surrender them. I give you my word I will order my men to help you leave Satan's Saddle in peace."

"The word of a Berber has never been a coin of the realm."

"You are now in the realm of the Amazigh Berber, and my word is law."

"Are you the Sharif?"

"I am so taken by all in the Maghreb."

"You can't expect us to travel any caravan trail without weapons. Give us a shield and sword."

"A long knife for each man. You are professional warriors."

"How do we know you will keep your word?"

"Because by killing you I would lose all your horses and booty. Some of my men would be killed or injured. I will remain your hostage until you reach Esau's waterhole behind you."

"You trust me not to kill you?"

"Not really. But on foot, without swords, arrows and long shields, your men would be finished by my men. Killing me would be the supreme act of stupidity. I already have the means of killing you. Ask your men to choose: fight here and die or take your chances going back along the caravan trail. You might meet another caravan to plunder."

"I decide, not my men."

"Choose, then: life or death?"

"One more question. Why do your women warriors fight without covering their breasts? It's very distracting."

The old chief chuckled. "That's why."

CHAPTER 5

THE BATTLE AT ESAU'S CAVE

Aksil's warriors made every effort to reach the cave before the bandits, but they saw what appeared to be twenty ghostly men and horses crowded at the water's edge. Unaware of Aksil's approach the bandits washed off the dust from the avalanche. They were so intent on clearing their noses and throats of dirt and grime they never heard his order to charge. He led his men at a gallop.

Ten bandits were cut down. The others fled to join those straggling back from the caravan. They stood off three hundred yards away, a large band of ghostlike figures mounted on grey beasts with wide frightened eyes and lolling tongues. More men straggled out of the canyon on foot. Bandit leaders formed up their rear guard on horses. Aksil was outnumbered four to one. He had to buy time until the old chief could send help. He lined his men arm's length apart. Their right flank protected by the pool of water in front of the cave and his left flank curved back to the rocky cave entrance. He and his men unsheathed the Takoba, a three foot straight sword, and jammed it point first into the sand. Then planting their large shield in front of that, propped it up with a seven foot lance and two small javelins. They unslung their bows. Strung them and took positions behind the shields.

Aksil sent one man racing forward on his horse. When about fifty yards from the waterhole he reined in and planted his lance with his turban tied to the top and raced back to his position. Aksil ordered, "Notch your arrows. When the enemy line reaches that lance, shoot. I don't care if you kill men or horses. Bring down meat! If they try to break through our lines, plant the shaft of the lance in the ground and set the point chest high to their horses. Do not drop your lance until the horse is impaled or knocks you on your ass. If they do break through, retreat to the cave entrance. There we stand or die. May the gods grant us an honorable death!" The men silently arranged their defense.

The ghostly force of eighty bandits lined up on horses. Their leader signaled and they approached at a canter. Some had swords others, javelins or long knives. They increased their pace to trot, then a gallop. The thunder of hoofs merged with their battle cry. The defenders notched their arrows and let them fly. Some horses and men went down but it did not check the charge. They were desperate to take the water hole. Two more flights of arrows flew into their ranks. They kept on coming. Those on foot behind them followed taking weapons from the dead and wounded. The line of horseman hit the Berber wall of shields at full gallop. The impact echoed through the canyon. The line of shields burst open. The bandits were through. The defensive line collapsed in the center. Aksil's men holding the right flank were outmaneuvered as the charging horsemen splashed through the shallows and turned the flank with ease. About to be surrounded. He signaled and the ram's horn sounded the retreat to the cave's entrance. It was a disorderly withdrawal leaving Berber dead and wounded behind. The oncoming bandits cut the throats of the living and dead. They hacked off their heads and threw them at the double line of Berbers standing shoulder to shoulder at the cave entrance.

Then the bandits stood off and taunted the Berbers. They picked up bows and arrows and hit three Berber warriors before Aksil organized the remaining shields to the front row. Everyone hunkered down behind them. Arrows and stones from slingers were no longer a threat.

Aksil checked his men. Eighteen remained. They had two javelins each, the long sword and knife strapped to their left arm.

"Those bastards have us trapped," Aksil growled. He pointed to the horde of bandits crowding the water pool. "Very well, let them be. Don't antagonize them. The longer they wait the better chance we have the old chief will send help."

The bandits drank, watered their animals and washed themselves. They shouted taunts and curses at the Berbers. Occasionally they shot arrows or threw stones. Aksil's men remained silent. "We aren't going anywhere," he said. "Everyone who has food, share it now. I want the second rank to wash, drink and relieve yourselves inside. Come out and take over from the front rank."

The men heading back into the cave joked, "If we're going to hell we might as well look nice."

One of the men guarding the entrance said. "'They are starting fires. That's a good sign isn't it?"

"They are butchering the dead and wounded horses," Aksil explained. "It gives us more time."'

Food shared among the Berbers was sparse. Everyone was thankful to the wife who packed a bag of sweets for her husband, and the man known as the village drunk had two skins of wine to share. Others told of their fathers eating their boots on campaigns. Jokes were made, but fell silent when the bandits were said to have cannibalized their victims. A gloomy silence was intensified by the aroma of roasting meat from the bandit's cooking fires around the pool.

The bandits had wine enough to enjoy their feast. Their leader was watchful; he placed guards facing the cave and on either flank. These men fired an occasional arrow to harass the Berbers. A halfhearted foray was beaten back by Berber javelins. But now most men had only the sword, knife and shield. There was no wood inside the damp cave. The evening breeze picked up and the men pulled their clothing tighter. The sun sank below the western cliffs. Aksil addressed his men. "I believe they won't attack until morning. They will try and keep us awake all night with arrows and stones. I have no solution. I know it was a terrible ride to reach here, but we must stay awake. In the morning, if help doesn't come, pray to your gods and prepare to die." Aksil leaned forward, and his white teeth shone. Through curled lips he growled, "Kill as many of the dogs as possible. That will guarantee you a place in the Heavenly Garden. And if the gods challenge you, tell them you are a member of Aksil's Chawia Berbers—who died fighting!"

At the head of the canyon the bandit chiefs conceded defeat to the old Berber chieftain. From mid-afternoon into the evening, the bandit leaders at the head of the wadi brought their horses, camels, sheep, goats and pack animals to a gap made in the Berber wall across the canyon floor. The animals were herded into the box canyon where the Berber horses were. The old chief looked on and said nothing to the bandits guarding him.

The surrender went on until midnight. When it was complete, the bandits were ordered to walk back to the avalanche and climb their way out and on to the water hole. The old chief had arranged for him and the three bandit leaders to keep their horses. They rode a mile and a half back to the blockage in the canyon. The bandits there hid in the shadows of the starlit canyon. "What are you waiting for?" the scar-faced leader demanded. "Climb over and let's get to hell out of here."

One of the men pointed up. "They are shooting arrows and throwing javelins and stones."'

"What the hell are you talking about? We have an agreement. Are those slaves hiding over there?"

"Yes."

"Whip them up the rock pile, and we'll see."

Twenty slaves were forced out of hiding and up the rocky wall blocking the canyon. A flight of arrows came down amongst them screams and moans filled the air. A second flight of arrows rained down and there were only half the slaves left, standing or running in circles, afraid to return or go forward. Scar-face grabbed the old chieftain by the throat and snarled, "We have an agreement!"

"My life depends on it," the old man said. "Have your signalman blow three long blasts on the ram's horn, and have your men remain quiet so I may be heard."

The horn echoed through the canyon, and silence fell. Even the animals held their breath. The old chief cupped his hands around his lips and shouted, "Soon the moon will shine its light over the rim of the canyon walls. You will see these murdering bastards down here as in the light of day. Kill them all."

Scarface opened his mouth but at first nothing came out. "You promised!" he yelled.

"And you were right in the beginning," the chieftain said. "You can't trust a Berber. I lie. And that's the truth."

Scarface whipped his long knife across the

throat of the old chief with such force that his head was severed from his neck.

Above, the moon inched its way over the cliffs, illuminating the Berbers on the canyon walls. At the head of the canyon Berbers, now mounted, used their seven-foot lances to prod and pack the bandits closer together at the base of the cliffs. Stones, rocks and boulders rained down on them. Arrows were used on the more daring bandits attempting to climb the canyon walls. The bandits had no shields, nor animals to hide behind. The moon exposed every nook and cranny.

Berber horsemen charged the rear of the bandit column again and again, killing with lance and broadsword. When their arms grew weary they exchanged places with a fresh contingent who hacked and stabbed their way into the melee. From above, arrows and rocks and javelins tore into the crowd below. Two hundred bandits died in the canyon. The dry canyon floor was churned to mud with blood. The Berbers poured down from the heights or dismounted from their horses to kill survivors and search their bodies for loot.

Four in the morning was the normal time for caravan travelers to begin their day. The bandits surrounding Esau's Cave built up their cooking fires. Aksil watched the enemy but saw no preparations for an attack. His men had indeed been harassed through the night. Some had collapsed sleeping on the ground. Others were asleep standing and leaning on their shields. He believed even a halfhearted effort by the bandits would overrun them. He went to the rear of the cave, relieved himself, washed and returned. He would keep watch and allow his men to catch their last chance at sleep before they all slumbered forever. He saw a group of five stragglers coming from the canyon on foot into the bandit camp.

The guards stopped them, and shouted to bring the others. Soon there was a crowd around the stragglers. One bandit took charge and sent the others to rouse the camp. Men stopped tending their fires and food. Those with horses saddled and mounted with weapons. Those without horses took what weapons they could find and formed up on foot behind the cavalry.

Aksil woke his men. He slapped their cheeks until their eyes focused. There were only eight lances among the eighteen survivors to break the horses charge. It wasn't enough.

The bandit leader readied his men to signal the charge—then froze at the sound of a ram's horn.

Behind him he saw a bare-breasted Berber woman with seven-foot lance leading forty warriors into the attack. Their horses plowed through the bandits on foot. They rammed and stabbed the bandit horsemen from behind, throwing them into a panic. Aksil instinctively jumped out in front of his men shouting, "Charge!"

The Berbers did. They stabbed with spears and swords, threw the remaining javelins, and met Sharif Moshe ben Shimi in the center. The slaughter was quick and merciless. Not one bandit remained.

Aksil's men ran to the cooking fires for what food might have been left. Moshe's warriors slaughtered a wounded horse and served out the pieces. Aksil rushed to the Sharif and asked, "I left Cahena with five women archers. Where is she?"

"Hiding in the rocks at the base of the cliff. I didn't know if we would be in time to save you or if we would defeat them. They numbered twenty or thirty more than all of us together."

"You panicked them. Even on foot my men were able to help."

"May I go and retrieve your daughter?"

"She'll be relieved to know we won. Take my horse."

Cahena saw Aksil coming, and trotted her Mongolian pony out from behind some boulders. "Is my father safe?" she called.

"He saved us. It's over," Aksil said. "I will take you to him. Are you alright?"

"I'm fine."

"How did your father know to come and save us?"

"My pigeon told him."

"You said your pigeons can't talk."

"But my father can count. When he read of three hundred and twenty men, twice as many horses and camels as we'd expected, he realized that they wouldn't all fit into the trap you planned. The survivors of the landslide would make for the waterhole. You would either try to defend the waterhole or harass the bandits there."

"How could your father and his warriors make that journey over the cliffs at night? It was difficult during the day."

"Our chief of Jrawa scouts has green eyes; she claims to see in the dark. The stars and rising moon helped."

The two arrived at the Esau's Cave, but Cahena dismounted and hurried away from Aksil to see the wounded. He wanted to bring her to her father in the cave, but he realized she was in a trance.

She walked through the wounded men and women, and touched each one with the palm of her right hand. Each one she touched appeared to be calmed and relieved of pain. Some smiled. One man was holding his entrails in his hands. She smiled down on him, said a few words and kissed his forehead. He smiled up and spoke to her. Aksil went over to ask the man what was said, but the fellow was dead.

Moshe ben Shimi was informed of the slaughter in the canyon, the old chief's death and his lying to the bandits. It was considered an honorable thing among Berbers; a leader sacrificing themself for the tribe was heroic.

Moshe summoned all the chiefs for a meeting in Esau's Cave, and with them arrived two problems. There were more than a thousand captured horses, camels, and as many sheep, goats and donkeys at the head of the canyon. The herds, the bandits' loot and slaves made it the greatest wealth any of the three tribes had ever known. There was enough water in the canyon but not enough fodder. In three days the horses would die, then the sheep, goats and camels.

The second problem was Selim. Moshe's future in-law showed up after the fighting with his men. He had them help with the animals in the canyon and came with the leaders to the meeting in the cave. Moshe and the tribal leaders believed Selim wanted part of the loot. As leader of three tribes, he was invited to sit in council. He did not hesitate to state his claim even before the discussion began.

It caused an uproar. Only Moshe's authority as Sharif stopped a knife-fight. Aksil was foremost in wanting to slit Selim's throat. Moshe shouted, "Sheket!" in Hebrew. Most didn't know the word but understood the meaning: "Everyone sit!"

He nodded to Selim. "My friend and future family member, I am certain you will recognize the complications of your request. It is not bitterness against you; it is against the bandits who killed thirty-six of our warriors and wounded twice that number. Would you kindly step outside and allow this council to establish the reward due you for supporting us?"

Appeased by the Sharif's word, Selim led his chieftains from the cave. Moshe arranged for a banquet of fresh horse-meat to be grilled over the open fires around the outside pool. Captured bandit wine was distributed and kept in good supply for the Helawi.

Angry faces challenged Moshe ben Shimi in Esau's Cave. "Now hear me out!" he said.

Aksil shouted, "That Helawi bastard has no honor! I lost half my men in this fight. Damned if

I'll give him the sweat off my ass."

"Bravery is to be admired," Moshe replied. "Stupidity will get your balls cut off and shoved down your throat. Do you remember who said that to you?"

"The old chieftain," Aksil recalled.

"Sit down and listen. Your bravery is not in question. We respect you; your actions and those of your men in this battle make you a man to be called upon. However, to be a good leader you most look for the opportunity in every problem."

"I see no way of improving the situation," Aksil said. "Selim wants booty he is not entitled to."

"The youngster's right," the chiefs grumbled. "Aksil's tribe suffered the greatest loss."

"I agree," Moshe said. "Aksil is right. But—" He held up his finger and pointed at his chest. "—I am not wrong. No one wants to openly insult Selim and the Helawi."

"How can you pacify him and satisfy us?" They grumbled, "Sharif, explain yourself."

"According to your accounts we captured over six hundred horses, twice as many camels, donkeys, goats and sheep. They lack food. The animals will start dying in three days. Instead of dividing up between our four tribes, we add the Helawi to share in our prize."

"Horses, camels and livestock are wealth," a chieftain said. "The Helawi didn't earn it."

"There are more than enough animals for everyone. The Helawi will be responsible for feeding their herds, but not in our territory. That makes it easier on us." Moshe pointed outside the cave. "You hear the drums and flutes, smell roasting meat, and the Bandit's wine will be served without stop for two days..."

Aksil jumped up and shouted, "You're a genius!"

"Why am I now a genius?"

"Because we will have two days to cull the herds for the best animals, give the others to the damned Helawi, and move before the last fodder runs out."

"Now you are thinking like an old Berber chieftain,'" Moshe said. "I order each tribe to select its best herdsmen to cut the worst one fifth of the herd for the Helawi, so that our herds will be ready to move as soon as possible."

Two days later Selim left Esau's Cave to take charge of his animal herd. In the blind canyon the four tribes had already divided and repacked the spoils of war, and moved out.

The finest horses, camels and other animals became the breeding stock that would improve Berber herds in the Maghreb for the next one hundred years. The four Berber caravans leaving Satan's Saddle stretched three miles. The pace was leisurely to allow the captured livestock to fatten on the grassland. As each tribe reached its road they saluted their Sharif and moved off with loot and herds.

Aksil approached, placed the fingers of his right hand to his forehead, lips and heart, then bowed in the saddle. "Sharif," he said, "I am honored to serve you."

"And I am honored to serve with you. You and yours will always be welcome in the Jrawa tents."

"Your daughter is a most unusual child."

"In what way?"

"She is only nine, but her thoughts are of an older and wiser person."

"Yes," Moshe nodded. "I am aware of this."

"She is also a healer. After the battle I saw her touch men, and they immediately appeared better. Many will recover. She spoke to them. They answered, but when I questioned Cahena she would not answer and the men remembered her but not the conversation."

Moshe sighed, "I have heard these stories. Do they call her a witch?"

"No. They refer to the white streak in her hair as a sign of the high priestess. Your father's name sake, Shimi, served in the holy temple in Jerusalem. They believe she is a reincarnation of him. They call her Cahena: priestess."

"I am always afraid she will be accused of witchcraft."

"Not while I'm around." Aksil held out his hand. Both men clasped each other's forearm. Aksil said, "May I ask a personal question?"

"You've earned the right."

"Why did you engage your daughter to that wet rag of a Helawi son? His father dominates the boy."

"But my daughter will decide to live in my camp. I will become Sharif of seven tribes, and then of all the Berbers in the Maghreb. My daughter will be queen. She can divorce him after a suitable time."

"I would be interested in a marriage arrangement."

Moshe ben Shimi patted Aksil's shoulder. "You'll have to get in line. Cahena will make her own choice of her next husband."

CHAPTER 6

TO CARTHAGE

Oil lamps lit the interior of the Sharif's tent, where Moshe ben Shimi sat across from his daughter. "It is with a heavy heart I send you to Carthage," he said. "Five years without your presence is a painful thought."

"Allow me to remain with you."

The father wagged a forefinger. "That cannot be. You are destined to lead the Berber tribes. You must know the enemy. Learn from the Romans, their strengths and their weaknesses. One day we will face them in war."

"But they are paying for my education!"

"In hopes you will be impressed by their power, culture and science. They have noted you as a future leader. They hope you will become a surrogate for them in the Maghreb."

"Why?"

"Good question. Remember, he who questions controls the conversation. The answer is that the Western Roman Empire in Europe was overrun by the Germans and Northlanders, and has never recovered. These barbarians will turn their attention to Constantinople, capitol of the Eastern Roman Empire, soon enough. The Muslim religion is gaining strength, and it is only a matter of time before Muhammad and his general, Khalid ibn Al Walid, direct their forces against Constantinople. You heard of Muhammad's plan to build a fleet of ships in Tangiers."

"Yes. But why, if the Romans hold Carthage, don't they enter Tangiers and wipe them out?"

"There is a saying in the study of Talmud, of which you are delinquent: 'A good question holds fifty percent of the answer'. Think!"

At first Cahena appeared perplexed. Then her face brightened. "The Romans are weak."

"That is why your marriage to the Helawi. The Romans want an alliance with me and the Berber tribes of the Maghreb. When our tribe and the Helawi are united, other tribes will join us. The two Roman legions based in Carthage, and our warriors, will sweep into Tangiers, kill the Muslims and take their ships. Then we will control the seven seas—and inland from Morocco on the Atlantic Ocean to the Nile River in Egypt, from the Mediterranean Sea to Nigeria, the breadbasket of Africa."

"Will Constantinople share power with Berber tribes?"

"Only as long as it suits their purpose."

Cahena blanched. "Father," she whispered, "The things you speak of are enormous. They will change the lives of millions of people. I am only a child."

The Sharif leaned forward and kissed her forehead. "That, is the most mature thing you could have said. Now go out and learn. Soon the great spring caravan leaves the Atlas Mountains. Berbers send their goods, animals and foodstuff to be sold along the thirteen-hundred-mile route to Carthage. You will be assigned slaves, plus five warriors: three women and two men. Ahmed the mute will tend the Camels and donkeys with your possessions. His mother insists on going; she will cook for you and the others. I want a correspondence by pigeon while you are away. Can you arrange that?"

"Yes. It will be the end of summer before we reach Carthage."

"And the greatest learning experience you will ever have. How many birds do you require?"

"All. New ones will have to be trained."

"Are your people able to do that?"

"Yes. There are several slaves whom I will take to man the stations along the way."'

"Can't you give the message to one bird and fly it here?"

"From Carthage it will require 20 stations."

The tent flap parted and a short block of a man entered. He appeared as wide as he was tall, wore a turban entwined with pearls and a colorful brocade cloak that reached his toes. He had a full beard as thick and black as pitch. His dark eyebrows raised to the turban on his enormous head, and he bowed to the Sharif. "You called?" his voice boomed, and Cahena sat straighter.

"I want to introduce you to my daughter. Cahena, this is the caravan master. For the next few months Benyamin will be lord of the trail. He is a Jew from Spain."

The man gave a cursory bow. "Is it true you cured warriors at the battle of Esau's Cave?'

"Some people were helped."

"I may call upon you during our journey. Donkeys and camels kick people. There are snake, spider, and scorpion bites, especially amongst the children. Can you cure *shil-shul*?"

"What is that?"

"It's Hebrew for diarrhea," her father explained.

"Ozeret, my Nanny, used dried pomegranate skins made into a tea."

"Bring a large supply of those skins. Some wells will be polluted. One of the worse things you can have is several hundred camels with the shits. Oy! What a mess."

"I would like my daughter to learn more about our religion while she is with you."

"This is a *mitzvah* I will enjoy."

"What does that word mean?" Cahena asked.

"A good deed, in Hebrew. It is also a Torah commandment. 'And you shall teach it to your children when you rise up, when you walk by the way and when you sit in your house'" Benyamin pointed a stubby finger at Cahena. "You are expected every Sabbath eve in my tent. You will sleep over, and join the family in prayer on Saturday mornings. Thus you will learn. My caravans do not travel on the Sabbath. We eat Kosher."

Cahena looked at her father. "I'll explain," he said.

Cahena employed half of the slaves in camp making cages, training pigeons, and selecting handlers and their families she would drop off along the route to establish pigeon stations.

The Jrawa contingent numbered a hundred and fifty-eight. Some were assigned to the camel herds at the rear of the caravan. These animals were for sale. With those captured from the bandits, the herds were larger than usual. The caravan was the largest ever to set forth from the foot-hills of the Atlas Mountains.

Bearded tribesmen with skin coats of bear, snow leopard and wolves, straggled down from the snowcapped mountains to assemble on the plains below. Benyamin assigned camping places and positions in the caravan. The land had long ago been stripped of trees by animals and man; dried camel dung was used for fuel. Children followed the camels and made briquettes of the dung with their bare hands.

The last rains of winter swept down the mountain and inundated the plains. The caravan master had selected the camping sites well; not one person was lost in the raging floods that thundered down the wadis, through ravines and valleys. Within two days the Maghreb came alive. Grass peeked from the arid soil. Wild roses lifted their buds to the warmth of the sun. It was the thirtieth of March and the first day of spring.

At four in the morning Moshe ben Shimi woke Cahena. "My little dove," he said, "It is time for you to leave the nest. My heart hurts when I think I will not see you for five years."

Cahena and her father hugged.

Outside he introduced Cahena to the warriors and explained, "You have slaves and servants. These five warriors are for your protection; that is their sole function."

He introduced each of the three women and

two men. "Bow your heads," Moshe ben Shimi said, then he read from an old scroll no larger than the palm of his hand.

"The Wayfarer's Prayer:

'May it be Your will oh Lord our God and God of our fathers that You lead us toward peace, direct our footsteps toward peace, guide us toward peace, and help us reach our desired destination for life, gladness and peace.

May You rescue us from the hand of every foe, ambush, bandits, and evil animals along the way, and all manner of punishments that assemble to come to earth.

May You bless our handiwork and grant us grace, kindness, and mercy in Your eyes and in the eyes of all who see us.

May You hear the sound of our supplication, because You are God Who hears prayer and supplication.

Blessed are You, Lord, Who hears our prayer.'"

The Sharif clasped each warrior's forearm, hugged Cahena, and whispered in her ear, "It is time for you to go out in the world and learn its ways."

She mounted her Mongolian pony and left without looking back, but the nine-year-old shed soul-wrenching tears into her scarf.

The trail from the foot-hills was deserted. Earlier the Jrawa had sent their camels for sale to the rear of the caravan. Ahmed and the pack camels, loaded with trade goods, food, and tents went ahead to an assigned position in the caravan's center. Cahena and her warrior escort moved at a leisurely pace down the slopes of the Atlas Mountains. The caravan was expected to stretch three miles long while on the march: their arrival was timed to join Ahmed while on the march.

The caravan cooking-fires appeared like stars on the plain below. Behind them the sun sparkled off the snowcapped eastern peaks of the thirteen-thousand-foot mountains. The morning light caught up to Cahena's party as they came onto the open plain.

The curtain of darkness withdrawn, the Maghreb displayed herself in all its spring beauty. The new green carpet of grass highlighted the red and yellow flowers. Small multi-colored birds flew from wild roses to fields of lavender. High overhead Cahena watched flocks of storks search for a lake to feed in. She looked back at the snowcapped mountains separating the Mediterranean plains from the Sahara Desert. Some of the highlands were so rich with iron that rust covered their slopes.

An eagle swooped low over the horseman. Cahena put two fingers of her right hand into her mouth, covered them with her left hand, and gave a high-pitched whistle. The bird hovered nearby. Cahena whistled again and offered her covered forearm. To the warriors' amazement the eagle flew to the offered perch. The bird examined Cahena and she memorized every detail and shade of black and white feathers and their patterns on legs, wings, head and breast. With her free hand she dug out a piece of beef jerky from her pocket and carefully held it to the sharp curved beak. It was snapped up, and the bird flew away.

Cahena removed her left foot from the stirrup and folded it behind two of the four horns of the Roman saddle. With a piece of charcoal she sketched the bird on parchment. She called it the Booted Eagle because of the black-feathered legs. The warriors were startled at the accuracy of the drawing and the fierce eyes of the eagle, and they looked with more respect on their young charge. Cahena was oblivious of their reactions; she was absorbed in the abundance of plant and animal life. She concentrated on the birds.

She had never before traveled south, nor ever met Berber farmers. They wore no weapons or shoes. Their clothing was minimal and brown with dust. Donkeys were used for hauling loads. There were no horses but healthy herds of sheep, goats and some cattle. The fields were irrigated by a complex design of trenches. Water was diverted from the rivers and controlled by a series of wooden gates raised and lowered by hand. The people spoke a dialect of the Berber language Cahena could understand. The farmers lived in small groups of five or six families. They traded foodstuffs for wares found only in towns they would never see.

Cahena questioned the flags being flown from several of the houses. The blue, she was told, indicated a boy and the white a girl of marriageable age. Cahena realized that two things were required to establish a settlement: water and a crossroad. The more trafficked the latter and abundant the former, the greater the size of the settlement.

The caravan traveled at two miles an hour. By mid-afternoon it stretched some three and a half miles. Everyone walked but the caravan guards, wealthy merchants, small children and the elderly. The dust set up by the column could be seen for miles in all directions. Benyamin, the Caravan Master, seemed to be everywhere at once. He occasionally nodded to Cahena but today he reined in his horse and boomed, "It's

Friday. Come early to my tent. Bring clothing to sleep over. You will bathe with my wife and children." Then he was off at a gallop to attend something ahead. Cahena realized he used up two or three horses a day. She had no idea what the bathing was about. She bathed on the full moon every month whether she needed to or not.

Her guards escorted her to Benyamin's tent. The caravan master's wife was busy directing slaves in preparing food for the Sabbath meal. The tent was warm with smells of roasting meats, boiling soup, fish, onions and garlic. Baked goods were being prepared for the ovens. Bread was prepared by Benyamin's two daughters. They made twenty large circular loaves by braiding the dough. These were set aside, covered with damp cloth and allowed to rise before going to the ovens. There the surface of the dough was dampened and sprinkled with sesame seeds. Prior to putting the loaves in the ovens, Anav, the mother, brought Cahena together with her daughters, said a prayer, pinched off a piece of dough and threw it into the fire. When questioned by Cahena, Anav did not know why she did it. Her mother and grandmother taught her. When asked what the prayer was, she said it was in Hebrew and she didn't know what it meant. Cahena tried but failed to interpret it.

Cahena questioned about bathing. Anav said, "It is in preparation for the Sabbath. Since the destruction of the temple, the Sabbath table in every Jewish home becomes the altar on which we offer sacrifices to the one God. The bread is a representation of the *Mana* God supplied us with during our forty years in the desert. We bathe to make our bodies as clean as possible before attending our offerings to God."

They reached the river where other women entered and left the water. They all knew Anav and her daughters, and everyone was curious about Cahena. When told she was the daughter of Moshe ben Shimi of the Jrawa, she was greeted heartfelt warmth. Anav and the girls dropped their clothes and waded naked into the river chest high. They repeated Hebrew prayers whose meaning was unknown to them, rubbed their bodies with the chilling water, interlocked the fingers of both hands, put them on top of their heads and ducked under the water until their hands were covered. They snorted some water into their nose, swished some in their mouth, spit it out and hurried out of the water to vigorously rub themselves dry. Cahena duly copied them.

On the way back to camp they passed the

men going down to the river for the same purpose. The men had been at prayer and were singing the song to the Sabbath Bride. The women joined in. Cahena knew the words from her father, who sang it every Friday evening before blessing the bread and wine, but she had never heard it sung by forty men and women. Benyamin's voice boomed over all others and Cahena found herself singing with joy and moving to the rhythm of the song.

> *Shalom Aleichem mlachai ha malachiym ha kadosh baruch hu!*

"May your coming be in peace, o angels of peace, Angels of the Exalted One–from the King who reigns over kings, the Holy One blessed be He..."

On arrival at the cooking tent, Anav and her married daughter lit candles. The mother explained, "The lighting used to be done by men, but it took too long for them to come in from the fields, bathe, dress properly and light the candles. About twenty years ago the Rabbis in Babylon and Spain ruled we women should do it."

The tent where the meal took place was several long tents tied together. Beautiful carpets lined both sides of the ground and several long tables linked end-to-end filled the center.

There was more than enough room for the one hundred and twenty adults and children. Benyamin returned, leading the men dressed in their finest cloaks and trousers and wearing colorful turbans. His booming voice greeted his family and guests with a hearty, "Shabbat shalom". He poured sweet red wine into a large silver goblet and blessed two enormous rounded loaves of bread. After sipping the wine he passed the cup down the table. Servants placed full wineskins all along the tables. Benyamin tore the bread into small pieces, sprinkled it with salt, and passed it down both sides of the table as he boomed, "Hearty appetite!"

There were deep-fried fish served on banana leaves, covered with cashew nuts and sprigs of parsley. Dates, almonds, olives and various pickled vegetables were nibbled between courses of roasted goat, lamb, and beef. There were great heaping trays of pilaf and couscous spiced with cumin, ginger, paprika, cinnamon and saffron. Fresh peppermint, parsley, and coriander were also side dishes with chili paste and peppers and mounds of olives preserved in various ways. Nuts, fruits, and sweet cakes soaked in honey, served with thick black coffee, completed the feast.

During the meal Benyamin had little to say, for his mouth was always full. He listened to his family and guests. Their major topic was the caravan dust plume. It could be seen from miles away and could attract bandits. Benyamin continued eating and would nod now and then. The large wine cup was returned empty to him. He filled it, and in one draught drained the silver vessel. He took a fistful or raisins mixed with almonds stuffed his mouth and nodded to his guests. He washed that down with more wine and said, "Tonight we are honored to have at out Sabbath table Cahena, daughter of Moshe ben Shimi, a Jew and Sharif of the Jrawa tribe. Cahena's father and mother were both from families of the high priests in the Holy Temple. She will travel with us as far as Carthage where she will study at the Roman school."

"You mean the Byzantine school," someone corrected.

"I keep forgetting that Rome as a power is no more. On our return trip we will make the three thousand mile journey to the Byzantine capital city of Constantinople. I gave my word to Cahena's father to teach her about Judaism, so forgive me if I keep my word." He turned to Cahena. "Questions?" he asked.

"How do you get enough fresh fish to feed so many people?"

Benyamin rocked back and roared with

laughter. "I'm expecting a Biblical question, and what is the subject? Fish!" He dried his eyes and said, "A good observation. We always travel alongside a river, stream or other sources of water. My father and his father's before him were traveling these routes since our expulsion from Jerusalem. We carry wicker baskets in the shape of a cone, and when we halt we place the wide end facing upstream. The water goes through and the fish are invited to dinner."

"Your wife tears off a piece of bread dough before baking and throws it into the oven fire. Why?"

"That is to symbolize the burnt offering which was made in the temple. Since the holy temple was destroyed, we consider the Sabbath table our altar."

"And why do some of your slaves wear a copper ring in their right ear?"

"Indeed I am going to be pressed trying to educate you. The slaves with pierced ears are those who chose to remain slaves."

"Who would choose to remain a slave?"

"Someone who would rather that another person make decisions for him, and be responsible for his or her welfare and that of their family."

"That doesn't make sense."

"Because you were raised as a Berber, the

Free People. Berbers go where they want and when they want. The Romans, or Byzantines, will soon put a stop to that."

"Why?"

"So they can tax you."

"Why can't they tax us now?"

"They can't find you. And when they do, they aren't certain who they've got. They are not powerful enough."

"I don't think they will tax us for another five years."

Benyamin's dark eyebrows lowered, and his bearded face looked grim when he said, "It is time to bless the Lord for his bounty. *Rabbotai n'vorache*." Men at the table who knew the Hebrew prayer replied, and Benyamin led the concluding service. He motioned for Cahena to see him later.

She joined the guests and slaves clearing the food, cups and platters. The carpets were dusted and replaced for the meal after morning prayers. The other guests duly filed out.

Benyamin called her aside, and walked her to the unmarried women's tent. "You are a very intelligent girl," he said, "And your father allowed you to sit in on important meetings. It would have been a grave mistake to explain why the Berbers have five years before being taxed."

"You know the reason for my marriage to the Helawi."

"Yes: a consolidation of the tribes. But you must be careful who hears you."

"But aren't they all Jews at your table?"

"No. Several Pagan dignitaries and Muslims share our Sabbath meal."

"Muslims? I thought they have their own laws about food."

"With revisions, those were taken from our Torah. Their animals must be slaughtered by a believer in one god who makes a blessing at the time of slaughter."

"Can they eat Christian food?"

"No."

"Why?"

"In Allah's name, Muhammad declared the Christians to be idol-worshippers. They worship three gods at once: the Father, the Son of God, and something called the Holy Spirit."

"Do we Jews consider them idol worshippers?"

"Some do and some don't."

"What if a Muslim were starving? Could he eat forbidden foods?"

"It's a Jewish commandment they adopted, called the Law of Necessity. That which is necessary makes the forbidden permissible. For Muslims, it allows one to eat pork or carrion, but not to drink wine even if one is dying of thirst. We Jews can drink as much wine as we like. Enough questions for tonight. You will be awakened for prayer service and afterwards we will eat."

Cahena found the Morning Prayer service unique. There were over forty men and women. The children were unsupervised and entered or left the tent as they wished. An old Moroccan Jew led the service, and he was easy to follow. A Torah scroll was opened and read. Those males from families of the priestly class blessed the congregation. Prayers concluded with children singing the familiar hymn, *Adon Olam*: Lord of the World. Each head of household gathered his family to him, spread his prayer shawl over their heads and blessed them. Benyamin invited Cahena to his family blessing and she felt secure.

It was midday when they walked back to the food tents. The servants had placed steaming cups of thick black caffa for them, a short stump of sugar cane by each cup. Anav showed Cahena how to dip the sugar cane in the caffa and suck the sweetness from it. After a while the coffee became cool and sweet enough to drink. It revitalized her. Anav cautioned against a second cup, "You won't be able to nap after eating."

Servants went to the baking ovens in pairs. It took two men to lift each of the four large pots and carry them into the tent. The pungent smell escaping with the steam from the covered pots set the juices flowing in Cahena's mouth. "What is it?" she asked.

"Hamin," Anav said. "It cooks for twelve hours."

"What's in it?"

"Do you want me to start from the top layer or the bottom?"

"I'll never get to the bottom of that pot."

"The family eats leftovers during the week on the trail. On top, what appears like large sausages is kishke. I learned it from a Khazari family. It is flour mixed with the cooking fat, spices and whatever snippets of meat comes to hand. It is stuffed into cow intestines. Alongside the kishke are eggs in their shells and stuffed peppers, eggplant and zucchini. Then comes a layer of red beans, a layer of white beans, a layer of chicken, a layer of yams, a layer of lamb, a layer of rice, and a layer of beef, and finally the bottom layer of chickpeas. I spice it with garlic, onions, cinnamon, ginger, and black pepper. I add cumin, hot peppers, and a large dollop of honey."

"...That will indeed feed us all for a week."

Life on the trail fell into a routine: up at four, feed and pack the animals, eat breakfast and step out onto the road. Watch the birds and sketch new ones. Ride on her pony up and down the caravan speaking with people from far off places.

There were several families from Chengdu, China; they had traveled through India, Iran, Iraq, Arabia, crossed the Red Sea into Ethiopia, then Sudan, Egypt, Libya and now in Algeria traveling to Carthage. They had been in caravans for five years. They expected at least three more years traveling through Italy, Greece, Turkey and Russia before returning home. They were trying to establish contacts for trade similar to the Silk Road, but according to Benyamin it was a scheme to cover their mapping the area, noting what governments or tribes were strongest, and where food and water could be attained to support large numbers of troops.

"Why don't you report them?" Cahena asked.

"To whom?"

"The Romans."

"They have as many spies in this caravan as I do. I eat once a week with the Chinese. They keep pork, cat and dog off my menu, but they eat anything that moves or grows. Sometimes it's disgusting, but they have a way of frying rice and roasting duck that is the best. And you want to see how well they eat with two little sticks. They think we are crude to eat with our hands, and the Romans with a knife."

Cahena found that Benyamin was right; the Chinese food was delicious. She joined him once a week at their tent for an evening meal. She mastered the eating sticks after being given her own pair and three beads. She practiced picking up the beads and moving them about to specific places on the exquisite blue-and-white ceramic plates with images of two graceful women crossing a wooden bridge spanning a stream where an old man fished. She learned of the variety of teas available which were never served with sugar cane. She preferred Yasmin tea; the flower buds opened in the hot water and the fragrance heightened the taste. Cahena dispensed her own tea of dried pomegranate skins.

Diarrhea was common in the caravan, but not among the Chinese. She questioned what medicine they used. They rarely had the problem, but when they did, used chamomile tea, rice soup or hyacinth bean soup. The Chinese believed it was their tea prevented diarrhea. Cahena gave this much thought. It didn't seem logical; the Muslims in the caravan drank tea and coffee, but they rarely made soups along the trail. The Chinese always served soup, breakfast and dinner. She found that the Chinese women made an overabundance of boiled water for soups and teas, and they used the excess water to fill the water skins for the day.

The one thing common between the soups, tea, and drinking water was that it had all been boiled.

Cahena tried to convince Anav to have the servants boil water for drinking. She was told that it would take too much time. She approached Benyamin, who begged off. "I only go to the kitchen to eat. Once I open my mouth, it takes in food. I don't suggest anything to Anav. She can be dangerous."

Life in the caravan became routine. Farmers along the way lived in mud huts with thatched roofs on a slope forming an inverted 'U' with the open end pointed toward the caravan trail. Matching the number of families able to support themselves from the land was the number of huts. The smallest was five huts; the largest, thirty. A shallow trench bordered the inside of the U in front of each house. A stream flowed in from the top of the U and down both sides to a channel through the caravan road and into the fields of wheat or barley. People washed, urinated, slaughtered animals in the stream and drank from the same water. Caravans were an extra source of income and welcomed.

They also provided loot for farmers adventurous enough to take the risk.

It was after midnight. Ahmed the mute had attended the birth of a camel when he saw two men crawling into an area where the camel loads were kept for the night. He informed his mother who alerted the guards.

The thieves were captured with their loot of rugs from Persia. They were bound and held for trial. Benyamin the caravan master was judge, jury and executioner. He delayed the trial until the inhabitants of the two settlements nearest the line of march were brought to witness the proceedings. A special chair was brought out, called Elijah's throne, and Benyamin sat in the ornately carved straight-backed chair. Cahena had seen it used during circumcision for male Jewish children.

Benyamin motioned the two thieves be brought forward. They were tied around the chest and upper arms, and did not raise their heads when Benyamin questioned, "Do you admit to stealing from my caravan?"

Both men nodded in the affirmative.

"Did you know the penalty for thievery on the trail?"

Again they nodded in the affirmative. One

man raised his head and pleaded. "Kill us please. We are not strong enough to suffer a life as outcasts. We are not courageous enough to kill ourselves."

"May the Almighty give you the strength to do what is right. It is my role to administer and implement a just decision: guilty, by your own words." Each thief was held by two men who kicked them behind the knees. They dropped to the ground, and Benyamin approached. He was given a large piece of cloth in his left hand. He grasped the thief's right ear and sliced it off with his knife. He placed the bloody cloth over the thief's nose and cut the tip off. He then clasped the man's right hand with his left hand, covered them with the cloth, pulled the hand as straight as the ropes allowed. A guard stepped forward and slashed the hand off at the wrist. Benyamin held the severed hand aloft, threw it to the ground and boomed, "Know by these signs that this man is a thief. Beware of him."

Guards tied a bandage around the bleeding stump and another around the man's head, covering the nose and severed ear. Benyamin stepped in front of the second man, who collapsed and stained himself. The caravan master signaled the guards to hold him upright on his knees and preformed the same ceremony.

Cahena had watched her father institute this

tribal justice. The taking of the right hand meant the thieves were forever forbidden to take part in any communal or family meal. People ate with their right hand and cleaned themselves at toilet with the left. The two would be forced to scavenge with the dogs and jackals for food. Cahena wondered if using the Chinese eating sticks would alleviate the problem of them eating with their family.

Then it was reported that a pack of wolves had attacked the rear of the column. They killed one shepherd and carried off a three-year-old boy. Wild animals were being drawn to the caravan. Benyamin sensed that wild men were also coming. His feelings were soon confirmed.

At dusk the following day two Bedouin approached the caravan riding camels that had been driven hard. They were small, thin wiry men with dark piercing eyes. They used Benyamin's name and demanded to meet with him. The caravan master embraced both men. He led them to his tent while shouting for food and wine to be served. He also called for Cahena.

She entered the tent and remained silent in the shadows. It was obvious from the conversation that the men were in the pay of Benyamin and reporting a serious threat by two groups of bandits who had combined for a major attack on the caravan.

"Come forward," Benyamin ordered Cahena. He introduced her to the Bedouin, gave her lineage and that in five years she would be queen to the Jrawa Berbers. The two men stood and she was taller than both. One said, "I saw your Father at the Battle of Satan's Saddle."

"Our scouts never saw you."

"They weren't supposed to. How old are you?"

"I just turned ten."

"The Jrawa certainly grow their women big."

The other Bedouin said, "I don't know whether I'd rather clothe her or feed her."

"You'll never get the chance," Benyamin chuckled. "You two Pagans marry your own kind. This is a Jewish Princess."

Both men sat down to their food. "Cahena," Benyamin ordered, "Go with Ahmed the mute and cut out two of the fastest camels in the herd. Use the saddles from the run-down animals these two came on." He turned to the men and said, "This Ahmed can't speak a word. He uses a whistle and is the best damned camel man I ever saw. He can make his camels dance."

Ahmed and Cahena approached the camel herd at the end of the long column. It was dark but he knew exactly which animals he wanted.

They could be found at the rear of the herd, and with the aid of three guards he pulled aside the two sleek creatures. They were of medium size with no distinguishing marks. He patted their stomachs, sides and humps; certain they were well fed and watered, he coaxed them away from the herd and put on harnesses. He and Cahena mounted them and rode bareback. On their return, he saddled the animals and through his mother told Cahena that the two worn-out animals should be slaughtered and made into a feast for the Pagans in the caravan.

The two Bedouin gazed with satisfaction at their new mounts, which looked like the two they had ridden in on, were the same size and appeared to have fast lines on fore and hind legs. Cahena noticed a new purse at the waist of each man. She reached down, took some dirt and rubbed the purses with it. The men understood and bowed their appreciation. One of the Bedouin asked. "Are the animals fed and watered?"

Cahena grinned, "We just finished bricking them."

"What do you mean?"

"You take the camels to water, get two bricks, sneak up behind them and bang them on the balls..."

The two men almost broke their faces laughing. "When you become queen we will scout for you," they pledged.

"I will keep you to that promise."

The scouts had said the bandits' attack would take place the coming Sabbath Eve. The outlaws would wait for the Jewish men to bathe in the river. Those bandits already in the caravan would signal when the Jewish guards were in the water and most vulnerable.

Benyamin and his lieutenants had no idea who the spies were, so he ordered his men not to show preparations for the assault. Benyamin tried to calculate the losses he would take in men, money and livestock. He couldn't possibly defend the entire column. The scouts estimated to two hundred bandits; he had eighty fighting men plus another fifty or so who could protect their families, and they were spread out over three miles. His people would be overwhelmed in the first rush.

While contemplating the oncoming catastrophe he spied one of his outriders racing back along the caravan trail whipping his horse into a lather. The scout reined in before the caravan master in a cloud of dust. "Romans!" he shouted. "Three hundred marching to meet us."

"Did you ask them why they want to meet

us?"

"I stayed away from them. We are headed straight for them."

Cahena and Benyamin were on their way to eat with the Chinese. She brought her pony to Benyamin's side and said. "God is smiling on us."

"A Roman smile I can do without. They tax everything that moves."

"They can save us from the bandits."

"Why should they?"

"For money. My father told me the soldiers and officers get paid for fighting. If they live, they receive a pension after sixteen years of service. Be certain to invite them for the Sabbath Eve when the bandits are expected."

Benyamin spread his hands and said, "Sabbath, them?" He pointed to the oncoming column led by an officer on horseback. He was followed by three standard bearers and four columns of troops with red and gold shields marching toward them. Benyamin looked down from his horse at Cahena who said, "If you pay the scouts, you can pay them."

"You can't always tell about Romans. If the commander considers my offer an insult, he'll cut out my stomach to see the back of my belly button."

"Then don't insult him. Make the offer large

enough to bribe him."

Benyamin spurred his horse forward to meet the Roman officer. He spoke in Latin offering the honorific greetings and requesting that his caravan keep moving. "We do not seek you," The legion commander said. "It's bandits we're after. We are the first cohort of the Seventh Legion, based in Carthage. My other cohorts are two days out on your eastern and western flanks."

"I may be of some help to you," Benyamin said. "We are expecting a visit from a large group of bandits this Friday."

The Legion commander's eyes brightened.

CHAPTER 7

THE SABBATH EVE BATTLE

Benyamin ordered those in his caravan to share their food with the soldiers. Fresh bread, meat, vegetables and sweet cakes instead of sour wine, hard-tack biscuits and beans delighted the Romans. The officer and three Centurions accompanied Benyamin to his family, where they were served what remained in the hamyin pots. They ate as if they had bottomless stomachs and drained jugs of wine. Their mouths were always full, so they listened to Benyamin about the expected attack. The Legion Commander conferred with his officers and presented a plan, to which Benyamin agreed.

He introduced Cahena, who would be a guest of the Roman Prelate in Carthage. The officer revealed it was one of his centurions who had brokered the marriage agreement. Cahena was delighted to meet with the soldier in charge of the Roman messenger pigeons. In their short time together they shared information that helped Cahena afterward. They even addressed a letter to their commandant saying she was in the caravan and would arrive toward the end of June.

Cahena was shocked when the Romans formed up on the road and marched off. Benyamin explained to Cahena that had the Romans remained, spies in the caravan would have warned the bandits. "There is a Cohort of 300 men on our east flank, and another cohort on our west flank. They will move in when signaled."

"How do they signal each other?"

"During the day, by polished shields reflecting the sunlight. At night with fire, and in combat by trumpet."

"But how do we know where the bandits will attack?"

"We already know it will be Friday at sundown. The Romans are certain they will attack our camel herd in the rear. Our wealthiest travelers and most precious cargos of spices, silk and salt is the center. They will attempt to kill me and my family. That would leave the caravan leaderless and forestall attempts to trail them."

Benyamin included Cahena in the consultations with his men, who appreciated the child's insight. Sometimes her thoughts were naïve but more often they highlighted a problem or hinted at a solution. She was too brilliant to be excluded.

He had river sand spread out on the floor of his tent in an eight by three foot rectangle. With a staff he drew a line down the length of the center of the rectangle. "This is our caravan, traveling south. According to the Roman commander, there is no way to defend our three mile long column. Similarly the bandits, who number two hundred, cannot attack the entire caravan. They will attack our wealth. That is the animal herds in the rear and our rich merchants in the center. The bandits are mounted on camels. The three Roman cohorts number nine hundred, But they are tracking the bandits on foot. One cohort is behind the bandits on our eastern flank and one unit on the other side of the river on our western flank. The commander with the first cohort is following two miles behind our herds.

"The plan is to suit up for battle. Wear our daily clothes over our armor. We go to the river after the women have finished bathing. The Romans on the other side of the river will hide on the banks until the attack begins. Half of us help the Romans to cross the river by throwing ropes to them and pulling them over. We must do that quickly. They will be in full battle armor and cannot swim. The other half of our men form a protective perimeter in front of the women."

"How many men will we have?"

"Less than eighty."

'Why so few?"

"The Romans in the rear need fifty of our horsemen to stop those attacking the herds."

"That leaves us naked against the outlaws! We need horsemen to stop their attack."

"Drastic times call for drastic measures. I believe the Romans planned correctly. We leave the front third and rear third of the caravan unguarded. We concentrate our men in the center. And hold until the soldiers cross the river."

"It means you are handing over the herds to the thieves."

"And what must they do with them?"

"Gather them up and drive them away.'"

"Which way? They can't cross the river with two thousand animals. They must return to their last camp. They won't hurt the animals. The first cohort in the rear will deploy across their path of retreat, while our horsemen race about the slower camel riders picking them off."

"What is the second cohort doing on the eastern flank?" Cahena asked.

"Coming up behind the attacking villains in the center, to trap and kill every last one of them."

"What happens if the Romans crossing the river don't reach us in time?" A man asked.

Benyamin's chest heaved, and he emitted a deep sigh. "Sit on the ground, pull up your knees, put your head between your legs and kiss your ass goodbye." He pointed to his men. "The bastards are coming to kill us, rape our women and sell them, and our children into slavery. One slave is worth three camels. One dead bandit is a good bandit. No quarter will be given."

The sun lingered above the western horizon, and Jews in the caravan prepared for the Sabbath. Fires were built up and banked for the night. Cahena accompanied the women to the river. There was little discussion; the children played, unaware of the danger. Cahena and many of the women had coils of rope wound about their bodies which they removed and left at the river's edge. The women waded naked into the water and Cahena thought she saw a movement in the underbrush on the other side of the river. She completed ducking under water saying prayers taught to her by Anav. They waded out and dried themselves.

"Hurry!" Anav called. "The men are on their way."

Benyamin appeared leading the men. He looked wider with his armor underneath his clothing. The sun rested on the western skyline. A ram's horn sounded: one long blast and a staccato burst of short blasts. It was repeated by other ram's horns up and down the caravan.

The attack had begun. Across the river a brass trumpet sounded, and the bushes came alive with Roman soldiers smiling from ear to ear. The women blushed. Legionnaires plunged into the water grasping the ropes thrown across by men of the caravan. It took only minutes for the Roman cohort to form up, shield to shield, in three ranks of one hundred men each. The officers shouted commands, and the three ranks spread to double arm's length. Each man held a shield on the left arm, two javelins in the left hand, a long spear in the right, and buckled at their waist the famous Roman short-sword. Behind this cohort were twenty archers from the caravan's guards.

Screams and shouts of terror from the unsuspecting members of the caravan came out of the dark as they fled to the river. They stared in fright at the line of Roman soldiers. Benyamin and his men encouraged them to pass through the ranks of soldiers to the river. The first of the bandits were heard whooping and screaming war cries from their perches atop charging camels. The fastest of them caught up to some women and children and speared them with lances or threw feathered darts into their backs. The camels were trained to stamp on the fallen. There were over a hundred attackers.

So intent were they on instilling fear into the hearts of the travelers that they didn't see the cohort of armed Romans facing them until the last minute. They reined in their camels fifty yards from the Roman battle line, and formed a confused mass of animals and men. The Roman commander raised his arm. Trumpets sounded, and the right and left flanks of the Roman line began to encircle the confused bandits.

Leaders among the brigands attempted to organize a charge into the Roman ranks. Twenty camels came loping forward. The trumpet sounded. Roman soldiers closed ranks and planted the butts of their lances in the earth, with the heads pointed to the oncoming charge. They hunkered down behind their shields as a flight of twenty arrows flew overhead into the oncoming charge.

One bandit was knocked off his mount and two camels went down from multiple arrows. A second flight of arrows and three more camels went down before the main body crashed into the wall of shields and spear points. Three bandits broke through and were quickly pulled from their mounts. Seeing the carnage ahead of them, the remaining bandits abandoned the idea of another charge, their expectation of an easy kill forgotten. They were being outflanked on the right and left.

They fell back through the caravan, retreated across the road and into the fields, only to be met by three more ranks of Roman soldiers. The Romans advanced from east and west all in perfect step, keeping cadence by banging their lances on against their shields. The sound frightened the camels. The bandits were driven together and encircled by the two cohorts.

Six hundred men used their lances to unseat the riders, and the short swords to kill them. The ground became muddy with blood. In short order, the whole bandit horde was dead.

The soldiers picked the bodies clean of valuables and weapons, and piled their loot to be divided later. Benyamin's men stayed clear of the foragers. They rounded up the frightened camels and put the badly wounded ones out of their misery.

The Roman commander mounted two hundred men on Benyamin's horses, and they searched for attackers in hiding. The two cohorts formed up to march to the rear of the column, but one of Benyamin's guards came racing up on a lathered horse, shouting, "It's all over in the rear! We picked them off their camels, and those we missed were caught by the Romans of the first cohort. The animal herds are safe. We lost three men killed and several wounded. The soldiers killed everyone they caught."

Cahena was impressed by the discipline of the Roman soldiers. They moved without hesitation to verbal or trumpeted commands. They were a powerful weapon in the hands of their commander. He could wield his units with speed and precision. Her wild Berbers and Tuaregs could never be trained to obey like that.

Anav called her to attend a wounded Roman; he had been kicked in the stomach by a camel and slashed on his forearm with a scimitar. Although he was suffering more pain in his stomach, she first stopped the flow of blood from his arm. He lay on his side in the fetal position and she asked him to roll over on his back. With painful effort he did, but could not straighten his legs; the pain was too great. She undid his tunic, and saw that the skin above his navel had turned blue and purple. She began speaking to him in a soft low voice. He could not understand her, and when questioned later she did not recall speaking. The man's face slowly changed from a teeth-grating grimace to a placid smile. Slowly his knees straightened and his legs lowered. He felt less pain, and thanked her. She attended others, and all expressed gratitude.

Wounded camels were slaughtered and butchered to be roasted on open fires for the troops. Benyamin came to an agreement with the Legion commander to buy the captured bandit camels and weapons. Both would be sold on the trail to Carthage. The Roman commander had his men set up a place to trade the valuables collected from the bodies for sale to merchants of the caravan. He and his officers were invited to Benyamin's Sabbath table.

During the meal Cahena questioned Benyamin as to why camel meat was not served. "The camel," she pointed out, "chews its cud, like a cow or a sheep, and has cloven hooves."

"Have Ahmed the Mute show you the bottom of the hoof of a camel. You will see that there is a pad that connects the split hoof. It makes it possible for the animal to walk on sand without sinking in. It also makes the beast non-kosher."

"Where do you Jews get all these rules?" the commander asked.

"From the Torah—the first five books of the Bible."

"Is it for your health?"

"It could be, but for certain rules, like our diet, no reason is given. It's a commandment; we must follow it."

"Isn't that difficult to live with?"

"Not really. For someone like me, who is always traveling to foreign lands with different gods on the other side of every river and ways of worship, I don't have to worry. Elohim, the one God, is the only one I serve."

"We Romans have many gods, of many different sorts. I pay attention to the important ones."

"We know," Benyamin said. "Your Emperor made himself a god and wanted us to worship him."

The commander grinned, "Some of our gods are fallible."

"Elohim is infallible."

"Be that as it may," the commander pointed across the table, "This young lady impressed my men and earned their gratitude, and mine, for healing a number of them." He bowed his head to Cahena. "I thank you for your ministrations to my soldiers. Do you have experience with 'Ghebbe Khalesseh' fever, also called 'Bad Air'–Malaria?"

"What are the symptoms?"

"Fever, headache, chills and vomiting, recurring every forty-eight hours. My best soldier in the legion is stricken with it. He is our aquilifer and carries the Legion's Eagle."

"The fever is common in the Maghreb," Cahena said. She had helped Ozeret brew tea from a certain tree bark to treat the condition. She also knew that the recurrence of attacks within forty-eight hours meant he had the more deadly type of disease. She mentioned this. The Commander understood, and after the meal personally escorted Cahena to the tent where his man was being cared for.

The man was wrapped in animal skins near a fire, yet he was shivering and perspiring at the same time. Cahena took a cloth and dried the puddles of sweat from his eyes and ears. She smoothed his damp hair, and with the palms of her hands caressed his forehead and cheeks. Slowly at first, the man stopped shivering. She dried his face twice more, and he stopped perspiring. Within ten minutes breathing was normal. He pushed off some of the animal skins. His sallow cheeks took on slight blush of color and the commander said, "If I didn't see it with my own eyes, I wouldn't believe it. We were going to leave him here to die."

"That could still happen," Cahena noted. "I've never attended anyone so ill."

"What did you do?"

"I don't know. I never did this before. He is not fit to leave with you tomorrow."

"Obviously. I will speak with your uncle Benyamin. Josephus will travel with your caravan to Carthage, if he lives. That is our home base. I hope to see you there."

The commander left Cahena and made straight for Benyamin's tent. "There is one more piece of business that must be dealt with," he said. Benyamin got up from his Sabbath meal and went outside where he and the commander would not be heard.

"Do you know who the spies in your caravan are?" the Roman asked.

"No."

"I do."

"Who?"

"The Chinese."

"How can you be certain?"

"My men geometered the signal coming from your caravan to the bandits; it came from the Chinese. When the attack took place, the Chinese wore red clothing or held red cloth flags— and were never touched by the bandits. They must be executed."

"I cannot do that on the Sabbath."

"I can. We leave tomorrow morning. Say the word, and I will kill them all."

"Could you save their cook?"

"They all look alike to me. Their jewelry and money belong to my men. Sell their animals and bring the money to Carthage. You take the tents, stores and trade goods."

"Agreed."

Two hours before sunrise the first cohort surrounded the Chinese tents. Including slaves, fifty people were marched into the field where the bodies of the trapped bandits lay. They were made to kneel, and their heads were cut off. Their wealth was carried away by the legionnaires.

The bodies were left where they fell, for all to see Roman justice.

The legionnaires traveled the caravan route back to Carthage, spreading the story of the fighting strength of the Jewish caravan. During the remainder of the trip there was no attack by armed groups, and thievery was at a minimum. Cahena set up her pigeon stations in the larger settlements of Tipasa, Cuicul, northeast of Sétif and Thamugadi southeast of Sétif. Benyamin suggested that those Berber families and slaves that manned the stations utilize the goods of the Chinese and the weapons left by the bandits as stock to trade with passing caravans. These he would charge to her father. It would not be in conflict with local traders, and would act as a legitimate explanation for settling there.

The caravan passed through Algeria's agricultural heartland, where the prosperity of the towns depended on wheat. Known as the Granary of the Roman Empire, wheat fields stretched further than the eye could see in all directions. They exported to Italy, Greece and Constantinople. Closer to the towns were orchards of pomegranates, dates, olives, figs, grapes, fields of melons and beans. There were terraced spice gardens for paprika, cumin, ginger, cinnamon and saffron. Fresh peppermint, parsley and coriander were harvested and dried for export.

It was a wonderland of discoveries for Cahena. She supervised the pigeons and the sick Roman soldier while taking in the people and sights along the trail, and caravans traveling the opposite direction. Friday evenings and Saturdays were taken up with praying, and lessons on Jewish history and religion from Benyamin. Ahmed and the five warriors guarding her were always nearby.

The Roman soldier recovered enough to travel by horse. He was a tough grizzled veteran, thirty-four years old, a rugged square man with deep-set dark eyes, a bent nose and curly black hair. Josephus was a Christian, born in the mountains of Calabria, and one of the few

Italians employed in the Eastern Roman army. He had joined at age sixteen and could have taken a pension two years ago, but was offered the honor of carrying the golden eagle standard for his legion. He followed Cahena around like a puppy dog. He not only owed his life to her but felt she was a Biblical prophetess and messenger of God.

He responded with delight to Cahena's request that he teach her the use of the Roman short sword, shield and javelin. She was as tall as Josephus, but half his weight. At first when he used the shield as a battering ram or a club she was knocked down or thrown off balance. He taught her the proper response for each move. He made her exercise her hands and forearms by placing a cloth on the ground. With her hand on top of the cloth and her forearm on the ground, she had to ball the cloth up into her hand without lifting her arms.

She became so muscular she could crack dried walnuts in the crook of either arm. Before Ahmed's mother made their evening meals, Josephus took Cahena on six-mile runs around the caravan. After two months, she wasn't even breathing hard when she sat down to dinner. She was only ten years old, but she became so proficient with the short sword and shield her guards refused to joust with her. She was taller and used her size and the large shield to bully them in mock combat.

In the town of Sétif she used Ahmed's mother to buy a shack and set up a stall to sell to caravans, become a waystation for pigeons to fly back to her father, and send other pigeons in passing caravans to Carthage. She now used Ahmed to manage the training of the pigeons. The negotiations completed for the stall and house, Cahena and her guards were leaving when they heard a commotion nearby. They walked over.

People had pinned a man to the ground, spread-eagled, face up. His hands and feet were then tied to wooden stakes. Cahena questioned bystanders and then explained to Josephus, "The man on the ground fought with another man, and inadvertently took out his eye. Now he is going to lose his."

"How?" Josephus asked.

"Shhh! The shaman is talking."

"What's he saying?"

"The usual stuff. Neighbors should not fight, peace is the best thing—but even in a case of inadvertent damage the price must be paid: a tooth for a tooth and an eye for an eye."

A man with a bandage covering his left eye came forward. He knelt by the head of the man tied on the ground, and held up his right thumb for all to see. He put his left hand on the man's forehead and hooked his thumb into the eye of the screaming man. He tried once, twice, and on the third attempt the eyeball popped out. It was still attached by nerves, and slipped out of his hand onto the man's cheek. The victim passed out as the aggrieved man cut the bloody tangle of nerves. His family helped him stand, holding the eyeball which he would pass on to his children. The man on the ground was unbound and his family allowed to care for him.

"We Christians," Josephus said, "Are taught to turn the other cheek, but I think this is a more practical solution."

"Agreed," Cahena said. "The Christian way, you get a lot of sore cheeks and nothing changes. This way people learn not to fight."

"What do you Jews do?"

"According to my father, until recently we followed what happened here. But the rabbis in Babylon ruled that the value of damage should be assessed and money paid, not an eye for an eye. It does more good for the injured party."

"Does that work?"

"Among the Jews it is accepted, except in the case of a death. If blood is spilled, it is up to the family to spill the blood of the offending tribe."

"Is that what is meant by blood feuds?"

"And they go on for generations. It is a matter of honor to seek retribution and remove shame from the family name."

"I've heard my commander say that this is the reason we Romans control the Maghreb, although the Berbers and Tuaregs a far more numerous than the Legions. They're always fighting each other."

"It's true."

The Roman influence became more and more apparent the closer the caravan came to New Carthage. The towns were larger, the crops healthier, the people more affable and better clothed. The streets were arranged in a grid pattern, with a place for pedestrians to walk on one side and not in the middle where the animals defecated, urinated, and churned the dirt into a smelly mess. Roman towns were always established on a slope, with a spring diverted down both sides of the main street and channeled off to all the streets for fresh clean drinking water. Punishments for contaminating the water in any manner or form were harsh and immediate: twenty lashes of the cat-o-nine-tails for a first offense, and death for a second. Designated areas were set aside for toilets, washing clothes, skinning and butchering. Places on the outskirts were selected for the animal herds. Guards walked during the day and were doubled at night.

'Orderly' was the word that came to Cahena's mind when they passed a Roman-supervised town. In contrast, those overseen or built by the local tribesmen maintained very organized fields, orchards and gardens, but the towns were open cesspools and under-populated. They required more servants than citizens. In these Berber towns Benyamin's caravan received the highest prices for slaves.

It was the beginning of June, and the beautiful weather conspired with the approach to Carthage to display nature in all its splendor. Everything was growing. Perfume from fruit orchards filled the air. People looked healthier, dressed better and acted more openly. The first major caravan of the year from the north was warmly greeted by merchants, business people and the public. Buyers came out two weeks before the caravan was due in the great city of Carthage to bargain for animals, materials and merchandise. Groups often left or joined the caravan on its way, and Benyamin collected his fee from all.

He was in good humor. Carthage was within a day's horse ride, his journey a success, with added profits from the bandits and transactions with the legion in selling their loot. His reputation as caravan master grew. He could charge more for the caravan to Constantinople.

The road to Carthage was safe; Roman laws governed everything and everyone, and the penalties for breaking them were swift. There were always thieves and cutthroats, but they avoided Roman authority.

CHAPTER 8

CARTHAGE

Cahena established her last pigeon station along the caravan route in the city of Neapolis. Benyamin helped her finalize the agreement. "If you are overwhelmed with the buildings and number of people in this city," he said, "remember that Carthage is larger, with half a million people, and is second only to Alexandria in population, wealth, and power."

"What about education?" Cahena asked.

"Education is power. That is why you were sent to Carthage. The Vandals and Goths destroyed Rome; now Athens, Carthage and Constantinople are the centers of learning. Recently a synod of Catholic bishops met in Carthage to amend and add to religious requirements. The Emperor Justinian may be about to declare himself a god."

"That upsets you?"

"It should upset you. For a Jew there is only one God: not Allah, Jesus, his father, or the Holy Spirit."

"I don't know how much of a Jew I am. Why can't I worship idols? What if you are wrong, and some of these gods I pray to can help me?"

"Heaven forbid!"

"How to explain my ability to heal people? Where does it come from?"

"God almighty! The one and only true God!"

Cahena did not respond to the anger in Benyamin's voice. He resumed his talk about the city. "Soon, I will show you a wall that will astound you. It never ceases to amaze me."

True to his word, at eight that morning—as they traveled along the coast of the Mediterranean Sea and the sun climbed into a cloudless blue sky—there appeared an unnatural structure rising from the sea. It was Benyamin's wall, forty feet high and thirty-six feet thick. Fighting turrets were evenly spaced down its vast length.

"Did I exaggerate?" The caravan master asked.

Cahena shook her head in wonder. "How long is it?"

"Twenty-three miles to Carthage. This is Roman power. The wall makes Carthage impregnable. The entrance to its two harbors is secret; only specially trained pilots can navigate ships into them. It will take two days for our caravan to arrive at the end of this wall. A third day is needed for me to bring the rear of the caravan to rest, and a fourth day for the animals and slaves going to market."

The closer they came to Carthage the more people they encountered. Cahena's Berber guards closed in about her, Ahmed and Josephus. The sound and presence of people talking, hawking their wares and bargaining, was exciting and a bit frightening. So many things were going on at once, so many choices of goods, fruits, vegetables and butchered animals. Tall brown dogs displaying bony ribs roamed about people's feet looking for scraps and avoiding kicks. Children played tag, blindman's-bluff and hide-and-seek. Strolling musicians with a monkey, dressed up dog, or talking parrot entertained for coins. In the midst of this multitude of people and disharmony of sounds, storytellers held people captivated for copper coins.

Cahena sent Ahmed and Josephus to buy baked sweets for her and the guards. They were made of deep fried dough, dipped in honey and covered with shredded coconut. They all licked their fingers and Cahena ordered tea from a man carrying on his back a large polished brass *autepsa*, a samovar, with a fire under its bottom. He filled four cups, served them and said, "Drink up. Hurry now!"

He was an old man, so Cahena spoke gently. "Your tea is tasty. But it is improper for you to rush us."

"I only have four cups, and you paid for eight."

Cahena laughed for the first time since she left her father. She had a good feeling about Carthage. "Here, Grandfather." She slipped a coin into his hand, and he blessed her in the names of the goddess Astarte and the god Baal while refilling the cups.

Before they reached the wall, the road swung down to the sea. It was her first view of the Mediterranean. Her father had told her what to expect, but the vastness of the blue waters was overpowering. She saw ships with one, two and three masts gliding north and south along the coast. Men and women on shore unloaded fish from smaller boats. Their catch was laid out on the beach and sold to the highest bidder. Absorbed, she was startled by a young man named Yaakov, from Benyamin's family. He explained the caravan master was busy, but he would lead her to the villa where she would stay.

"I expected to live and study in the gymnasium with the other students."

'Impossible. Do you speak Greek?"

"I do."

"The emperor Justinian requires that all learning and official business be done in Greek. What is the meaning of gymnasium?"

"It's a place where people study to train their minds and perfect their bodies."

"What is the root of the word?"

"I never thought about it. It means the naked body."

"Correct. And that is how the students, all boys and young men, spend their entire day: naked. You would create a sensation going in there naked. Is it true you are only ten years old?"

"Yes."

"I am fourteen, and you are taller and look stronger than me. May I touch your breast?"

"Why would you want to do that?"

"Because you wear an open vest, and although they are small they look nice."

"Alright."

He raised his hands and put the palms of both hands over her breasts. "Oh!" she exclaimed.

"Did I hurt you?"

"No. It tickles."

"You are beautiful. Can I kiss you on the lips?"

"That's for big people."

"I'm older, and you are bigger than me."

"Alright."

He leaned forward and pressed his lips to hers. She watched him close his eyes and look very serious. After a moment, she pulled away. "I don't see what kissing does," she said, puzzled.

"Maybe I'm not a good kisser," he said. "Men and women like to do it."

"I think you should lead us to our new quarters."

Cahena mounted her pony and her entourage surrounded her, pressing past the caravan with the view of the sea being blocked by the great wall on their right. The wall itself had stalls, shops and restaurants along its length. Fountains with clean drinking water and latrines for public use were regularly spaced. Animal dung was swept up by children who made briquettes for the fires and sold them. Beggars were everywhere and very forward in demanding charity. Cahena commented on their aggressiveness.

"The Christian patriarch of Carthage complained about the beggars to the Roman commander," Yaakov said. "He banned all beggars from the beginning of the wall and south through Carthage. The city people agree with you. Those outside the city protested. There was a near riot."

"What were the people outside the wall angry at?"

"They no longer had anyone to give charity to."

"Pagans want to give charity?"

"Oh yes. It is very important to them, Eastern Orthodox Christians, and Muslims too."

"Muslims live here?"

"Not enough to make a difference. I don't mind as long as they keep their midnight and early morning call-to-prayers quiet."

"You live in Carthage?"

"Second generation. My father is a merchant; he selected your villa. It's in the Jewish sector, at the beginning of the city. The Romans are paying for it. My father rented a beautiful villa for you."

"Are there many Jews?"

"Two hundred. Another fifty families own homes, like my uncle Benyamin, but they live most of the time abroad or on the caravan trails. You and your people are invited this Sabbath eve. The whole family will be there. Everyone wants to meet Cahena, daughter of the famous Moshe ben Shimi, Sharif of the Berber Jews."

"On Friday evening do the women go to the river and bathe?'

"No, we have a synagogue and a *mikvah*."

"What do those words mean?"

'Synagogue is Greek and means a council or gathering. It is the name for a Jewish church, mosque, or temple. We pray and study there. In the rear of the synagogue there is a separate room with a pool of fresh-flowing water for ritual bathing. My sister will take you. This Friday will be the biggest family affair ever. Uncle Benyamin, my father Yeshia and their families will all be there."

"How many people do you expect?"

"Mother is preparing for three hundred and fifty."

"All family?"

"No. The entire Jewish community wants to see you and hear stories of the mountain Jewish Berbers."

"I am not used to speaking to groups of people."

"Don't worry, we're all Jews. You'll be lucky to get in a word."

"I don't know how Jewish we Jrawa are, compared to you."

"Don't talk about religion, then. If you can, speak about trade, politics and fighting. We have heard stories of the Jews defeating Pagans and Romans and Persians. We Jews keep a low profile under Roman law. Our men guarding the caravans and ships can fight but always in defense."

Josephus rode up, requesting to speak with Cahena alone. "I must report to the legion," he said. "The road to our camp is here. My enlistment is finished; I will ask for a discharge with full pension and Roman citizenship. I would like to return as your personal bodyguard and advisor."

Cahena pointed to the Berber warriors. "I have bodyguards, and on what will you advise me?"

"These men are paid to protect you; you saved my life, and I am destined to save yours. You are more than just a smart little girl—not so little; you are taller than me. I believe in the Christian gods; I can accept that there is one God greater than the rest. Maybe it's yours. Whoever or whatever it is, I swear by him to serve you until my death. I believe your God has touched you, and I want to be close."

"You've thought more about my God than I have. My future is in school, then marriage; it's not very religious, and could bore a fighting man like you."

"To die in your service is the honor I seek."

"Speak to your legion commander. He believes you're the best soldier he has."

Josephus departed.

The caravan passed villas large and small.

Trees showed their heads from behind whitewashed walls.

"We turn off here," Yaakov said. "Your villa is further up the hill. It is above the height of the great wall, so you will get the sea breeze."

"Does it get very warm?"

"Carthage has wonderful weather. Tunis is just across the lake from us, and theirs is even better. July and August are the hottest months."

"Why did the Romans choose New Carthage?"

"For the two harbors, the great wall makes the city impregnable from the sea. Between Carthage and the fleet in Constantinople, the Eastern Roman Empire controls the five connecting seas."

"What if an enemy approached by land?"

"Emperor Heraclius stationed twenty thousand infantry, four thousand cavalry, and three hundred elephants to protect this city."

"Oh, elephants! I want to see the elephants! I heard about them. When can we go?"

"Your man Josephus will be the best person to arrange that. But tomorrow you are invited with Uncle Benyamin and aunt Anav to visit the Cohanim of Djerba."

"Why would I visit the priests?"

"Because you are the daughter of Moshe ben Shimi, a direct descendant of the high priest of Israel. They want to see you."

"I'd rather see elephants. Why can't they come to the party?"

"The elephants?"

"No. The priests and their families."

"There are eight hundred of them. They live on Djerba Island. And our food isn't kosher enough for them."

"What if they find out I eat camel with the hair on?"

"I wouldn't mention that. Uncle Benyamin says you are very smart; look, I'll be near you. Watch my eyes. If I roll them, change the subject."

"I'd still rather see the elephants."

"That's your villa on the right. That giant fig tree shades the portico, and your bedroom."

The villa's walls formed a moderate-sized quadrangle. The outer walls of the rooms also made up the outer walls of the compound. Windows were covered by curtains inside and ornate iron grills outside. The walls themselves were three feet thick to protect against the heat of summer and retain warmth in winter. The arched entrance had two large wooden doors and a smaller door from which a guard appeared. He called behind him and the two doors were opened. The horses were taken outside to the rear of the villa. Cahena sniffed. "What is that beautiful smell?"

"Lemon trees," Yaakov said. "Outside there are two each of pomegranate, apple, plum trees, four varieties of grapes and the large fig tree which cools everything."

"Where is my room?"

"You have two rooms, each five meters square, in the rear of the quadrangle. Come, I'll show you." He pointed to the well on the left of the entrance. "That is for the kitchen. The well up forward is for everyone. There are fourteen rooms in all. Clay Roman pipes carry the toilet water from the rooms, downhill to the cesspool outside the wall. It helps water and fertilize the fruit trees."

Cahena gasped at the sight of the interior; the walls were painted a very light blue-white, so it looked like an ice palace inside. The domed ceiling was twenty feet high. Brass food trays with intricate engravings leaned against the walls. Small colorful rugs were scattered on the blue and white tile floor. An arched storage space with shelves covered by a curtain was built into the wall. To the left was a second room. It too was spacious, painted ice-white, with a high vaulted ceiling. "I have never had such luxury," she almost whispered.

"My father's house is three times the size of

this."

"How did he become so wealthy?"

"Uncle Benyamin and he both inherited the caravan business from their father. The family hauled salt from the Sahara desert, through the Atlas Mountains, into the Maghreb. They made good profits. Benyamin decided to sell in Carthage, where they received twice the usual price. They agreed to make five times as much by selling the salt in Sicily. My father suggested they buy a boat and sail to Marsla. They bought the boat, but Uncle Benyamin became seasick. He made another trip to the salt mines, and my father went to Sicily 380 miles across the Mediterranean. My father knew nothing about boats or navigation, so he hired a Jew who did. The Jew took him to Palermo."

"Why?"

"That was where he was from, and wanted to get home.

"It turned out that salt in Palermo was worth more than silver, and almost as much as gold. He went to the synagogue on Friday. When the Jews of Palermo heard he needed a navigator they found an excellent one. When they heard my father was returning to Carthage empty and looking for ballast, they convinced him to fill his boat with Palermo wine, the best in the region. He bought the wine for what the barrels alone would have cost in Carthage. When he entered Carthage, word spread of the Palermo wine. He couldn't get the barrels out of the hold fast enough to satisfy the buyers. That was the beginning of our success. He is now having a large ship built in Bombay, India."

"Now I understand what your uncle Benyamin meant when he said your father does as much right by mistake as he does on purpose."

"He learned to navigate, sail, barter, bargain and trade on the seven seas, and in as many languages."

"What time do we leave tomorrow?"

"We catch the outgoing tide at five in the morning."

"I've never been on a boat."

"Don't worry, just don't eat too much for breakfast. May I touch your breasts again?"

"No."

"Why not?"

"The look you had on your face."

"Oh? What did it look like?"

"Like you went into a trance and were very happy."

"Is that bad?"

"I wasn't happy and still don't know why you were. Goodnight."

Cahena slept well. Attuned to caravan time, she

woke at four. Breakfast was served in the other room, and she ate frugally. She heard Yaakov assembling the men, and went out to her pony. Two outriders with torches led the way to the seashore, where Uncle Benyamin and Aunt Anav were waiting on the boat. Slaves led the horses away. Cahena's guards examined the craft above and below deck before allowing her to board. She felt the boat shifting under her feet, and noted that the feeling was much like riding a horse or camel. The tide turned and the boat tugged at its mooring lines. "Cast off!" Benyamin bellowed. and went directly down below deck.

"Where's he going?" Cahena asked Yaakov.

"To the cabin. He'll lie down for the remainder of the trip. He gets sea-sick."

"How long a trip is it?"

"A little over an hour. Look: the sun is rising. See the snow-covered mountains in the east."

"And on the other side is the Sahara Desert."

"I never saw the desert," Yaakov said.

"And I never saw the ocean. Look: birds are flying out from shore."

"They think we're a fishing boat and that they will feed from our catch."

"I wish I brought my pad and charcoal."

"Let me see if there is some in my father's cabin."

Yaakov returned with a pad and charcoal sticks. Cahena began sketching the birds, and Yaakov watched them come to life on the top sheet. Cahena stopped sketching and ran her fingers over the surface of the sheet. "I never worked on anything so smooth," she said. "It's more flexible than papyrus."

"That's paper," Yaakov said. "It comes from China by way of the Silk Road."

"I wish they'd come nearer."

"A minute!" Yaakov shouted, and ran off to return with a loaf of bread. He stood next to the helmsman and threw out pieces of bread to the birds. They flocked in closer. He stopped throwing bread and held it out to individual hovering birds. He fed each one until Cahena nodded. He then enticed a different species.

They entered Djerba harbor where the birds settled on the beach, and the paper was stored below deck. Benyamin, looking a bit pale, came up from below and was first to disembark. People awaited them on the quay. They had come to see Cahena, but were more taken by the Jrawa bodyguards who preceded her—especially the women warriors who wore short unbuttoned vests revealing their ample breasts. Uncle Benyamin roared orders to the crew, who brought out small woven carpets used as Muslim prayer rugs and draped them over the shoulders of the women guards.

Cahena was introduced to the people and leaders. There were two distinct groups: the larger group of priestly families, the smaller of Israelites. All were descendants of a military garrison sent by King Solomon, sixteen hundred years ago, to protect against barbarian pirates from the mainland and Sicily. They lived in two separate villages. The rabbi pointed to a long stone aqueduct stretching from the island to Tunis, three miles across the sea. "The Romans built that so we could continue to live here," he boasted. "It brings fresh water to us."

Cahena observed the lush fields of leafy vegetables and orchards behind the houses. "How can you afford water to grow so much?" she asked.

"You are a most attentive young lady. King Solomon was considered the wisest of men. Throughout building of the Holy Temple in Jerusalem there was a lack of water during the dry season. He devised a way of digging cisterns, very large cisterns under houses to store water. The ratio was one cistern to every three rooms. He had two problems: first, how to catch enough water during the rainy season. Do you notice the flat roofs here and in Carthage?"

"Yes, and domed ceilings inside."

"Pipes run from the flat roofs that catch the

rain, through pipes in the walls down into the cistern underneath the building where the watered is stored."

"You mentioned a second problem."

"Water can be stored only so long, except where it rests in limestone caves. Solomon experimented and made a mixture of limestone into paint. The walls of a new cistern are plastered with limestone. To this day, every year before the rains, throughout the entire middle-east people clean and repaint their cisterns."

"He was a wise king."

"And we hope you will remember us Djerba Jews when you become Queen of the Berbers."

"I will remember you and this story. But there is something different about your fields of vegetables and fruit trees. They look healthy enough, but the fields alongside the caravan trail were more orderly."

"I told you she was smart," Benyamin bellowed.

The high priest smiled. "Your guardian is right and you are not wrong. The plants, flowers and trees are planted in circles, not rows. As much water as we have, we still must be careful and use it sparingly. Solomon also taught us to make giant clay pots, fire them lightly so they remain porous, bury the pots in the ground, fill them with water, cover and plant around the porous pots. The roots of plants, shrubs and trees seek the moisture and only take as much as they need to remain healthy. We don't plow our fields in straight lines but in circles around the covered pots."

They were led to the main synagogue, which was a large building with high vaulted ceilings. A brief prayer service was held, and Cahena was invited to the raised speakers' platform in the center of the synagogue. Benyamin suggested she take questions from the audience, and she prepared for religious questions. The people were most interested in how many Berber Jews there were, and what was their feeling about Jerusalem and returning to Israel.

"We observe the Sabbath," Cahena said, and knew the only thing her father and others did was to light candles on Friday night and celebrate Rosh Hashanah, Yom Kippur and Simchat Torah—the giving of the Torah. "There are no synagogues or rabbis to teach us. Some parents teach their children, but we have no Jewish schools."

"It is much like that on the mainland," the high priest said. "Assimilation is rampant."

"We heard the Berber Jews defeated a band of three hundred robbers," an elder asked. "How did that come about?"

Cahena told the story. There was some commotion at the beginning of her tale.

When she concluded a man said, "We are not used to hearing of Jews fighting for themselves. It was very thrilling. But tell us more about your pigeons. If you had not received word of the bandits planned attack by pigeon, you would have been defeated. We know the Romans use pigeons to communicate. They won't share their secret with us."

"Others use pigeons," Cahena said.

She explained her use of the birds to communicate with her father. Benyamin added that he was informed by the feathered messengers of favorable trading opportunities. The excitement about the pigeons overrode the possibility of embarrassing questions about religion. Cahena agreed to take some slaves back to Carthage and train them with the pigeons. She would return and set up a post in Djerba.

She asked, "Why did Solomon send a military garrison to this island? And later, why did the Romans think it important enough to build a three-mile aqueduct to bring water year round? And why do the Romans allow you to rule yourselves?"

The high priest pulled on his beard and gazed with respect at the young girl. He rocked back and forth muttering indistinguishable words into his beard. "Good questions deserve proper answers. In Solomon's time the Phoenicians occupied Tunis and Carthage. They requested the King's assistance against the pirates of Sicily; he dispatched a contingent of our forefathers and their families. To live as Jews, we had to be separate from the population. This island served as an ideal location standing between Sicily and the mainland. The Phoenicians promised to supply us with water. They eventually became a major power under Hannibal's leadership and defeated Rome twice. The third time the Romans won and destroyed the Phoenicians, their fleets and armies."

"Is it true the Romans salted the land so it could never be used again?"

"Your Uncle Benyamin can answer that."

"That was a lie by the Romans to frighten other rebellious countries," Benyamin said. "The cost of hauling salt in those days was higher than it is today. It would have been like throwing gold on the ground. You saw the wheat fields, orchards and livestock entering Carthage. If salt had been used there, the place would look like the Sahara Desert."

"Why do the Romans leave you alone today?"

"We work to protect them in this area of the

Mediterranean," the priest said. "There are still pirates in Sicily, Sardinia and Corsica."

"But your people are not warriors?"

"No, but we provide a neutral place for the pirates to sell their loot, the Romans to buy it, and both maintain peace in the Tyrrhenian, Ionian and Mediterranean Seas as far as Malta. Beyond that there is Roman law. And now, there is a banquet of welcome we prepared for you. Please join us."

Lambs had been roasted through the previous night, and vegetables, including sweetened rhubarb, which Cahena enjoyed. Afterward, the people sent bundles of rhubarb down to the ship. The Israelites from the smaller village insisted she visit them. She agreed, and they led her to a similar collection of houses, fewer in number but neat and in good repair. Their synagogue was smaller. They explained that there was marriage between the two villages, but every time a male priest married a female Israelite she went to live in his village. "Over sixteen-hundred years there have been born more males to the priests and more women to us," explained the mayor.

Benyamin said, "Your religious practices differ."

"We follow the more archaic form practiced

in Jerusalem. When confirmation or clarification on Torah law is required, we accept the Jerusalem ruling. The priests accept rulings from Spain; they are more modern and contemporary in their decisions. Their religious ritual is modified, and Spain is closer."

"Have you ever thought of returning to the land of Israel?"

"That is all we think of. We pray for it twice a day." He quoted the familiar prayer: "'If I forget thee, O Jerusalem, may my right hand forget its skill.' But we must wait for the Messiah."

"I've heard my father say that. But he says the Messiah is a period of time, not a person. In Messianic time the Jews will rise up and return to Israel."

"Moshe ben Shimi thinks that? When the priests hear that, they will blush."

"Why?"

"They accept the usual version; a man will lead us back, and he will be the Messiah. We have to wait for him. That is why we are excited about you becoming queen of the Berber Jews. Possibly you or your husband could be our Messiah."

"I've seen our Berbers fight, and also watched the Roman legion destroy a gang of bandits. There is no comparison. The Romans fight like a machine, crushing and killing anything and everything."

"The Roman Army is no longer Roman. Their legions in the east are made up of professionals from various countries. They swear allegiance to Rome but would not do so without pay, pension, and citizenship if they serve sixteen years. They were defeated by the barbarians from Europe. Think of it. How much can you pay a man to die? There is a saying. 'If the rich could pay the poor to die for them, there would be no poverty.'"

"We must leave," Yaakov said. "The tide will soon turn."

CHAPTER 9

ROMAN CARTHAGE

Cahena woke before the sun. She bathed, dressed, and tip-toed past the guards to feed her pigeons. She required more birds for relay stations to her father and for the people of Djerba, but most immediately she had to acclimatize her birds to this station. Once oriented, they would be sent to Djerba and the stations along the caravan trail.

She wrote her father about her visit to the Jewish island, their hopes and prayers for his success. She made copies of the letter and sent her three strongest birds on the thirteen-hundred-mile journey, though she had little hope of their safe flight to the Atlas Mountains. She prepared a fourth message to send when she would receive birds from the nearest station to Carthage.

She had bought a long bamboo pole, tied a rag to it and released her flock of birds. They swooped up, happy to be free, but as quickly sought the safety of the cage. Cahena waved them away with the stick and ragged flag. Eventually she was able to guide them into a circular flight pattern. She found a ladder and climbed onto the roof. With the stick she sent the flock higher.

She had been flying them for a half hour when from the corner of her eye a brown streak stained the blue sky.

"Pow!" the sound was audible as pigeon feathers exploded in the air. Another streak. Another sound and more feathers. She saw two falcons follow their prey to the ground. Cahena dropped her pole, curled her tongue behind her teeth and whistled. The flock came down and lined up to enter the main cage. One of the hawks attempted to follow the flock. Cahena beat at it with the bamboo pole.

"Please," a male voice called in Latin, "Don't hurt my bird! She's a great hunter."

"She'll be a dead hunter if I get her!"

"Be careful. My little girl can be dangerous."

"Yes, I can be."

"Oh, I meant the bird. Here, I'll take her away." He blew on a peach-pit whistle, and the bird snapped to attention. Another whistle and she flew to the leather gloved hand of a well-built man in his forties. He had a healthy sunburn and balding head wreathed by short-cropped white hair, and wore a Roman toga and sandals. He held the bird up with one hand. With the other, he slipped a hood over its head. He whistled up the second hawk, and repeated the procedure. "Now we are safe. My name is Linus Crassus, senior medicus surgeon for the Legions in Carthage."

"I am the girl whose birds you killed."

"Ah yes. And I do apologize. I fly them against the sea birds. They are more challenging than pigeons. My pair couldn't resist the easy targets. I live across the way." His eyes widened. "Are you the Berber Princess?"

"I am Berber, but not a princess."

"We are supposed to meet tomorrow at the camp. I spoke to Josephus yesterday and the commander of the Seventh Legion; they told me about you. Especially I would like to know how you cured malaria."

"Could we discuss my pigeons first?"

"How old are you?"

"Ten."

"By the gods above and below! You are as tall as I. and look almost as strong. ...And you have a quick wit. Are mountain Berbers all like you?"

"No. They are bigger and smarter."

He caught the glint in her eye and rocked with laughter. "Good girl. Come! As partial payment for your birds, you will have breakfast with me. My house is close by."

There was a sumptuous breakfast laid out on a table: fruits, eggs, sliced meat, fish and delicious looking baked stuffs. Cahena ate and left, hoping to arrive before she was missed.

The guards were unaware of her departure, and they'd thought she was still sleeping. She explained, saying that while the guard was looking the other way she childishly sneaked out to her pigeons. It was a female guard who had slept on duty, and later that day Cahena took her aside and said, 'You were asleep on duty. If it happens again, you are dead."

The woman dropped to her knees and kissed Cahena's feet. The girl pulled away. "Do your duty," was all she said.

"Yes, my Queen."

It was the first time anyone had addressed Cahena with that title. She walked away.

The following morning, Linus the Medic arrived in a chariot and invited Cahena to ride with him. Three mounted Berber guards accompanied them to the army base outside the city. Cahena kept up a stream of questions about the chariot, its effectiveness in war and use in peace. Was it true large knife blades could be attached to the wheels to maul enemy infantry? How accurate were bowmen from chariots? What defensive tactics did Roman infantry use against them? Linus was delighted to answer.

They arrived at the entrance to the Roman army camp, where the guards snapped to attention and shouted, "Corporal of the Guard, visitors from Carthage." The Corporal of the Guard stepped out of his small tent and relayed the message to the Sergeant of the Guard, who repeated it to the Commander of the Guard, who bellowed, "Allow them to enter with honors." The guards withdrew their swords and saluted.

From within the compound a bugle sounded. There was a drum roll. Commands were shouted. The doctor sent his chariot forward to the center front of the parade ground. There were gathered a group of men with ornate battle uniforms and helmets, covered with leopard, lion and tiger skins. Linus whispered to Cahena, "This is for you and your uncle, the caravan master. In the history of our occupation of Africa, no one legion has brought back as much loot—and combined with Benyamin's sale of camels and goods, you have made the Seventh Legion the wealthiest on this continent." He reined in. "Meet the commander of the base, General Antonio Basso."

The general, draped in a lion's skin, stepped forward. "Young lady," he said in a strong voice, "I want to convey my appreciation for your efforts on our behalf. I speak not of the wealth my men reaped; I refer to your ministrations to our wounded—especially your treatment of malaria. ...Doctor Linus, I thought you said this girl is ten years old."

"She is."

"She is built very solidly, and is as tall as I am."

"Elephants!" Cahena shouted, growing impatient. "Are there elephants?"

"Yes child, there are," the general smiled. "They will pass in review after the troops. They have a habit of shitting on the parade ground. The men get upset trudging through the muck."

"Oh, I want to play with the elephants."

"Your man Josephus will introduce you to them."

"My man? Has he decided to leave the Legion?"

"He wishes to serve you."

The Seventh Legion marched by in full battle gear. Their heads snapped to the right when they passed Cahena, and their officers saluted.

The elephants—enormous gray beasts—followed, led by Josephus. He carried a long wooden pole, and stepped out of formation leading a large beast with a baby running under her belly and between her legs. Josephus raised his hand in salute and smiled. "You can ride Momma or play with Baby. Let me introduce you to Momma so she will let you touch her child."

Cahena forgot about the dignitaries. She played and frolicked with the elephants until it was time for Baby to feed.

She was invited to lunch with the officers, and sat between Linus and the commander at the head of the table. The senior commander questioned her about the number of mountain Berbers, the tribes and their allegiances. What was their relationship to the Berbers of the Maghreb and the Tuaregs? Cahena listened and attempted to frame intelligent answers that would favor her father.

"There are fifteen tribes considered mountain Amazigh, or Berbers. Three of the larger tribes are led by my father. When I marry and my father becomes sharif of seven tribes, he will command some twenty thousand fighting men and women warriors."

"Is it true your women fight and bear up under battle conditions as well as men?"

"Yes. Three of my guards are women, and they are among the best of the Jrawa tribe. But your question about allegiance raises a problem. The word *Amazigh* means 'Free People'.

Each Amazigh is free to lead or follow whom they wish. They may be loyal to my father or they may decide to go hunting. But once an Amazigh, or Berber to you, swears allegiance he will fight to the death to maintain his oath."

"Then your father does not have complete control of his tribes?"

"Only by virtue of his personality and his birthright as a descendant of the High Priest in Jerusalem."

"Will the Berbers swear allegiance to you as queen?"

"That is my father's objective. If it happens, more than one million Berbers, Tuaregs and Bedouin will band together."

"Let's hope it comes about, and you accept advisors from the Corps Africanus of the Imperial Roman Army."

"My father sent me for that purpose: to learn from you."

The general smiled.

The conversation turned to lighter subjects, and Linus invited Cahena to see the base medical facilities.

The hospital's layout was an inverted U shape of three buildings. Each room facing the inside was private. Behind it was a long barrack room with doors facing outward and straw mattresses lining both sides of the room. The center building at the top of the U contained operating rooms, kitchens, baths, a dispensary, latrines and a mortuary.

Linus explained that cleanliness had to do with contagion. "We know it happens, but not quite how. We know that things which smell bad cause contagion, but those are not the only sources. Our water comes from uphill wells of clean water. Certain rooms are isolated, and those are used mostly by malaria cases. That is our major problem. In the rear we have herb gardens that are used for medications. We grow hemp, fennel, sage, garlic and others to treat patients. For pain we give opium and henbane seed. Brewed willow bark and vinegar reduces infections."

"Everything is so clean," Cahena noted, "Yet when we entered this surgery room I saw moldy bread on a table. Why is that?"

"There is a patient with an infection we haven't been able to stop. Some medicus have had success by covering infected wounds with moldy blue bread. It's our last chance to save him."

He showed her scalpels, hooks, levers, drills, probes, forceps, catheters and arrow-extractors. The latter held her attention. She memorized the shape and questioned Linus about its use, and questioned why they boiled instruments before and after use.

"I don't have a medical answer. Our battlefield surgeons find the cleaner the wound and the instruments the less chance of infection. The public call us doctors 'butchers' and 'thieves'. Some doctors do shamefully deserve the title. They charge excessive prices for worthless medicines, and treat diseases they do not understand. We medicus in the army have been recognized for our dedication, study and the survival of our patients. Wounds are washed in vinegar, stitched with sheep-gut thread, and kept covered against flies. Broken bones are placed in traction. I have learned to extract eye cataracts with a special needle."

"What is a 'cataract'?"

"A film that grows over the eye. Some call it 'cotton eye'."

"We have people like that."

"If I ever get up to the mountains I'll help them see again."

"Those people you help see again must be very grateful."

"Not always," Linus sighed. "Sometimes they become accustomed to living within a limited world of sight. When I take the film from their eyes they have to cope with, and be responsible for, a much larger and more complex world. Most are initially upset. Later on they praise me."

"Do you believe that illness is caused by demons?"

"I never saw a demon, only the effects of dirt or cleanliness. But the public's order of priorities for treating illness is faith first, magic second, last of all doctors. They'll seek a priest or magician before a medicus." He sighed again. "I have a patient suffering from malaria. He is a friend and high ranking officer. Would you please see him?"

"Josephus told you?"

"Yes."

"Did he tell you I don't know how I did it?"

"Please try. I don't expect he'll live another day."

Cahena stood in the doorway of a private room. A male attendant was placing another blanket over the patient. With several blankets covering him he continued to shiver. He convulsed and had to be restrained lest he roll off the mattress.

Doctor Linus watched the girl carefully. He was very taken with folk medicine, but found most healers to be frauds.

She walked to the bedside and there was a change in her expression. It became calmer, and instead of her outside beauty, she emitted an inner glow. It expressed itself with a beatific smile. She used a towel to dry the perspiration from the man's face, neck and forehead. She then soaked the towel in water and dabbed his face. She began speaking to the man. Linus didn't understand a word, and doubted the patient did, yet he responded in garbled unintelligible Latin. She passed both her hands over his forehead, then down his cheeks and neck. His breathing eased, his face relaxed, and slowly the body tremors reduced until they were gone.

"If I didn't see it I would never have believed it," Linus murmured. "The moment you placed your hands on him the fever began to break. I have three others. Would you please visit them?"

Cahena worked her charm on two, but collapsed before reaching the third man.

She was taken to private room to rest, with her Berber guards and Dr. Linus at her bedside. She slept. She ate at the base, and returned home after dark.

When she entered her bedroom she questioned one of the guards about a pile of clothes tumbled against the wall.

Before he could answer, the clothes moved, then stood up.

"Ozeret!" Cahena shouted. "How did you find

me?"

"Everyone's talking about the future Berber Queen. I just followed the stories."

"I'm so glad to see you. I have many questions."

"As do I."

They talked through the night until Cahena fell asleep in mid-sentence.

She awoke to an argument between Ozeret and Ahmed's mother as to who would make Cahena's breakfast.

"If I understand," Cahena settled the matter, "Mother has already prepared breakfast. Ozeret, you serve it."

When Ahmed's mother left, Ozeret asked. "Don't you like me to cook for you?"

"Not really. Your cooking tastes like your medicine."

"This is the thanks I get for walking the long caravan trail, suffering thirst and hunger to be with you."

"I'm certain you traveled quite well, and earned some coins along the way."

"I expected joy, smiles, and happiness; I get anger and sarcastic remarks."

"You asked; I told the truth. Your medicines are excellent, but your cooking is terrible."

"I know," Ozeret grinned, "but let's not talk about it. Your breakfast looks tasty."

"Let's share. I could use your help on something else."

Between mouthfuls, Ozeret grumbled, "After insulting me you ask for help?"

"It has to do with malaria. I have the talent to break the fever."

"I told your father you're a natural healer. I will show you other unknown gifts you possess."

"I break the fever but the condition returns."

"That's the nature of the sickness. I have nothing to prevent that."

"There was a Chinese group in our caravan. Like you, they had a supply of medications."

"I would like to see their tools, and talk to them."

"They all died in the bandit raid."

"Too bad. Do you have any of the medicines I left with you?"

"Waiting in the storage bin. I asked the Chinese if they had a cure for malaria, and the woman claimed they did. They called it the Qinghao plant."

"Must be a Chinese word. I've never heard it."

"They showed me an envelope with dried leaves and seeds. The leaves were to be chewed and the seeds brewed as a tea. There was a drawing on the envelope of the plant."

"Can you draw it?"

Cahena took a piece of paper. Ozeret touched it. "What is that?"

"'Paper'. The word comes from *papyrus*, but it's much better. The Chinese make it from wood-dust."

"Clever, the Chinese."

Cahena drew a picture and handed the paper to the hunchback. The older woman looked, turned the paper around, gazed, and turned it around again. With a toothless smile she said, "You've drawn two different plants. One is sweet sagewort and the other is mugwort. We use these to reduce fever. It's logical to use it for malaria, but no one I know ever tried it."

"Will you help me try it on the Romans?"

"Why not? I wouldn't mind killing some of them."

"What have you got against them?"

"They aren't Berber."

A commotion outside the quadrangle brought Cahena to the gate, where she faced a Roman centurion. He led a five-camel caravan carrying one hundred pigeons in bamboo cages. "This is a present from Dr. Linus and our camp commander," he said. "Thank you for your helping our soldiers. Where can I put them?"

For a week Cahena's time was taken up with

training her slaves and those sent from Djerba to feed, fly and care for the birds. She then showed how to tie messages to the bird's leg. She took the birds three, five and ten miles away, then releasing them on orientation flights. The slaves recorded the order and time of their return. Ten percent were lost in flight, but she continued flying them until all returned. She then traveled with them to the sea and launched them one, then two miles from shore, and then from Djerba beach. The second week she flew her birds from the station in Djerba. She did not know if they would orient themselves. The old grizzled veteran in charge of the Legion's birds told her, "The smart ones will come home. The others will take a bath."

Nineteen birds made it back within a half hour. One was found with a broken wing two hundred yards from home.

Linus and Cahena came to an agreement about times of flying their birds. He was put in charge of organizing her education, which would take place in her villa.

"Education," Linus said, "Is like climbing a ladder. If a rung is missing, you will always falter when taking that step. You will be examined on basics in Latin and Greek: you speak both languages fluently, but with an outlander's accent and minor errors. As queen you will negotiate with emissaries of foreign countries; your speech and presentation of ideas will influence the acceptance of your concepts. Although you will be taught by a Greek, Roman education has a different goal. The Greek goal is to perfect the body and soul for the wellbeing of the person and community. Romans educate for one purpose: to benefit the whole empire."

"Will you be one of my teachers?"

"I will introduce you to Roman life in Carthage, our ancient and modern history, and specifically the plan for domination of the Maghreb and North Africa by Berbers and Romans—including Egypt, Babylon and Persia."

"Muhammad and his people are converting those areas."

"Which is why we are courting you Berbers. We require a buffer against the Muslims until we are ready to wipe them out, for they are a mad, cruel and dangerous people."

"Who will teach me besides you?"

"Andronicus, a Greek freed-man. He's on his way from Gaza. He shall examine and hire teachers who specialize in mathematics, astronomy, geography etcetera."

"Those subjects appeal to me. Grammar, rhetoric, mythology and philosophy seem a waste of time."

"Those, Andronicus will teach. From a soldier's point of view I agree with you. However you are being groomed for political power. You will have the opportunity to move people with your thoughts. If those come out of your mouth like the words of some uneducated shepherd, only the sheep will listen. The second you speak, people classify you. The words you use, their order, tone of voice and position of your body will dictate the influence you achieve."

"I am only ten and doing quite well, thank you."

"People are impressed by the child with ideas of a mature intelligent woman, who expresses herself in a childlike manner and level of language. Five years from now, if that is still the case, they will make fun of you."

"As queen, I will order them to obey."

"And they will, but they will seek someone better prepared to fill your position. You have led an idealistic life with little discipline. Now is the time to develop your self-discipline. When you have trained yourself to do the most abhorrent task, and do it well, that's self-discipline. With it you can change the world. Without it you cannot change your own mind."

"When do I start learning?"

"Tomorrow. I will stop by at six in the morning. It is getting hot in the afternoon, and I've become accustomed to the local routine of eating a large meal in the afternoon and sleeping from two until four."

"I'll be ready."

"I would like to make a suggestion. Your Mongol pony is cute and sturdy enough, but your stirrups almost touch the ground. For appearances sake you should have a full-sized horse."

"He's like a little doll to me. I never had a doll, but I always had him."

"Retain him as your pet, but get a bigger mount."

"Is this one of my self-discipline moments?"

Linus shrugged. "We'll see."

CHAPTER 10

SCHOOL DAYS

Cahena chose one specific guard, a tribal horse wrangler, to accompany her and Linus. At her request, Linus led them to a horse trader. The owner was exercising some twenty horses inside a corral when her chosen guard approached the trader. They looked over the herd and cut out four animals to be looked at. Before going to examine the animals, Cahena's wrangler whispered, "Insist on a white horse." He had cut out two sorrels, a black and a grey. The trader beckoned Cahena and said, "Any one of these four animals will serve you well."

With a petulant look and tone of voice, Cahena replied, "I want a white one."

"You heard my mistress," the guard said.

The trader kept eyeing Linus in Roman military uniform as a source of danger. He sent the four animals back to the herd and cut out two white horses. The guard pointed to a third animal. "But she has black spots on her rump and foreleg," the trader said.

"Bring her anyway." The guard examined the three horses and began haggling for two of them. He put the animals through their paces and made an offer for two. "I only use one horse at a time," Cahena murmured.

"Let your man negotiate," Linus said.

"I'll give you your full price," the guard continued, "But I want all three for that much."

"Which gods do you Berbers pray to?" The dealer lamented. "They must be the cruelest in the heavens. Your offer is insulting."

"Far be it from me to insult a brother Pagan. We thank you for your time and effort..."

"Why are you leaving? We've just begun to talk."

The guard's terms were eventually agreed upon, and they left with three horses.

"Why did you have me insist on white horses?" Cahena asked the guard as they rode away.

"You are Cahena, the priestess. Everyone knows the redeemer will come on a white horse."

"You think I am a prophetess?"

He smiled, "Just in case."

"Then why did you insist on the spotted mare?"

"She's the best of the lot. And I can powder over her black spots."

"Your man is right," Linus said. "You may do some hard traveling and require more than one mount a day. Now let's settle these at home and then go see Carthage."

Linus spoke further as they traveled south on the caravan rode. "Two hundred-seventy years ago, Constantine became Emperor. Because of the invasion of Franks, Germans and Goths he moved the capital from Rome to Byzantium."

"I always wondered where that name came from."

"The emperor gave it his name, Constantinople. This second Rome is strategically located on the trade routes between Europe and Asia, and between the Mediterranean and the Black Seas."

"How did he become Christian?"

"He battled Emperor Maxentius at the Tiber River's Mulvian Bridge in 312 AD. Before the battle Constantine saw a flaming cross in the sky bearing the words, 'In this sign thou shalt conquer'. He had his men make the sign of the cross on their shields, and from that time forward they were always victorious."

"That sounds like one of our Berber legends."

"Good girl. Greek historians agree with you. They claim it was a political move to gain Christian recruits for Constantine's army. His mother Helena may already have been converted. We know she went to Jerusalem where she too had several visions. At each place where these revelations took place she built a church. An engineer once pointed out to me that each of the seven churches commanded the high ground and were built in a manner making it easy to defend."

"You mean she was having these revelations at places to defend the holy city?"

"They formed a convenient chain of forts. The following year Constantine signed the Edict of Milan. It ensured religious tolerance for Christians, which brought an end to the Age of Martyrs, begun after Jesus' death. In Carthage the primary gods are Baal and his wife, the goddess Tanit. There have been and still remain Christian writers and philosophers—Saint Augustine, and in the Eastern Orthodox Church, Constantine is also a saint. Now Constantinople is more important than Rome, and so is Carthage."

"How did Rome defeat The Carthaginians?"

"It was a battle for our survival. We Romans do not care so much about the gods other people worship as long as they obey our laws and pay taxes. Hannibal led the Phoenician army from Carthage to Italy, twice. He was far more brilliant a general than he was a politician."

"Why do you say that?"

"He only knew how to win at war, not negotiate peace. The Italian people were prepared to pursue him. Wheat was in short supply. The Emperors had taxed the people to penury and beyond. Hannibal did not take advantage of these feelings. Our Romans banded together from necessity, attacked and defeated the Carthaginians. Thousands were slaughtered, and fifty thousand Carthaginians sold into slavery. All of North Africa came under our rule."

"Not all of the Maghreb."

"Another reason for our courting the Berber tribes. Did you understand my use of the word penury?"

"I believe it means poorness."

"Good. Poverty, would be a better word. I will use a higher form of the language. Feel free to question."

"Why did the Romans destroy the city and then rebuild it?"

"Two of the finest harbors in the world: one used for commercial shipping, the other for our battle fleet. From here and from Constantinople we control the seven seas."

"How did you take it from the Carthaginians?"

"The flaw in their defenses was the deep salt-water lake with access from the sea. Their fortifications faced seaward. We sailed behind them, landed our troops and attacked their undefended rear."

"That's the reason you built the twenty-three-mile long wall!"

"An engineering marvel. Carthage was founded by the King of Tyre's daughter Elissa. She fled from Lebanon when her brother killed her husband and was trying to catch her. With a small fleet of ships she reached this area. She recognized the two best harbors in the Mediterranean and attempted to settle. A local Berber chieftain gave her an ox-hide and stipulated she could have as much land to live on as she could cover with it." Linus pointed the tallest building. It had four spires with a cross atop each. "It is located on the highest point of land on the coastal plain. She laid claim to that entire mountain."

"How could she do that with only one ox-hide?"

"She had her people cut the ox hide into thin strips and put them end to end around the hill. The Berbers were impressed by her solution, and she held the high ground in a fight. The Berbers also appreciated that the Phoenicians were ages ahead in education, technical and military innovation. They built fleets of ships that sailed around Africa, into the Mediterranean and as far away as England."

"What is that building with the crosses?"

"A church. This is the most Christian city in Africa. Muhammad wants to destroy and convert them, and the Pagans as well. It served as the Necropolis and the seat of the Carthaginian government until King Constantine donated it to Roman Christians. It is built on a Pagan temple to the Goddess Tanit."

"I have a small statue of Tanit with my other gods."

"And I have my Roman gods. On the left you see the circus, behind that the amphitheater. Behind the Citadel on the Byrsa is the key to development and security of Carthage: the La Malga Cisterns, a row of giant cisterns storing clean water the year round. From there you have the Baths of Gargilius, el Karita Basilica, the Baths of Antonius Pius and the Governor's Palace. The private houses you see are different neighborhoods of villas. Behind their walls are lush gardens, and miniature orchards."

"Outside looks rather poor."

"'Stark' would be a better description. The word means glaringly poor. But I assure you, inside wealth is displayed in architecture, furniture and wall hangings."

"Why so?"

"Because Roman tax collectors are forbidden to enter the private residence of a Roman citizen, so they tax from their view of the outside."

"Which is stark, and costs less."

"Good girl. Now for our last visit of the day: the Temple of Eshmun, the Phoenician god of healing. With your special talents, it should interest you."

They mounted sixty steps. The sanctuary boasted an esplanade and a grand court, surrounded by huge limestone terrace walls that supported a large podium with two marble thrones. Both were in a state of disrepair. A series of ritual basins were fed by channeled water from the sacred Yd'il spring. "The water," Linus explained, "is used to purify, and is believed to contain therapeutic value."

"Have you tested it?"

"It keeps the sick cleaner. That is the only benefit I see."

"It looks as if those two thrones behind the podium were vandalized."

"'Vandalized' is a good word. Instead of the words 'looks as if' try the word, 'appears'. The statues were of the god Eshmun and the goddess Astarte. Two years ago Muhammad's followers came overnight and chiseled the statues out of their marble thrones."

"Why?"

"Muslims abhor any depiction of the human form, in painting, tapestry or sculpture. If you ever see a statue with its nose chipped off you know a Muslim was there. The Legions' senior engineer said if he could find the perpetrators he would hire those who desecrated the statues. They completed a massive amount of work in only ten hours."

"Did you find them?"

"Crucified them all."

On their way out of the temple Cahena bought a clay statue of the god Eshmun. The old woman who sold it asked in mountain Berber, "Won't the Cahena Princess visit the Zaimph?"

"I am no princess."

"You are the daughter of Moshe ben Shimi, and will one day be queen of all Berber tribes in Andalusia, Africa, Egypt, Persia and the Levant."

Cahena didn't translate the last part but asked Linus about the Zaimph. At the same time a messenger arrived with an order for Linus

"There is a city meeting I must attend," he explained. "I will leave you with Josephus and your bodyguards." He dropped a copper coin into the lap of the vendor. "This old woman can show you the Zaimph."

The Zaimph was not a statue but an ornate veil, adorned with precious and semi-precious stones and woven threads of gold and silver. It was draped about the statue of the goddess Tanit in the sanctum sanctorum of the temple. "The veil," said the old woman, "and not the statue, is the city's protector and guardian. Touching it brings death."

"Why, if the Muslims ruined the other two statues, didn't they steal the veil?"

"One tried," Josephus said. "His body was found at the feet of the goddess Tanit." He gave another copper coin to the woman and dismissed her. "That's how we found the rest of the group. We interrogated his friends. It wasn't the curse that killed him; his friends did that to stop him from touching the veil. Medicus Linus investigated the situation. He walked up to the statue, took the veil in both hands, and kissed it. He's still alive."

"I would have thought he would tell me a story like that."

"He is a Roman and you a Berber. He tells you what he wishes you to know. He always has a reason."

"But you're a Roman."

"To you I am. To Linus I'm a Calabrese from the mountains of Italy. They call us thickheads, slow to learn. Linus is one of the few true Romans in the legion, born and educated in Rome. He thinks of you and your people as barbarians."

"That isn't apparent."

"He's clever. The Latin word 'barbarian' is like 'Berber' to them. You may speak Latin or Greek better than every Roman, but they will always look down on you as a Berber, barbarian."

The return to the quadrangle was done at a leisurely pace with Josephus at Cahena's side. He explained that the genius of Rome was not only its military, but its ability to seek out future leaders of potential enemies and influence them in favor of Rome. This they accomplished by education, economics, force, and bribery.

"They are grooming me by education?"

"And bribery."

"I accepted no bribe!"

"You took one hundred pigeons for two dead ones. Linus paid for your three horses. There will be other gifts. Don't refuse them. Recognize them for what they are."

"And what is that?"

"A means of getting you to eat from the Roman plate. When it becomes a habit, like your pigeons, you belong to them."

"At first I thought you foolish to follow me." She reached out and touched Josephus' shoulder. "I am fortunate to have your loyalty."

A message from Moshe ben Shimi awaited Cahena. It had traveled thirteen-hundred miles and more than twenty stations to Carthage in five days. The message was in Hebrew so no casual bystander could comprehend it.

> *"My dearest Daughter, May the Almighty bless you as Sarah, Rebecca, Rachel and Leah. May He shine his countenance upon you. I wish you health and everything that is good. My attempt to unite the Berber, Tuareg and Bedouin has met with some success. This inspired many to join me, others to oppose and many from Morocco's' Amazigh Berber to question my intentions. The latter are the wealthiest and most numerous of the tribes. I require you to convince these tribes of the Maghreb that the Muslims will soon be breaking into their homes and giving them two choices: convert to Islam or die. I offer the option of a powerful Berber Kingdom and free-*

dom. This is not an easy task for one so young, yet I have no one else to represent me. I must take the two-thousand-mile journey through the Atlas Mountains to speak with the hill tribes, then meet with the Ait Haddidou, on the Imilchil plateau in the Atlas range for the annual Moussem Festival. Meet me there September 8th."'

Two more birds flew in with the same message. Others contained instructions: which cities to visit and names of people to speak with and what points to stress. Cahena contacted Benyamin.

"I am going in the opposite direction," he said. "I will find a safe caravan for you to travel with to Tangiers. Your father's plans are known to me. I will speak for him to the tribes along the trail to Constantinople. I would like you to see the Strait of Gibraltar."

"What's there?"

"The end of the world. They call it an ocean, far larger than any of the seas. If you turn right in the Atlantic Ocean you see the coast of Spain. If you turn left, the coast of Africa."

"What if you sail straight ahead?"

"You fall off the end of the earth."

"Has anyone tried it?"

"They never returned."

Cahena consulted Ahmed, Josephus and her guards, who agreed they would join a caravan selected by Benyamin. It departed in two weeks. They prepared fifteen camels, as many horses, and ten donkeys. In the middle of these preparations Linus appeared with a tall lanky man in a Roman toga. He had the largest sandaled feet Cahena had ever seen. He squinted at Cahena and his Adam's apple jumped up and down. "Are you really only ten years old?" he asked.

"Who are you?"

"You will be taller than me."

"I asked you a question!"

"This is Andronicus, from Gaza," Linus said. "Your teacher."

Cahena eyed him up and down. "He looks... appears to have been in a famine."

"And your uncle Benyamin looks as if he caused it," Andronicus the teacher replied.

Cahena burst out laughing. "So you've met my uncle?"

"And I am prepared to start teaching."

"I fear that won't be for some months," Linus said. "Cahena has been ordered to Imilchil Plateau by way of Tangiers and Marrakech."

The tall thin teacher cocked his head, rolled his eyes and said, "I always wanted to see the end of the world. I detest camels. Ugly beasts. I can teach from horseback."

"If Cahena is satisfied," Linus said. "I will make the arrangements."

"Lessons will pass the time," Cahena said. "Welcome to our caravan. We are about to take a long journey from Algeria to the far end of Morocco—three and a half months."

"I require one camel for my books and one for my personal things," Andronicus said, "Plus three horses. Gentle ones."

Cahena had no time for her teacher. She trained pigeons to take with her, others to return with messages to Carthage that could be forwarded on the thirteen-hundred mile route to the foothills of the Atlas Mountains. She also trained pigeons for those on the island of Djerba

CHAPTER 11

ON THE TRAIL AGAIN

The caravan master referred to Cahena as Benyamin's niece. "I have great respect for your uncle," he said. "Binyamin is one of the great caravan masters of our time."

His cheeks were puffed from betel leaves tucked inside, and his lips red from the color. Ozeret hurried to him with a palm leaf, into which he could spit the betel leaves. The man was just over five feet, slim and energetic. He spat into the palm leaf and continued talking.

"You and your people will find life with my caravan different than with your uncle's. We move faster, and all seven days a week. No Sabbath. No time for illness. The dead are buried where they fall. Mourners must catch up or are no longer under my protection. I pay certain tribes to pass unhindered through their territories, but I cannot pay everyone. My guards will do what they can to protect you, but you must be ready to fight for yourselves if necessary. Your warriors are a welcome addition to our group. Your uncle says you make a tea to prevent the shits in both people and animals?"

"Yes."

"It probably won't be needed during our first month, as we will be following the seashore, and the wells are many, clean, and regulated by Roman law. When we leave Casablanca in Morocco the wells are sometimes unclean. That is where Roman law stops and it pays to be vigilant."

"But you have only five professional guards?"

"Which brings me to another subject. I would like to hire your man Josephus to train the travelers in our group for self-defense. I will add five more professional guards in Casablanca, and he will take charge of our security until we reach the place of the Berber Moussem festival."

"Josephus is a free man. You must discuss this with him."

"Casablanca is the end of all law; from there on your people reign. Berbers, Tuaregs and Bedouin control everything into the desert and the Atlas Mountains until Numidia. I am hopeful your Berber ancestry will work on my behalf and the tribes won't attack."

"I will be speaking to the tribes on our way.

They know I am coming. To be certain there is no misconception by local Berbers, one of my warriors will always be up front with your scouts to tell them The Cahena is in your caravan."

For the first time the caravan master bowed, touched his heart, lips and forehead in a sign of deference to the young girl.

Similar to Benyamin's caravan, at four o'clock travelers began their morning tasks of feeding and loading the animals, stoking the cooking fire with dried camel patties, making fresh bread and boiling water for the strong black kaffa whose beans they roasted and ground. The pace of the caravan was faster. Stragglers learned to keep up, ride or be left behind unprotected. The elderly and children rode.

The landscape was richer in orchards, fields of wheat, vegetables and livestock. There were few settlements, more towns and villages. They were Berbers: farmers who went out to their fields, here and there a blacksmith, cobbler and carpenter. They hired professional guards for their villages. Roman law was evident by the orderly placement of homes, wells, sanitary facilities and occasional crucified body rotting in the sun. Josephus insisted on Cahena's morning and evening runs, and when others hid from the midday heat he trained her with javelin, shield and short sword.

Andronicus had to give his lessons from the saddle when Cahena wasn't training or tending her birds. She found time to sketch birds on paper given her by Yaakov. Andronicus helped her to arrange a more orderly classification of the birds, and medicinal plants collected by Ozeret. The three tried with little success to unlock the secrets of the Chinese medicines taken with them. Cahena was prepared to abandon them. Ozeret insisted they be kept.

Andronicus set ironclad rules for teaching: no interruptions. "I am your teacher, not your friend or playmate. You wish to learn, I wish to teach; it should be enjoyable for both. Everything should be questioned."

"Even the gods?" Cahena asked.

"Especially the gods. You may not be satisfied with the answers, but we work with the knowledge we have. By writing it, we pass the information on to future generations."

"For what purpose?"

"To make a better life for those who follow."

"What if I suspect my conclusions may be proved wrong?"

"Erroneous is a better Greek word. If you fear the validity of your conclusions, put a date on your document. You can always say, 'On this day I believed so and so, but now I am convinced otherwise'. Linus informed me he compared education to ascending a ladder. If steps are missing you will always falter until they are repaired. He says you are intelligent, but that doesn't indicate what might be missing in your basic education. Jews start teaching their children at age three. Is that what your father did?"

"I doubt it. I was five when he taught me to write."

"The children of religious Jews are given a scroll with a dollop of honey on it. The child is given to lick it from the scroll, and their education begins." He held out his hand with a piece of honeycomb on a palm leaf. "Eat, and we will investigate the world."

After the morning chores and exercises, Andronicus and Cahena rode to the front of the caravan with Josephus and two guards. They found a shade tree and studied. When the rear of the procession approached they returned to their position in the center.

Andronicus tested Cahena in reading, writing and mathematics. He experienced two conflicting emotions at the same time; he wept and laughed. He shed tears that wet his shirt front, and howled with joy at what he discovered. "The girl is a genius!" he shouted. He squatted in the field and tried to stem the tears and control the laughter. "How will I teach her? Most of what I prepared on the voyage to Carthage is irrelevant. She is missing a plethora of basics but is a mental trap, grasps whatever is taught. She examines, contemplates, questions and decides. Oh, what a joy. Oh, what work! Am I capable? Can I help her? Challenged by a ten year old girl! She has the natural capacity of intellect, in creative and practical thought. Most mathematics she does in her head, on introduction to geometry dealing with angles, surfaces, and solids—considered by Greek scholars to be the benchmark of intelligence. She understood as if born to it. She could visualize shapes and forms described in words."

This led Andronicus to fulfill a promise to Cahena's father, to map the country they traveled. The girl was so much more adept than he at reconfiguring the roads, towns, wells and bridges onto animal skins with consistently scaled diagrams of significant geographic features. He reminded her to indicate the time of year, as trees with foliage would change their appearance in winter, or could supply food in season. He introduced her to astronomy.

"Often in the desert you will travel without roads. Sleep during the heat of day, using only the stars to guide you at night."

She charted the heavenly bodies and learned to navigate by the stars. She attempted to create a map of the heavens by pricking holes in an animal skin to align with the stars. Andronicus had seen it attempted by one of the king's astronomers in Athens, and fail. He said nothing. The concept was worthy, its implementation faulted. She would learn as much by her mistakes and failures.

Cahena was occupied every minute of the waking day. There was no time to train pigeons as they never stayed in one place more than a few hours overnight. Andronicus helped her draft her first talk to the Berbers of the city Hippo Regius. Neither was satisfied with the speech. It was being given by a ten year old girl whose ideas were couched in modern seventh century Greek, translated to ancient Berber. The idea of a ten-year-old giving advice to tribal elders about the future confederation of Berbers extending throughout the Maghreb and beyond appeared illogical to teacher and student. But her father's instructions were clear and defined.

They needn't have worried or prepared. In every town and city the Cahena was greeted by elders and chieftains followed by pilgrims come to pay homage to the High Priestess of the Berbers, Daughter of Moshe ben Shimi, leader of the Amazigh Berbers. They'd come to greet the future queen of the Berbers, the mystical High Priestess, Cahena. They sought her healing power. She couldn't attend the needy, speak with tribal elders, continue her daily routine and keep up with the caravan.

She and her group stayed three days in Hippo Regius. Cahena pardoned herself from the elders and tended the sick. Ozeret helped by giving a placebo to those she felt were shamming for attention. Ozeret often advised a treatment or recommend a potion to relieve pain or fever. She and Josephus helped with setting bones and using the tools donated by Medicus Linus to extract arrows or cleanse infections. Here and there an amputation was required. It was done with a special Roman medical saw and the skin tied with sheep's-gut thread while the patient was sedated with opium. Some died, others were successful. All were soothed by the touch of Cahena.

The majority of patients suffered from malaria. Those stricken with the disease wanted the touch of Cahena and declined offers of help from Ozeret. By the third day Ozeret managed having the patients placed in rows on the ground. Cahena passed by briefly touching each one's forehead. She remained a little longer with those about to die. All appeared to benefit from her attention. Mugwort was distributed by Cahena's guards. Ozeret described its intensive use to the shamans of the tribes. Word spread of the Cahena's mystic powers. People came to worship outside her tent.

They required two days rest at a Caravansary, a travelers' hotel with protective guards and meals provided. They were now three days behind their caravan. Catching up would not be difficult nor safety a problem; word of the Cahena proceeded them. She questioned her guards as to how the towns ahead of her knew she was about to arrive. The answer was: "Your godfather, Abu Abak the Storyteller. He has been telling wonder tales about you." Cahena smiled and was certain her father was instrumental in the storyteller's version of events.

With Andronicus as her advisor she sat with the tribal chieftains, briefly explained the message of her father to all Berbers: "Prepare for war. Train your young men and women. It will be another five or six years before the call to arms will come, but come it must. The Romans need our assistance to hold off the Muslims. Learn from the Romans. One day we will use that knowledge against them. Send spies amongst the Muslims. They are certain to invade the Maghreb as a stepping stone to attack Catholic Spain from the Strait of Gibraltar. They will attempt to conquer Orthodox Christianity in Constantinople, from Islamic Thrace just across the Bosporus. Your young men must learn military discipline and how to wield weapons of war. At the same time you must continue to grow and store food for our army when we come, and come we will. Your young men will form auxiliaries to guide and advise our commanders on the lay of the land, the attitude of its inhabitants and the strength and weakness of the enemy."

In this way Cahena relayed her father's message and received vows of loyalty to the future Queen of the Berbers. She stopped in two more towns where the exact same scene was played out as in Hippo Regius. The populations came out several miles to greet The Cahena. As before many sought cures.

Andronicus quickly understood the need for a more orderly approach. He requested Cahena call a meeting of those who left the Atlas Mountains with her, Josephus, Ozeret and himself, Ahmed, his mother and the guards. He addressed the group, "Our journey together has been successful, but we must revise our travel plans. Not even Cahena's father considered such fierce loyalty and devotion among the distant Berber people. They were waiting for a prophet, and Cahena fits their expectations. We cannot stop at every town and reach the Grand tribal grounds in September." Andronicus said, "She is being received as the High Priestess of the Holy Temple in Jerusalem. Already people follow us. They call her a prophet, healer, a Hebrew seer, the reincarnation of Shimi HaCohen, the High Priest of Jerusalem."

"How can you stop the people from coming out to greet Cahena or joining us?" Josephus asked.

"I do not wish to stop them, but her appearances must be more orderly, less strenuous. She is about to collapse from exhaustion."

"How can Cahena appear before the people and keep up with the caravan?" a guard asked.

"We will leave the caravan," Andronicus said.

"What of security?"

"With dedicated Berbers following us, and those coming out to greet us, we are protected on all sides."

It was agreed to leave the caravan and send messengers ahead to inform the people, The Cahena would only be stopping at the cities of Cirta, Saldae, Lol, Cartena, Russadda and Tinglis at the Strait of Gibraltar and the end of the world. Her priorities were ministrations to the sick and injured, discussions with the tribal chieftains about preparations for war, and discussions with the shamans about treating malaria.

Ozeret convinced Cahena that the shamans were as important as the chieftains regarding a future war with the Romans and Muslims. Even farming Berbers considered themselves Free People, capable of making their own decisions—which was often influenced by the shamans.

Andronicus arranged a more orderly approach for Cahena to minister to the sick and convey her father's war message to the tribal leaders.

Everyone in the party but Cahena was disappointed in their visit to the Port of Tinglis. They were more impressed with the shoreline of Spain just seven miles across the Gibraltar Strait than they were with the end of the world. They hired a ship to take them out into the Atlantic Ocean, but they saw only more ocean. The captain turned back as he explained that the end of the world could be close, and once trapped in the ocean currents no ship could save itself. They would fall off the end of the earth. Andronicus wanted to proceed but was shouted down. He was not reconciled by the Captain's explanation, "Some ships have sailed two months due north and returned without finding the end of the world. The border to Hell varies."

Cahena busied herself with the Chinese paper sketching birds. Andronicus helped identify and classify the flocks from Spain migrating to Africa for the summer: hundreds of thousands of Cory's and Balearic shearwaters, Audouin's, yellow-legged and lesser black-backed gulls, razorbills and Atlantic puffins. Andronicus pointed out the larger eagles, buzzards, kites and vultures using the midday thermals to soar and glide on their way to Africa. Called by Greeks, 'the Magic Corridor', the short distance between the continents gave access for smaller birds to summer in Africa.

In Casablanca, Andronicus approached Cahena and spoke of Numidia. "In cities we've visited the chieftains recommended you attempt to enlist the aid of the Numidian Army."

"I never knew there was one."

"Four hundred years ago they considered themselves Berbers. The Romans know of them as fierce fighters. They were hired by Hannibal and helped defeat the Romans twice. The Romans hired them in the third Punic war, defeated Hannibal and destroyed the Carthaginian Empire."

"Tell me more."

"The Romans tried converting them to Christianity, but had limited success. Numidians are fiercely independent. Their religion incorporates Christianity, Paganism and whatever appeals to them at the time. They are of the black race."

"I never saw a black Berber."

"That is why you are making this trip. It is part of your education. Unlike those blacks from southern Africa, who wallow in mud huts, Numidians have developed a highly organized society. They educate the young. They are divided into social, merchant, religious and military classes supporting the monarchy. I studied their military tactics against the Romans and against Hannibal. They are fearless in battle. Convince them to side with you against the Romans or the Muslims, and you would gain a powerful ally and eliminate a possible foe. The Muslims will convert or kill them. The Romans will hire them to fight you."

"My father hasn't the money to bid against Rome."

"Numidia is a desert kingdom. The infertile land is unable to supply food for basic living. They have no natural resources."

"How do they survive?"

"They supplied Rome, now Constantinople, with military auxiliaries. There only export exotic animals from southern Africa: lions, leopards, elephants, and all manner of birds.

They are fighters. Their main source of income is from the services of their soldiers to the highest bidders in Spain, Europe and the Middle-East. The soldiers send the money back to the King. He uses it to implement what he believes is worthwhile for his kingdom."

"Is he a fair ruler?"

"He thinks so."

"You must believe I should meet with them."

"I do."

"Can you arrange it?"

"Yes. Approach them as you would a king of a powerful monarchy. These are intelligent leaders; play on their Berber heritage. You are young and disarming. Your willingness to help the poor and infirm will not be lost on them. They are a proud people. In addition to their Berber heritage you have two things in your favor.

"They have a historic memory of betrayal by the Romans. Eight hundred years ago Rome defeated Hannibal with the help of the Numidian cavalry. Rome promised them all the seacoast towns and plains from Tinglis to Carthage, plus they were to be given the fertile plains of the Maghreb two hundred miles inland. This stretch of land is the lushest place on earth. The Romans reneged on that treaty and kept the Numidians in the desert. The nation harbors a blood feud with Rome. The Numidians have their own religion. Their priests and temples are free from Numidian taxes, but they are taxed by Rome. The clergy are a powerful class, influencing the King. They will fight to the death against Islam. Promise the Black King to honor the eight-hundred-year-old Roman agreement about land. Then promise the priests that you will not promote Judaism or Christianity, continue their generous tax status, and absolve the Roman tax. Do this and you may acquire the finest light cavalry in the world."

"How large a force are they?"
"Significant. And..."

Introduction to the desert was a gradual process in Numidia, where the desert meets the lush farmlands of the Mediterranean coastal plains. The caravan trail increasingly became the dividing line between the sand on the left and cultivated land on the right. Here and there, white sand fingers reached across the road into the fertile fields.

From the Atlas Mountains streams and rivers marked long green limes through the undulating dunes. These waterways irrigated the rich farmlands known as 'The Bread-Basket of the Roman Empire'.

All but the hardiest of those who followed Cahena's caravan dropped away as the landscape became more stark and forbidding. It was midsummer. Temperatures reached 120 degrees. Movement during the day became impossible, so they traveled at night. Andronicus taught Cahena to use the stars as guides when the trail disappeared. Further into the desert the sand and wind wiped out the trail and withered the fields.

Those twenty camp-followers who remained were incorporated into Josephus's guard contingent. He was a strict taskmaster and trained them at every opportunity. He stressed repulse of an armed cavalry charge. His aim was to convince these men and women that horses were at a disadvantage when charging trained, properly equipped infantry. He purchased weapons from passing caravans moving in the opposite direction, buying helmets, daggers and swords, but his main objective was shields, javelins, and the four-meter-long contus or thrusting spear, to repel cavalry. Cahena questioned, "Why do you train with the contus and javelins? I thought the sword and shield more important."

"In normal terrain, yes, but attacks in desert fighting are rarely done on foot."

"Then why are you teaching them to defend

as infantry?"

"In the desert, raiders must travel by camel or horse. Mounted men always feel superior to foot soldiers. They are not. The horse is a very skittish animal; when faced with a solid wall of shields and spear-points it will always turn aside or stop. In either case, those mounts charging behind them must stop or turn even more quickly to avoid collisions. Experienced cavalry try to strike fear into their foes so they break and run."

"And if they don't break?"

"The cavalry must turn a minimum of one-hundred feet before the enemy line, half the cavalry to the right and half to the left. They then attack the flanks or complete what is called a double envelopment, attacking the rear, hoping to cause panic and a route."

"What if they did break into the ranks? Couldn't they cut the infantrymen down?"

"It looks good in paintings and sculptures, but a mounted man is at a disadvantage. If he is right-handed, I move to the left side of his horse. I have dropped the long spear and now have two seven-foot javelins. I can bang his horse in the nose with my shield and pick him out of the saddle with the javelin. If he is right-handed he cannot use his sword against me."

"If what you say is true, then why are the

Numidian Cavalry considered to be so important?"

"They are the best at instilling fear. It takes courage and training to hold your position against charging horses. The Numidians throw spears, shoot arrows, and howl before they turn away. If they sense the slightest weakness in the enemy lines, they will exploit it. I watched them cut apart a thousand Vandals; they were like a pack of wolves on a wounded deer. They are fast, ride bareback, have no bit, bridle or armor for their horse or themselves. That is why they are called 'Light Cavalry'."

"How do they control the animals?"

"With their knees and their heels. They have a rope around the horse's neck, used to pull him up short. Their archers are exceptional at full gallop, and effective with javelins. They never attempt to breach a solid infantry formation. But once enemy foot-soldiers break formation, they slaughter them."

The third night on the caravan trail took them out of the fertile region. Now to both the right and left were sand dunes. Under a carpet of stars and a bright half-moon Andronicus continued his lessons in astronomy.

It was close to sunrise. The moon's radiance waned and the stars began to blink out as the sun glowed behind the Atlas Mountains on the left. Cahena saw a line of fifty horsemen silhouetted on the left. She turned right and fifty more paralleled the right flank. "Josephus!" she hissed. "Look!"

"They've been with us for several minutes. There are more up front and behind. If they wanted to attack we'd be dead already."

Andronicus heard the conversation and whispered, "They may be our escort to the Numidian King. Have one of your guards speak Berber to them, but under no circumstance are you to speak. You are the queen."

"Not yet."

"In all the Maghreb, that is how you are called. Have one of your guards negotiate."

As the sun topped the snowcapped mountains, murmurs ran through the caravan. The silent sentinels on either side were black men. Their hair was wild and unruly. Most had short mustaches and pointed beards. They wore simple full length cotton pullovers. Behind wooden shields they held two javelins, swords belted at the waist, with bows and arrows over the shoulders. Some held the ropes around their horse's necks in their teeth. They rode silently without casting a glance to either side. The sun continued to climb. The senior guard came alongside Cahena and asked, "What should we do?"

"Nothing!" Josephus hissed. "They are Numidians, and they have twice the men we do. Let them decide."

"Look ahead," the guard said. "See where the sun is lighting that green spot among the dunes? It gets brighter and larger every minute."

"It looks like a giant emerald," Cahena said.

Josephus stopped his horse and stood up atop the saddle. "You are looking at an oasis."

Andronicus went into his teaching tone of voice. "Most people think an oasis is any place in the desert with water. The biblical city of Jericho is an oasis because it can support more than ten thousand inhabitants. That is about how many it takes to protect a city from desert raiders and bandits. Any smaller population is called a water hole. The green of the date palms is dazzling. And look, they have a manmade lake. It feeds off that river. What are those white mounds surrounding the edge of the oasis?"

"Bee houses," Ozeret said. "Maybe they will part with some honey."

"The green is so bright it hurts the eyes," Cahena noted.

"It contrasts with the whiteness of the dunes. This must be the city of Ben Abbas, the king's home."

A delegation met the column. Cahena's senior guard, a woman chieftain, spoke with the Numidians. They had food and tents prepared; they expected the caravaneers to eat and sleep during the day, then attend the king's welcome in the evening.

The temperature dropped twenty degrees under the canopy of tall palm trees that hung heavy with dates. The desert wind was cooled by fields of grain and the artificial lake. These were protected in turn by carefully groomed orchards of plums, pomegranates, oranges, lemons and orderly rows of large leafed plantain plants. Herb gardens bordered the paths between the trees, lush vegetable gardens encompassed the western border of the oasis, and beyond this bright green canopy and carpet of green were the rolling waves of pure white sand that marched to infinity under the ever-burning sun.

The sound of rushing water distracted Cahena. She guided her horse to a beautiful twelve-foot waterfall. She came close enough to feel the coolness of the spray. Her horse whinnied and grunted in pleasure as the cool mist engulfed them.

Trees shaded the tents, which contained plush mattresses, pillows, cool drinks and trays of fruit. One of Cahena's guards choked and spit out a mouthful of plantain. Josephus laughed, "Try eating it without the skin."

Andronicus was excited at being amid the tribe he had studied in Greece. He went around touching everything and naming it. Sleep for him was out of the question; he wandered off to explore the oasis. Ahmed and his handlers unloaded the camels and took the livestock to a corral north of the orchards.

Sleep came easy to the rest of those of the caravan, for the last three hours of the journey had been tense; being hemmed in by the silent black sentinels who appeared out of nowhere had been unsettling, and they slept well.

The cool evening desert breeze awoke the guests. They were shown where to bathe and informed to dress appropriately. Gershom, King of Numidia would receive them.

Ahmed's mother and Ozeret fussed and fretted over dressing Cahena. They were interrupted by the King's messenger with a gift for the High Priestess. It was a necklace of several rows of golden coins minted under King Massinissa. Andronicus explained. "He was the greatest king of the Berbers. King Gershom sent this particular gift so he can impress you by telling the history of his people and himself. He is considered the wisest of men. Everything he says will have meaning. You are young and untested in diplomacy. My advice is to listen as though each word he utters is golden. Flattery goes a long way, even with the wisest of Kings."

"How old is this king?"

"Thirty-six. He speaks Latin, Greek, and of course Berber."

"What subjects should I raise?"

"Only those you know well. This first meeting is a test; he must be asking himself why your father sent a ten-year-old to carry his message."

"How can I impress him?"

"Don't try. He's been approached by the most sophisticated. Stick to your subjects, and your intelligence will shine through."

"And if it doesn't?"

"Be yourself. He'll sniff out any falsity on your part."

The music of lutes, lyres and bull-headed harps sounded. A nye-flute, blown through the nostrils, combined with the wildly plucked strings of a table-lyre. A Roman brass trumpet followed the melody.

Cahena and her group were led from the tents to the Cardo. This main thoroughfare was lined with torches that lit up the night. Before the torches stood rows and rows of people, all dressed in full-length pullover linen shifts of exotic colors and designs. The beat of the music was set by the drums. Two lines of warriors appeared, holding shields and javelins, who marched in front of the crowd until they reached the king's tent. They stopped, turned inward and grounded their weapons in the short guard position. Following them came two lines of nubile maidens whose bodies were outlined through the thin linen by the light of the torches. They stood before the young warriors. The music ceased except for a solitary small drum tapped with a curved stick. The King appeared and before him walked a Christian priest chanting, "Behold the Lion of Judah, Inheritor from Ethiopia, Descendent of King Solomon and the Queen of Sheba, Inheritor of Ethiopia's mandate from Egypt to the Mediterranean, to the great ocean and to the end of the world."

Not tall or physically exceptional, the king moved with grace and power. His lion-skin cloak, golden crown and silver thread sandals enhanced his natural dignity. He exuded power by his posture, eyes and confidant step. The warriors beat their javelins on their shields in time to the drum. As the king passed the maidens fell to their left knees, threw rose petals from their right hands beneath his feet, bowed their heads and held their fists over their hearts in salute. When the king came parallel to Cahena he indicated she should join him, and she walked on rose petals to the throne.

The seat of power was carved from a single trunk of a walnut tree. A plethora of Numidian fighting hawks was depicted in the carvings. Gems of rubies, diamonds and sapphires were embedded in the wood. The throne was polished every day with goat's milk to bring out the richness of color and grain, and to highlight the workmanship. Cahena sat alongside the king. The people bowed, touching their foreheads to the earth, and remained so until the king waved his horsehair scepter. This was also a sign for the young women to move to the center of the path, followed by warriors carrying strings of red and yellow flowers which they draped over the shoulders of their female partners. The men stepped back and began to chant, swaying from side to side, and the young women took up the chant and movements. Several young women entered, swinging golden incense burners in one hand and spreading the scent of myrrh, jasmine, and roses by fanning with ostrich feathers in the other hand.

The dancers grew stimulated, their movements quicker and more frenetic, until they lost control and fell to the earth in sexual embraces. Cahena watched the faces of the onlookers mesmerized by the performance. The king reached over and touched Cahena's arm. "This is in your honor," he said. "All female children conceived this evening will be named Cahena."

"What of the male children?"

"Gershom."

"An illustrious name," Cahena said.

"I was told it was an Egyptian name."

"In Hebrew, *mashah* means, 'to draw out of the water'. When Moses was saved by the princess of Egypt, she named him Moses because she pulled him from the river. His first born son was named Gershom." Cahena paused. "You could be related through Zipporah, Moses' wife. She was a black Midianite."

"We have many Jews in Numidia. They usually argue among themselves."

"About what?"

"Religion: those who say they must adhere to the old ways, those who accept the interpretation from rabbis in Babylon, those who incorporate the Christian religion and those who worship our Pagan gods."

"I am in the latter group."

"And I am for whatever works best for my people."

"And I am here to bring my father's message of consolidation of the Berber people, so once again we can live as 'The Free People'."

"I can't believe I am having this conversation with a ten-year-old! Are you truly a genius?"

"I wouldn't know. I never met one."

"Nor I, until possibly now. See these coins around your neck? They were stamped by the greatest King of Numidia, Massinissa. He was a genius. In addition to physical strength he was fearless, devious and diplomatically skillful. He conceived the idea of bringing the native tribes together and forming a nation. He developed agriculture and commerce in addition to a powerful military. He was recognized first by Hannibal and then by Rome. The Italians hired him away from Carthage with promises of the fertile plains you passed on the way here. They reneged, and forced us into the Sahara desert. Our civilization is older than the pyramids! Romans hunted pigs and Greeks swung from trees by their tails when Numidians were trading silver, gold and precious gems. Today the Romans tax everything. All that rich farmland you passed on your journey no longer belongs to us. The Romans distribute it to their retired soldiers in place of pensions. We can no longer graze our livestock on what was once tribal land."

"Then my father's plan for Berber independence should interest you."

"Interest and implementation are two words which carry the death penalty regarding a Berber state. I have ten thousand troops patrolling for the Romans throughout the Sahara, another ten thousand for the defense of Constantinople, and the same amount somewhere near Poland keeping the Huns and Vandals in check."

"And here?"

"Fifteen thousand, and several thousand more fighting men in the string of oases that lead across the Sahara in the direction you are going."

"How is it you know where I am going?"

"Everyone knows. You think the Romans aren't spying on you? Your godfather Abu Abak has been here."

"Did he tell the story of how to brick a camel?"

King Gershom had just taken in a mouthful of plump pomegranate seeds. He laughed so hard the seeds shot out of his mouth. He choked. The music stopped, the Numidians froze, and Cahena's people stared in fright.

The king regained his composure and bellowed, "Did you hear this young one? She wanted to know if Abu Abak taught us how to water a camel!"

The Numidians roared back, "Brick 'em!" and

then laughed uproariously.

The king used his sleeve to wipe the tears from his eyes. "I haven't laughed that much since he told that joke."

"Did he tell the one about a little girl named Petal?"

"Not that I can remember. You tell it."

"A Roman Catholic priest came upon a little girl playing with her dog on the steps of the temple of Venus, the Roman goddess of love. He asked her, 'What is your name, little girl'?"

"'My name is Petal', she said."

"'And how did you come to have such a beautiful name?'"

"'My mother and father were making love under a flowering tree, and a delicate pink petal drifted down on them when I was conceived.'"

"'That is beautiful. And what is your dog's name?'"

"'Porky!'"

"'Why call a dog Porky?'"

"'He likes to fuck pigs.'"

The King laughed so hard he held his sides. "No more! No more. I have been keeping you from the food."

The food was assorted raw vegetables served with hot-spice, honey, and vinegar dipping-sauces, sliced apples on goat cheese, with plump figs drizzled with honey. Then came beef ribs roasted to a crackling spicy crust, sliced tongue and deep-fried breaded chickens, sweetbreads, roasted carp on plantain leaf with crushed cashew nuts, a bowl of blue-eyed prawns with sweet and spicy dipping sauces, deep-fried rolls made of thin pastry filled with beef, lamb, vegetables, cheese and plantains, then skewers of meat and vegetables roasted over open fire pits. There was wine chilled in the waterfall, salads served on palm leaves, iced raspberry wine for dessert with a multitude of cookies topped with honey nuts and cherries. The festivities went silent as everyone concentrated on the feast.

Cahena turned to the King. "It is a complement to the host," she said, "When his guests are quieted by the quality of the food and the generosity of the one who provided it."

"Your father did well to send you. We shall talk again tomorrow, and I would like you to see my military units in action."

CHAPTER 12

THE BERBERS

When Josephus learned what was planned, he went directly to Cahena and told her, "Ask King Gershom to allow me to deploy my men against certain formations he is going to display tomorrow."

"For what reason?"

"Except for your guards, most of the twenty followers I am training are farmers. Another twenty who work for Ahmed are herdsmen. None ever fought in a battle in formation, or withstood a cavalry charge. They need experience."

"How can they get that?"

"Ten years ago I witnessed a Berber show of strength for the Legion's commanders. They will display light infantry and cavalry formations and impress you with signal mechanisms. I would like to put my men in a defensive position against their light cavalry."

The following morning after a dawn breakfast of

fruits, wine, and roasted pigeons, Cahena was escorted to a large elaborately decorated tent set up on the edge of the oasis facing the desert. The sides of the tent were rolled up, and she was seated at the right hand of the king. "Have you ever heard the song of the sands?" he asked.

"What is it?" Cahena said.

"Under certain conditions of temperature and wind, the sands begin to move. That movement causes a weird undulating sound we call the song of the sands. Some people believe it is Satan whispering."

"And you?"

The king steepled his hands before his lips. "I believe in what I can see and touch."

"And God?"

"That is why I remain a Pagan. This Jesus who is supposed to have risen from the dead? Ha! Who has seen him? Or Allah or your invisible god Yahweh? They mean nothing to me."

"What of the Bible?"

"Which one? The Holy teachings, Christian, the Torah? The Hindus, Babylonians and Chinese have holy books more ancient than yours."" He handed her a plate of figs and pistachio nuts. "Let's watch." He waved his horsehair scepter.

Atop the dunes appeared a lone horseman.

He raised a large curled ram's horn to his lips and sounded three distinct blasts. From the right and left moved infantry formations. At commands from their officers the formations changed shape while maneuvering to attain a superior position. Then they engaged in a mock battle, and on command disengaged.

"Have you ever witnessed a real battle?" the king asked.

"My first was at Satan's Saddle, where our tribes destroyed a large band of marauders. On the caravan trail to Carthage, I watched the Roman Legion massacre two groups of bandits."

"Then you recognize the signals that changed the formations?"

"I saw flags displayed and units move in response."

"Good. How did the Romans signal?"

"With trumpets."

"That must have been at night. They too use flags in daylight. Do you know what a rhombus is?"

"In Euclidean geometry, a rhombus is a simple quadrilateral shape whose four sides all have the same length. Another name is equilateral quadrilateral, which includes a square. A rhombus is often called a diamond shape."

"You studied geometry?"

"With my teacher Andronicus."

"The Greeks have a saying, 'Those who do not know geometry may not enter a house of learning'. What you will see next is the Sacred Band, my personal guard. They receive the best equipment for heavy infantry. Their weapons and training are similar to the famous Greek Hoplites; they carry a fourteen-foot spear, two javelins, sword, shield, breast-plate and greaves. They form a square, and stand shoulder to shoulder. Their shields interlock, protecting them from slingers and archers. We place them where we think the fighting will be most fierce. They use the Roman innovation of rotating fresh troops to the front line every ten minutes. Watch their change of formations against flanking enemy horse or attack from the rear."

After executing various formations to repel flanking and enveloping attacks, the Sacred Band marched off.

A straggling band of sixty, wearing mismatched helmets, breast-plates and weapons, led by Josephus, walked onto the field. They marched out further into the desert and formed in a square with their long fourteen-foot spears pointing to the dunes ahead. Cahena's untrained eye detected the difference in physical attitude of her group as compared with those of the proud Numidians. There was no energy in their step nor arrogance in their stance. Josephus addressed them and explained once again the advantages of infantry over cavalry. To achieve that advantage they must hold their formation and break the cavalry charge. When the charge was broken they must attack the confused horsemen with the long spears and javelins. He waved his shield.

At this signal a line of horseman appeared on the summit of the nearest sand dune facing them. They were followed by a second and then a third line of cavalry. A ram's horn sounded and the cavalry charged down the slope. At three hundred yards from the defenders the Numidian horsemen emitted loud war cries and banged their shields with their javelins. The defenders began to shift. One man broke then another and another. The attackers bulled their horses past the long spears and into the ranks of the defenders cracking heads with their shields or beating men with their javelins. Those defenders who fled were met by Cahena's five guards wielding short whips and beaten back into ranks.

A horn blew and the Numidians horse left the area. Josephus addressed his men. "Not as easy as it was in training, is it? Even though you knew this was an exercise, some of you broke and fled. Cowardice is the shortest path to hell! Every fight is a fight to the death. Don't worry about a grave; the wild animals will chew your bones—unless you hold your ground!

"We will try this again, with one difference. The five guards will put aside their whips and take up their bows. I have given orders for them to kill any man who flees. You take one step back and you will look like a hedgehog! Now return to your formation. There is a second group of cavalry waiting to kick the shit out of you."

This time Josephus' guard performed a lot better.

King Gershom and Cahena left before the warmth of the morning sun became unbearable. "What do you think of our tribal society?" he asked.

"It is more sophisticated than I or my father ever imagined. My first impression of wild-haired men riding horses without saddles or bridles was confusing."

"I always want to see if my guests look down on us. It places me in an advantageous position from which to judge them. The Romans still make that mistake."

"They look down on everybody."

"And it cost them their western empire."

"You helped them save Africa from the Vandals."

"Only because, like your father, I want it for my people."

"...this white tower we are passing: there is no entrance or ladder, only small holes with birds nesting."

"It is one of the keys to the natural wealth of this string of oases. We call them the Shit Towers. We make the holes small enough for pigeons and doves, but too small for predators. Mostly pigeons nest there and always face outwards. They shit into the tower, and we open it up every three years. The manure is dug into our soil to fertilize our crops and hold back the desert."

"This morning we had roast pigeon for breakfast."

"I hope it was satisfactory?"

"Very much so, but I have a different idea for the use of your pigeons."

Cahena explained how she used them in the battle of Satan's Saddle, and how the people of Djerba were using them for commerce. The king listened intently.

"You are an amazing young lady. I must admit, my primary reason for inviting you had little to do with your father's dream. Please accompany me; I wish to introduce you to my son."

The king's tent was protected by two guards at the front and rear entrances and one guard at each corner. "You see all my tent flaps are up. Like the founder of your tribe—Abraham, father of Israel—I too receive guest from whatever direction they arrive and whatever beliefs they have. Ishmael!" he called. "I have brought a guest for you to meet. She is your age. and her name is Cahena."

A boy stood up, holding on to the center tent poles. A slave girl went to take his hand but he brushed her aside asking, "Where is she from?"

"The mountain Berber tribes. Her father is Moshe ben Shimi."

"The prophetess you told me about?"

"Yes."

"Prophetess, will you help me see again?"

"From the way you hold your head and walked sideways toward me, you have some sight."

"True, but I am losing more and more. Soon it will be dark."

"May I touch your hand and look into your eyes?"

"Of course."

"Would you mind lying down?"

The slave girl spread a sheepskin and silk pillow, upon which the boy rested. Cahena drew closer and looked. The pupil of his left eye was covered by a milky white growth, and the right pupil was partially covered by a similar growth.

Cahena released his hand and said, "Please close your eyes." The boy did.

She placed her right hand on his forehead and her left hand over his heart. His breathing changed from shallow rapid breaths, to slow, deep even ones. In a few minutes he was asleep. She removed her hands, stood and motioned for the King to go outside with her. She had tears in her eyes when she said. "I never treated anyone with such a condition."

"He rarely sleeps so deeply," said Gershom. "He wakes up with nightmares of being totally blind. My son is intelligent enough to know there is no place in our world for a blind man. I am afraid he will commit suicide."

"Allow me to think."

"You shed tears for my son."

Cahena choked back a sob, and left to consult Andronicus, Ozeret and Josephus.

"Under no condition can you promise a cure," Andronicus stated. "And if you recommend Linus Crassus, let it be thought he is in the service of your father."

"We have another problem," Josephus said. "We cannot return to the coastal route and arrive in time for the annual ingathering of the

Berber tribes."

"Which we must do," Cahena said.

"It can only be done if we leave yesterday and cross the Sahara desert."

"You exaggerate," Cahena snapped.

"I made this desert crossing with the Legion. It was brutal; we lost fifteen men to the heat."

"We leave tomorrow evening," Cahena said. "Ask the Numidians' advice with preparations for the desert crossing. I must see the king this evening."

With the help of Andronicus and Ozeret, Cahena prepared for her meeting with the king. She brought with her the last six pigeons, and left the caged birds outside the reception tent. "I cannot cure Ishmael your son, but it may be that one in the service of my father can help."

"Whatever needs to be done, I will do it."

"I am compelled to explain the procedure. You may not wish to subject your son to it."

"Without sight he is dead."

"I never saw the operation performed. It and the equipment were explained to me. It is not pretty."

"Continue."

"Your son will probably not feel or remember anything. A drug—grown in India, and used in China—called opium puts the patient to sleep.

A small, smooth curved piece of horn is inserted into the eye socket next to his nose. The eye is pried out and while still attached to blood vessels and muscle. The eye is placed in a special cup rested on the cheek of the patient."

"Will he bleed very much?"

"There is very little blood, as no cuts are made to the skin or the eye."

"How do they remove the milky stuff?"

"With hot needles."

"In the eye?"

"He cuts or burns a circle around the white substance. Then, with a tweezers, peels it off."

"And how do they put the eye back?"

"They push it in."

"And my son will live through that?"

"Hopefully."

"You are uncertain?"

"Several people died from shock, but none from loss of blood or damage to the eye."

"How many people regained their sight?"

"All who lived."

The King paced back and forth mumbling. He wiped sweat from his forehead with his ornate jeweled sleeve, and drew blood. Cahena handed him a scarf as the droplets ran down his nose. He asked, "Is there much pain?"

"They relieve it with opium. He is required to remain in bed with his head held steady by sandbags for two weeks."

"How long before they know if he can see again?"

"A week."

"How long before he can travel?"

"Two weeks. But if the first one is successful I recommend you have the second one done soon after."

"This is mad! My little boy..." The king beat his fists on the sides of his head. "This is my only son. Leave! Leave now!" he ordered. "I must think this through."

Early that evening Cahena was summoned. The Numidian ambassador to Constantinople was in attendance. "The ambassador will accompany my son and my wife to Carthage," said Gershom.

"I will also send my last six pigeons to Carthage," Cahena offered. "It will take your son three or four months in caravan to reach the city. I cannot guarantee the pigeons will successfully make such a long flight. But I will ask the doctor to prepare and practice, on slaves if necessary. I am also asking the Jews on the island of Djerba to send a delegation of people trained in flying carrier pigeons to return with your son, and set up pigeon relay stations from Carthage to this Oasis. They will also train your people in the use of flying messengers."

"So you believe my son will survive the ordeal?"

"I pray to my God."

The king grunted and indicated the ambassador should speak.

'This oasis is the largest of seven that lead to your destination on the plateau for the Moussem festival. The king has provided guards to accompany you from oasis to oasis. You will be hosted on your journey and supplied with the necessities until you reach the last haven in the desert. From there you must travel alone. Your Roman Josephus is correct in training your men; there are still bands of Vandal marauders wandering about, and they are vicious people. Our agreement with the Romans precludes our fighting men moving into the desert beyond the last oasis. There is a Roman outpost at the Wadi Amra leading to the Imilchil Plain. I suggest you stop there; they will guarantee safe passage through the wadi."

"Who must the ambassador see in Carthage?" Gershom asked.

"His name is Linus, a medicus with the legion, trained in Greece and Rome." Cahena handed a scroll to the ambassador. "This contains instructions to my people. My home is yours. Whatever you require, my people will comply."

The ambassador was half listening and examining the scroll at the same time. He held it up to the light. "What is this written on?"

"Paper, made in China, from wood dust."

"Enough!" the king said. "Young lady, you have made a lifelong impression on my heart. Pray to your God Yahweh for my son. And take this as a token of the esteem in which I hold you and the father who created you, Moshe ben Shimi."

The Ambassador held out a ornate jewel box. Cahena took it and lifted the lid. Diamonds, rubies, pearls and green sapphires sparkled atop bright gold Roman coins.

Cahena was about to speak, but stopped when the king put his finger to his lips and shook his head. He held out both arms and embraced Cahena. "Now I know why the storyteller Abu Abak adopted you. I will always think of you as my daughter."

"I prefer to have the King's word that he will join the confederation of tribes my father is organizing."

"I know. But even if my son's life depended on it, I could not do so. The future of my people depends on me choosing the right side in the coming war. My heart is with your father. He must show me strength, numbers, and the benefits of joining him. Prove it, and a hundred thousand Numidian warriors will march under his banner."

CHAPTER 13

THE SAHARA

The cool evening wind swept the Touat Oasis, and camels grunted in anticipation. Ahmed blew his whistle. Cameleers shouted, armed guards moved into position, and scouts on swift camels set out into the sea of sand. They trod a path dictated by the stars, where there was no trail or sign of habitation, human or animal. Here and there under the heavenly lights of stars and moon the tracks of a snake could be seen in the smooth desert sand. The pace of the caravan was set by the scouts, who were military men and moved fast. The jostling of the camel was unfamiliar to Cahena and her group, but they endured.

There was no stopping. They ate in the saddle. Those who hadn't slept during the day, did so while riding. They had covered twenty-two miles when the sun topped the dunes. Ahead of them was a burst of green in the middle of a sea of white sand. On their arrival, food was waiting. The camels were unloaded and taken care of. Tents awaited, and they slept until late afternoon. Hot food was prepared. Their camels were replaced by fresh ones, all packed and ready to leave. Once again they followed the scouts into the trackless desert under a canopy of stars and a bright moon.

They made five more journeys and as many stops to reach the last oasis.

The senior officer of the military contingent accompanying them approached Cahena and said, "My king has instructed me to say you have his blessings and best wishes for you, your family and your people. You and your men know how to read the stars. The direction is straight forward. Orient yourself from the North Star and travel directly south. The entrance to the wadi you seek is a mile across. On the western slope is a small Roman fort. They will see you before you see them. Do not avoid them. Ask their assistance passing through the Wadi Amra onto Imilchil Plain. Keep strict water discipline. Two Bedouin scouts have reported a marauding group of Vandals chased into the desert ahead, so be on guard. These two Bedouin wish to speak with you. They said something about rocking a camel to make him drink more water?"

"They are friends," Cahena laughed. "Send them to me."

Ozeret and Ahmed's mother set out fruit, nuts, wine and meat left over from the evening meal. The two wiry little men entered, looking fresh, with clean clothes and a spring in their steps. They embraced Cahena and she them. "What news do you bring?" she asked.

"That is the sad part," one of the scouts said. "We have been waiting five days for your arrival."

"How could you know we would travel this way? We didn't make that decision until a week ago."

"We sought your original caravan."

"Where are they?"

"In the bellies of buzzards and jackals. A gang of Vandals wiped them out."

"All of them?"

"They tortured some. Others they played a game with. One man cut off the captive's head and the other dropped a small red-hot plate on his neck. They would bet how far the body could move before it collapsed."

"You witnessed this?"

Both men shook their heads.

"How did you know we would take the desert route?"

"You weren't among the dead, and you must reach Imilchil plateau by September. The desert route would be the only possible way. We will guide you to the Wadi Amra and would like to accompany you to the festival."

"I will feel more secure with you two leading us. What other news?"

"Berber tribes are speaking of Moshe ben Shimi and his daughter, the future queen of the Berbers."

"That is encouraging."

"Yes and no."

"Explain."

"On the one hand, your father is making allies. On the other hand, the Romans have taken note and have spies everywhere."

"Even among the Berbers?"

"You can't believe that every Berber is honest. There are those who would sell their souls for a couple of Roman coins. Your Roman traveling companion is the chief suspect."

"Josephus? I trust him with my life."

"My princess Cahena, you are wise beyond your years but untouched by the betrayal of those closest to you. Your personal group has access to you and must always be considered a source of danger. You are spoken of by the desert tribes as the High Priestess of the Berbers, able to cure by the laying on of hands, with the ability to travel in soul flight and observe your friends and enemies."

"Do you believe that?"

"It would be true if you allowed me to teach you," Ozeret said. "That Greek teacher of yours is too concerned about the stars. You have slaves who can do that."

"Be quiet, old woman. Take these two sons of the desert and see they are given fresh camels and any equipment they require."

Everyone on the oasis came to bid farewell to Cahena and her caravan. Led by the two scouts, they set out into the sea of sand.

It soon became evident why the scouts had twenty-foot bamboo poles with flags on them. Ten minutes into the journey and their camels were out of sight. The flags were visible above the dunes and they signaled one another and Ahmed which trail to take. Cahena's five guards served as outriders. Josephus commanded the remaining men. Most were busy with the animals. All carried weapons and shields.

Midday temperatures reached one hundred and twenty degrees. The air was so dry that if a cloth wasn't covering the mouth and nose, the nose dried out within minutes. The small hairs stiffened like needles inside the nostrils. Accustomed to sleeping in the shade of date palms for the last two weeks, all suffered a sleepless first and second daylight sleep. The water supply was sufficient. Ahmed seemed to be everywhere at once. He checked and double-checked the loading and unloading. If one of the animals became feisty he grunted to him in soft tones. If that didn't help, he hit him in the side of the head with a club.

The second night the wind picked up and the temperature dropped forty degrees. During the day the sun returned with its unbearable heat. Cahena had a dream of heavy rains and a wall of water sweeping down on them. It was so vivid that she told Ozeret. They continued south through the sand. Unpacking, setting up tents, eating in the morning, again in the late afternoon and repacking the animals became routine. They relished the cool evening breeze. Andronicus continued to teach astronomy and history of the Numidians. Cahena agreed with him that King Gershom could be the answer to her father's dream of uniting the Nomadic people of North Africa. The heat of the day wore down the travelers.

Josephus became more and more irritable keeping his people alert during the hottest temperatures of the day. Beyond two hundred yards, heat waves distorted ones vision. At night those who stood guard during the day slept in the saddle. Two people fell off their animals and remained asleep in the sand. The rear-guard saved them. Some had to be tied onto their camels. The scouts came in to report signs of a large band of unidentified horsemen. The daylight guard was doubled. Cahena's five guards spread further out from the main body at night. Word from the scouts they were approaching Wadi Amra.

"How can they tell?" Cahena asked.

"Haven't you noticed the stones here and there in the sand?" Josephus asked. "When it rains in the mountains, the water rushes through the wadis in a great wall. It can roll and throw boulders as large as a house into the air. Smaller stones are carried further. I can't wait to reach the safety of that Roman fort. Heat waves during the day make it impossible to see very far. Our guards fall asleep while standing up."

That morning, as the sun topped the Atlas Mountains and the veil of night withdrew, Ahmed froze in the saddle. He blew a high-pitched screeching sound on his whistle and pointed to the scout's flags revolving in a circle: it was the signal for danger, to form a defensive position.

The guards on the outskirts saw it, and raced back to the column beating their camels. Josephus slid off his camel, tumbled in the sand and came up shouting. He directed Ahmed where to hold the animals and put Cahena in the center of the formation. He ordered the long fourteen-foot spears to be distributed as he shoved, kicked and shouted people into position.

He formed his men in the diamond formation, and now had a small but solid unit facing all four directions. The flags of the scouts disappeared. The guards had not seen anyone or anything. The sun was rising and Josephus ordered a double ration of water for everyone. His men in ranks were fidgeting, and Josephus knew that even veterans got anxious before a fight. He shouted "You are about to have your first engagement. Luck is where preparation and opportunity meet. I have prepared you. The opportunity may come in the next few minutes. If anyone leaves the formation, these five archers will kill you. Don't try to be a hero. Stay behind your shields and make the enemy come to you."

Josephus knew waiting for the action was difficult, and barked further commands. "Long spears! Attention!" The iron-headed spear points gleamed in the morning sun. "Long spears! Long guard!" The spear points from all four side of the diamond lowered to a forty-five degree angle. "Short guard!" The spears lowered another 15 degrees. "Prepare to repel the enemy." The men obeyed. Josephus shouted,

"'You did well. Rest in place. Drink and we'll pass out some bread."

"The waiting is the most difficult," Josephus explained to Cahena.

Andronicus pointed. "You won't have to wait any longer."

Atop a sand dune in the west appeared a solitary horseman. He brandished a polished brass trumpet over his head then blew one blast. Fifty horsemen carrying lances and shields appeared on the skyline to his left. He blew the trumpet again and even more horsemen appeared silhouetted against the clear blue sky to his right.

"Men," Josephus bellowed, "take heart. They are trying to frighten you so they don't have to fight you. Obey my orders and I'll see you through this battle."

"Is that true?" Cahena asked quietly.

Josephus covered his lips and whispered, "No. These must be the band of Vandals that slaughtered our caravan. Their horses should be weakened by this desert, lack of food and water. But that means we are the only thing between them and death in the desert."

"You mean we have food, water and camels."

"I mean we are their food if they win. They are cannibals."

"Our men are getting nervous."

"So am I. These Vandals have been in a hundred fights like this. They will toy with us hoping the weakest will break and run."

"Why not entice them to attack?"

"Because I'm afraid they'll break through."

"According to you, they have no alternative—so let us make them attack us where and when we are strongest."

"What are you thinking?"

Josephus explained Cahena's plan to his men, and they broke formation. Some sat. Others lit cooking fires, most milled around looking aimless.

Josephus took Ahmed, the woman chieftain of the five guards, Andronicus and Cahena aside. "There is a possibility for our princess to escape. The enemy is certain to break through on the first or last attempt. They are seasoned warriors and outnumber us. Ahmed, you prepare nine of your swiftest camels. Each will carry water, the extra camel carries food for five days. If you can't find the Roman fort by then these Vandals will hunt you down."

"I am not leaving my people," Cahena said.

"Yes you are." The woman chieftain said. "I promised your father."

"But their horses are faster than our camels."

"Only when they are healthy," Josephus said. "They cannot be in such good shape running around this desert."

Josephus took Ahmed and Cahena aside. "Explain to Ahmed. I cannot include his mother in this escape."

Ahmed nodded his understanding and went off to organize his animals.

"They are getting ready to attack!" one of the guards shouted. The sun was burning bright in the sky. The enemy trumpet sounded. The line of cavalry started forward at a walk.

"If those horses were healthy," Josephus shouted, "The attack would have started at a trot. Everyone to his position! They have horses, but we have Cahena!"

The men took up the chant and rushed into formation. "Long spears! Attention!" Josephus ordered. "Long spears! Long guard!"

The enemy horse was at a full trot. Trumpets sounded, the charging horsemen shouted and beat their bows onto their shields.

"Long spears! Short Guard! Stand strong, you sons of dogs! Ground the butts of your spears, and hang one of these devils on the point!"

"Will they turn as you predicted?" Andronicus asked.

"If they're smart."

"Then we have a chance."

"Not much."

"Why?"

"If their horses give out as I expect, they will fight on foot with swords. Our men are not trained for that. They will be slaughtered."

Josephus and the five guards encouraged the men to hold their ground as the line of more than a hundred horsemen bore down on them at a full gallop.

"Hold! Hold! Hold!" Josephus chanted. The line of horsemen stretched way beyond either side of the diamond formation. At one hundred feet the lead horses veered to the right and left. A few animals and riders went down in collisions. But the double envelopment movement was carried off with practiced efficiency. They swept to the flanks and were met by the same phalanx of long spears. Seeing no opening and signaling on the trumpet, the horsemen unslung their bows and let their arrows fly into the caravaneers. Josephus shouted the command, "Turtle!"

Using their shields the men covered themselves and each other from the shower of arrows.

Cahena heard a gurgling sound behind her. Andronicus was attempting to remove an arrow from his Adam's apple. He was dead before he collapsed.

The five guards loosed their own arrows with deadly accuracy. Josephus ordered javelins thrown which caused more casualties among the horses than the enemy, but it drove the attackers off. They regrouped just outside the range of Cahena's bowmen.

"Their horses are in worse shape than I thought,' Josephus said. They've abandoned most of them."

"What are some of those men doing to their horses?" Cahena asked.

"Drinking their blood," Josephus said. "Their next attack will be on foot."

"We should leave now," the senior guard said.

"Too late." Josephus pointed. "They are marching toward us." He bellowed, "Long spears to the third rank! Pass all javelins to the first and second rank! When these bastards come within range, throw to kill! Keep your shields raised to protect against arrows."

The Vandals moved forward more like a mob rather than a military formation. They carried various kinds of swords, axes, spears and wooden clubs with spikes. Each had an ox-hide shield they used to deflect the javelins thrown at them. Their clothes were stained with horses' blood and the sun beat down on them as they charged.

Josephus turned to the woman chieftain and said, "If I fall, get the queen to safety." He rushed forward pushing through the ranks of the diamond formation to the point closest the enemy. He reached in a pouch on his belt and scattered all his caltrops on the ground before him. They were five-pointed sharp metal stars that, no matter which way they landed, one of the points would always be upward. He drew his sword and thrust his shield forward knocking a vandal backward. He stabbed another. The long spears from the third rank kept many at bay. The stars had effect on those attackers with thinned soled boots. The crash of shields was audible. Then the clanging of crossed swords and axes wielded on armor. Men shouted, cursed and died.

Josephus felt himself being pushed backward. His years of experience in the ranks served him well, but when he cut one man down two took his place. He initially gave heart to his men but he and they were being forced to retreat by the larger force. He was about to be pushed over backward when he was pushed upright from behind. The five guards entered the fray led by the woman chieftain. She wielded a Vandal ax and cracked skulls, chopped off arms and legs.

The defenders took heart again, and fought even more fiercely. Their response was so vicious it stopped the Vandal advance in the center. Slowly the enemy retreated. Finally they broke and ran. Josephus had all he could do to stop his men from chasing the more numerous Vandals. Who would have turned and slaughtered them. "Back! Back! Into formation!" he shouted.

The five guards helped him reform the men. Cahena and her chieftain met with Josephus and asked, "What now?"

"We run. Leave nothing for them to drink. Hopefully they will waste time plundering before they come after us." Josephus pointed at the stunned group and snapped, "Do it! Now!"

Cahena grabbed Josephus' arm. "I suggest you leave the wine behind. There isn't much. They will fight each other for it and give us a few more minutes."

"Done!" Josephus said.

The wounded were quickly tied onto camels and placed last in the line. While the Vandals milled around three hundred yards away, Ahmed led the first camel south. Josephus and the guards went around hamstringing the excess camels. The noon sun was boiling hot.

The noise of the wounded camels alerted

the Vandals. When enough of them gathered they broke into a run to intercept the caravan. Halfway to their target some warriors broke away from the group to plunder the caravan camp. Others followed. The leaders of the group stopped. They saw men drinking wine from goat skins. Then all of them rushed the abandoned camp.

Ahmed set a fast pace. From the summit of the first large sand dune he could see no one following them. He led on, gaining confidence upon finding more and more stones washed down from the mountains. It indicated the wadi was close.

Atop the next sand dune he turned to look back, and was shocked. Twenty Vandal horsemen were closer than he expected. On either side of each horse was a warrior holding the stirrup and a third holding the tail of the animal as they ran through the desert.

Josephus shouted, "At this rate they'll catch us. I'd hoped their horses were gone. Now I've got to delay them."

He turned his camel to the rear of the caravan. He selected the most severely wounded man, cut his throat, hamstrung his camel, and returned to the head of the column. The downed man and camel disappeared behind a sand dune as the caravan raced on.

"Was that necessary?" Cahena demanded.

"They will stop to drink the camel's blood, open up his stomach and take out what water remains. That should give us another mile. The longer we keep them in the sun, the better for us."

"We are boiling under the same sun."

"We have water. They need it."

"What if they catch us?"

"We die."

"Look!" Cahena pointed to the dune ahead.

Two men on foot were silhouetted by the setting sun.

"How could they have gotten in front of us?" Josephus said.

"It's not them! It's *them!*'

"What are you saying?"

"It's my Bedouin scouts!"

The two men trudged down and were helped the last part of the way. They were too parched to speak until their thirst was quenched. They'd had to kill their camels and drink the stored water in their stomachs. Cahena briefly explained the cat-and-mouse game taking place with the Vandals.

"You are close to the wadi on the eastern side," the scouts said. "The Roman fort is all the way over on the other side. We suggest you climb the canyon walls, as high and fast as you can. There was a great storm in the southern mountains two days ago, and we expect a lot of water in the wadi. The Vandals will have to attack uphill."

"Agreed," Josephus said. "Let's move."

'Give us two camels, and we will guide you.'

The only camels available were those carrying the wounded. Josephus selected the two men most severely injured, cut their throats, and presented their camels to the scouts. They went off into the night. Ahmed followed. The five guards moved back as rear guard of the column.

Cahena rode in the center next to Josephus. "You were praying when you killed those wounded men," she noted.

"Nothing of the kind. I said what I have said to legionnaires: 'Those who die may also serve their comrades'."

Cahena waved her hand in disgust.

"Possibly you think I did it to save them from torture, and that is true, but those bastards coming after us, who would drink the blood of camels and horses, will also drink the blood of men. They will eat the flesh of men—and take slices from their bodies while they are still alive. They will be delayed by ravaging the corpses."

"I didn't know that."

'You are wise beyond your years and you

have mystical talents, yet there is much for you to learn. The loss of your teacher Andronicus damages your future. He was very learned."

"Ozeret is waiting to teach me."

"I don't trust that humped-backed witch."

"She thinks you are a Roman spy."

He grunted and turned to check the rear guard.

The gait of the camels changed as they moved up the eastern side of Wadi Amra. They slowed as the slope steepened. The sun illuminated the desert and the following band of marauders. They were closer than expected. Several attempted to reach the rear guard with arrows but failed. Josephus warned the guards to keep their arrows for a last stand. They sent word to him, "The Vandals are getting ready to charge."

"This is a good place to defend," Josephus told the scouts. "We can leave the camels in that clearing behind those boulders."

"Leave the camels, yes," the older scout said, "But we climb higher."

"What do you see up there that makes it easier to defend?"

"It's dryer."

"What are you talking about?"

"This area will soon be flooded."

"Are you crazy?" Josephus pointed at the

Vandals struggling up the rocky slope under a barrage of stones thrown by those in the caravan. "They would sell their souls for a drink."

The scout pointed into the wadi. "See the wind rustling those bushes? We have no wind up here."

"So where does it come from?"

"A wall of water, made by the rainstorm two days ago. That wall of water is so high it's pushing the wind out of the wadi."

As the scout spoke, the wind whipped out of the deep narrow canyon and the sands of the Sahara began to sing. It sounded more like a moan. The scouts shouted, "Up! Up as high as you can go!"

The wind reached a screaming pitch. Vandals who were beginning to climb the slope dropped to their knees or were toppled over by the force of the wind. They scrambled and clawed their way over the rocks. Fear drove the attackers as well as those in the caravan. A distant rumble grew louder and louder until shouting wasn't enough to be heard. The earth trembled. The five guards formed a line up the slope and passed Cahena from one to the next until she was on the highest ledge they could reach.

What appeared was unbelievable. A wall of water one-hundred-and-twenty feet high burst out from the narrow canyon walls. Boulders thrown by the huge wall of water smashed to earth only to be raised again and catapulted forward. The height of the wave lowered by twenty feet as it spread out in the mouth of the wadi, but the volume and power of the water behind it forced it to rise again. It drove its way up the slopes at sixty miles an hour.

It engulfed the rear guard of Vandals trying to reach safety. The raging water raced up the slope picking off Vandals like fruit from a tree. Horses and men were swept away into the desert. Those Vandals higher up the slope dropped their weapons and scrambled upward—only to be met by javelins, swords and spears. They too were carried away by the flood. The caravan defenders climbed as high as possible, and watched their camels picked up and carried away.

There was a moment of eerie silence, then a great sigh as the water spread out into the desert. It receded from the slopes leaving a sea of featureless mud below. The five guards turned to Cahena and began chanting: 'We have Cahena! We have Cahena!" The survivors took up the chant. The guards threw themselves face down on the ground. Everyone prostrated themselves before the ten year old girl. She looked to Josephus for help, but he was on his knees, making the sign of the cross.

The two Bedouin scouts approached Cahena and bowed. "Cahena, daughter of Moshe ben Shimi, you have defeated the enemy, but danger is all around. We have no camels. Our water is limited and food none."

Cahena was stunned by the obeisance of the survivors. She indicated with her hand that the scout should continue.

"We must reach the Roman fort. It is a mile away, on the other side of the wadi, and between us and it is a sea of mud. It will be difficult to get through. Most dangerous are patches of quicksand; they can swallow a man in minutes and leave no trace."

"What do you suggest?"

"Allow us to scout a path to the other side of the wadi, then follow us across."

"Help me get these people up on their feet, then do as you've said."

Descending the slope was more difficult. Boulders, rocks, and stones, large and small had been loosened or washed up by the flood. It was more a process of slipping and sliding down the hill. Minor avalanches and rock slides were the greatest hazards. On reaching the muddy plain the first thing Josephus ordered was for all the good water to be combined in the goatskins and the empty goat skins be filled from muddy pools of standing water before they disappeared under the desert sun.

The scouts hadn't gone one hundred yards before one of them became trapped in quicksand. He was sucked down to his knees and was waist deep by the time his companion and the guards reached him. They made a rope of their waist-bands, and with great difficulty pulled him out. He had to remove his clothing, for the mud was already drying and would irritate his skin. He washed his clothes in a pool of water, and the two continued across the flatland. After two hours under the blazing sun, all signs of standing water disappeared and the mud hardened, slowly reverting to sandy clay. Quicksand remained a problem, for only a crust formed on its surface. The scouts used javelins to test the ground.

Halfway across, Josephus saw a flashing signal from the slopes of the western side of the wadi, and recognized the legion's heliograph signal. "They see us," he shouted. He undid the chain holding the sickle-moon medallion awarded him as bearer of the Legion's Eagle. He spat on it, rubbed it clean with his sleeve, then pointed it toward the sun. He held it at arm's length and positioned himself so that the sun threw his shadow directly on it. He looked behind him to see if he was in line with the flashing light, then moved so his shadow no longer covered the medallion, and flashed the sun's reflection back. There was then a long series of flashes from the Roman fort.

"Can you read what they say?" Cahena asked.

"Yes, but I can't send. They can't come out to us because of the mud. We must go to them."

CHAPTER 14

RENDEVOUS

The sun was resting on the western horizon when the survivors entered the Roman fort. Josephus was greeted by several men who knew him from the ranks. The survivors were fed, washed and clothed. Space was found for sleeping quarters. Extra rations of wine were served to all in celebration of the defeat of the Vandals. This Roman unit had chased those very Vandals into the desert, and was delighted to hear of their ultimate defeat.

The survivors slept through the night and into the afternoon.

"I reported to the fort commander," Josephus told Cahena. "He wishes to meet you."

The base commander was a young centurion.

"We were informed that you were killed in the massacre of a caravan," he said. "Then two Bedouin told my interpreter you were not among the dead, and were probably taking the desert way to the annual Berber gathering on the Imilchil plateau. Our accommodations in this outpost are meager. You have twenty-six people. We cannot feed them. You must move on."

Cahena indicated that Josephus should speak. "We have no camels," he said, "Nothing but water-skins and weapons. How shall we travel?"

"We captured a small herd of horses from the Vandals when we chased them into the desert. If my men could earn something from their loot..." The officer spread his hands and said, "Everyone would be satisfied."

"My people can't ride bareback."

"They left saddles and harnesses, everything you need, including horse blankets. If it's profitable enough for my men, we may be able to part with some food for your journey."

Cahena nodded. "We accept."

Josephus said. "I know your wrangler, and will introduce him to Ahmed. They can sort out the horses."

Cahena produced gold coins from King Gershom's jewelry box. She also visited the fort's infirmary, where she and Ozeret tended to the ill. Most suffered from malaria and diarrhea. One trooper, kicked in the head by a horse, was made more comfortable by Cahena's touch. He died later that day.

The twenty-six survivors on horseback entered Wadi Amra at first light. The high walls protected them from all but the noonday sun, and the earth remained damp from the flood. There were standing pools of water, and green shoots of grass and brush for horses to nibble.

At noon they came across two separate set of tracks entering the wadi from the south, and another sign of camels joining from the north. The scouts proclaimed them peaceful caravans on the way to the ingathering of the Berber tribes. They caught up to the three caravans in the evening.

It became dark early in the wadi. Firewood was plentiful, as the flood had brought down full grown trees from the mountains in addition to everything else in its path. Far above an entire thatched hut, teetered on a rock ledge.

Two of the guards purchased provisions from the other caravans. When the people heard Cahena was with them, they gathered their sick and lined up outside her tent bearing food. Josephus, the guards and Ozeret brought some order to the excited group, and the guards decided who would be seen first. Ozeret helped Cahena with diagnosing and preparing medications.

To Josephus fell the task of dentist. Ozeret taught him to pull a tooth by wrapping string around it and every hour push the string further down into the gum. With his calloused thumb and forefinger Josephus then rocked the tooth sideways and back to front until it was loose enough to pull out. He was bitten several times. She showed him how to make a poultice for drawing pus from the gums. He used bread and milk wrapped in light gauze and applied it to other infected areas if the body. People came to him with boils on their neck and legs. He used the same poultice with some success. He achieved better results when Ozeret had him incorporate clay from the Chinese medicines in the poultice.

Cahena became so adept at reliving pain and symptoms, and here and there an instant cure that she no longer questioned the source of her gift. She sensed herself as a tool being utilized by a higher power. Ozeret observed her young charge with admiration. She made plans for teaching her the charms, spells and curses of a sorceress and magician.

In the next three days they overtook a fourth caravan with the same experience of healing. With one exception. Josephus fingers were seriously bitten. Ozeret helped train another to replace him. After a week of trekking up the Wadi Amra a messenger from Cahena's father arrived to guide her caravan to an especially appointed place for the Jewish tribes. They exited the wadi ahead of the plateau into a green, lush valley with a wide shallow stream. As far as the eye could see tents were pitched on both sides of the valley and up the slopes. The tents glowed in the darkness like large lanterns. Food and tents were waiting. The survivors were shown to an area in the center of the valley close to the river. Moshe ben Shimi was waiting there, arms spread wide to receive his daughter. Women greeted them with the high pitched undulating sound. The men chanted, "We have Cahena. We have Cahena." Father and daughter embraced. "'My God," Moshe said. "You are going to be taller than I. Whatever they fed you, it made you grow."

"Father, why are we separated from the main body of Berbers? Is something wrong?"

"Don't you know the date?"

"Late August."

"Very late. September fifth to be exact. Tomorrow evening begins Yom Kippur."

"We forgot to celebrate Rosh Hoshanna!"

"Tonight you will. Food is on the way. Let us go into your tent; I wish to hear everything that happened from the day you left."

Voices came toward them out of the dark. Cahena felt her father stiffen. He called, "Greetings to Selim, chieftain of the mighty Helawi tribe. Have you come to welcome my daughter, future bride of your son Ali?"

"My son and chieftains come with me to welcome the Cahena, princess of the Berbers," said Selim. "We wish to bless the prophetess who has raised the interests of the western and southern tribes of our peoples."

"Father," Cahena asked, "How can you know so much about our caravan?"

"Pigeons. Your pigeons brought word. We haven't had any for some time, and became worried."

"But not to worry," Selim chortled. "Your daughter is now with us. I would like to hear of her adventures."

"As would I, but she hasn't yet celebrated our Jewish New Year. You will pardon us if we keep this tradition in the family."

"How could I be so intrusive? Daughter-in-law to be, may the gods bless your coming in and going out, and may Yahweh bless your family past, present and future. I anticipate hearing of your adventures."

Selim and his men left.

"Father, you seemed upset when Chieftain Selim appeared." Cahena noted.

"I try to hide it. He's organizing a faction of Tuaregs, Berbers, and Bedouin to oppose my becoming leader of the nomadic peoples."

"Hmmm. I have positive news about the Numidians."

"Come! Let us celebrate the Rosh Hashanah feast and your safe return. Tomorrow at sundown we begin the twenty-four hour Yom Kippur fast."

A brief prayer service was conducted by the rabbis under the stars. The ram's horn was blown, the Kaddish for the departed chanted, and seven-hundred people entered the line of tents erected for the occasion.

The tents were redolent with the smell of roast squash, stewed lamb heads, roasted mutton and beef, long strings of sausages, baked chickens and grilled ducks, carrots, spinach, peppers sweet and hot, trays of mounded couscous sprinkled with pecans and cashew nuts, pickled vegetables, olives, dates and honey. Aromatic spices of cinnamon, coriander, ginger, saffron, turmeric, and paprika scented the air. Dried figs, apricots, prunes, raisins, sweet and tart pomegranates were plentiful, as were salads fresh and cooked.

But the most welcome of all was the presence of Abu Abak, Cahena's godfather. He sat next to her in the head tent. The Rabbis blessed the congregation, the food and wine. There was much talk, laughter and good-hearted singing. Between courses, rabbis took turns espousing teachings from the Torah, but the last speaker of the evening was Abu Abak, Pagan storyteller and historian of the Maghreb. Everyone quieted as he stood up and began to speak.

"This is the time of year when Jews prepare to atone for both their individual and communal sins committed over the course of the previous year. I respect the Jewish attitude toward sin. They cannot ask forgiveness or expect forgiveness for sins committed against a fellow human being or any creation of God.; that means an offense against your fellow must be settled between you and the injured party. Tomorrow at sundown Jews will beg forgiveness from the Almighty for sins they have committed by not carrying out the dictates of their Holy Torah. Not only are you responsible and pleading with God to absolve you of your individual sins, but you beg him to forgive the sins committed by your community. You may be innocent, but you are accountable to your God for the actions of your leaders and your people. As with individual sin, forgiveness is not given by God for communal sins committed against an individual or another community. These offenses must be worked out between the parties involved.

"You Jews have a legend of God keeping accounts in what is called 'The Book of Life', where he inscribes your fate for the coming year. The evil decree can be changed by an individual or community by doing good deeds and acts of kindness. So, although your fates are written they can be rewritten and avoid the evil decree. The Jews traded their slave status to Pharaoh and became servants of the one God. The need to serve God is stressed time and again, over and over in your Holy Book. The non-Jew asks, 'For what purpose?' The answer is, to perfect creation. God who created the heavens above and the earth below and formed us in the image of himself could certainly have created a perfect human being in a perfect environment. Instead, he gives us trees and we build houses. He gives us animals, which we teach to serve, clothe and feed us. It is told that during the exodus from Egypt, God fed you Jews for forty years with Manna. So why didn't this almighty creator make a bread tree? Instead he gives us wheat and we make the bread. The question is, why? What does God really want from the Jews?" Abu Abak challenged the audience with his eyes. 'I believe God wants a friend. Jews believe God is one—the only one. I believe he created man in his image to eventually become an equal—a child, a friend—and he specifically chose the Jews to fulfill this task first by becoming a light unto the nations."

The Rabbis and many Jews promptly began discussing, then arguing, until no one could be heard. Moshe ben Shimi signaled his musicians, who rapped the drums and clanged brass cymbals until quiet was restored.

"Wise man of the Maghreb," ben Shimi said to the storyteller. "You have spoken so intelligently. Then you concluded by putting man on an equal basis with God. You must know we Jews would be offended."

"I did, but felt I must say what is true. Tomorrow I will fast with the people of Israel and plead with your God that he writes me well in 'The Book of Life'."

Cahena asked, "If you respect our religion that much, why not become a Jew?"

"Your rabbis discouraged me. They told me that, as a Pagan, I was only responsible for the seven laws of Noah—which are similar to your Ten Commandments: I must not commit idolatry, blasphemy, sexual perversion, murder, theft or animal cruelty, and must establish courts to enforce these laws. The rabbis explained, if I converted to Judaism I'd be responsible for all six hundred and thirteen commandments in your holy book. I could work only six days a week and no longer eat horse, camel, pig, or mix meat and milk. Those I might have endured, but the commandment of circumcision? Oh no! No! No! I am not prepared to shorten my manhood when I can more easily qualify for heaven by remaining a Pagan."

Moshe and Cahena laughed merrily and refilled his cup.

Then Moshe ben Shimi and Abu Abak questioned Cahena about her journey. The tale lasted well into the night, and resumed again after breakfast. They told her stories they heard from travelers about the Cahena. She could cure the sick and wounded, tell the future and even levitate. She was the Jewish sorceress who influenced the weather to destroy an army of Vandals. The requests for conversion by the nomadic tribes increased. It was to be a topic of discussion before the Jewish tribes prior to the Yom Kippur fast. Cahena and all women were invited to take part in the discussion.

The dale formed a natural amphitheater where the discussion took place. Those who traced their lineage to the ten tribes of Israel were in the majority, and sat in the center facing seven rabbis. To the right of the makeshift stage were the Levites. On the left were the Cohanim, direct descendants of the high priest, led by

Moshe ben Shimi.

There was visible unrest in the audience. The Rabbis looked to Moshe ben Shimi for permission to begin. He nodded. The senior rabbi spoke. His words were repeated by people throughout the audience so even those seated furthest up the slope could hear.

"Brother Hebrews. I should include our sisters also, for that is what is causing dissonance among our congregants. We are gathered here, hours before the holiest day of the year. Soon we shall stand in judgment before Almighty God. We each pray to be written well in the Book of Life for the coming year. We will fast from sundown to sundown. No food nor drink of any kind must pass our lips. As a direct descendant of the High priest Aaron I will plead with God on our behalf.

"We have gathered here to discuss a problem that has developed because of Cahena. She is known throughout the Maghreb and beyond as The Cahena. She and many other women are present today. It is their presence that is creating the discord.

"It is thought by many that women cannot be any kind of teacher, let alone rabbi. However, the Babylonian Talmud and the Spanish Jews of Toledo have both ruled that rabbinical ordination for women is permitted. Women should be educated equal to men, and therefore women can teach."

There was a negative response from a portion of the audience.

The senior rabbi continued: "This ruling is based on our Holy Writings. A teacher, male or female, who misinterprets a Biblical Law while teaching is required to bring a sin offering to the Temple. If a woman is obliged to bring a sin offering for having taught something incorrectly, it means she is allowed to be a teacher and assume most rabbinical duties. Therefore women may participate and vote in this forum."

The conservative members of the audience were bewildered, then angered. The majority of those present considered themselves Jews but did not observe all the commandments. Most, like Cahena, kept pagan idols. It was they who raised the cry, "We need more Rabbis!"

Everyone knew that there were only seven ordained rabbis in attendance and another five throughout the tribes.

When order was restored the Chief Rabbi addressed the people. "You are right, and the Babylonian and Spanish religious courts are also correct in their ruling. We require more rabbis to teach."

Someone in the crowd shouted. "Will that include women rabbis?"

"It may."

"And if it does, don't send a she-rabbi to my tribe."

"There is little danger of that. We have problems of sending our best students to Spain and Babylon. They usually do not return from those two centers of Jewish learning. Life and living in those modern cities is far more rewarding intellectually, socially and economically. Throughout all of Africa there are only twelve qualified rabbis."

"Then how are you going to convert all those Pagans crazy enough to want to become Jews?"

"Moshe ben Shimi will explain."

"Not to me he won't!" The chieftain signaled his people to stand. "Either the women leave or we do!"

Moshe ben Shimi stood at the Rabbi's side and said. "It is a Halachic ruling, and now part of our oral law. Women may be ordained as rabbis and qualified to teach."

Other tribes in the audience joined the dissenters and left. They represented twenty percent of the congregation.

"Brethren," Moshe ben Shimi said. "We have queried the academies in Babylon and Spain about the ritual of conversion. Both synods responded. The prospective convert must accept Jewish beliefs and laws, and after being taught the key elements of Judaism and passing a test on this knowledge. A convert to Judaism must undergo immersion in a mikvah and circumcision for men, as conditions for the conversion. This is the Spanish view. The Babylonian approach is less stringent. It agrees with the teaching and testing but says circumcision can be no more than 'making a mark', which may be no more than a single cut, upon the foreskin. "

Cahena was thinking about her godfather. Would Abu Abak convert if he didn't have to undergo circumcision?

She heard her father say, "We are here to make a decision. Do we require only immersion in the ritual bath or do we also require those who wish to become part of the Israelite people to have a token circumcision, or a full circumcision and removal of the foreskin?"

The crowd erupted in arguments. It was difficult to speak to one's neighbor over the noise. Cahena tugged her father's sleeve. "Your option is predetermined," she said.

"What do you mean?"

"If those wishing conversion learn it is possible to become an Israelite without removal of the foreskin, just a drop of blood, they will naturally elect ritual immersion."

Ben Shimi raised his finger and was about to argue with her when he realized she was right. Most important would be the teaching and the testing. The people separated into several groups. The most animated and loudest claimed there was no true method of converting anyone into the Jewish religion.

The chief rabbi and Moshe ben Shimi finally brought about order. The Rabbi addressed the people. "It is good that we argue. Only through debate will the Lord's truth be known to man. Argument for its own sake is of no value; argument for the sake of heaven is the objective. The question in dispute is, do we have the right to convert heathens, Christians or Muslims? The answer is yes."

One of the Rabbis seated behind the speaker demanded, "Where is such a right conferred?"

"The Book of Ruth," the Chief Rabbi answered. "It is written in a style similar to a Greek morality-play. It is meant to prove that conversion is a legitimate function of our religion."

"What is a morality-play?"

"An acting-out, where characters are given names of social attributes. For instance, two men named Good and Evil walk down the path of life. They come across greed, avarice, morality and virtue. Each selects what is most important, and the story goes on."

"I thought we were forbidden to convert. How can you claim the Book of Ruth promotes conversion?"

"Two reasons: one historical the other literary. Historically we did convert non-Jews. That is why there is a Roman law prohibiting conversion; we were too successful. The old Roman Pagan gods, as in a morality-play, personified civic virtues and demanded civic duties. The Romans feared that converts would abandon those duties, so they forbade conversion. The penalty for converting a Roman is death, so our leaders forbade it. Bur western Rome has been destroyed by the Vandals, Huns and Visigoths. The Eastern Roman Empire is now Christian. We should once again promote conversion."

A chieftain from the mountains challenged, "You may be historically correct, but that does not give you the authority of changing a rabbinical ruling centuries old."

"The antiquity of a ruling does not enhance or detract from its legitimacy. At Sinai God gave us the written Law. He also taught Moses the oral Law. Moses taught the Elders, and we continue to teach the interpretation of the oral Law. God did this so we could adapt to everyday conditions and live by these laws."

"And how do you find the Book of Ruth proves this?"

The Chief Rabbi motioned the people to be seated. "This holy book presents characters in action. The author not only portrays experience but gives his or her moral viewpoint on these experiences. The book becomes a demonstration of human practice."

"But wasn't the book written by God?"

"No. A human being wrote the book of Ruth. The author never signed it. Those of you who can read, do so in Greek, Latin or Berber. This book was originally written in Hebrew. I will do a brief translation of the names and function of the characters. You decide the purpose of the author.

"The Book of Ruth begins with Elimelech—which means Father King—married to Naomi—Pleasantness. They live in Israel, the land of milk and honey, but there is little milk, no honey, and wheat is scarce. Elimelech dies. Naomi takes her two sons—Mahlon, sickness, and Chilion, death—to live in Moab. Of all the enemies of Israel, Moab is the most detested. Prophet after prophet predicts their doom and destruction. Jews are forbidden to mingle, no less marry into that hated tribe. The offspring of a Jew and a Moabite is forbidden to enter the congregation of Israel for ten generations. Yet the two sons of Naomi marry Moabite women: Orpah—to turn one's back on you—and Ruth—companion, friend. Shortly after, the two sons die. Naomi decides to return to Bethlehem from whence she came. Orpah turns her back and remains in Moab. Ruth says, 'Whither thou goe'st I will go. Thy God shall be my God and your people my people.' This has become the accepted statement required by a proselyte to vow before acceptance into Judaism. Ruth marries Boaz and they become the great grandparents of Israel's greatest King, David—predicted by the first name in the Book, Avimelech, father-king. He is the forefather of David."

"How do you know this wasn't written by God?"

"Because the Almighty didn't say so. Because the elders at the time it was written examined and debated as we doing are now, and because the author was known to them."

"Then why didn't they name the author?"

"The author wished to remain anonymous. Secondly he wanted to indicate to future generations that this book was written in antiquity. Ancient writings carry with them the authority of time."

"How can you know that the writing is more modern?"

"The author revealed it when he explained that Ruth and Boaz were the great-grandparents of David. It meant that the author was born after David was King in Israel, though the Book of Ruth supposedly predates this."

"Then the book is false."

"On the contrary, it is true and most relevant to our discussion. Do we convert or not? The Book of Ruth promotes conversion into Judaism by making the Moabite Ruth the great-grandmother of Israel's greatest king."

Another Rabbi addressed the people. "What was just said is generally accepted in rabbinical circles. The question debated between the academies of Shammai and Hillel was, which form conversion should take. The more restrictive requires teaching, declaration of intent, immersion and removal of the foreskin. This is mandated by Shammai. Hillel required teaching, declaration intent and immersion?"

"You are saying a male can become a Jew without a circumcision?"

"We do not circumcise female converts, therefore as the Law applies to one gender so it should to the other, the same as the ruling on ordaining female teachers and Rabbis. Qualification should be judged by intent and knowledge."

Moshe ben Shimi stepped forward, ""People

of Israel. The sun is receding. We must bathe and eat before the fast, so discuss this amongst yourselves. When the ram's horn blows, those who agree with the more liberal interpretation of Hillel's acceptance into Judaism, move to my right. Those who believe in Shammai's version requiring circumcision of the entire foreskin move to my left. Those who are against conversion remain in the center. You have fifteen minutes."

The discussions were heated. People shouted, cajoled and pleaded their case. The Ram's horn sounded, and the people separated. The center group of conservatives against conversion was the smallest, as a large group had walked away from the meeting earlier. The difference in numbers of the two groups remaining could not be determined by sight.

Moshe ben Shimi was about to start counting when the Chief Rabbi stopped him. "Counting was forbidden to Moses in the desert, Saul in Canaan and David in Israel, lest a plague ravage the people. Hosea 2:1: 'And the number of children of Israel shall be as the sand of the sea, which shall neither be measured nor counted.' Have each person place a stone in one of two baskets. We then count the stones."

"'Father," Cahena grumbled, "If I weren't already a Jew I would not become one with all these superstitious rules."

Her father indicated she be quiet.

Baskets were passed around then brought to the Rabbis. The Chief Rabbi called for order and announced, "The Hillel conversion ritual is accepted. There need not be any form of circumcision, only teaching and immersion." The chief Rabbi nodded to Moshe ben Shimi. He raised his hands, the crowd became silent as he blessed the congregation then said, "Go now to bathe. Cleanse your body. Eat and prepare to stand before God and cleanse your soul. God will then pass judgment on us. May the Almighty's ruling be merciful."

"Amen," muttered Cahena.

At sundown the Israelites in the valley gathered for prayer. Moshe ben Shimi led them in appeal to the Almighty. Not all the Jews attended; a significant number slipped away to join the festivities on the Imilchil Plateau. Word spread among the Berbers on the plateau that one could incorporate the Hebrew God of the Cahena into their lexicon of gods by immersion in water. No circumcision was necessary. Upon hearing this Selim, Chieftain of the Helawi, summoned Shamans from the three tribes he governed. He asked, "What does this immersion consist of?"

The Shamans whispered among themselves and finally said, "It is the same as the Christians baptism. A holy man places them in moving water..."

"You mean a river?"

"Yes. And he asks them if they accept Christ? When they say, 'Yes.' He pronounces them Christian. And so it must be with the Jews."

"Are you and your colleagues holy men?"

"Of course. We are shamans who have served the nomadic tribes since the beginning of time."

"Then go out and convert as many as you can to Judaism. For each one you make a Jew I will give you a copper coin."

"And if we were to convert a thousand?"

"Plus one gold Roman coin. On two conditions: convert me first, then tell those you convert that I, Selim, Chieftain of the Helawi, is the high priest of their new God."

Fifty thousand nomads occupied the Imilchil Plateau, and word spread like a wildfire. Shamans from other tribes began converting. Christian priests joined in by immersion and swearing fealty to the Father, Son and Holy Spirit. The rivers were full of people. Those wet by the waters from the Atlas Mountains believed themselves to have a new god to be worshipped with the others. People gathered in and around the Helawi encampment.

They were prevented by Helawi guards to approach Selim who was busy paying the Shamans. He ran out of money, and asked the Shamans to be patient while he sent out a box of jewels to be traded for coins. In the meantime he approached the senior Shaman, Lila. She was officially the head of this secret occult society, and he asked how to worship this new god.

"Leave it to us." Lila said. "Each shaman of each tribe will control his people in the best way to maintain our power and yours."

"I pray that it is so," Selim answered. "Your life and those of your fellow Shamans depend on it."

For Jews in the valley the day passed quietly in fasting and prayer. It was only after the ram's horn was blown, closing the Book of Life in which God wrote the future of the world, that word spread through the encampment as to what had taken place on the Plateau. Moshe ben Shimi and the three rabbis dressed in the garb of Berber tribesmen went up to the Imilchil Plateau.

The sun had gone down and the fast was

over when Cahena learned of her father's departure. She called in Josephus, Ahmed and Ozeret to accompany her onto the Plateau. They too dressed inconspicuously.

The full moon and bright stars revealed the well-traveled road up the slope. Ahead the night sky glowed from thousands of campfires of the nomadic tribes of North Africa. Each tribe had its own encampment circling the stalls, booths, entertainment tents, camel market and storage shelters on the plateau. Passing through the tribal areas children played tiddas (jacks), melghas (hide and seek), albanaban—blind man's bluff, almoma and solag (wrestling for boys and girls), and sellendoug (tag). They came to the adult area where men gambled, throwing stones for wagers. They wrestled and bet on camel and horse races. The shamans set up wagers for the game of takadant, which consisted of telling a person what they were thinking. Ozeret said, "Most of them are frauds. They have people in the audience who are their agents. Others make bets for the shaman and the audience is fleeced when the collaborator admits his mind was read."

"I'd like to have some fun with them," Cahena said.

"No!" Ozeret snapped. "For them this is not a joke. You ridicule them and we might have to leave quickly."

"I agree," Josephus said. "Don't spit into the plate they eat from."

"But it's what I want to do."

"Not if you want to see the rest of the festival," Josephus said. "We can stop on the way back."

They entered the souk market area, where oxen, horses, camels and donkeys were corralled on the outskirts, followed by two other corrals of sheep and goats for sale. These were often sold at impromptu auctions.

Then there was the salt market, which was a combination of buying and trading. Then the food markets with sought-after Tuareg cheese, butter, dried meat, millet and other foodstuffs. Behind these stalls butchers slaughtered fresh meat to order. The Street of Garments carried everything worn by man, woman or child: leather products including sandals and boots, silk turbans of all colors, and the favored ostrich feathers to keep away the flies on the caravan trail. There was a long row of entertainment tents that had waiting lines in front and in back; the lines in the front were people waiting for seats, and those in the back were for men seeking male and female prostitutes.

Somewhere between the camel market and the entertainment center Josephus disappeared. He rejoined the group listening to music outside one of the tents.

"You're drunk!" Ozeret accused.

"You're right. I have every right to be snoggered." He held up a bottle and said, "I found two of these filled with grappa from Salerno. In the legion I could get a lot of money for these. Want a taste?"

"What's it like?" Ozeret reached for the bottle.

"Taste don't matter. It's like drinking bottled bear. When it hits your throat it's like drinking hot lava; then it explodes in the stomach and you get all warm and fuzzy."

"I've drunk some of the worse concoctions in the world." Ozeret said. She used both hands to tip the large bottle up to her lips. She tried to throw the bottle from her but Josephus dove and caught it while rolling on the ground. He never spilled a drop.

"Holy shit!" Ozeret gasped. She tried to say something but her vocal chords wouldn't function. She began pointing to her stomach and her eyes began to bulge. Children pointed at the funny little hunch-back lady hopping around the street fanning her mouth and trying to cleanse her tongue on the two upper teeth. Ahmed returned and handed Ozeret a cup of goat's milk. She guzzled every last drop, fell to her knees, looked up at Josephus with her bulging eyes and cursed him. "May a thousand fleas infest your cruddy crotch and your arms be too short for your hands to scratch."

Josephus raised the bottle to Ozeret. "I'll drink to that!" He emptied it and passed out.

"I won't carry that drunken slob." Ozeret said. "He must weigh a ton."

Ahmed soon returned with a horse blanket. He rolled Josephus onto it and signed to Cahena and Ozeret help him drag Josephus. It worked. They reached the tribal tents and the shamans were still entertaining the crowd with their mind reading act. Ozeret and Ahmed attempted to dissuade Cahena but she resolved to have her own fun. She stood at the edge of the crowd watching and waiting. After the female shaman had correctly read the minds of two of her stooges from the audience Cahena volunteered to have her mind read knowing the shaman would fail to do so and her coworkers in the crowd were betting against the Shaman.

"What is your name?" The Shaman asked.

"Miriam," Cahena answered

"And from what tribe are you?"

"Amazigh.'

"From the northern mountains. Do you believe I can read your mind?"

"I would like to find out."

"Are you prepared to wager money?"

"I have two coppers."

"Put them on the ground in front of you and I will match them with these two coppers." She produced two coins as if plucking them out of the air. Cahena had been taught this sleight-of-hand by Ozeret, and was not impressed. The crowd muttered in awe.

The shaman said, "Concentrate on something you did this past week that made you happy. Close your eyes and concentrate. ...You are making it difficult for me..."

The shaman's colleagues working the betting in the audience found it difficult to get bets until the shaman brightened and said. "Now that's better. I can see you in the Street of Garments." The crowd's money was being bet on the Shaman accurately predicting the girl's thoughts. But when asked if that was correct, Cahena refused to answer and the betting subsided until Cahena brightened when the shaman mentioned the Street of the Jewelers. More bets were made in favor of the shaman, until she shouted, "You have switched your thoughts, but cannot fool me. The thoughts in your mind are of the very dress you are wearing and bought two days ago in the Street of Garments!" The Shaman wagged a finger at Cahena and said, "Naughty, naughty girl."

"But I thought the truth. And you read my mind correctly the first time. This is the dress!"

The shaman's mouth opened and closed several times before a word came out. It was low moan lost in the clamor of the joyous crowd who bet on the shaman reading correctly. They roared their delight and lined up to be paid. "How can it be?" the shaman blurted out.

"Because you are so wise and learned in the occult," Cahena said. She pointed down, "Take your four coppers. Unless of course you would like to wager them, that I can read your mind?"

"Why you young twerp! You make fun of me and disrupt my presentation of mental and spiritual conception."

"I will tell you for nothing what you are thinking." Cahena threw back the shawl covering her head and her long black hair flowed down her back to her waist. It reflected the torch lights.

She stepped closer to the shaman. "I will tell you for nothing what you are thinking, because your thoughts are worth just that. Nothing! You are wondering; 'Who is this girl from the mountains that disrupts my attempt to steal money from these poor gullible tribesmen. Now you are thinking why is she doing this? Does she want money?'"

The shaman was stunned into silence. Cahena had spoken the thoughts of the woman.

The bets were still unpaid to the crowd and fighting erupted. Knives were drawn.

A woman as tall as Cahena entered the torch light. She wore the tribal colors of Moroccan Berbers but in the Spanish style. Her glistening black hair fell straight down her back to her heels. There were touches of gray at the temples but not a line on her smooth bronze face. She was thin and straight as a warrior's lance.

The people recognized the senior sorceress. The shamans, including Ozeret, bowed. It was Lila, the same woman who represented the shamans in the meeting with Selim, Chieftain of the Helawi. She motioned the shaman to pick up her four coppers and said to those in the crowd, "Pay the wagers."

She approached Cahena and walked around her until she stood in facing her. They locked eyes and a test of wills took place. Each pressing to enter the others thoughts while fending off the attempt to read theirs. For the first time Cahena experienced a power stronger than her own. She tried to avoid it. Failing that she resisted. Her confidence waned to the power challenging her. She looked away and broke the spell.

"Your name is not Miriam," the elder Shaman whispered. "It is Dihya."

On mention of the secret name Ozeret leapt forward and cautioned, "Not outloud!" The shaman dismissed Ozeret with a flick of her hand and she was pulled back by other shamans. The chief shaman said, "My name is Lila. You are known as The Cahena, the priestess or queen of the Berbers. We've been waiting for you."

"How could you know all this?"

Lila disregarded the question. "You will remain with me. I've glimpsed into your mind. It indicates vast potential."

"I must return to my father."

"Your father and the rabbis are quite busy. He is here in the encampment. I will send word."

Ozeret sidled up to Cahena, "It is best you heed this advice. No harm will come to you."

"The mute will remain with the drunken Roman," Lila said. "Your foster mother will accompany us. But first I wish to see the healing powers people speak of. Come."

They walked between the dwellings of different tribes until they reached a compound surrounded by live cactus so thick a snake would have trouble getting through. The entrance to the shaman's compound was guarded by two old men without weapons. There were a combination of straw huts and tents large and small inside the ring of cacti.

Lila led the way to a small hut in which two women lay, both obviously ill. Lila pointed to one who had a severe case of malaria. Cahena gently dried the woman's face with a towel. Put her hand on the fevered brow. In seconds the woman stopped shaking. Color returned to her pallid face and she asked for water. Cahena motioned Ozeret forward and said, "Mugwort."

Ozeret pulled some of the dried plant from her pouch and explained to Lila. "This young one has learned to use some Chinese medicines." Lila questioned Ozeret about the Chinese remedies, then immediately sent someone on an errand, and directed Cahena to the second woman.

This one was in her thirties and had no visible signs of injuries or illness. She didn't respond to Cahena's questions; she lay unmoving with eyes open. Cahena passed a candle in front of the woman's eyes. She neither blinked nor did her irises respond. The woman's forehead was normal temperature. Cahena concentrated on entering the woman's mind and reading her thoughts. Instead she found herself in a long empty corridor made of two walls without doors ceiling or windows. She attempted to look behind her but couldn't because she was being pulled away. Cahena opened her eyes and was looking into the fractured irises of Lila who asked, "Do you remember what you said?"

"She never remembers," Ozeret answered. "And I never heard that language. Yet the sick answer her in that tongue and they too do not remember.

"It is the language of the soul. Very few ever reach understanding." Lila led Cahena to a Zebra skin to rest upon. "I must consult with my colleagues," She left the hut.

It was thirty minutes before she returned, leading an oriental woman into the hut. "This is Mai Li," Lila said to Ozeret. "She is Chinese, can read and write that language and Berber too. She has no background in medicine, and is a slave. I give her to you in hopes she can translate the medicines and their applications from their scrolls." She put the young Chinese woman's hand in Ozeret's hand and said, "You two will go outside." She looked over at the woman suffering from malaria and said, "She appears well enough. Take her with you."

Alone with the other sick woman, Lila sat cross-legged on the zebra skin in front of Cahena. "I have only glimpsed into your mind. That brief sortie revealed an intelligence I never encountered before. It is beyond that of most wise men. You must learn to harness this intellect. The gods have given you natural talents it has taken me a lifetime to acquire. If you do not learn to yoke these gifts, one of two things will happen. Either you will lose them or they will destroy you. I have received permission from the council of shamans to take you on a spiritual journey few have ever traveled."

"Where are we going?"

"To the spirit world."

"Why?"

"To find her soul." She pointed to the woman lying motionless nearby.

"How can a person lose their soul?"

"That is the reason for this trip: to reveal your lack of knowledge." She led Cahena off the zebra skin onto the hard earthen floor. They sat facing each other, legs crossed, knees touching, backs straight and chins up. Lila leaned forward and touched the silver streak in Cahena's hair. "The sign of a shaman," she murmured.

The fractured irises of Lila locked onto those of Cahena. The older woman said. "Once we begin our journey we will speak to each other in our thoughts. There is no reason to be frightened. I am your spiritual guide. Close your mouth and take a deep breath through your nose. Draw the air down into your belly below your navel." Lila placed her hand on Cahena's lower stomach. "Try again. Yes, that's it. Now continue inhaling and fill your upper belly. When you have that down, fill the air pockets around your neck and shoulders. Now do it again and hold the air in. Now let it out through the nostrils. Repeat this five times and keep looking into my eyes."

Cahena did as instructed. She could not remember taking the last breath as she fell into the limpid darkness of Lila's pupils. It was murky but not frightening. The world was turning. There was no air rushing by nor temperature felt on her skin. Suddenly she was again in the long corridor with high ceiling, no doors and no windows, but now it was full of people. But they weren't people; they were like small, dark, triangular silk kites flying about. "You are right." Lila spoke in Cahena's thoughts. "They are people, or rather the souls of people. They were here when you last visited, but were invisible."

"How can you possibly find the lady's soul among the thousands that are here? They all look alike."

"And each is the image of God." Lila held a small bone. It was hollow at both ends. She put one end to her lips and blew a short tune. Every soul in the long corridor froze in place. Lila blew the same notes again. The souls separated to the left right, above and below. Now there was a portal down the entire length of the endless corridor. Cahena saw a dot in the center coming toward them. It was another small kite. As it approached it grew larger. It hovered in front of Lila who again played the tune. The kite chirped the same tune. The second it finished Lila inhaled through the bone. She sucked the soul into it and clapped her hands over both ends. There was a distressed sigh throughout the long hall. "We must leave quickly," Lila said. "They don't approve."

Cahena felt herself in the whirlpool of darkness and questioned, "What is so pleasant about flying around a place like that? I wouldn't want to stay there."

"You only see what they want you to see. There is more to the heavenly realm than that."

Moshe ben Shimi was seated to the side of his daughter and the chief sorceress when they returned from their astral journey. He had been cautioned not to approach or address either until they acknowledged him. He watched Lila rise up with the bone held between the palms of both hands. She bent over the sick woman slipped one end of the bone down onto the woman's chest, placed her mouth over the other end and give a mighty puff. The patient did not move. Lila stood and faced Cahena's father. He asked, "What was all that about?"

"An unusual ritual. It is rarely performed, and never before witnessed by one as young as your daughter. She is a very special girl. You should treasure her."

"I do. That is why I forbid her to see you again. We are Israelites. You call us Jews. Our religion forbids sorcery and magic."

"Your religion is no longer your daughter's religion. Before she came to me your little girl visited places and cured people that Hebrew mystics only dream about. If you respect Cahena's intelligence and her desire to do good, then let her study with me. Not to do so would put her in great danger."

"What danger?"

"Have you witnessed your daughter's ability to heal and read other's thoughts? How she communicates with birds and animals? She may already have unknowingly destroyed the Vandal band at the entrance to Wadi Amra by controlling the weather two or three days in advance. If she does not learn to govern these powers, they will rule her. That would be a disaster for your child, and the Berber people."

"What on earth are you talking about?"

"In less than four years Cahena is to marry and become queen of all the Berbers. You are canvassing this encampment making alliances to assure she will reign with power. Why don't you tell your daughter the real motive for making her queen?"

"If you can read people's minds why don't you read mine and you tell her?"

"Be careful what you ask for, Moshe ben Shimi."

"Nobody in this world but God Almighty knows my plan. Tell me, and I give my daughter to learn from you until her marriage."

Lila put both her hands to her temple, rocked back and forth weighing the necessity of teaching Cahena to control the powers that would surely destroy her, against the love of her father for his daughter and their religion. She said, "From your book of Hebrews, Jephthah swore to sacrifice his daughter."

"I am aware of Jephthah's vow."

As if Moshe ben Shimi had not spoken, Lili continued, "He sacrificed her by fire because of a vow he made to God to help him in battle. Are you also willing to make a vow?"

Now Moshe ben Shimi filled with righteous anger answered. "The rabbis teach; 'you are where you are supposed to be and you do what you are supposed to do. What happens is God's will'!"

"If I predict correctly your ulterior motives to make your daughter queen, she will then be an apprentice to me until her marriage?"

"I do so vow."

"Then hearken unto me. Your daughter is the reincarnation of your ancient ancestor and namesake, who was in line to become the high priest in the Jerusalem Temple. He was away in the land of Moab when the Romans sacked Jerusalem and burned the temple, killing all the priests."

"That story is common knowledge amongst the literate."

"What is not known is your plan to control the Berbers to field an army of half a million strong, including the Numidians. You will use them to defeat the Byzantine Roman forces in Africa, then defend against Mohammed and his general, Khalid ibn Al Walid. To accomplish your master plan you must invade Egypt and eliminate the Muslim regimes in Iraq and Iran."

"With your intelligence system of shamans, you could have pieced this together."

"That is why you sent your daughter alone to raise up the tribes and the Jewish consciousness throughout the Maghreb and beyond. She succeeded beyond your wildest dreams. Even these so-called conversions my shamans performed work in your favor."

"But your people took money to commit them to Selim, Chieftain of the Helawi."

"Selim wouldn't know a Jew if his son married one."

Lila smirked, and it angered Moshe ben Shimi. He snapped, "My daughter will marry his son, and I will see he converts if I have to circumcise him myself."

"The marriage will not be consummated."

"You also claim to see the future?"

"Let's remain on the subject."

"If you are through, you have lost your wager"

"I haven't finished and will not lose."

"Then what do you claim is my goal for gathering and utilizing such an army to defeat the Roman's and stop the Muslims?"

"To conquer Jerusalem and rebuild your sacred temple."

Moshe ben Shimi blinked, his knees buckled. He fell on them. His face turned deathly pale. He looked around for help. There was none. He reached out to Cahena. She hurried to her father and he wept. She had never seen her father shed a tear. She cried with him. He muttered, "I've failed you. I've failed my little girl."

He looked up at the chief sorceress who said, "It is best for your daughter, your plans, and your people that Cahena remains with me."

Moshe swallowed, marshaled his thoughts attempting to find a way out of his solemn religious vow. He mentally reviewed Biblical arguments and the story of Jephthah, a judge in Israel who promised God to sacrifice the first thing he saw when he returned home victorious. It was his daughter who led the people to greet him. "That's it"! Moshe shouted and stood putting Cahena aside. His face shone as he wiped the tears with his sleeve. "Our agreement and my vow was that of Jephthah. But Jephthah excused his daughter from fulfilling the vow, And so I now I excuse my daughter from my vow."

Moshe ben Shimi didn't catch the hint of a smile on the sorceress' lips when she said, "Then let your daughter decide."

"I can't!" Cahena blurted out, and then said. "I want time."

"For what?" her father demanded.

At that moment the woman who had retrieved her soul stood up behind Lila and interrupted, "I feel much better now." Her eyes were bright and her face a healthy color. "May I leave?"

Lila nodded toward the door and Cahena took advantage of the distraction to slip out of the hut. Her father shouted, "Meet me back at the camp."

Moshe ben Shimi returned to his tent elated he had outwitted the sorceress. Cahena awaited her father in dread. He burst into the tent and dismissed the servants. Alone with his daughter he asked, "Why did you not tell that witch your desire to remain with me? I need you now more than ever. The convenient conversion of the tribesmen by Selim can be worked in our favor."

"How?"

"You continue healing people. They will flock to you and acknowledge your leadership rather than his."

"Father, is it true that the purpose of making me queen is to recapture Jerusalem and rebuild the Holy Temple?"

"I would have revealed this to you in time. It is the dream of every Jew. It is why we exist."

"It has never been my dream."

"For that I am at fault. I should have remarried and had a Jewess raise you rather than the Witch of the Maghreb."

"Father, I repeat your words; you are where you are supposed to be and you do what you are supposed to do."

"Are you actually thinking of apprenticing to that witch?"

"Father, on my journey with her I learned far more than to see souls. The life Lila wishes to train me for is one of dedication, responsibility, service and an enduring commitment as a healer to all people. I will learn dream shifting.

This entails astral travel and observing others without their knowledge. Lila may have been right about me controlling the weather without realizing it. Two nights before the Vandals were wiped out by the flood. I dreamed of a great storm in the mountains. I was in the dark clouds and made them come together. There was lightening, thunder and rain came down in blinding sheets."

"You believe this witch?"

"I believe there is more to Pagan shamanism than Judaism explains. I know she is right."

"Right, about what?"

"If I do not learn how to control the powers gifted to me, I will destroy others and myself. Father I am frightened by the power. I also think I may have been chosen by God to consolidate the Jews in exile, possibly even to fulfill your plan re-establish the Temple in Jerusalem. But that can only be achieved with the support of the Nomadic tribes in Africa and my control of these powers."

"Are you telling me you have decided to apprentice yourself to this Moroccan witch?"

"Father, on my astral journey I learned that the human soul is divine and immortal."

"We Jews believe in the immortality of the soul."

"But reincarnation is not accepted by many,

and I absolutely believe it. I know I am the reincarnation of the high priest for whom your father was named."

"Reincarnation is a delusion," Moshe ben Shimi proclaimed.

"Father, a human being is a source of energy. We are dependent on God to identify and direct that energy for the good of mankind. I have been given unusual powers. Lila is correct; I do not know how to control them. It frightens me. As my spirit guide, she will teach me to avoid the dangers and achieve success. Those achievements will include your plan to unite the tribes, defeat the Romans and Muslims. I can only help you rebuild the temple if I learn to control these special abilities."

Father and daughter embraced. They wept.

Early the next morning Ahmed, his mother, Josephus and Ozeret helped Cahena carry her belongings and theirs to the Shaman's compound. Moshe ben Shimi stood at the entrance of his tent and waved goodbye. He thought of the old proverb, "Man plans and God laughs."

CHAPTER 15

THE PROPHET

In Mecca, fifty-one years before Cahena apprenticed to Lila the Chief Sorceress, Muhammad ibn Abdulla was born. His father died before his birth and his mother gave him over to a wet nurse. When the child was five years old the nurse returned Muhammad to his mother claiming he was possessed by demons. Two years later his mother died.

His grandfather took him in. He also died.

In 595, twenty-five year old Muhammad married his employer and distant cousin, Khadijah. She was forty years old and wealthy, he twenty-five and poor. He worked as a salesman. She was twice divorced and had two sons and a daughter. She ran the business and he traveled, buying and selling.

In the year 610 he received his first revelation. The angel Gabriel said he was chosen to be the Prophet of Allah, meaning 'the Lord', and carry the Almighty's teachings to the world. He thought his wet nurse had been correct; he was possessed by demons.

He attempted suicide. The angel Gabriel stopped him.

It took Muhammad three years of study to gain the confidence to preach Allah's word publicly. He was ignored by most, called a plagiarist by some and a trouble-maker by others. Mecca was the center of the Pagan religion, with the Kaaba—a great black meteoric rock, originally sacred to the sun-god El-Lahga-Baal—as its focus. His own uncle derided him in public saying, "We Meccans ask for miracles, and the prophet of Allah has none."

In 615 Muhammad raised the ire of Meccans by attacking native Pagan beliefs. He developed a small following that was harassed, then hounded, for supporting him. He sent them to safety in Abyssinia while he remained in Arabia. His wife Khadija died in 619.

The Prophet had been brought to deep sorrow when Lady Khadija, his wife of twenty-five years, died. The messenger of Allah said: "God Almighty never granted me anyone better in this life than her. She accepted me when people rejected me; she believed in me when people doubted me; she shared her wealth with me when people deprived me." The Prophet called it the Year of Sorrow.

An uncle who helped support him also died,

leaving Muhammed pinched for cash; he had been preaching rather than selling with the unswerving support of his wife. In less than a year he wed the six-year-old Aisha, daughter of Abu Bakr, who was wealthy.

That same year, while preaching in Mecca, the Prophet uttered the words of "satanic suggestion" for divine revelation: "Have ye thought upon al-Lat and al-Uzza and Manat, the_third, the other? (53:19,20)" These were the names of three female Pagan goddesses, believed by Pagans to be the daughters of the Lord.

Muhammad yearned to convert his kinsmen, neighbors, and all Meccans to his new faith: Islam, "submission". His followers were shocked at his statement of the three goddesses, for he had stated repeatedly that there was only one God, Allah; none other was acceptable. The Pagan merchants of Mecca were ecstatic by the Prophet's remarks, for Muhammad had spoken harshly about their gods; they could now conduct business with Muslims and incorporate Allah into their pantheon of gods.

Then the angel Gabriel appeared to the Prophet and said, "Those two sentences you uttered were not given by Allah. They were from Satan! If these words are accepted, it would call into question the infallibility of the Prophet and Allah himself."

Gabriel then revealed the following verse to the Prophet: "Satan made a suggestion respecting his desire, but Allah abolishes that which Satan spoke. Allah establishes His instructions, and Allah is all-knowing and wise. Know thou that Allah is able to do all things. The Prophet is infallible and has divine protection from all mistakes."

Less than a year later the Prophet made his famed night journey on his winged steed Buraq, from Mecca to Jerusalem to Heaven in one night. There he was instructed in the holy teachings and met the prophets of old. He told about Moses weeping because there will be more Muslims in heaven than Jews. Inspired by his journey, he enthused others and caused more friction between his followers and the more numerous Pagans.

In 622 he led his people to safety from Mecca to Medina. He also consummated his marriage with the nine-year-old Aisha.

Exiled from Mecca, the commercial center of Arabia, Muhammad was dependent on the largess of Medina's inhabitants and his followers, which wasn't much. The need for income was dire.

He formed a small band of fighters and sent them to reconnoiter the caravan trails from Mecca to the sea. This group set up at a crossroads outside of Mecca. They spied a caravan with seven heavily laden animals getting ready to pitch camp. On their own initiative they attacked the traders, even though it was the Pagan's holy month when violence was forbidden. It was a very rich cargo his men brought to the Prophet in Medina.

He scolded his men for attacking during this sacred month, but they replied that Muhammad himself had set the new Islamic calendar, and to respect the Pagan one seemed contrary to holy teachings. The Prophet meditated on the problem. The following morning he convened his followers and explained. "If you are questioned about fighting during sacred month of the Pagans, answer thus; yes it is a great transgression, but greater still are the transgressions imposed by the idol-worshippers. They prevent us from visiting the Kaaba in Mecca. They drove us Muslims from our homes. They obstruct those seeking the path to Allah. And their greatest transgression is to prevent man from following Allah; It is worse than killing a person. They are murdering the immortal soul. Therefore you may keep the goods, but do not sell the animals. I wish to expand our military."

Several more minor raids were made on merchant caravans from Mecca.

Muhammad initiated a strategy to isolate the

Meccans. He approached those tribes surrounding that city, always with an overwhelming show of force. He then negotiated a peace treaty ensuring safety for their caravans. He set up an intelligence gathering group to report on the activities of friend and foe. Finally he placed his armed men in strategic positions to control the busiest caravan routes. Either the caravan master paid tribute or was attacked, his men and travelers converted, killed or ransomed.

The Merchants of Mecca had dealt with bandits before. They soon realized the Prophet was more interested in their spiritual self than their money. He began by taking the latter but would soon come for their soul. The merchants resisted by making their own tribal alliances, hiring professional fighting men and expanding their armory. They were supported by Arabian merchants, ship owners, importers and exporters on the Red, Arabian, Mediterranean Seas, the Gulf of Aden and the Persian Gulf.

On one occasion Muhammad himself led two hundred fifty men in an aborted raid on a large caravan. They were beaten off by professional guards. The Meccans retaliated with a successful raid on the Muslim livestock grazing outside the city of Medina. There were several more skirmishes.

In the beginning of March 624, Abu

Sufiyan—chief of the Umayyad tribe and respected Meccan city official—led a caravan from the Port of Jeddah to Mecca. His seventy camels were loaded with the wealth he had traded for the merchants of that Holy City. Muhammad's agents in Jeddah sent word of his departure, and the Prophet decided to take the wealth by force. The trail used by the caravan was a major one, but its direction was determined by accessible water holes. The Prophet set his scouts to fill the wells along the route with sand. They left wells open that would lead the caravan to a place advantageous to his Muslim fighters.

Abu Sufiyan and the merchants of Mecca also had agents who informed the Caravan Master of the danger. Mecca sent out a mounted force on horse and camel of more than one thousand men. Muhammad went forth with three hundred men prepared, even eager, to die in this Holy War (Jihad) to support the Messenger of God.

Tuesday the 13th of March in year 625, in the Hejaz region of Saudi Arabia, an important battle was about to be fought. The Muslims were confidant in Jihad; to die in battle meant to spend eternity in heaven with rewards of women, riches, and eternal pleasures. Mecca, the richest city on the Arabian Peninsula fielded an army three times larger than the Muslims. They carried heavy weapons while the raiders had only light weapons and armor for a quick raid and early escape.

When Muhammad learned of the disparity between the opposing forces he consulted with his God. Allah told him to challenge the idol worshippers, and thus began the Battle of Badr. The Islamic force was stationed on a hill side looking down into the valley. They had only two horses and seventy camels for three hundred men. They had to march ninety-four miles to the place the Prophet had chosen. Men rode three astride every camel and alternated with those who walked until they reached the high ground.

The Meccans arrived, took their time to set up their tents and with the greatest confidence prepared their morning meal. Their scouts reported the Muslim force only the three hundred on the hillside.

Muhammad's men were anxious to begin the battle. He cautioned patience. As was the tradition each side sent out three champions to face each other prior to the battle. These men were chosen for their oratorical skills as well as their swordsmanship. They insulted each other, their tribes and their ancestors. Then the three joined battle as one group against the other. The Prophet had advised his three men: Hanya,

Ali and Ovadia. "Two of you always attack one of them. Move him so he is always between you and one other opponent. Ovadia, you are the youngest. You will engage their third man. Take defensive actions until Hanya and Ali have eliminated one after the other. Then the three of you finish off the third."

The champions from both sides marched out to the valley floor. The Meccans strode to the sounds of drums and trumpets the three Muslims to the chant of their brethren, "Allahu Akbar!" They engaged as the sun climbed higher in the sky. The men were equally matched but the tactics of the Muslims proved effective. Two men attacked one keeping him between them and his partner.

Ovadia entered single combat with an old veteran. At first his strength and agility allowed him to escape the vicious onslaughts of the Meccan warrior. But as the sun burned brighter he began to whither under the fierce attack of the veteran. The first wound was a slash to Ovadia's neck. The second penetrated his chest armor. But he succeeded in delivering a powerful blow to the head. At that moment Hanya and Ali finished off the second man and rushed in to kill the Meccan warrior. Ovadia died. His last words were. "Thank you for allowing me to serve the Messenger of God."

The Muslim rank and file awaited Muhammad's signal to attack. He looked up at the sun, unrolled his prayer rug and gave thanks to the Almighty. All others in ranks put down their javelins, spears and prayed in the face of the enemy.

Among the Meccans there was a murmur of wonder at these Muslims who prostrated themselves to God before they would be killed. Some urged the attack while they were praying, but others said no. A group of two hundred, having witnessed the defeat of their champions and the unswerving faith of the Prophet's followers, abandoned the battlefield.

Muhammad stood from his prayer rug, looked up at the sun, gauged the distance to the enemy below and ordered his men to arms. He marched them some fifty yards forward, then commanded his archers and slingers to fire. Their first volley caught the Meccans with their shields down and took a devastating toll. Meccans raised their shields and their more numerous bowmen fired, but they and their slingers were shooting uphill. Their arrows and stones fell short. Another barrage of arrows and stones pounded the Meccans.

What happened next is described in the holy teachings, though nowhere else. The Prophet ordered his men to attack the larger, better-equipped force in front of them. As the three hundred warriors shouted "Allahu Akbar!", Allah sent three thousand angels—led by the angels Gabriel and Michael—to help the Prophet and his companions to show the world that Allah is God, the only God, and Muhammad his greatest and final prophet. Even though the Meccans had the swifter horses they could not escape. They were in complete disarray, and even though mounted on horse and camel were hunted down and slaughtered by the angelic host. No survivor of the battle told any different story.

The Battle of Badr established Islam as a significant military force and Muhammad a wise combat leader. The Prophet preached, "It was not you who slew them, it was God...in order that He might test the Believers by a gracious trial from Himself" Koran, (8:17).

Among the captives was the storyteller Abu Abak. He had accompanied the Meccans so he could tell the story of the battle. Muhammad was informed that the storyteller, an avowed Pagan, had made fun of Islam. When the Prophet asked what he said, his captors refused to answer because it was too sacrilegious. Muhammad said, "I must have some indication to judge the man fairly."

The guards consulted each other and each repeated a joke told by Cahena's godfather.

"The Prophet Muhammad was riding the caravan trail with thirty of his followers. He turned to his men and shouted, 'Do you believe Allah is the one true God, the only God?' The companions shouted, 'Yes we do.' 'Then stand up on your camel's back and shout it!' They did—and fell off their camels.'"

Muhammad grunted and motioned to the second man. "Oh Messenger of God," said the man, "Forgive me for the unclean words I am about to say. The storyteller of the Maghreb said he told a Muslim Imam he did not understand why Muslims do not drink wine. A cup of wine a day, he said, has wonderful benefits. 'Like what?' the Imam asked. 'Well,' said the storyteller, 'It keeps you from becoming a Muslim.'"

"These were his exact words?"

Both men nodded.

"Kill the infidel."

Abu Abak was dragged through the sand, tied hand and foot. He was forced to kneel before Muhammad's tent. The flaps were open. The Prophet nodded, and a warrior chopped the storyteller's head off.

The Battle of Badr established Muhammad as a force to be respected. His tribal alliances were strengthened. The capture of the treasure caravan provided funds to feed the poor, better arm his men and pay them.

The Prophet preached to the Jews of Medina, inviting them to join Islam. Few did. He preached and he badgered them, emphasizing the heavenly deliverance by God at the Battle of Badr. The Jews were polite but adamant. They did not flock to Islam. Muhammad intensified his efforts to no avail. This angered him. He ordered every Jewish male in Medina, adult and child to be murdered.

As the order was about to be carried out, one of his closest companions—Abdullah ibn Ubayy—reasoned with the Prophet that if the females remained they would inherit the land and wealth, "Whereas, if we just confiscate the properties and exile the Jews, it will fill the Islamic coffers." And so the Prophet decreed expulsion.

A year later, March 11, 625 AD, the Meccans sought to avenge their losses at Badr and strike back at Muhammad and his followers. The Prophet was prepared; he had a smaller but more dedicated army. The two militias fought on the slopes of Mount Uhud, and the smaller group of Muslims initially broke the enemy line. When victory was within their grasp word spread the Prophet had been killed.

They lost heart and were routed. Muhammad had been hit by a slinger's stone; he was seriously wounded on the forehead and scalp. Muslim warriors lost heart and abandoned the battlefield. The Prophet and his troops retreated to the safety of Medina.

The Triumph of Mecca over Islam at Uhud encouraged the Pagans to attack Medina two years later, at the Battle of the Trench in late January of the year 627.

The Meccans marched out with ten thousand men, six hundred horses and more camels. The Prophet commanded three thousand men with only a hundred horses and twice as many camels. Muhammad's genius was instrumental in the outcome. He did not go out on the plains to meet the Medina Army; rather he used the natural lay of the land and an important ploy to negate the superior cavalry of his enemy. The mountains behind Medina formed a horseshoe around the city. The highlands were impossible for cavalry to deploy and difficult for infantry to navigate. Muhammad ordered a wide trench dug across the open ends of the horseshoe and the dirt piled high on the inside. Chariots could never pass and horses would flounder trying to climb the high side of the great trench while Muslim archers and slingers could pick them off at their leisure. It was the end of a harsh winter and the Meccans came to do battle. They were forced into a siege situation. unprepared with clothing, food and fuel for the bitter winter weather. Twenty-seven days later they straggled back to Mecca.

One result of the battle was that Muhammad accused the Jews of Banu of attempting to betray him. All the Jewish women and children were sold into slavery or traded for weapons and horses. The males were beheaded.

Many of the horses used by the Muslims were foals birthed to the Berber horses that were captured from the bandit's years earlier, and sold to them by Cahena's uncle Benyamin. The remaining residents of Banu had to pay Muhammad for every camel, donkey, or horse that moved in or out of their city.

CHAPTER 16

SELIM OF THE HELAWI

In April of the year 627, in accordance with Berber tradition, the bride's family held a three-day feast for the groom's family. Outwardly there appeared no problem between Selim's Helawi and Moshe ben Shimi's Amazigh tribes, yet an underlying tension existed.

It was acerbated by Cahena's apprenticeship to Lila, Africa's senior sorceress. The shamans who were paid to convert the nomads to Jews and swear allegiance to Selim defaulted on their promise. On Lila's instructions they advised people to pledge loyalty to Moshe ben Shimi and the future queen of the Berbers.

On the Imilchil plateau the three days of feasting, trading, paying respects, attending horse and camel races, wrestling, archery and javelin throwing contests were held. While Moshe ben Shimi negotiated with Selim for the marriage of Cahena to the future king of the Helawi, Moshe had not seen his daughter for four long years. He sent and received brief messages by carrier pigeon. He yearned for her. Every morning he tied on his phylacteries saying special prayers for her wellbeing. At noon and at night before retiring he prayed for her happiness. On Holy days when he led the congregation in prayer he composed special pleas for God to protect her. He composed a prayer before welcoming Selim into his tent for the pre-nuptial negotiations.

He was aware of Selim's bogus conversion to Judaism and desired that Cahena had the freedom of Berber law for women in marital relationships, mainly that the woman chose her spouse, which Cahena had already agreed to for the benefit of her father's plan. She maintained the right to divorce and remarry. He was surprised this was not protested by Selim. The Helawi Chief had other plans. He sat his son between him and Moshe during the festivities.

The only minor problem came about in arranging the groom's hosting of the bride's more numerous family prior to the wedding. Selim had insisted the marriage ceremony take place at the annual gathering on the Imilchil Plain. For reasons that were unclear and appeared unimportant he wanted the Helawi to host the Amazigh and the chieftains of all tribes to this three day feast. To Moshe ben Shimi it seemed out of character for Selim to take on such an expense. They were both in competition for the loyalty of other tribes. Moshe assumed the Helawi chief was trying to influence nomadic leaders. With Cahena and the help of the shamans, Moshe felt confident he could manipulate the situation to his advantage. As queen, Cahena would lead the unified tribes. Her husband to be was not known to assert himself. He rarely spoke except to agree with his father.

The Jewish holy days had come early this year. The Helawi and the Amazigh camped in the same valley where Moshe and Cahena had parted four years ago. He was informed by Ozeret that his daughter would arrive soon. He tried to question the hunchback to no avail. The only answer she gave was, "You will be proud."

The person entering the tent had to stoop down. When she straightened up her face was creased with a large smile of bright white teeth in a sunburned face of angelic features. They were enhanced by wide-set penetrating grey eyes framed by long, straight, glistening black hair. "Aba," She said in Hebrew. She rushed forward, knelt and kissed his feet. He raised her up. Tears filled both their eyes and wet their lips as they rained kisses on each other's faces. He grasped her head and lowered it so he could kiss her cheeks, nose and forehead.

"Oh daughter dear," he wept, "My little girl,

every day was like a year, each year a lifetime. Did you learn what you expected?"

"Far more."

"Were you happy learning?"

"Not at first. It requires much self-discipline."

"Most worthwhile things entail strength of mind." He stepped back. "Look at you. How you have grown! You could eat apples off my head."

"I wish to hear words from your lips. Father, how are you?"

The two talked all night and into the morning hours. Moshe had taken a tribeswoman as a wife, but she died of malaria six months later. The carrier pigeons kept him informed of the latest news from all over the Maghreb, but he found it difficult to visit all the tribes and request their allegiance. Selim took advantage of every possible opening to forge agreements of mutual interests and have his son and daughter-in-law to reign as king and queen of the North African nomads.

"Father, the tribal shamans claim the people are more interested in your leadership and my becoming queen than anything Selim can offer."

"We'll know after the wedding. I was disappointed that Gershom, King of Numidia didn't forge an alliance with me. His son was healed by that Roman Medicus in Carthage. He can see again."

"Gershom will swear allegiance to you and no other. I invited him to the wedding. He is most grateful."

"I never received a word from him."

"He is watched by the Romans. They use falcons to stop his pigeons. The Romans are preparing to move against the Muslim ship-building in Algiers. They want the Numdians to join them in wiping out the Muslims and burning or capturing their ships."

"The Romans approached me," Moshe said. "The Emperor in Constantinople wants us to oppose the invasion of the Maghreb by Islamic forces."

"Why should we go to war for the Romans?"

"They promise money, slaves, land and booty captured from the Muslims. We will obtain preferred shipping prices in the seven seas. We also control and collect all import and export taxes from the Maghreb to the sea."

"Being tax collector for the Romans would create enemies amongst the tribes."

"Exactly. There is every indication the Muslim fleet will defeat the Romans in Constantinople. This Muhammad is a very clever military leader, as well as being politically astute and religiously infallible. The Romans are weak in Africa: only two legions in Carthage and a third stationed in small garrisons throughout the country."

"They just defeated the Persians after decades of war."

"How could you know that? It just happened."

"I saw it."

"Daughter, you couldn't possibly have witnessed that battle. Nineveh is a thousand miles away. Only two days ago we were informed by pigeon."

"You asked me what I have learned. One thing was astral travel. I need more experience. Lila took me on the journey."

"You traveled through the air to Nineveh?"

"My astral body did."

"Cahena, the Torah forbids sorcery."

"Do you wish to hear what I saw?"

"Yes, but only if you believe it is the truth."

"I speak only the truth. Lila said the Persians had defeated the Romans time and again over the centuries. They had a collection of five hundred Legion standards captured in battle. Heraclius the Roman Emperor led his troops into battle. He placed his less competent men in the center. There was a brief vicious fight until the Roman center collapsed."

"Where were you when you saw all this?"

"Floating above, but I could not see my ethereal-self or Lila. We communicated in thought.

She explained that the Roman's had planned the collapse of the center and the retreat appeared real. It was a trap to bring the Persians onto a field where the Roman square could be employed to its maximum effect. The Persians, although more numerous, were being slaughtered by the Roman war machine. Rhahzadh, General of the Persian army challenged the Roman emperor to single combat before their troops. Heraclius slew the Persian with a single sword thrust. The Persians withdrew. The Persian King was murdered by his son, who sued for peace with Rome. Both parties retired from occupied territories. It was a Roman victory."

"If it was a Roman victory why didn't they pursue the Persians and sack their cities? Constantinople could use the wealth. The Vandals, Goths and Huns are battering their northern borders."

"I never gave it a thought."

"Think. Now that the Persians are neutralized, what or who is the greatest threat to the Romans in the east?"

"You and the alliance of nomadic tribes."

"There is a more imminent threat, not only to Rome but to the world."

"Islam!" Cahena said.

"Correct. Muhammad's disciples are preaching and making converts in Iraq, Iran, Syria, Egypt andi Arabia. That is why the Romans need us and the Numidians to take the shipbuilding port of Tangiers. They made peace with Persia so they could concentrate on defending their northern border against the Vandals and Goths. To do that they must neutralize the Muslims, or the future belongs to Muhammad."

"The Romans are no longer the force they once were," Cahena said. "They have only three legions in all of Africa. One is defending outposts, and two are in Carthage. If we align ourselves to them we could lose everything."

"And if we don't, we could lose it all to the Muslims."

"What do we require to fend off the Muslims and be independent of Constantinople?"

"Five years to build up our forces. We will discuss it after the wedding. I do not understand your ability to fly about and see things. I believe what you told me, but Jewish law forbids me from believing how you know."

Josephus entered the tent. "The Helawi are getting anxious for the bride to appear," he said. "The guests are lined up for the gift giving ceremony. With the Amazigh, the Helawi and the other tribal chieftains, there are a thousand. You don't need a torch to walk with. The night is lit by fires roasting everything but camel and pig. Selim wants to keep the feast kosher."

For three days and nights the bride and groom sat at the main table with their fathers. Selim always arranged the seating in the same manner: he sat on the right with Cahena on his left, and they shared food from the same platters. His son and Moshe ben Shimi sat to the left, sharing their platters. Then came King Gershom, Lila, and other chieftains. In this order they received guests and presents.

The crowded tent went silent as two men in pure white silk turbans and linen robes, of Muslim fashion, approached the bride and groom. They bowed to the bride and groom. Each presented a book, saying in unison, "The Holy teachings. A gift for the future king and queen of the Berbers from the Prophet Muhammad, may his name be blessed."

The groom accepted the gift and handed it back to a servant. Cahena tapped the cover of her book and asked, "Is this the book dictated by God to the prophet?"

"It is."

"The same Prophet who ordered the murder of the storyteller Abu Abak?"

The emissaries shifted uneasily but answered forthrightly, "The old man was given the same choice as all others: Islam or death."

"Abu Abak was my godfather. He didn't choose death. Your prophet did." Cahena dismissed them with a wave of her hand. She instructed Josephus to escort them safely from the camp.

The guests were so many and their gifts so plentiful a special tent was erected to hold them. Behind the tent was a large corral built to hold the horses and camels. Three scribes were charged with recording the gifts, their value and who gave them. It would be an insult if the king and queen favored these tribes with a smaller gift on a similar occasion.

Two bedraggled Bedouin had somehow inserted themselves in the line of gift givers. Their appearance caused Cahena to break out in laughter. She stood and had to bend down to embraced both men at the same time. With one in each arm she lifted them kissing their weather-worn cheeks. When she put them down they bowed and said, "Our present to you and the groom." They each held out a ten inch knife with a shiny thin polished blade and rawhide bound handle. "Many years ago we tracked a shooting star into the desert. We found the metal and have worked on it ever since."

The scouts each pulled out a square of sheer blue silk and lofted them in the air. As the cloth settled down they whipped the knife blades through the silk. They parted into four pieces floating to the floor. The scouts placed the blades on the backs of both hands and bowed presenting them to the bride and groom.

"That you have come to celebrate with us is present enough." Cahena motioned for the two sit behind her.

The Helawi were the last to attend the bride. Selim orchestrated his gift giving to achieve maximum effect. It was two in the morning. He had musicians play loudly to wake up the wine-drugged sleepers. His wranglers drove two hundred horses almost into the reception tent. They were followed by four hundred camels. Selim himself came forward and presented the couple sugar for a sweet life, salt for a long life, bread for a life of plenty and milk for a life of purity. He waved forward a line of tribesmen carrying jewelry, bolts of cloth, caftans, beautiful slippers, handbags, saddles and perfumes. His men then marched in with a full set of new armor for horse and warrior, plus swords, javelins, long spear and dagger. "These," Selim pointed out, "are for our new warrior queen. They are made for your great height and strength, but made in such a way that they can be enlarged as you continue to grow. May these vestments of war protect you throughout a long and prosperous life."

Cahena, her father and the entire bridal party were duly impressed by the largess of the Helawi chief, and said so aloud. Ahmed recognized the herds or horses and camels as the same undesirable ones he and the chieftain Aksil selected for Selim after the battle with the raiders in Satan's Saddle. Now they were four years older and in worse condition.

The guests returned to their tents. Tomorrow was Tuesday, specifically chosen for the wedding day as a good omen, for when God created the world after each day of creation He saw it and said, "It was good." On the third day He repeated the phrase twice. Tuesday was considered an auspicious day for weddings.

The Night of the Bath, Jewish women of the Helawi and Amazigh escorted Cahena to the Mikvah. The outer room was a Turkish bath. A giant oven held heated boulders upon which were thrown buckets of water creating steam and raising the temperature of the room. The room was packed with naked women, all sweating and trying to wish the bride well. Cahena was led into the clear pool, then rushed naked into another room with a pool of ice cold water from the mountain snow melt. The shock of the cold on her heated body turned her skin a fiery red. As instructed, she clasped the fingers of both hands on top of her head and submerged until the water covered her hands. She repeated the purification prayers. She was hustled out of the water and covered with towels and rubbed dry.

Garbed in a hooded woolen cloak, she was led outside where tables laden with food awaited. Behind the tables were henna experts. Cahena was seated, her feet raised on a footstool and her hands resting on the arms of the chair palms up. Four henna artists, using yellow, black and red Henna, began the intricate designs to ward off evil spirits. They painted the bride's palms and the soles of her feet. Yellow and red dots formed a triangle under each eye. There were forty more henna artists to accommodate the women of the bridal party. Cahena fell into bed at five in the morning.

Ozeret wakened her at eleven for the first of seven different dress changes that would take place prior to the wedding ceremony. Six of the dresses were from mothers, grandmothers and great-grandmothers of both families. The seventh was the wedding dress, an original made especially for Cahena, to be passed down to her heirs. The remainder of the day consisted of the bride and groom being carried in two special chairs through each of the tribal areas and up onto Imilchil Plain. Fifty thousand Berbers were gathered for the annual festival and wedding that would form a monarchy to govern and empower the tribes.

Men now entered the vacated Mikvah. For most it was the first time. The newly converted used it to sweat out the wine and make room for more. Outside they ate, drank and toasted each other's health, then they followed the bridal party to the main camp grounds. The bride and groom were separated and could not see each other before the ceremony.

The fathers met in a special tent to negotiate the ketuba (wedding contract). The amount of dowry had been agreed upon prior to this meeting, as was the settlement in the event one party wished to dissolve the marriage. The only remaining issue was about levirate marriage. He questioned of Selim, "What if, God forbid, your son dies? He has no brothers to marry Cahena and carry on your family name."

"You are right," Selim answered. "The rabbis pointed out that like you, I might marry again and have a son. In that case he would be obligated according to this ketuba to marry Cahena and carry on my family name. Without an heir my name is lost."

Moshe consulted his two rabbinical advisors and concluded. "I see nothing awry, and wish all here a long and healthy life." The contract was signed and countersigned by one man from the tribe of Levy and another a Cohen, direct descendant from Aaron the high priest.

Sweets and wine were brought in and the two families toasted each other.

In the bridal tent musicians and singers entertained Cahena and her party. Special songs where sung for the bride and a hamsa—a five-fingered silver filigreed hand—on a chain was placed around the bride's neck for protection against the Evil Eye.

Those in charge of coordinating the wedding ceremony took over. They began to dress Cahena in pure white silk. The dress had gold brocade and a golden cummerbund that accented her waist and voluptuous breasts. She stood as a giantess who dwarfed the matrons attending her. A small star of jewels was centered above the bridge of her nose and between her eyes. Another jeweled star was placed on her chin pointing up to her ruby red lips. An ancient silver crown worn by Berber queens long forgotten was placed on her head and thin veils draped over it and her face.

A loud discussion erupted at the entrance to the bridal tent. Ozeret hurried to Cahena, saying, "King Gershom of the Numidians insists on seeing you before the wedding."

"By all means."

"It is bad luck."

Cahena showed her henna markings on the palms of her hands and pointed to the filigree Hamsa around her neck. "I'm protected."

The king entered. He bowed before Cahena, then fell on his knees in front of her saying, "I, Gershom, King of the Numidians, come to thank you with all my heart. Your doctor saved my son's eyes. He can see. I have an heir. You gave him to me. I wasn't at the gift-giving celebration, for I wished this to be a private presentation between you and me."

He looked around at the women in the room and Cahena dismissed all but Ozeret. The king stood. "Please hold out your right hand."

The silver and gold brocade rustled as Cahena raised her arm and extended her henna-painted hand palm up. The king dropped a smooth river stone into her hand saying. "This is a simple pebble taken from the stream where David King of Israel took the stone that killed the Philistine giant Goliath. It has no intrinsic value to anyone but you. It represents a wish. If it is my power to grant, or that of my son who will succeed me, the Numidian people will carry out your wish to the death."

Cahena was shocked into silence.

Ozeret said, "This is no time to talk of death, when we're about to celebrate a wedding and the creation of life."

The king took the hem of Cahena's dress, kissed it, and left.

Cahena was still staring at the pebble in the palm of her hand when Ozeret handed her a small pouch. "Put it in here," she said, "And keep it close. It is the most valuable gift you will ever receive."

Four turbaned men chosen for their strength entered the tent. Their bodies had been anointed with oil and the muscles in their arms and torsos rippled in the firelight as they set down the bride's chair. Cahena's handmaids and wedding organizers escorted her to the chair. She was lifted shoulder high. The upper entrance of the tent was opened to allow her to pass through. Outside, Lila and Ozeret waited to accompany the bride, acting as her mother and mother in-law. Thousands formed a mile-long lane to the bridal canopy. Musicians were stationed on the route. Professional singers serenaded the bride. Flowers, petals, and rose-scented water sprinkled the path. The Hebrew Berbers stationed themselves closest to the bridal canopy. There were several thousand of them wearing their finest and displaying all their jewelry. Their musicians and singers took over. They altered two songs, sung on the Sabbath to fit the occasion.

"Y'did Nefesh נֶפֶשׁ יְדִיד

"Yedid nefesh, Av harachaman,

"Lover of my soul, merciful God,

"Bring Your servant close to Your will.

"Your servant will run like a gazelle, to prostrate before Your glory.

"For Your companionship is purer than any fine taste or flavor.

"Perfect, pleasing, radiance of the world, my soul desires Your love.

"Please, God, heal her now, as You show her the pleasantness of Your light.

"Now, strengthen and heal her, and she will be for You an eternal servant.

"Ancient one, may your mercies be made manifest,

"And have compassion on the child of Your lover,

"For it is so long that she has faithfully waited, to see the glory of Your strength.

"Please, my God, the desire of her Heart, hurry and do not hide!

"Please, my beloved, reveal yourself and spread over her the shelter of Your peace.

"Fill the world with the light of your

glory, so that we may rejoice and be happy in You.

"Be quick, my lover, for the time has come, and have mercy on me for all time."

And this was followed by:

"Lecha Dodi דּוֹדִי לְכָה

"Lecha dodi likrat kala, p'nei Shabbat n'kabelah!

"נְקַבְּלָה שַׁבָּת פְּנֵי. כַּלָּה לִקְרַאת דּוֹדִי לְכָה:

"Come, my Beloved, to meet the bride; let us welcome the presence of the Sabbath.

"'Observe' and 'Remember the Sabbath day,' the only God caused us to hear in a single utterance: the Lord is One, and his name is One to his renown and his glory and his praise.

"Come, let us go to meet the Sabbath, for it is a well-spring of blessing; from the beginning, from of old it was ordained,—last in production, first in thought.

"O sanctuary of our King, O regal city, arise, go forth from thy overthrow; long enough hast thou dwelt in the valley of weeping; verily He will have compassion upon thee.

"Shake thyself from the dust, arise, put on the garments of thy glory, O my *people! Through the son of Jesse, the Bethlehemite, draw Thou nigh unto my soul, redeem it.*

"Arouse thyself, arouse thyself, for thy light is come: arise, shine; awake, awake; give forth a song; the glory of the Lord is revealed upon thee.

"Be not ashamed, neither be confounded. Why art thou cast down, and why art thou disquieted? The poor of my people trust in thee, and the city shall be builded on her own mound.

"And they that spoil thee shall be a spoil, and all that would swallow thee shall be far away: thy God shall rejoice over thee, as a bridegroomm rejoiceth over his bride.

"Thou shalt spread abroad on the right hand and on the left, and thou shalt reverence the Lord. Through thy offspring we also shall rejoice and be glad.

"Come in peace, thou crown of thy husband, with rejoicing and with cheerfulness, in the midst of the faithful of the chosen people: come, O bride; come, O bride."

On the singing of this verse thousands held out their arms and turned to Cahena as she was carried by, and followed her with their eyes, hands and hearts to the wedding canopy.

> *"Come, my Beloved, let us welcome thy presence."*

The groom, flanked by his father and future father in-law followed the candle-lit path to the wedding canopy, escorted by warriors from both tribes. He was greeted with similar songs ending with the verse, "Come my beloved and greet your bride to be."

The Rabbi placed the groom and the fathers facing Cahena and the mothers. The groom had to reach up to raise Cahena's veil. This tradition dated back to Father Jacob, who had been tricked into marrying Leah instead of Rachel. The groom held a cup of wine to her lips and she drank.

The veil was replaced and the rabbi read the Ketuba aloud. Seven blessings were said by Selim, Moshe, the king of Numidia and other dignitaries. Escorted by Ozeret and Lila, Cahena was led three times around the groom reciting blessings. Rings were exchanged. Shouts of Mazel Tov and Simon Tov were shushed by the rabbis. The groom wrapped an empty glass goblet in a cloth and set it on the floor.

The rabbi said aloud, "Ín our joy and at the height of our happiness, we must always remember the destruction of our Holy Temple. May it be rebuilt speedily in our day."

He signaled to the groom who brought his shoe down smashing the glass. The crowd burst into song, and everyone crowded in to wish the bride and groom long life.

It was two hours before the wedding party was seated in the main tent and the food served. Meats, vegetables, fruits nuts, baked and pickled delicacies followed one after the other, tray after tray. Selim saw to the seating arrangements, as before, with Cahena on his right and her husband and her father Moshe sharing the same food trays on the left. Lila thought it odd that the bride and groom did not eat from the same trays. Cahena ate with Selim from his tray and her father with the groom, then Lila and Ozeret, the Numidian king and his wife.

Suddenly the groom stiffened and fell over backwards. His legs remained crossed and up in the air. Moshe ben Shimi went to catch the boy—and collapsed on top of him.

It took several seconds for people to react. First were Cahena and Lila; together they pulled Moshe off the groom and laid him on the carpeted floor. Josephus was at their side helping. Lila wiped a froth from Moshe's lips. She pulled back his eyelids and only the whites were showing. Cahena was crying "Aba, Aba, speak to me!" Lila examined the groom with the same results.

Josephus whispered to her. "I've seen this before in the legion."

Lila said, "Poison."

He nodded, and she left him to examine the food tray the two had eaten from. Ozeret was already picking through a leafy vegetable salad the two had been eating. She pointed to several small black seeds. "The Devil's snare."

Lila picked out a green leaf and used the Spanish name, "Toloache."

"*Tolgucha*," Josephus corrected. "My Legion served six years in Spain. The Latin name is *datura stramonium*. We called it loco weed. I've seen it kill horses."

Lila heard Cahena weeping hysterically, begging her father to speak with her. Cahena leapt from her father's side grabbed Lila, picked her up and threw her at her father's feet. "Help him!"

"I cannot. He is in a coma."

"You saved that woman the first time I met you!"

"That woman was in a self-induced coma."

"What caused this coma?"

"Poison."

"Who? How? You must know an antidote?"

"The leaves and seeds in the salad plate were especially selected by an expert for their deadliness."

Cahena had thrown off her bridal crown and veils. She pushed Lila aside, placed her hands on her father's chest and sought the spirit that had guided her so many times when healing. She made the connection and began to speak in a language no one understood. She moved her hands over her father's body from head to toe. Again and again she attempted to contact him. Three hours later Moshe ben Shimi's body and that of the groom began to stiffen from rigor mortis. Cahena collapsed and was carried to her tent.

CHAPTER 17

THE BURIALS

A delegation of the five leading Rabbis met Cahena to plan the funeral. A grassy knoll overlooking the valley was chosen for the grave site. Hundreds requested the honor of pallbearer. She chose Aksil, Chief of the Chawia, King Gershom, Ahmed, Josephus and the two rabbis who remained by her father's side. One of the three rabbis who remained with the Helawi suggested, "Selim would bring more honor than the mute."

"That son of a dog poisoned my father."

"That can't be!" the rabbi said. "His own son died by the same poison."

"Then let him carry his son to the grave."

"Selim has a request. He wishes his son to be buried next to your father."

"No!" Cahena shouted. "That Helawi bastard is responsible for my father's death! I will kill him for it."

"Consider the request withdrawn," the chief rabbi said. "The two men will be buried separately, according to Jewish custom. The burial ceremony will take place at noon today. Your father's body is being washed as we speak. As per your tradition, he will be daubed with ochre and placed, fetal position, in a rock-lined hole facing Jerusalem—the city he wished to restore."

Tens of thousands attended Moshe ben Shimi's funeral. They covered the valley floor and up the slopes to the burial place, and as many joined the groom's cortege two miles away. So many stones were placed on each grave that they became separate monuments to the bodies they covered. The shivah, seven days of mourning, were held in the separate tribal camps.

Cahena sat on the floor. She wore sackcloth. Ashes were poured over her head and shoulders. She was forbidden to bathe or do any form of work. Food was brought to her. Despite the encouragement of Lila and Ozeret, she ate little. The multitude of guests paid homage to the new Berber queen. She remained silent. Her unblinking blue grey irises stared into space.

Ozeret and Lila remained at Cahena's side with Josephus and Ahmed. They posted and inspected guards around the tent day and night. After the last visitor had left on the evening of the sixth day, Cahena ate her first full meal. She summoned Lila, King Gershom, Ozeret, Josephus, Ahmed and the two Rabbis. "I know Selim of the Helawi is responsible for my father's death," she said.

"Do you have proof?" Gershom asked.

"None that I can show you."

"That is the only kind that is acceptable."

"Unless you have two witnesses who will testify under oath," The chief rabbis said, "You cannot convict for murder."

"It is my intuition."

"No Jewish court will accept that," the rabbi said. "What could Selim possibly gain by killing his own son?"

"I don't know."

"You are now queen," Gershom said. "You have absolute power. If you begin your reign by corrupting your own law and not providing proof as required by Torah, your rule will be tarnished and short-lived."

"That is why the chief sorceress is here; to take me on an astral journey to recall the past."

"Yes.' Lila said, "But where in the past would you like to go? Whom would you like to observe?"

"I do not know."

"Me neither. If I could put Selim under hypnosis..?"

"He'd never allow that," one rabbi said. "He hates you and your band of sorcery. You turned his conversion scheme to benefit Cahena. We rabbis are also against magic and conjuring."

"Why can't I accompany you in astral flight?" Cahena demanded.

"You could, but wouldn't understand a thing. Reviewing the past in spirit flight is like watching a thunder storm. Do you remember being taught to watch the clouds? When you see the lightning, count the seconds until you hear the thunder. Each second represents a hundred feet distance between the lightning strike and you. When recalling the past, you see it—but several seconds or minutes or even hours later you hear what was happening. It's garbled."

"If you learned to interpret it, I can."

"I didn't learn. After years of watching, it just came together."

"Is it possible for you to translate for me so I can be certain who murdered my father?"

"Yes. But you would have to name the conspirators and tell me where they met."

"Selim is my first choice. Does anyone have a second?"

Ahmed hesitantly raised his hand and indicated by tapping his forehead he wished Cahena to read his thoughts. He sat before her and she looked through his eyes into his mind.

There he showed her a pigeon and message from Carthage five months ago. The message read that Selim, chieftain of the Helawi was on a visit to that Roman city.

"If we can find out who he met," Lila said. "I might be able to conjure up the past."

For an hour the possibilities were discussed and dismissed. Again Ahmed approached Cahena to enter his thoughts. She turned to Lila and Ozeret. "Ahmed wishes to know more about the type of poison that was used.

"It's a common plant we use in healing." Ozeret said. "It's dangerous if not handled properly. Lila can explain."

"There are five different parts of the plant that are used. Roots, stems, leaves, flowers and seeds. Each has a varying degree of strength. The strongest being the small black seeds and the leaves. We found them in the salad on your father's tray. The person who chose them was an expert. The leaves were small and young. That is when they are most dangerous. The seeds had to be harvested months ago then dried to increase their strength."

"Shamans!" Cahena said.

"My thought exactly," Lila said

"Selim has some shamans working for him," Ozeret said.

"I will question each one of them," Lila said. "I'll know if they lie."

"That may not be necessary," Josephus said. "Ahmed gave us the right question. Why was Selim in Carthage? That's a hell of a long trip to enjoy the sea."

"You know something?" Cahena said.

"I know where the expert in the use of this loco weed lives. He used it to assassinate tribal chieftains in Spain."

"Who?" Cahena demanded.

"Your friend and mine, the medicus, Linus."

"How could a doctor who saved my son's eyesight be guilty of such a crime?" King Gershom demanded.

"My life was spent with the legion." Josephus said. "I laugh at Greek historians who put Roman military victories up to discipline and our military college. No doubt they were important, but the critical part of the Roman war machine is its politicians. They were trained from childhood to lie, deceive, murder and achieve. They hire one tribe to fight another, then come in and enslave both. Think of the Roman military as a large business. They would rather make deals and money than war. When they do make war they try to have others fight for them. Preferably enemy tribes fight each other. How do you think the Huns, Vandals and Goths overran Italy and

Roman Europe? After a thousand years of Roman politicians playing off one tribe against the other, the north-men got smart. They banded together and attacked in force."

'Selim and Linus the Medicus met in the city of Carthage." Cahena said to Lila. "Is that sufficient?"

"It will have to be," Lila said. "I want everyone but Ozeret and Cahena to leave the tent. Josephus, post guards outside. No one is to enter. Cahena and I must prepare for the journey. Ahmed, have the slaves bring enough water for Cahena and I to bathe. We must be clean."

Lila instructed Ozeret to make a fire, with stones around it for incense. She instructed Ahmed to open the smoke flap and place two blankets facing each other on opposite sides of the fire. Cahena and Lila bathed. It took time to clean the ashes from her long black hair.

Lila sat opposite Cahena. Both women crossed their legs under them. Lila held her hands over the flames palms down, and Cahena did the same. The rising heat prevented them from touching hands. "Ozeret," Lila said. "You must prevent anyone from disturbing us while we are on this spiritual journey. If someone does, we will die."

Lila signaled Cahena, who stared across the

fire into Lila's eyes. The two women remained with their hands raised over the fire. Ozeret moved around the fire sprinkling incense on the hot stones and rose water on the fire. It created a heavy scented smell and dulled the fire. The two pairs of hands came closer and closer as the heat diminished. Ozeret chanted incantations keeping time with a gourd rattle as her deformed body attempted to follow the rhythm.

The hands touched. The two bodies stiffened. Ozeret fell to the floor exhausted. They were on their way into the past.

Lila's right hand clasped Cahena's left hand and they arose on the smoke through the top of the tent. They weren't outside but in inside of what appeared to be a volcano. Above them a circular hole in the cone top displayed a clear blue sky. They floated up and through the hole and were outside. Cahena did not recognize the place. It might have been the foothills of the Atlas Mountains in spring. Lila's thoughts indicated they were in the Northern Maghreb and Carthage was west. They flew over hills and meadows, lakes and rivers. Their passage did not disturb the animals nor draw attention from the occasional caravan. Lila followed the main caravan trail that paralleled the Mediterranean Sea northward until the great city of Carthage came into view. "How can we find them if we don't know when and where they may have been?"

'I must contact their spirits and recall them to a time when the two men met... If they ever did meet."

"Can you do it?"

"I'm trying. Concentrate your thoughts and project them through your hand into my body." Cahena focused her thoughts in the center of her forehead. When she had gathered as much power as she could control she directed it down through her neck into her left shoulder and through her hand clasping Lila's. The effect was instantaneous. Images of the past came hurtling at them until Lila could eventually control the speed of the past. "I know what Selim looks like, but you will have to describe or show me Linus the Medicus."

"Can you find the legion? He always wears his uniform."

It took several minutes, and then images from the legion's camp began to appear. "There!" Cahena said. "The group of officers on the parade ground. The tall one with steel grey hair carrying a hooded falcon on his arm."

Lila remained silent for several minutes and the images of the past stopped. When she established contact with Linus' spirit she sought Selim's. "They did meet! Can you see them?"

"Yes, and I know exactly where they met. See the jeweled veil covering that statue? That veil is the good luck omen of the city of Carthage, and considered holy by the Berbers. It's in a public building at the southern end of the city."

"Good, now I must not be disturbed while I try to coordinate their actions and their speech. You can watch. Their voices will be garbled. Concentrate on what I say. I will translate for you."

"Selim and Linus are exchanging salutations. It appears Selim has been in contact with the Roman Legion by carrier pigeon regarding your father. The scroll he is handing to Linus is proof of your father's betrayal of Constantinople and the Roman Emperor. It is signed by one of the chief rabbis."

"What does it say?"

"Quiet! It proclaims that your father will assemble all the Berbers (one million) under the Star of David and recall the Jews from Babylon and throughout the world to march on Jerusalem and restore the Holy Temple. From what is being said Linus appears to be aware of your father's plan. He asks Selim if he can guarantee his son's compliance with the Roman administration. 'Yes,' Selim answers. 'But you must advise me how to administer the poison.' Linus explains, 'Place the seeds and the leaves on a salad plate. To the untrained eye they will blend in.' Selim asks if he can be given the poison now.

"'No, I must take the seeds and leaves at different times and send them to you by pigeons just before the wedding.' Linus then asks, 'Is it necessary to kill Moshe ben Shimi?'

"'If you want to prevent an uprising of the Jews and attack on Jerusalem. My son is not a strong personality. His wife-to-be is a dominant character. Her father controls her. I believe she will control my son.'

"'With Cahena's father dead, can you control your son?'

"'This I guarantee.'

"'You believe his wife will dominate your son yet you will control him? That's not reasonable.'

"'I will lead the Berbers.'

"'How can you lead when your son will be king?'

"'I will be king.'

"'How can that come about? Rome is not prepared to back your leadership of the Berbers without absolute guarantees.'

"'Send enough poison for two. I will be crowned king. That I promise. Before he beds that big Amazon bride he will rest next to his new father in-law. May God bless their souls.'

"'You would kill your own son?' Linus asks.

"'Your Roman emperors have done it often enough.'"

The two men clasped each other's arms and parted.

Lila and Cahena began the return journey.

Ozeret was alerted by an argument taking place outside the tent entrance. She examined the two seated figures facing each other. Their hands remained clasped and lowered into the cold ashes of the fire. Two men wearing Helawi tribal colors burst into the tent, swords drawn. Ozeret whipped out her knife and took a position between the warriors and her two charges. Josephus and Ahmed were shoved into the tent at sword point by two more warriors, followed by Selim and three rabbis.

"What do you want?" Ozeret shouted.

"To speak with our queen." Selim pointed at Cahena.

"The two women are in a trance. To disturb them guarantees their death. The Maghreb Berbers will tear you apart."

"I don't want to kill her," Selim smirked. "I wish to marry her. I am fulfilling a religious Jewish obligation."

"And we are fulfilling an ancient Berber tradition." The two Bedouin scouts and Aksil had slipped into the tent behind Selim. Two Bedouin knives pricked each of Selim's kidneys. He went pale.

"Have your men put down their weapons," Aksil commanded.

Josephus and Ahmed immediately picked up the swords. They backed the warriors and Selim out the tent entrance. Josephus called for his men to triple the guard around the tent.

An hour before cockcrow Lila and Cahena returned from their journey. They were weakened from the experience and slept until ten.

Cahena was awakened by Ozeret to eat something and meet the delegation of five Rabbis. They officially ended the period of mourning. Aksil and Josephus with a number of guards and two rabbis took Cahena on a walk around the Amazigh compound. It was the traditional reintroducing the mourner back into the community of the living. Everyone who passed bowed and wished her, "Long life." A message from Selim awaited Cahena. He requested an audience with the queen. Cahena questioned the Rabbis and they explained, "A clause in the wedding contract gave Selim the right to be your husband."

"But I thought that took place only with the brother of the deceased?"

The Chief Rabbi explained, "The institution

of Levirate Marriage, called *yibum* in Hebrew, requires that a man marry the childless widow of his brother to produce a child who will carry the deceased brother's name, so that the deceased brother will not be forgotten. This is detailed in the Book of Deuteronomy, 25:5: 'If brothers dwell together, and one of them shall die and have no child, the widow shall not be married to another man who is not his—her husband's—kin. Her husband's brother shall... come unto her, and take her to him as a wife, and perform the duty of a husband's brother unto her. And it shall be that the firstborn that she bears shall carry the name of the brother that died so that his name not be blotted out of Israel.' If the brother of the deceased refuses to marry, the widow must go to the gate of the city where the Elders sit. The Elders must call the brother to them, and if he states, 'I will not marry her', the ceremony of the Removed Sandal—*halitza*—takes place. In this ceremony the widow loosens or removes the brother-in-law's shoe, spits in his face, and says, 'So shall be done to a man who refuses to build up his brother's house.' Only after this symbolic act is the widow free to marry."

"But there is no brother," Cahena said.

"True, but Selim is invoking an ancient custom in the absence of a brother a kinsman may take on the obligation."

"Can I refuse?"

"Choice in marriage is a Berber custom for women. Judaism rules in favor of the departed."

Cahena remained silent for several minutes. No one in the tent moved or spoke. "Out!" she ordered. "I want the tent cleared. I must meditate."

Word spread through the Amazigh camp. People gathered outside the queen's tent. Two hours later Cahena appeared, and said, "Tell the Chieftain of the Helawi that I will receive him."

She instructed Aksil that only he and Josephus were to be with her when she received Selim, adding, "Send for the two rabbis now."

The Helawi chieftain arrived with his warriors and three rabbis. His face was drawn and his body tense. Aksil allowed only Selim to enter, unarmed. The young girl towered over him. He showed no fear, and said, "I assume the Levirate marriage was explained to you?"

"It was."

"Do you accept so my family name may continue in the house of Israel?"

"I accept."

"You accept!" Selim repeated. "You accept?"

"It is only proper."

"I thought you objected to me?"

"I thought you instigated my father's death."

"What made you change your mind?"

"Abraham was stopped by God from sacrificing Isaac. No Jew would kill his son, even for a kingship."

"Well, yes, that is true. I am pleased you accept me as a Jew. And surprised."

"I am bound to fulfill my father's dream. By uniting our tribes and all the Berbers, we can once again become a nation among nations."

"When would you prefer the ritual to take place?"

"Tonight. A private affair."

Selim beamed. His voice took on the tone of authority. "Of course. As you wish. Tonight then. We'll keep the celebrations at a minimum?"

"If you would be so kind."

"My chieftains and yours, with the rabbis, will make the arrangements."

Cahena nodded approval.

Fifty thousand Berbers on the Imilchil Plain watched the night sky for the first two stars. Their appearance signaled the beginning of the wedding ceremony. Selim, dressed in the most ornate groom's attire, was escorted with drums and cymbals to the wedding tent. Cahena concluded a conversation with Aksil, Josephus and Gershom.

"About an hour after midnight, have your Numidians surround the Helawi camp." She placed a stone in the palm of his hand. "This is my wish. If the Helawi do not swear allegiance to me by the old gods and the new, kill them."

Gershom looked into Cahena's eyes then down at the stone. He returned it to her. "If I understand what you intend, this is not a favor you ask. It will be my pleasure."

"The groom is approaching." Ozeret said.

Lila sought out Josephus. "Tonight, after the wedding, be certain your warriors are armed and alert. Place another forty men suited for battle within hailing distance of the wedding tent."

"What kind of trouble are you expecting?"

"The kind where men like you are needed."

"Is there anything else?"

"You might ask the Numidian king to keep his men ready."

"He has already been alerted. You can see into the future. Will it be war?"

"Possibly."

Cahena was escorted to the bridal canopy by Lila and Ozeret. The music accompanying her approach was soft and subdued. The rabbi read the wedding contract. Seven blessings were said. Cahena was escorted three times around Selim. Vows were taken, the glass broken and a joyful shout went up from the Helawi tribesman. "Long live Selim King of the Berbers!"

The Amazigh replied, "We have Cahena! Queen of the Berbers." It might have come to blows but Selim soothed his tribesmen and invited everyone to the wedding feast. Ozeret made certain that bride and groom ate from the same trays. The feast was quieter but the fare no less sumptuous than the wedding eight days before.

It was after eleven at night when Cahena said to Selim, "Isn't it time for us to retire?"

His smile almost cracked his cheeks. He announced their withdrawal to the wedding tent.

The guests formed two lines several men deep leading to the bridal tent. Josephus and Aksil were at the entrance to greet her. Cahena whispered to Josephus and he replied, "All the guards are my men. Aksil has forty more warriors nearby."

"No one is to enter the tent until I appear, no matter what sounds you hear."

Selim turned to address the well wishes, "It is time for me to bed my queen. Please give us some privacy." The people shouted well wishes and prayers for a male child. When all but Josephus's guards were gone Selim smiled, stroked his beard and took Cahena's arm. "My dear it is time to enter the nuptial bed."

Cahena brushed his hand from her arm and picked him up like a child, cradled in both her arms. "It is the Amazigh custom to carry the groom over the threshold."

"I never heard anything like that!"

"I just began the custom." She brushed through the pavilion flaps and into the center where the fire was burning. "I understand the groom must have a certain amount of stimulation before he gets an erection." Before Selim could answer she lofted him like a sack of grain onto the fire. He landed back first screaming and rolling out of the fire. Glowing coals clung to his clothing. He burnt his hands brushing them off. Cahena pulled off her bridal gown and stood naked in the firelight except for a leather belt with two holstered knives.

Selim was awed by the beauty, frightened by the fire he stammered. "What kind of Jewish ritual is this?"

Cahena stepped over the fire and slapped Selim with her right hand then her left. Over and over again and again. He threw up his hands in defense to no avail. He fell to the floor on his knees bleeding from the mouth, nose and ears. She grabbed a crop of his hair with her left hand and flattened his nose with her right fist. Still holding his hair she dragged him to his feet and slapped him until he regained consciousness. "You want to know why I am acting this way? I saw you meet with the Roman Medicus, Linus. I know you killed my father and why. But how could you murder your own son? He would have done your bidding."

Selim spit out a broken tooth. "He was weak. You would have influenced him."

"So you blame me for his death? No matter. I want to be certain you know what is going to happen to you in case there is no life after death. These two knives," she removed the knives from their holsters on either hip, "were given as wedding presents to your son and me. I will place both into your belly button and cut outward at the same time. Then I will wait until you're almost finished writhing in pain. And cut your head off. I will then bury your body without your head. Your name will be lost forever. Your tribe will become members of my Amazigh. No longer will your people exist."

Before Selim could say a word she drove the points of both knives into his navel. She drew them left and right. He doubled up and fell to his knees. His bowels poured into his hands. He looked up and begged to be killed. Cahena waited. When the pupils of his eyes begin to shrink she cut off his head.

Holding it by the hair she walked outside the tent, almost stark naked. She took a long spear from one of the guards, stuck the point through Selim's throat into his head and planted the butt of the spear in a fire. Her eyes had a wild look as she spied Aksil. She motioned him into the tent. "Josephus," she ordered, "Meet King Gershom, and help him to enlist the Helawi into the Amazigh or kill them."

"All of them?"

"That's the choice Muhammad gives."

She ordered the guards at her tent that she was not to be disturbed.

Aksil awaited her. "My queen?"

"I want to have sex with you."

Dumbstruck, Aksil stammered. "How can you think of sex now?"

"That's all I thought about since I saw you without your shirt in Devil's Canyon."

"You were only nine years old!"

"With a fine imagination. For my father's sake I accepted my first coupling with Selim's son. That was not meant to be. I want you—and I want you now."

"Your legs are covered with Selim's blood."

Cahena walked over to the large copper pot used for drinking water. It normally took two men to lift it. She raised it over her head and emptied on herself. The water washed down her glistening body. She undid the holster belt and dropped it, revealing the dark nest of her pubic hair. The thick curly hairs sparkled with drops of water like gemstones. "You are married," she said. "You must know how to do sex."

"Yes."

"You will have to explain what I am supposed to do."

Aksil undressed, revealing a muscular hairy body. He kicked off his sandals and approached her. She looked down on him but was swept up into his arms. The sensation was new. Since her childhood, few people including her father could lift her. He carried her to the bridal bed and gently laid her down on the silk sheets and feather mattress. He smiled down on her. "You are beautiful. I once asked your father to be your suitor. He said, 'Get in line.'"

"What do we do now?"

He leaned down and kissed her lips. She put her hand behind his head and kissed him. His tongue entered her lips. Their tongues met. Like a bolt of lightning both bodies were magnetized to each other. She felt his erection probing the inside of her thighs and she spread them wider.

He entered her slowly at first, a little deeper with each stroke. She felt an instant's pain, and then the most pleasurable feeling. He stroked in and out, up and down. "Faster!" she cried.

"Faster, deeper! Oh! Oh!"

She wrapped her arms around him, thrashing up and down now. She rolled over on top of him and pounded the breath out of him, both of them shouting mindlessly, then swooned. His arms dropped to his sides. She looked down at him with concern, and asked, "Are you alright?"

He nodded and smiled. "That was the most wonderful thing I ever experienced," he panted.

"Me too. Can we do it again?"

"I must wait a little while."

"I can feel it shining inside me. Can't you keep it stiff?"

"It will take a while."

"May I see it?"

"You must get off me."

Cahena rolled to her left and sat up. She lifted his limp penis and said, "It has a little hood. Jewish penises do not have that." She manipulated the foreskin up and down. "Oh," she said, "It's growing again. It's getting stronger and harder."

"You keep rubbing it like that and it will explode."

"I want it inside me."

"Get up on your knees, now bend over."

He came from behind and entered her.

"Oh! Oh, this is also nice. Keep doing it. I love this. Why did I have to wait so long?"

"Tradition."

He reached over and manipulated her nipples. Her back arched, her head came up she sighed, "Do it more. Faster. Faster!" There was another burst of mindless delight. She collapsed on the pillow. "I always wondered why women became prostitutes. This is wonderful. You have captured my liver."

"And my liver pines for you," Aksil replied

CHAPTER 18

PLANS AND PLOTS

King Gershom postponed his return to Numidia for two months. His first concern was establishing Cahena on her throne as acceptable to all the Berbers, and the only real problem came from the Helawis. Even they grew subdued upon learning the extent of Selim's crimes. Under Josephus' watchful eye, backed by Amazigh, Numidian and Aksil's warriors, Selim's tribe took an oath of loyalty to Cahena and accepted the Amazigh tribal name. It was only when they were forced to move their camp and combine with the Amazigh that real assimilation began.

Cahena returned to her former routine of healing the sick. Although most of the tribes had left the Imilchil Plateau many of the seriously ill awaited treatment from the Queen—or, as they began to call her, "The Cahena": The Priestess.

Lila, Ozeret, and several talented healers among the Shamans assisted her. The Chinese girl Mai Li was helpful in interpreting the scripts about the Chinese medicine, but she had little understanding of the Chinese medical terms. Lila, witness to this weakness, heard of a group of male oriental slaves for sale. With Mai Li to translate, she bought a nineteen year old male, Wa Ling, who had apprenticed for ten years with a Chinese apothecary. He proved himself knowledgeable in the medicines available and their application under various conditions. He attempted to explain another form of treatment using needles pricked into the body, but no one including Mai Li could make sense of what he said. He had only the rags to cover his nakedness and couldn't show them. Cahena became impatient. She ordered him to marry Mai Li, but he refused. "I am Chinese," he said. "The children of this marriage must be mine. They cannot be sold."

"Perform your work well, train two of my people in your craft, and I will apply Hebrew law to your servitude," Cahena said.

"We don't know what that means," Mai Li answered.

"After seven years he will be given the choice of going free with a year's salary and his children, or if he chooses, to remain a slave."

"As his wife, does it include me?"

"Of course. Families cannot be separated."

The two promptly agreed to the bargain.

From the first day of her rule Cahena was beset by people requesting answers regarding law, sanitation, education, and everything relating to a community. There was a never-ending line of people awaiting her decisions.

It was here the rabbis stepped in. They reminded Cahena of Moses in the desert being overwhelmed by the legal decisions, and his father in-law, Jethro the Midianite, advised him to share his labors with the elders. He would rule on that which they could not.

King Gershom reinforced the rabbi's advice. For two months he sat at her right hand. He donated the services of twenty of his best people in agriculture for two years advisory service, and as many from the military. For repair and construction of roads, bridges and sanitation, he recommended employing retired engineers from the Roman Legion living in Africa. Josephus helped with that. It was agreed that courts of law would be a parallel system of Pagan and Jewish law, with a court of arbitration available, comprising both. "Education," Gershom said, "Will determine the effectiveness and continuity of your reign. The best teachers are Jews. They teach all the males to read and write. They also preach religion to the children."

"They will also teach females," Cahena decreed.

She selected Uncle Benyamin and his brother Yeshia to administer trade by land and sea. The two rabbis, Lila and her shamans organized the courts, and the litigants would choose which court to be heard in. Cahena gave Ahmed responsibility of the tribal horse and camel herds. She freed a slave who had coordinated the pigeon stations from the Amazigh camp in the Atlas Mountains to Carthage, and from there to the Imilchil Plateau over the Southern Atlas Mountains into the Sahara Desert and Numidia, and set him in charge of training new pigeon-handlers. It took time for her people and their offices to function properly, but there was a sense of organized chaos—and the Berber people were becoming united.

The year was 628. Cahena was seventeen. She lived with Aksil but did not marry him. King Gershom remained a month longer, and was there when pigeons began to arrive with messages about Muhammad making a treaty with the Meccans.

The messages were necessarily short and did not always arrive in order, and there was confusion interpreting them. Cahena convened her counselors attempting to make sense of the situation. The agreement appeared to favor the Meccans. Yet they had been defeated in two of the three battles by the Muslims. Muhammad made unexpected concessions. What and how they applied remained unclear.

A messenger from Uncle Binyamin arrived. The caravan master sent four men to deliver it. Two died of natural causes and one was murdered on the four-month journey. They rode the fastest animals money could buy. The lone survivor was hospitalized in serious condition.

Uncle Benyamin regretted the assassination of Moshe ben Shimi and Cahena's groom, and he agreed with the death penalty for Selim—but would have preferred that, as queen of the Berbers, Cahena have had someone else inflict the penalty. "You are now ruler of a million souls," he explained. "Things that were once appropriate for you, as the daughter of a tribal chief, are deemed unsuitable in a queen.

"Now, I and my brother are honored to serve you. If it is acceptable, we prefer to work from Carthage; it is centrally located and the largest trading port in Africa. The death of your godfather Abu Abak was a shock. He was on in years, but engaged with life. He had many more stories to tell. Even Muslims were upset that the Prophet would kill such a man for telling jokes—but Muslims will not say so in public. Make no mistake; Muhammad is a very clever man. That is why most people are confused by his acceptance, or more correctly his proposal, resulting in the Treaty of Hudaybiyah.

"It is six years since the Meccans drove Muhammad and his Muslims from their holy city and the Kaaba, the prehistoric sacred Pagan shrine. This Pagan temple, sanctuary, or whatever you wish to call it, is considered the center and most important holy place in Islam, though the logic escapes me. The Prophet and his supporters yearned to see the Kaaba and make the walk around it called the *tawaf*. The Muslims may have defeated the Meccans twice, but the Prophet knows he does not have the men and equipment to launch an effective siege of the city. He tried to purchase siege engines from the Roman Legion in Carthage, but they would not sell.

"Muhammad had a dream in which he led his followers to perform the *tawaf* in Mecca, and pray by the Kaaba. This encouraged him and his followers as a test of faith to make the journey. Even though they were in a state of war with Mecca, they went unarmed with only peaceful intentions. Fifteen hundred Muslims left Medina with seventy camels to sacrifice, it being an age-old custom among the keepers of the Kaaba that all pilgrims would be allowed to worship, and free to enter Mecca without weapons. The Prophet and his group approached the smaller city of Hudaybiyah hoping to avoid a conflict. The Meccan scouts notified their leaders who sent General Khaled ibn Al Waleed with a battalion of armed troops to stop their entrance into Mecca. To avoid confrontation the Prophet changed the route, and another general with armed men was sent against the Muslims violating the age-old Arab tradition of welcoming the pilgrim. General Urwahibn Masud was impressed by the devotion of Mohamad's follower's and their desire to worship at the Kaaba. He advised his leaders, "Let them enter Mecca," but was overruled.

"The Prophet then sent an emissary to plead his case. The Meccan leaders held him by force and circulated unscrupulous reports about his intentions. They spread word that the emissary was killed in hopes the unarmed Muslims would fear a battle and retreat. Instead the Muslims prepared themselves to die. The Prophet called on his followers to fight to the death with their bare hands. Fifteen hundred men swore allegiance to Muhammad. When the people of Mecca learned of the violation of traditional access to the Kaaba and the Muslim's vow to die for their beliefs, they forced their leaders to negotiate. They returned the emissary unharmed. General Suhayl ibn Amr negotiated with Muhammad. He reached an agreement with the Prophet. It certainly favors the

Meccans; see paragraphs three and four. Yet the Prophet claimed that Allah approved; it would be all to the benefit of Islam. Indeed, Muhammad was overjoyed; for the life of me I cannot understand why. I would appreciate the opinion of others. Note that the General who recommended the Muslims be allowed to pray at the Kaaba, General Suhayl ibn Amr, was so impressed by the Prophet he converted to Islam. By the way, they were sacrificing the camels they stole from the Meccans. Here is a copy of the treaty.

"The Treaty of Hudaybiyah

"1. There will be an armistice between the two parties and no fighting for the next 10 years.

"2. Any person or tribe who wishes to join Muhammad and to enter into any agreement with him is free to do so. Likewise any person or tribe who wishes to join the Quraish (Meccans) and to enter into any agreement with them is free to do so.

"3. If any Meccans went to Medina, then Muslims would return him to Mecca, but if any Muslim from Medina went to Mecca, he would not be returned.

"4. If any young man, or one whose father is alive, goes to Muhammad without permission from his father or guardian, will be returned to his father or guardian. But if anyone goes to the Quraish of Mecca, will not be returned.

"5. This year the Muslims will go back without entering Mecca. But next year Muhammad and his followers can enter Mecca, spend three days and perform the *Tawaf*.

"This agreement goes against the demands of most Muslims, but Muhammad declared it a great victory. By virtue of his holiness and charisma people accepted his ruling. Neither they nor I can fathom the Prophet's interpretation of the agreement as benefiting Islam.

"Your Loving Uncle Benyamin and Faithful servant to Cahena, Queen of the Berbers."

For two days and nights Cahena and her advisors attempted to understand Muhammad's interpretation of victory from what appeared to be a setback. On the evening of the second day

Lila recommended Cahena send everyone home to rest. Lila then said, "It is time for you to view the Prophet."

"You mean an astral visit?"

"This you must do alone. There are certain to be others in the Muslim camp attempting to understand Muhammad's acceptance of this treaty. Listen and observe. Above all try to take the measure of the man they call the last and greatest Prophet that has been or ever will be."

Lila brewed a tea for the queen. Ozeret sprinkled incense on the stones around the fire and Cahena meditated until she went into a trance. The floating sensation was pleasant. She flew over the grassy slopes of the mountains and the snowcapped peaks of Algeria, the deserts and cities of Libya, Egypt and Arabia. By concentration, she directed her spirit to Medina.

It was a city of merchants, located on the crossroads of three major caravan trails. It was a Pagan and Christian city, with several thousand Muslims living on the outskirts. Cahena visited tents and homes with the most horses or camels tied outside. She watched and listened to the conversations. Men puffed on their hookahs and conversed.

She then visited the tent of Muhammad the Prophet. He was of medium height, broad shoulders showing his age of fifty-eight. He had lost much of his black curly hair and was grey at the temples. His sunburnt skin was paler than most Arabs His features were obviously once handsome and retained an aura of virility. His eyes were brown and clear, the brows and lashes dark and defined. His voice was impressive; he spoke distinctly and drew the listener to him. The respect given the Prophet was of the highest order, and he received it in a most humble way, but the conversation in his tent was about everyday problems similar to those Cahena had delegated to others.

She found her answers at other gatherings, and returned to her body in the middle of the night. Ozeret and Lila were waiting with food. She ate and slept until noon when she addressed her counselors and tribal chiefs.

"The Prophet Muhammad is the most respected and holiest man in Islam. He is also an astute negotiator and politician. What appears to be concessions by him in the Treaty of Hudaybiyah are actually opportunities to expand Islam, infiltrate Mecca and eventually control the Kaaba—sacred to all but Christians and Jews."

"How can that be?" a chieftain asked. "Articles three and four say any Meccan who goes to the Muslims must be returned, and a Muslim who goes over to the idol worshippers will not be returned. Article five said they cannot perform *Tawaf*."

"Listen to the Prophet's answer to your question: 'if a Muslim flees from us to Mecca we don't need him, and if a Meccan wants to be a Muslim and comes to us in Medina, we shall return him. They did not stipulate how soon. When we do return him, he will preach Islam there and make converts for us among the Meccans.' Regarding Article five, performing *Tawaf* this year, Muslims received a written guarantee to perform it next year peacefully. The Prophet was determined to avoid bloodshed, and he succeeded in establishing the Muslims' right to pray and preach Islam—next year, and for nine years hence. Even more effective was the concession of the Meccans to allow Muslims to make any alliances they wish, with whatever tribes agree."

"The Pagans are forced to agree," a Chief shouted. "That Islamic bastard holds a knife to their throat and says, 'Convert or die!'"

"There is more to the cunning of Muhammad." Cahena lowered her voice and the people leaned forward to hear. "By concluding this treaty with the Prophet, the Meccans officially recognized him as the head of the people of Medina, and Islam as its religion. They also ended the state of war between the two cities for ten years. Muslims can preach anywhere they want. They can fight anywhere they want—and the first place they chose to attack were the Jews of Qurayza, an oasis ninety miles from Medina."

"What have they got there?"

"Wealth and livestock to support larger Muslim campaigns. They are Jews who rejected the Prophet."

Cahena dismissed all but her closest counselors. She had guards posted shoulder to shoulder around her tent several meters away so they could not hear. "My father was killed because someone he trusted told Selim of his intention to unite the Berbers to attack the Romans in Jerusalem and rebuild the Holy Temple. We must be careful. I believe it was one of the three rabbis that live amongst the Helawi. There is more to what I learned on my astral journey. This is for your ears only. I want your thoughts on the matter. Why did the Prophet agree to a ten year truce with the Meccans?"

"He wanted peace," King Gershom said.

"But the Holy teachings speaks of *dar al-Islam* and *dar al-harb*. The world of Islam and the World of War. There can be no peace between Islam and non-believers. There can only be a truce. The Treaty signed in Hudaybiyah was a legal fiction to give him time, to protect what?"

"His shipbuilding in Tangiers for the attack on Constantinople," Josephus said. "The Legions have begun training for this battle. Muhammad, like any good General, is protecting his rear and supply lines by making peace with the Meccans. His followers must already be marching from Egypt, Sudan, and Libya to Constantinople."

"From as far away as India, Iran and Iraq," Gershom said. "The Prophet wants to conquer the world. That is why he is putting so much into the attack on Constantinople. The two-headed dragon called Rome has only one head remaining. If he cuts it off, the Roman world belongs to Islam."

"The Romans will not go down without a fight," Josephus said. "I heard rumors they are also building a special war fleet called triremes and experimenting with some secret fire weapon."

King Gershom called for a map. "I will revise my former statement," he said. "The Muslims from Persia, Iraq and Afghanistan, Egypt, Arabia and the Sudan will not go to Morocco and the ships. They will attack overland through Turkey to cut off supplies reaching the Romans by land. Muslims more familiar with the sea, from Morocco, Algeria and the coastline of the Maghreb, will supply the crews and fighting men for the sea assault."

"Can you be certain the Muslims will send a force by land?" Josephus asked.

"Nothing in life is certain, "the King replied, "but my spies and scouts report that General Leo, the Syrian, has taken advantage of civil strife in Turkey. He is challenging Emperor Theodosius for the throne of the eastern Roman Empire. The commander of all the Muslim forces from India to Turkey is Maslama ibn Abd al-Malik. He was a protégé of Leo the Syrian until Leo converted from Christianity to Islam. Malik is certain to make a military agreement with the Syrian and combine forces to defeat the Romans on land. Together they will sweep the land clear of Romans from Syria to Constantinople. There aren't enough Legions in the world to stop them."

"Leo the Syrian would make a good Roman senator," Josephus said. "He betrays his own people without a blink of the eye. The question he must answer is, if the Prophet will accept him as Emperor."

"If the Muslims are so well prepared," Lila asked, "why did they need a ten-year peace treaty with the Meccans?"

"Because they know the Legions are preparing to attack their naval base in Tangiers," Cahena answered. "That port city is difficult to defend and most of the Muslims there are shipbuilders and sailors, not warriors."

"The Muslims will be looking for allies," Gershom said.

"They have already approached me," Cahena said. "Their most famous general Khalid ibn Al Walid will be here within the month. If what you say is correct, he will be looking for us to fight the Romans. Constantinople has already offered us trade, land agreements and self-government."

"Let's see what the Muslims offer," Josephus said. "I trust Muhammad more than the Roman Emperor. The history of Rome is one of law, order, and subservience. If you deal with them now expect to slave for them later."

"Are the Muslims any better?" Lila asked. "They will demand your soul."

"Let us dwell on the options," Cahena said. "Side with the Romans or the Muslims?"

The debate went on past midnight. Josephus and Gershom addressed Cahena together, and Gershom spoke for the two. "Without help, Muslim land forces will never reach Tangiers in time to save the ships. The two legions are sufficient to take that city. However, the Roman forces will be isolated in hostile territory in North Africa, and eventually wiped out or evacuated by sea. All of Africa is open to you, but the Berber people are not militarily, economically or administratively prepared to conquer and rule Africa."

"What are you suggesting?"

Josephus said. "If you support the Romans and defeat the Muslims, it is only a matter of time before Rome betrays you. They will have to recall the Legions from Africa to oppose the large Muslim land army in Turkey and the Syrian turncoat. That will leave you and your people surrounded by a sea of Muslims."

"What do you suggest?"

The king responded. "You require five years to put in place a valid civil administration. The same amount of time will be needed to train your warriors as a coherent fighting force. With the addition of my army we can hold the Maghreb against the Muslims. And if the Huns or Goths try to swim over from Spain we've got enough salt water to drown them all."

"Another reason to consider what the Muslims offer," Lila said, "is that your father was assassinated because of his plan to conquer Roman-held Jerusalem. Constantinople must suspect you of the same."

That night under the bed covers Cahena

asked Aksil, "Why didn't you join in?"

"There was so much new to understand. I am still awed by your ability to fly about like a bird and listen in on people. You are planning so far ahead. I am a warrior; give me an objective and I'll take it or die."

She pulled him close. "No talk about dying. Make love."

"I'm good at that too."

CHAPTER 19

KHALID IBN AL WALID

Cahena recalled the lecture by her godfather Abu Abak, about General Khalid ibn Al Walid. She questioned her counselors for updated information, for which her uncle Benyamin was her primary source. Merchants from the island of Djerba and her two scouts contributed their knowledge.

Walid's only weaknesses were partiality to good food and fair-skinned women. On the march he ate and bivouacked with his men, and he banned camp followers. His family was the army, his God Allah, and his master, Muhammad the Prophet.

The Caravan Master wrote, "I have not met a man more dedicated to his craft as a soldier or his religion as a newly converted Muslim. I negotiated with him on several occasions selling horses, camels for his cavalry and the white pantaloons and shirts for his infantry. They are made on the island of Djerba. Roman generals in Carthage and Constantinople evaluate General Walid as the finest military planner alive. His tactics surpass Julius Cesar. They compare him to the Carthaginian, Hannibal and the Macedonian, Alexander the Great. He is straight-forward in speech, forthright in action and honest to the point of embarrassing politicians no matter who they represent. He is not a humble man, but neither is he a braggart. When he tells you about himself, believe it. There are many myths about him, all built on facts. For instance, it is true he broke nine swords in the Battle of Mutah and wore out several horses in one day. He often challenges the enemy leaders to single combat and has never lost. He loves battle, but is not bloodthirsty and hopes to die fighting as a martyr for Allah and the Prophet. He is a very powerful spokesman for Islam. During the invasion of Persia he converted twelve thousands of the Shah's elite troops to Islam. They served him in conquering that empire. In Lebanon he converted four thousand Greek Christian mercenaries. They served in the conquest of Egypt. and helped him convert Coptic Christian soldiers. Do not under any circumstance allow Walid to address your troops, people or leaders. Aside from the Prophet himself, Khalid ibn Walid is the most persuasive man you will ever meet. He is also a man of his word. So is the Prophet. If Walid speaks in the name of the Prophet be careful. Muhammad is honest; he is also a farsighted, adroit politician and strategist. The Prophet sees beyond today. Keep any written agreements brief and to the point. Consider the future effects a treaty will have on you and your people. General Khalid ibn Al Walid is known as the Sword of Allah. He makes his own decisions. You on the other hand should consult your counselors before agreeing to any pact.

Your Faithful Uncle Benyamin, Minister of Trade."

Cahena received daily reports by pigeon of General Walid's approach. She sent Josephus and Ahmed with a contingent of her personal guard to meet his column at Satan's Saddle. Upon his arrival he and his three hundred men were billeted with those Jews who kept a kosher kitchen, so the Muslims could eat without violating their dietary laws. The five-times-daily Muslim call to prayer was taken some distance from the camp so as not to waken the Berbers.

Cahena questioned Josephus and Ahmed, who were privileged to ride along with the general for three days. Ahmed through his thoughts showed Cahena a man who sat his horse with dignity and strength. His green eyes picked up the slightest defect in men, animals or equipment. On the march he cared for his own animals, cleaned and kept his own weapons.

Josephus said, "In the legion there was much talk about him. Our officers considered him the greatest military commander since Julius Caesar."

"What is your opinion of him?"

"I was awed before I met him."

"Did you ask questions?"

"He ignored them and questioned me."

"Didn't you press him?"

"You don't press the Sword of Allah. I'm a good soldier with sword or lance. Not words."

"What can I learn from his questions?"

"He wanted to know everything: the farming season, crops, water, holidays, how and by whom the roads are maintained."

"What did you tell him?"

"The truth. That's what you ordered me to do. I told him the sheep and goats made the paths and we followed, and that's how they became roads. He asked about everything except our army."

"Because he already knows,"

"How can he know?"

"Spies."

"Among the Amazigh?"

"We've absorbed the Helawi and their allies."

"When you drag in garbage you're bound to

get dirty. How many?"

"Ahmed knows of two Muslim agents."

"You want me to take care of them before or after the General leaves?"

"Neither. Watch them. There may be others. The spies you know are worth more than the ones you don't. We will use them to pass on information we want General Walid to have."

"If your children come out as smart as you, they will rule all of Africa."

"Did Ozeret tell you I was pregnant?"

Josephus' jaw dropped. From his reaction and fluttering hands Cahena realized her mistake. She pointed at him and laughed. "I never saw you so off balance. Most girls my age have babies."

"But you're the queen," he stammered.

"Queens get pregnant."

"They usually have kings."

"Aksil doesn't want to convert. Unless he's a Jew, we can't marry."

"Why not? You aren't that observant."

"I promised my father to marry in the faith and name the first male child after his father."

"Won't that be a problem if we become involved in a war?"

"Berber women have been going to war when pregnant since forever."

"The blacksmith will have to let your armor

out in the front."

"That's his problem. Let us decide about General Walid."

A crier went before General Khalid ibn Al Walid and his guard of ten warriors, astride coal-black stallions in full burnished armor with sheathed swords, reins in the left hand, javelin in the right. The crier preceded the Muslim delegation on their way to Cahena's tent, announcing:

"When Allah decides a matter, it is done.

Our lives are dedicated to the way of Allah, Most High. Man intends one thing, but Allah intends another.

If you are truthful you will survive. If you lie you shall perish.

I am Khalid bin Al Walid the Sword of Allah!

I am the son of many chiefs. My sword is sharp and terrible. It is the mightiest of things. When the pot of war boils fiercely I am grateful.

I am the pillar of Islam! I am the Companion of the Prophet! I am the warrior, Khalid bin Al Walid!

I have received with gladness the invitation of your Queen. There is no resentment in my heart, for I know of her beauty and skill in matters of the Berbers.

We give tribute to the brave Berber warriors whose mounts carry lions in shining armor to meet their enemies.

"General Khalid ibn Walid will apportion three days to reach an agreement with the Cahena. If terms are not negotiated by then, it is the will of Almighty God."

"He thinks quite well of himself, "Ozeret said.

"He has every right," Josephus replied.

"Tie the tent flaps lower so he must bow his head to enter." Cahena ordered.

The tent flap was slashed by one of the general's guards. In walked the Sword of Allah, erect, shoulders thrown back and eyes taking in everything. He stood five foot nine inches, square head, face and body. His trimmed, dark curly beard and hair framed a sun-burnt face, clear green eyes and straight white teeth. He pointed to the torn tent flap, bowed to Cahena and said, "I bend my knee to a queen, not a tent."

"You have negotiated before, I am new at this," Cahena said demurely.

"How could it be otherwise? You are only seventeen years in this world."

"Please approach and explain why you have traveled so far and can remain only three days?" Cahena pointed to a chair next to hers. When seated most people appear to be the same height, but when standing she would towered over him. One mistake with the tent entrance was enough; she did not want to insult Islam's champion again. She remained seated. "We Berbers heard of General Khaild's ventures, and hoped to have more than three days of your company."

"I must be off to reinforce the city of Tangiers against the Romans."

"With only three hundred men?"

"They are all Muslims."

"The two legions from Carthage number four thousand."

"That is why I came to you."

"You want me to help you defeat the Romans?"

"Exactly."

"Have you any idea what they offered me to support them?"

"Yes. And I have permission from the Prophet to offer the same terms on your governing the Maghreb, shipping, trade and a five year truce. You will not have to become a tax collector for Islam as the Romans require."

"What if the Romans send ten more legions? They would defeat my people, take Tangiers and destroy your ships."

"They haven't ten more legions to send. The Vandals and Huns threaten Constantinople from the west. A Muslim army is already on its way overland from the east. They come from

India, Persia, Iraq and Arabia. They will be joined by warriors from Egypt numbering more than one hundred thousand fighting men."

"And they are going to blockade Constantinople?"

"By land. Our troop ships will soon be joined by fighting ships from Italy. Constantinople will be cut off by sea. That city will bow to the will of Allah."

"What will happen if I support the Romans?"

"I will die in Tangiers and consider it an honor. The Prophet will view your action as a betrayal. He will change the route of the land army and flood the Maghreb with Muslims. He will call on fifty thousand more of our faithful from Ethiopia and the Sudan. Africa will become a Pagan graveyard and a Muslim country."

Cahena expected the negotiations to be far less direct. General Walid stared unblinking at her expecting an answer. She felt off balance and replied, "I must consult my advisors. We shall meet again in the morning." Now she purposely stood and looked down at General Walid. He stood and still had to step back and look up at her.

He bowed and said, "I hope you are as intelligent as you are tall."

Cahena sorely missed King Gershom. In his

place she added three of her brightest chieftains as counselors. All but Lila were against accepting the Muslim offer. They wanted to join the Romans and sack Tangiers. Josephus was uncommitted It was sunrise when Cahena decided to postpone her meeting with General Walid until that evening. She sent everyone to rest and return with their recommendations.

Cahena had Ozeret prepare incense as she wished to mediate. She fell into a deep dream-filled sleep. Her journey was not in space but in the ideas that challenged her people. She was able to view the thoughts from outside of herself and from the point of view of the Prophet, Muhammad. He was playing the long game with the destinies of nations and a desire to conquer the world. She, on the other hand, was the defender of the Berber people. Over one million souls depended on her decision. She slept till after the Muslim noon call to prayer. Convened her counselors and called on the chieftains to present their view.

"We should refuse the offer of General Walid," the spokesman for her generals said. "He is an impressive man and a champion among warriors, but he said if we don't support him against the Romans he and his men will die and Tangiers will fall. It took five years for the Muslims to build their fleet. If they want to defeat Constantinople they will need ships to do it. That will take another five years to build. By that time the Roman army could rebuild itself to its former strength. We would be in charge of the Maghreb's military, economics, agriculture and military. I don't like the role of tax collector for the Romans, but their roads, sanitation and longevity of their citizens are the marvel of the modern world. If we Berbers are to establish a dynasty for the ages, we must increase the lifespan of our citizens. Our advice is to cast our lot with the Emperor in Constantinople. Join the Romans in conquering Tangiers and return with the booty of that city."

Cahena motioned Lila forward. The chief sorceress bowed to the queen and said, "There is much to agree with in what has just been said. Yet I am for joining the Muslims—and not because I believe in their Prophet or religion. Muhammad is a dreamer. He is dangerous to all non-Muslims. He offers a truce with us Pagans not peace. He cannot offer peace. It is against his holy teachings. There it is written *dar al-harb* and *dar al-Islam*: either the world of war or the world of Islam. Why then do I recommend we side with the Prophet against the Romans? If you believe General Walid, the Prophet will ensure five years of peace."

One of the chiefs interjected, "The Romans

offer ten years."

"I don't trust the Romans."

"Neither do I," Josephus said.

"To side with Constantinople," Lila said, "is to support a religious monarchy. Rome is no longer a republic. Its emperor is a considered infallible. His Christian god is infallible. We Berbers are Pagans, many are Jews."

"Why do Christians and Muslims hate Jews?" a chieftain asked.

"They both thought the Jews would come over to their faith," Lila said. "The Jews would have none of it. As long as the Jews exist they are witness that both those faiths birthed from Israel are false."

"The subject is not Jews," Cahena said. "Why do you recommend going with the Muslims?"

Lila adjusted her robe and said, "If you believe as I do, Muhammad will divert the land force of one hundred thousand warriors from Constantinople to Africa, and send another fifty thousand from the Sudan and Ethiopia, Africa will become Muslim. The Romans will be wiped out and we Berbers will pray five times a day or fertilize the Maghreb. To side with the Romans is only to delay the inevitable. Rome's rule is about to end."

Cahena motioned Josephus forward. "I

agree and disagree with both views. On the one hand Lila is right. One hundred and fifty thousand Muslims entering Africa, even the lions and sheep will kneel to Allah and his Prophet. On the other hand, that is one hell of an overland march. The Prophet is depending on civil strife in Turkey to weaken the Roman forces in his march through that country. To accomplish this, the Prophet signed an agreement with King Leo the Syrian. The Roman Army considers Leo a snake and would never take his word on anything, and less his signature on any document. It is true Syria is at odds with Rome. It is more economic a conflict than a political or military dispute; It has to do with Leo keeping all the tax money from Syria and the Lebanon. The Muslims have interpreted civil unrest as a revolution, but it is not. And if King Leo refuses to help the Muslims fight their way through Turkey, the Prophet is going to fertilize a lot of Turkish land with his people."

"Don't forget the murder of your godfather Abu Abak by Muhammad's personal order," a chieftain said.

"My godfather's murder will never be forgotten or forgiven. We also remember it was the Romans who supplied Selim with the poison and idea to murder my father and my husband. The Torah teaches us there is a time for everything. Now is not the time for revenge." Cahena sat on a raised platform in a large ornate chair. She looked at her advisors. "Thank you for your advice. I will now meditate on the matter." She closed her eyes and was silent. No one had permission to leave. Ten, twenty minutes passed then a half an hour, and she opened her eyes. "To ally the Berber people with the Romans would result in short term benefits. Such as the looting of Tangiers and ruling until the great Muslim army arrived. General Walid requires an answer. The Muslim army has just marched through Persia and is on the outskirts of Iraq. It must turn right to reach Turkey and left to cross through Arabia, Egypt and Libya to invade our Africa. An army that large will denude the land in a short time. They must remain on the move. I believe the threat of invasion by the Muslim army to be a real danger. We are not prepared to face an army that size in so short a time. If Josephus is correct regarding King Leo the Syrian, and Leo aborts his agreement with Muhammad, the Muslims will either be wiped out or too busy saving themselves to think of us. If the Muslims succeed in launching their ships with fifty thousand Ethiopians and Sudanese, more power to them. I wish them success in the siege of Constantinople. There will be less Muslims in Africa to deal with.

Assuming Islam defeats the Christian Roman Empire, they will be so involved in converting and killing Christians. and at the same time trying to administer a caliphate with one hand and fight off the Huns, Vandals and Northmen with the other. They won't have time for us."

"What if the Muslims lose?" a chieftain asked.

"We still gain. The Prophet will have lost a major war and won't be looking for another one with us. The Romans will have suffered the siege and be weakened. That will encourage the European tribes to attack them. They will leave us alone for years to come. In the meantime I will depend on you to build us an army that has the flexibility of Berber style combat combined with the discipline of the Roman military and the dedication of the Muslims to their god."

"My Queen," the chieftain said. "You have made a decision to side with the Prophet. It is said you can see into the future. What awaits us?"

"I have the power to glimpse the future. What I see is not always what will be. No one understands everything. It is best for Berbers to support the Prophet."

That afternoon camels and sheep were slaughtered for a feast. Three hundred Muslims warriors were hosted by three hundred Amazigh. Cahena hosted General Walid, his staff and her counselors.

"Did you enjoy the prostitutes?" she asked.

"Your young women exceed their reputation. What happens to them when they get too old for the trade?"

"That is rare. Most are married by age eighteen. They are much sought after as wives."

"In Islam prostitutes are shunned."

"Why?"

"A wife must come to the bridal bed as a virgin."

"And the man?"

"His virginity is not questioned."

"Does he relieve himself by hand?"

"That is forbidden."

"In the study of Bible, that which is forbidden is taking place."

"He goes to prostitutes."

"Which Muslim enjoy. Then they curse these women who satisfied the man's lust."

"It is the will of Allah."

"How many wives has the Prophet?"

"He only had one until Khadija died. Now he has ten more."

"Is that also Allah's will?"

"Yes. But I suggest you refrain from expressing your thoughts about the Prophet's many wives. I might have to kill you as you did your husband, Selim of the Helawi."

"Thank you for the warning. Your terms for opposing the Romans are acceptable under certain conditions."

"They are?"

"I can only field thirty thousand fighting men."

"I am leaving tomorrow to visit Numidian King Gershom. He has a trained army of twenty thousand cavalry and twice as many light infantry."

"If I can secure the Numidian participation on your side will you accede to my requests?"

"I must first hear your wishes."

"No Muslims may enter the Maghreb or the Atlas mountains, from the Algerian and Libyan borders to the Mediterranean in the west and to the Atlantic Ocean in the south. This is Berber territory from now on. They will require my permission."

"I cannot give you that pledge. I have fifty thousand troops on their way from Ethiopia and the Sudan, to board our ships in Tangiers. They must enter the Maghreb to access that port."

"I will give my permission if you agree no Muslim shall proselytize within those boundaries. That includes you."

"That I can accept."

"Not good enough." Cahena said. "Your people are much like Vikings. It's your greatest wish to die in *Jihad* (holy war) as a *Mujahedeen* for Allah and the Prophet."

"What do you suggest?"

"Make it mandatory that anyone preaching Islam in my territory along with their family will be dishonored, purged and called a deserter from Islam."

"That is a most terrible thing," Walid said.

"I am not negotiating. If you want the Numidians to join us against the Romans that is my first demand."

"How can you speak for King Gershom a thousand miles away?"

Cahena held out her right hand with a small gray river stone in her palm and explained.

"I accept that you can bring the Numidians to assist us in the taking of Tangiers. What other demands have you?"

"All that you have said regarding trade, a government by me of the entire Maghreb and the Atlas Mountains without tax collecting. I wish a ten year truce."

"That cannot be."

"Why not?"

"The Prophet received his instructions from God and I from the Prophet. Five years is what I can grant."

"Then your Imams will flood our land preaching Islam."

"The future is in Allah's hands. What else can I give you?"

"General, you have nothing to give. It is I who will be saving you and your fleet of ships."

"And only I who can prevent your people and land from becoming a vassal state of the new Muslim Empire. Is there anything else you wish?"

"Yes. In the defense of Tangiers the Numidians and Berbers will each receive one Roman gold coin for each man who marches."

"That is acceptable. But payment will come when we have gathered the funds."

"Payment within a year?"

"Yes."

Lila whispered in Cahena's ear. She listened then asked, "What happens to this treaty if you or Muhammad dies?"

For the first and only time General Khalid ibn Walid was taken aback. He organized his thoughts. The silence weighed heavy. "I welcome a death in battle. As for the Prophet, he is a man. I never thought of him dying. But one day he must leave us. All agreements accepted by me in his name will be honored. I was a Pagan most of my life. I have seen what shamans can do. I respect Lila. Has she seen into the future?"

"No," Cahena said. "She is also a good negotiator and asks that this be included in our treaty.

"Do so. I will sign in the name of Muhammad, may he be blessed."

"When your forces leave Tangiers, that city and all the cities along the Atlantic sea coast and inland will pay yearly tribute to King Gershom and the Numidians. All the cities along the Mediterranean Sea will pay tribute to me and my Berber state."

"Does that include Carthage?"

"Especially Carthage. The Roman garrison will try to defend it. We will take the city and other cities along the coast. My people will loot and take slaves."

"You will milk it like the Golden Calf for many years."

"Only five years, then you Muslims come hungering for our souls."

"You will eventually convert to Islam. It is the truth. Your gods are false."

Cahena held up her hand. "You agreed, no preaching."

"It is difficult to know the truth and talk with one so bright who is misled by idols who cannot see, speak or hear your prayers."

"That quote comes from the Torah. I have

one more request. As an expert in military tactics how best can we defeat the legions?"

"Then we have an agreement?"

"My scribes will put it in writing for your approval. Meanwhile please share your knowledge on tactics against the Romans."

General Walid was still giving instructions when he climbed into the saddle the following morning. "Don't rely on written communication by horse. Use a combination of smoke, reflecting mirrors and your pigeons during the day, fire or Chinese rockets at night. I will leave some rockets with you."

He bowed, "I pay homage to Queen of the Berbers who represents her people well. May Allah's blessing be upon you and your warriors and we next meet in victory on the field of battle."

"Sound the drums of war! Let word go out to every Berber, Bedouin and Tuareg," Cahena announced. "Their Queen summons them to war against the Byzantine Empire. We fight the Romans with the aid of General Khalid ibn Al Walid."

"I never expected to fight the Romans," Aksil said. "I thought the threat was from the Muslims."

"It is. We've made a temporary truce. In five years we will be fighting Islam. Do you and

Josephus recommend Walid's plan for combating the legions?"

"We do. He is utilizing our strengths and minimizing our weaknesses," Aksil said. "We Berbers are not good in pitched battles. Walid understands that is the Roman strength. They become a killing machine from their formations. The expanded five tribes of Amazigh can harass their supply and communication lines on the long march to Tangiers. Only when the Roman soldiers break formation to attack us do we respond. We pick up tribes along the Roman line of march. These tribes can feed us and join in expanded attacks. When we leave their tribal area they remain, and we absorb the next tribe using the same tactics, until we approach Tangiers. There King Gershom will be waiting. He'll have his heavy infantry on the Roman left flank and his light Cavalry hidden along the coast on the right flank. Our cavalry and men will be attacking from behind, and General Walid will be there with his men in Tangiers blocking the head of the Roman column."

"Can we be certain which route the Romans will take?"

"They built a thousand miles of road from Carthage to Tangiers," Josephus said. "It parallels the sea."

Cahena ordered, "Send agents and pigeons

to warn the people along the Roman line of march. They must hide their food and abandon their villages. When we come along there will be food for us. Order fishermen to either sail away in or destroy their boats, nets and equipment. Ahmed, you are expert in sign language. Set up signal systems from the hilltops. Aksil, you will be my military liaison to the chieftains. Work with Josephus in training our warriors. Lila, use your shamans to keep us informed of the Romans and attitudes amongst our people. Work with Ozeret and the Chinese couple in setting up a medical group to treat the wounded and bury the dead. We are going to war."

CHAPTER 20

THE COMBATANTS

Josephus expected the Legions to send out small units of men and animals with food and money, to purchase supplies in advance for the troops along the one thousand mile line of march from Carthage to Tangiers. They would establish hidden caches, located eighty miles or four days march apart. The men carried five days rations of wheat, beans and chickpeas, a flask of oil and a mess kit, one skin canteen of water and one of sour wine. They carried shields, weapons, wicker baskets for moving earth and a spade or pick, a woolen cloak, a blanket, and two wooden staves. The staves were sharpened and used to build a protective palisade at every bivouac. The shovels and baskets were used to dig a trench in front of the palisade to disrupt attacks. This was done every night and took between two and five hours to construct. The legion stopped marching during daylight to build their fortification, unless they had not covered their basic twenty miles. It would take fifty days to reach Tangiers

By pigeon Josephus informed his people to warn the villages along the Carthage-Tangiers road to flee the Roman advance. Pagans in the Maghreb had expected the Muslims. Suddenly it was the Christians. They obeyed the Queen's orders.

Josephus hunted down the road from Carthage paralleling the sea, searching for flat areas of at least two hectares square. The area he sought had to be located away from towns, and have sufficient fresh water for two legions of ten thousand men, six hundred cavalry, supply personal and their animals. That was the ideal location to bivouac, preferably with trees nearby for fire-wood. The centurion in charge of hiding the food caches in advance of the Legions would be looking for the same thing. Josephus briefed his spies on how and where to find these secret storage sites, and sent them out with a caravan heading west. Before leaving, Cahena gave them the names of villages where she had established pigeon stations. She also sent Amazigh prostitutes to join the Legion's camp followers and spy.

The Roman base camp outside of Carthage was put to the torch. Everything that could be utilized by an enemy was destroyed. Outposts throughout Africa were required to dispatch twenty percent of their fighting force to the Seventh and Ninth Legions, but the commanders of the outposts sent their weakest and most troublesome men. Three-quarters of the Roman force were not Italians; many were former enemies, forced to serve sixteen years in the army. These two legions had a four-hundred-year history of fighting for the empire. Behind the Golden Eagle were tens of banners awarded in honor of the services performed in battle by the legionnaires. Legatus Remo and Legatus Claudius addressed their legions separately with the same message.

"Legionnaires, we who brought peace and prosperity to Africa, clean water to its cities and towns, prosperity to its merchants and a better life to its people, are betrayed by those who benefited most. The Berbers, Tuaregs and Bedouin have declared themselves enemies. They will help the Muslim General Khalid ibn Al Walid to defend Tangiers. There a mighty Muslim fleet is being built to transport their warriors to attack our capital of Constantinople.

"We will attack Tangiers. It is a port city, and its wealth will be yours—plus the tribute from every town and village along the way. Then we will swing east and decimate the villages, towns and cities along the Atlantic coast. And there in the desert we will find the rich oases of the nomads—Known to you as Numidians. They have wealth beyond calculation. They are a formidable fighting force, but with two and a half legions we will chew them up and spit them out like pomegranate seeds.

"A letter from the Prophet Muhammad to Heraclius our Emperor reads; 'In the name of Allah, the Beneficent, the Merciful, this letter is from Muhammad the slave of Allah and his Apostle to Heraclius, the ruler of the Byzantines. Peace be upon him who follows the right path. Furthermore, I invite you to Islam and if you become a Muslim you will be safe, and Allah will double your reward, and if you reject this invitation of Islam you will be committing a sin by misguiding your subjects. And I recite to you as Christians, Allah's statement: "O People of the Scriptures! Come to a word common to you and us that we worship none but Allah and that we associate nothing in worship with Him, and that none of us shall take others as Lords beside Allah. Then if they turn away, say: Bear witness that we are those who have surrendered to Allah. We will defeat you.'"

The legion commanders continued, "When we capture this Prophet, as Christ and Minerva are my witnesses, I will personally shove this letter up his Muslim arse. Sound the trumpets, roll the drums. Seventh Legion: forward march! Ninth Legion: forward march!"

The noncombatants, foragers, and supply wagons followed with horse herds, sheep and goats. Traders, prostitutes and other camp followers brought up the rear of each column. The two legions marched independently of each other, commanded by men of equal rank: Legatus Remo and Claudius. Both aspired to the Roman senate, and glory in war would assure that position.

Approaching Tangiers, Khalid ibn Walid sensed a disaster in the making. No scouts or sentries challenged his three-hundred-man unit. Garrisons outside the cities were undermanned, the men sloppy in dress, cleanliness and everything military. He hung the first three commanders. Word preceded him and conditions improved.

Not so in Tangiers itself. He found soldiers out of uniform, carousing, drinking forbidden wine with civilians. Some guards even worked on the ships to earn extra money when they were supposed to be standing guard.

Public floggings reversed that. Training schedules were set. Twenty percent of the work force were selected by his officers to train for the ranks. He made it clear that work schedules would be maintained. The fleet would sail on time. His men educated the new recruits in a grueling program of exercises, with the javelin and long spear, to repel infantry and cavalry. They learned to march, form battle formations, and dig trenches to break up attacking enemy forces. They camouflaged traps on the approaches to the city; hidden underneath were pointed wooden shafts to kill horses and men. They learned to respond without thought to verbal commands, signal flags, or blasts on the ram's horn.

General Walid would place the weakest of them in the center of his formations, backed by his best men who would cut them down if they hesitated to engage the enemy. As construction of the ships was completed, more men became available to take up arms. His force expanded to three thousand new recruits.

He received word of a change in plan from Cahena; Josephus was to travel ahead of the Roman legions and raid their food caches. Aksil was more in tune with the Berbers method of fighting; he would lead the horsemen of the Maghreb. They were already on their way from the foothills of the Atlas Mountains. Aksil led five thousand horsemen onto the plains, and Cahena followed with several thousand. Like the snow-melt tributaries of the great mountain range, Berbers poured down the hillsides and through the valleys and waited along the roads to join Cahena's Army.

Berbers, Tuaregs, and Bedouin from the desert joined. Hearts swelled with pride. Men sat straight in the saddle, determination in the set of their jaw and glint in their eyes. By the time they bypassed Carthage, the ground shook from the weight of thirty thousand horsemen. Berber villagers came out of hiding to offer food, throw flowers, and sprinkle the warriors with rose water for luck. The heart of every man and woman swelled to bursting. Even their horses trotted to the chant.

> *"Cahena! Cahena! Cahena! We follow Cahena!*
>
> *We are her children. She is our light.*
>
> *We walked in darkness, but never in fright.*
>
> *We see the future with her as our guide.*
>
> *The gods will all bless us and fight on our side."*

From the lowest water carrier and hewer of wood to the greatest warrior, they felt themselves on a holy mission to throw off the Roman yoke and establish a kingdom of their own—to be a free people once again.

Josephus angled down from the mountains to get ahead of the Roman legions. He pushed his men and horses to exhaustion, traded and bought new mounts for his five hundred warriors. These men were selected by Aksil for their ferocity, experience in theft and smuggling. Josephus called in his spies; they told of known food caches and suspected Roman stores buried ahead of the legions. Of those storage sites unproven, he asked one question: "Where do the men dressed as civilians shit?"

If answered, "All over the place," he dismissed it. When questioned, he explained, "Roman soldiers may do many things, but they always dig latrines. Anyone not using it gets his arse painted with turpentine. Those who shit in the same place might be dressed as civilians, but they are from the legions. These we attack."

His officers questioned, "If we dig up the Roman supplies and haul them away, we'll leave a trail a blind man can follow. You told us the Romans have six hundred cavalry for each legion; they'll find us."

"Cahena made arrangements. Be certain to bring the Chinese rockets."

Cahena and her chieftains roamed up and down the ten-mile-long column of men, animals, and supply wagons. People of the tribes were conditioned to this lifestyle, but never a caravan so large.

Cahena regularly inspected the medicine tent. Although Ozeret was in charge, it was the two Chinese slaves who ran the unit. There she saw the Chinese male slave walking with a strange instrument, and thought it something to do with medical care. She described it to Aksil. "It's called a crossbow," he said. "I've heard talk of them by people who traveled the Silk Road."

"What advantage does it have over the regular bow?"

"It takes a year to train a mediocre longbowman: two years for him to hit a target at sixty yards, and a lifetime to hit a moving target at that range. They say a man can learn to shoot the crossbow in an hour, and become good at forty yards in a week."

"The arrow for the crossbow is shorter, about the size of Numidian arrows."

"That's good. They can use the enemy's longer arrows, but the enemy cannot use theirs."

"Who can fire more rapidly?"

"I don't know."

"Have two crossbows made and find out."

A rider handed Cahena a message that originated from the island of Djerba, from her uncle Saul: "My boats are moving into position. My brother Benyamin sends his best. May God bless you in all your undertakings. Your Humble Servant, Saul."

In 628 CE Khaybar was an oasis of fourteen thousand Jews and several thousand Pagans. In the battles with the Prophet the residents fought against the Messenger of Allah. There being no mention of Khaybar in the truce with the merchants of Mecca, the Prophet felt obligated to take revenge against the Jews for not accepting Islam and opposing his army. The Messenger of Allah besieged them for twenty days, and broke down their fortifications one by one. The strongest of these, with the most fighters, was a stronghold called al-Qumus.

Musa Bakr took the Islamic banner to lead the Muslims in battle. He returned defeated. The next day Umar ibn al-Khattab carried it. He too suffered defeat. This enraged the Apostle of Allah, who said: "I shall give the banner tomorrow to one who attacks, and does not retreat. He is one who loves Allah and His Apostle, and whom Allah and His Apostle love. He shall not return until Allah opens Khaybar at his hands."

Next morning people gathered around the Messenger of Allah. Sa'id ibn Abi Waqqas reported: "I sat facing him; I knelt, then stood up. He turned to me and said: 'Call Ali for me.' Men cried out all around: 'He is so sore-eyed that he is unable to see the ground under his feet!' The Prophet replied: 'Send someone to bring him here.' He was brought, and the

Prophet laid Ali's head on his knee and spat in his eyes. Immediately they became as clear as Yemenite glass beads."

The Prophet then gave Ali the banner and prayed for him. "Ali went out running," Sa'id said. "By Allah, even before I had reached the last men in the line of fighters, Ali had already entered the enemy stronghold." Jabir ibn Abdallah al-Ansari added: "He did not even allow us enough time to put on our armor. Sa'id cried out: 'O Abu 'l-Hasan, stop and wait awhile until the men are able to join you!' But Ali went on until he fixed the banner near the stronghold.

"A Jew called Marhab came out to meet him in single combat. He was well armed and surrounded by other Jewish fighters. Ali met him and they fought until Ali struck him with his sword, and cut off his leg. He fell down, and Ali with the other Muslims rushed at him, but he and his Companions fled quickly. Ali reached the gate of the stronghold, which was shut in his face. He pulled it off its hinges and used it as a shield. He then carried it on his back and broke into the fortification with great force. The Muslims then attacked. Ali threw the gate away from him, while a crier went out to announce to the Messenger of Allah that Ali had entered the fortification. The Messenger of Allah hastened to the spot and Ali went out to meet him. The Prophet said: 'I have learnt of your welcome news and your worthy deeds. Allah is well pleased with you, and I too am pleased with you.' Ali wept, and the Prophet asked: 'What makes you weep?' 'I weep for joy,' 'Ali answered, 'because Allah and His Messenger are well pleased with me'."

It is reported that among the captives whom Ali took was the beautiful Jewess, Safiyyah, who was wife of the leader of the Jews. Ali sent her to the Apostle of Allah, so that he might decide what to do with her. She was taken past her dead family on the way to the Messenger of Allah. Her husband, the Jewish leader, Kinana, was tortured and beheaded. She nearly died of weeping for them. The Prophet then chose Safiyyah for himself; he freed her and married her.

It is reported that after the Messenger of Allah had concluded the affair of Khaybar, he raised a banner of war and demanded: "Who will rise and take this, and be worthy of it?" He did this because he wished to send an army to join those from Persia, India and Egypt on their way to Turkey, where they would be joined by the King of Syria to lay siege to the capital city of Constantinople. The Prophet then said: "O Ali, rise up and take this standard!" He took it and set out. The Prophet then sent his Imams to Medina and other Pagan cities to preach the Holy teachings.

Josephus called in his chieftains and explained the strategy planned by Cahena, General Khalid, Aksil and himself. On the tent floor he drew a long line, and said: "This is the thousand-mile route of march for the two Legions. Cahena, with our largest force, is traveling behind the Romans. She will attack their baggage trains and food supplies, and avoid pitched battles. There will be fifteen buried caches of food for the legions along the line of march; each will be four days or eighty miles apart. We will sprint ahead and attack those caches two weeks in advance of the Legions. They will be hesitant to send their mounted troops to protect the other caches, but we will continue our attacks until they do."

"Then we attack them!" A chieftain said.

"No. We run." Josephus gave his broadest tooth-filled smile.

"Run?! I want to kill them!"

"And you will. We draw them to Tangiers, where General Walid will block the advancing Roman cavalry. They will have outrun their supporting infantry by then. King Gershom's Numidian cavalry of fifteen thousand will meet us and seal off the Roman left flank. With the sea at the Romans' backs, they have no option: fight and be defeated by the Numidian horse, or swim."

"They can retreat to their columns."

"Who is behind them?" Josephus asked.

"Cahena."

"Cahena will move her Berber horsemen forward to seal the trap. The Roman infantry will be too far away to come to their aid."

"Josephus, I asked this question before, and your answer was Chinese rockets. How can we avoid leaving a trail to where we hide the stolen supplies? Their cavalry scouts will easily track us."

"You are right, and my answer remains the same. Bring the rockets."

After the conquest of Khaybar, Muhammad declared a celebratory feast. Among those in the kitchen was a Jewess, Zeynab bat Harith. Women of beauty were spared to become slaves and concubines, though her family—along with ten thousand other Jews—had been massacred. She poisoned the lamb served to the Prophet. He ate a little and felt ill. Bishr ibn al-Bara, sitting to his right, died from the effects of this food. Zeynab was brought before the Prophet and asked why she did such a thing.

She answered, "My father and husband were leaders among the Jews. You killed them. You killed my children. That gave me the idea. But I wanted to find out the truth, If you are really a Prophet of God. Alas, he saved you."

"I have heard the following," said Shayk Muhammad Saalih al-Munajjid. "The Prophet ate two mouthfuls, then Allah caused the sheep to speak and tell the Messenger that it was poisoned."

The Prophet recovered. The woman was executed, and the Messenger of Allah addressed a more pressing problem.

In 628 CE, the Meccan tribe of Quraysh and the Muslim community in Medina signed a 10-year truce called the Treaty of Hudaybiyah. According to the terms, the Arab tribes were given the option of joining either of the parties, the Muslims or the Meccans. Should any of these tribes face aggression, the party to which it was allied would have the right to retaliate. As a consequence, Banu Bakr joined the Meccans, and Khuza'ah joined Muhammad.

They thus lived in peace for some time, but ulterior motives—mostly blood-feuds, stretching back for generations—triggered fresh hostilities. Banu Bakr, without concern for the provisions of the treaty, attacked Banu Khuza'ah in a place called Al-Wateer in Sha'ban. The Meccans helped Banu Bakr with men and arms. Pressed by their enemies, the tribesmen of Khuza'ah sought the Holy Sanctuary of the Kaaba, but here too, their lives were not spared; contrary to all accepted traditions, Nawfal, the chief of Banu Bakr, chased them in the sanctified area—where no blood should be shed—and massacred his adversaries. Khuza'ah at once sent a delegation to Medina to inform Muhammad of this breach of truce and to seek help from the Muslims of Medina.

After the incident, the Meccans sent a delegation to Muhammad, petitioning to maintain the treaty with the Muslims and offering material compensation, but the Muslim forces had gathered in strength to settle accounts with Mecca. Muhammad assembled a large army. The objective of the operation was kept secret, and even Muhammad's close friends and commanders did not know his plans. Muhammad intended to assemble and attack the Meccans by surprise. For further secrecy, Muhammad sent Abu Qatadah towards Batan Izm as a diversion.

The Muslim army set out for Mecca on Wednesday, the 6th of Ramadan. Volunteers and contingents from allied tribes joined the Muslim army on the way, swelling its size to about 10,000 strong—the largest Muslim force ever assembled in Arabia. The army stayed at Marr-uz-Zahran, located ten miles northwest of Mecca, where Muhammad ordered every man to light a fire so as to make the Meccans overestimate the size of the army. Meanwhile, Abu Sufyan ibn Harb travelled back and forth between Muhammad and Mecca, still trying to reach a settlement in order to avoid a battle. He found assistance in Muhammad's uncle Al-Abbas.

Mecca lies in the Valley of Ibrahim, surrounded by black rugged hills reaching heights of 1,000 feet. There were four entry routes through passes in the hills, from the north-west, the south-west, the south, and the north-east. Muhammad divided the Muslim army into four columns, one to advance through each pass. The main column, in which Muhammad traveled, was commanded by Abu Ubaidah ibn al-Jarrah. It was tasked to enter Mecca through the main Medina route, from the north-west near Azakhir.

Their tactic was to advance simultaneously from all sides, targeting a single central objective: the Kaaba. This would lead to the dispersion of enemy forces and prevent their concentration on any one front. Another important reason for this tactic was that even if one or two of the attacking columns faced stiff resistance, and became unable to break through, the attack could continue from the other flanks. This would prevent any of the Meccans from escaping.

Muhammad emphasized refraining from fighting unless Meccans attacked. The Muslim army entered Mecca on 18th of Ramadan. The entry was peaceful and bloodless on three sectors. The hardened anti-Muslims gathered a band of Meccan fighters and faced the Muslim column. The Meccans attacked, and the Muslims charged. After a short skirmish the Meccans gave ground after losing twelve men. Muslim losses were two warriors.

Most captured Meccans adopted Islam. They conceded their gods had failed them.

The Prophet proclaimed, "He who lays down arms will be safe." He also declared: "Allah has made Mecca a sanctuary since the day He created the Heavens and the Earth, and it will remain a sanctuary by virtue of the sanctity Allah has bestowed on it until the Day of Resurrection.

Fighting in it was not made lawful to anyone before me, nor will it be made lawful to anyone after me. Its game-animals should not be chased, nor should its trees be cut, nor its vegetation or grass uprooted."

Then, along with his companions Muhammad visited the Kaaba. The idols were broken and their altars were destroyed. Thereupon Muhammad recited the following verse: "Say, the Truth has come and falsehood gone. Verily falsehood is bound to vanish."

The people assembled at the Kaaba, and Muhammad delivered the following address:

"There is no God but Allah. He has no associate. He has made good His promise that He held to his bondman and helped him and defeated all the confederates. Bear in mind that every claim of privilege whether, that of blood or property, is abolished except that of the custody of the Ka'aba and of supplying water to the pilgrims. Bear in mind that for anyone who is slain the blood money is a hundred camels. People of Mecca, surely God has abolished from you all pride of the time of ignorance, and all pride in your ancestry, because all men are descended from Adam, and Adam was made of clay."

Then Muhammad turning to the people said: "Oh Meccans, what do you think of the treatment that I should accord you?"

The crowd responded: "Mercy, O Prophet of Allah. We expect nothing but good from you."

Thereupon Muhammad declared: "I speak to you in the same words as Joseph spoke to his brothers in Egypt. This day there is no reproof against you; go your way, for you are free."

Muhammad's prestige grew after the surrender of the Meccans. Emissaries from all over Arabia came to Medina to accept him and Islam.

Aksil wore out three horses a day. He inspected the column, goading his warriors to keep up the pace. He oversaw the training of his attack force of five hundred. He visited Cahena at every opportunity, and the first thing he did was to place his hand on her belly to feel if his son was awake. Both Lila and Ozeret claimed all the signs indicated she was carrying a boy.

Cahena became more sexually active in her pregnancy. Aksil enjoyed her need, but feared that he might be poking his son in the head when he entered her. Cahena told him that if he disturbed her baby, who was destined to be a great warrior, the child would grab his tallywacker and tie it in a knot. They laughed. He often fell asleep with his cheek on her belly, hoping to feel movement or hear sound.

Aksil fashioned a stool to help Cahena mount her horse. Her guards protested, as they vied for the honor of having her step on their backs to mount. Aksil worried that Cahena sitting astride the animal might somehow endanger her son. He got an idea from watching shepherds on horseback sitting in their saddles with their right leg thrown over the pommel, and had a saddle-maker fashion a larger seat for the saddle and a narrower pommel, so Cahena could ride side-saddle. Cahena only used it when he was near; she thought the spreading of her hips would make the child's exit easier.

Ozeret told Cahena a story about a pregnant woman about to give birth who hurried to the mid-wives' tent. Suddenly the child fell from her womb onto the ground, in the dirt. Ozeret asked, "What do you learn from that?"

"To wear men's britches."

"You're too smart for your own good."

"And you're too ancient to be telling old stories like that. I always heard that when you get pregnant you look beautiful, but I feel as if I swallowed a two-hundred-pound pig—with the hair on."

"Just wait. The last two months of turning over in bed is an experience you'll never forget. Then your son will be born, grow up, and fill in the last line of your jokes. He will cause you trouble and anguish."

"Are you wishing that on me?"

"No, I'm going to teach him how to aggravate you. Now go out and wish Aksil and his men good luck on their raid."

Cahena started out, stopped, and asked, "What happens if you and Lila are wrong, and I have a girl?"

"If she's as big as you were, I'll shove her back in. I'm too old to carry that weight.'

"I'd like a nice little girl."

"Little is fine, not a giant like you." Ozeret gave her gap-toothed grin and asked, "What do you do when your daughter's pregnant and says she hasn't slept with a man?"

"Tell me."

"Start a religion. The Christians did it."

"Come join me in wishing Aksil farewell."

Although Linus traveled with the Seventh Legion, he rode back and forth between it and the Ninth to observe the condition of the troops and those who presented themselves at the medicus' tent. There were the normal blisters to be lanced, sprained ankles supported, and twisted knees rested. Thus far hygiene was good. The Prophet's Revenge—the howling shits—was not evident. He wished to test Cahena's dried-pomegranate-skin tea against his concoction of chewing blackberries leaves and drinking tea made from its bark. In the old days he would have been inspired by the ranks of legionnaires. Today they were mostly men from defeated tribes who hoped to stay alive long enough to collect a pension. Some were good fighters and bad marchers; most were mediocre at both. Their shields and armor were wiped clean but not burnished to reflect the sun. In the old days the enemy was often frightened by the reflection of the shields and armor marching toward them, but no longer. There was no snap in the step or pride in the stance of these men outfitted like Romans.

Even in the officer's corps, native-born Romans like himself were rare; most were from Germany and Gaul. The ranks were filled by Turks or Byzantines. They were brave men, used to hardship, but lacked initiative. He discussed this with the generals, themselves native-born Romans with villas inside the walled capitol of Constantinople. They agreed with his assessment, but finding and training recruits was difficult, as throughout the empire people lost respect for the Emperor and the power of his army. Defeated by the European tribes, challenged by the Muslims, and betrayed by the Berbers, the Empire was in danger. He watched as the men stopped to dig their nightly fortification, and felt no confidence in the future.

CHAPTER 21

THE RAIDS

Aksil and five hundred men left Cahena and the main column. He already had five hundred more in the field: three hundred establishing a camp and a trap, two hundred keeping track of Roman scouts. The two legions marched separately, the Seventh in the lead, the Ninth three miles behind.

Every fourth day the legions came together at the caches to share the supplies. The troops marched more quickly than the camp followers with their sheep, goats, and horses. Those caught up to the troops when the men stopped to dig their nightly fortifications. On the fourth day the protecting rear guard of the Ninth Legion usually galloped forward to get their food and supplies and dig in for the night. Aksil's scouts were careful to avoid clashes with Roman scouts. They observed and reported.

Aksil's men were bewildered at the camp waiting for them. It was located on two opposing slopes at the end of a valley that led out onto the grass plains of the Maghreb, and pointed toward the Roman road five miles away. There were no shelters for men but empty corrals made from trees and branches.

From the moment of their arrival they began cutting trees and sturdy branches. Some were put to sharpening the ends and hardening them in fire; others set up a defense perimeter across the valley entrance with bowmen on either slope. The officers followed Aksil at a trot out of the valley and onto the flatland. A mile into their journey, two scouts led them to a hillock overlooking the encampment of the Ninth Legion. Except for several scouts and a few guards on horseback, the cavalry had moved forward to access the cache and get their supplies. The camp followers, their herds, wagons, and provisions were left unprotected. Aksil brought all his troops forward except for two hundred archers. They remained in defensive positions at the entrance to the valley.

The sky above was clear. A three-quarter moon peeked over the horizon. By the time his troops arrived, two stars could be seen in the night sky. Aksil addressed the men: "Kill all the soldiers, but do not kill the civilians. Drive off their herds. Leave no animal alive; if it cannot come with us, kill it. If you can't move it, break or burn it. Animals will be herded back to the corrals."

"Why not kill the civilians? Then they will fear us."

"No! They will be dead. Alive, they will want to eat. Either the legions will share their food or kill them. Josephus is several hundred miles ahead, conducting his own raids. Mount up."

Aksil's' scouts easily overwhelmed the few guards protecting the camp followers. Signal fires were quickly extinguished. People fled on foot to the safety of the soldiers four miles ahead. Aksil counted on at least a two-hour head start before the legion's cavalry could attack. He hurried his men collecting wagon loads of grain and dried beef, and barrels of wine, olive oil, garlic, and other foodstuffs. His men were already driving the herds of sheep, goats, and horses east to the valley. The elephants were ignored.

He started his column loaded with foodstuffs west to the Mediterranean Sea and gave the order, "Fire two rockets!" The rockets left red and yellow streaks across the night sky, then burst in a blue sparkling umbrella of flashes before the moon. Aksil drove his men and the captured supplies toward the sea. Men grumbled, fearing entrapment by the Roman cavalry against the water, but Aksil increased his efforts to move the captured goods at the fastest pace.

Two miles from the beach, he stationed five men on the trampled grass road to warn him of the pursuing Roman cavalry. A mile from the beach he placed another five men for the same purpose. As they spread out on the beach a group of torches floating on the water approached them. Saul Levy and twenty cargo ships ground their bows into the sand. With encouragement from Aksil, ships crews and his men loaded everything but the dray animals onto the ships. Yeshaya clapped his hand on Aksil's shoulder, chortling, "You would make a wonderful brigand on the high sea."

"We must leave. Can you take half of my men?"

"How many?"

"One hundred and fifty, with their armor and saddles."

"Assign seven or eight to a boat and they will help us push off."

Aksil and his officers organized the men. Each man left on the beach now held two horses, both saddled. He sent messengers to call in the guards from the road, and his officers assigned men to cut the throats of the dray animals. Aksil gathered his men and ordered, "Select which of the two horses you like best.

Saddle and ride the other one until he is dead. Change horses and continue along the beach, heading north. The Romans cannot follow you too far. When they break off the chase, be certain it is not a trap. Only when you are one hundred percent assured it is safe, fire two red rockets out to sea. The ships will return. Send out scouts to find Cahena's army so they can be resupplied."

"Where will you be?"

"At the valley entrance. The Romans will send cavalry to recapture their herds. That is why you dug trenches and traps in front of the corrals."

Linus was supervising the distribution of supplies to the Ninth Legion when the first civilians arrived. The Legatos ordered four hundred cavalry and five hundred infantry to attack the raiders, and both the horsemen and foot soldiers set off at a trot. The horsemen arrived first and found everything broken, burnt or dead. Two trails led in an opposite directions. The cavalry commander sent two hundred horses to follow the group to the sea, and led the pursuit after the herds. He left orders for the foot-soldiers to follow the path to the sea, as the wagons would be slower and they could catch up more quickly. Then he set off on the wide track made by the raiders.

His officers agreed that the attackers were an organized enemy; they destroyed everything, whereas common thieves would not have wasted time. Bewildering was the second track toward the sea; it should have been obvious that freight wagons and donkey carts could not outrun the Roman cavalry. When they arrived uninterrupted at the sea, a fire of burning carts on the beach revealed everything. The beach was littered with more than two hundred dead animals. The keel-marks of many ships remained in the sand and the footprints of those who had pushed them out to sea. The trail north of four hundred horses racing away did not trick the Roman scouts. They could judge by the depth of the hoof prints that half the animals carried riders and half did not. The commander sent only ten scouts to follow the trail. He wanted to know if they continued north or would circle back.

He dictated his report, sent it back to the Legato of the Ninth Legion, and returned to the point of ambush to follow his men tracking the captured herds. The infantrymen cursed the animal dung left by the captured animals. The track was a broad path through the short grass, under a moonlit sky leading to a mountain pass. The infantry followed the horsemen. Messengers from the advanced unit reported the raiders dug in on both slopes of the valley. The Roman cavalry was hesitant to attack, as the enemy was twice their number and dug in. They advised waiting for the infantry. The commander dashed forward to confirm the reports.

Not one arrow had been fired: no enemy encounters. Several Roman scouts were missing and presumed captured or killed. The enemy was identified as Berber tribesmen and women warriors. "Tell our men about the beautiful Pagan women," the Roman commander said. "They can keep all they capture, sell them as slaves or fuck them with the dying shivers."

"Sir, we haven't fought the Berbers for two hundred years. Are they good fighters?"

"I'm not that old. We'll find out in the morning. The infantry will start work after breakfast."

The ten Roman scouts ordered to follow Aksil and his men north along the Mediterranean coast were given two each of the strongest animals. They too flogged the first animal to collapse, transferred mounts and continued to track. Trails in the sand showed a small unit of horsemen had broken off and travel inland. Two scouts followed them. They were led to the outriders of Cahena's army.

They climbed date palm trees to see the enemy. The fires of the encampments were so many, they gave up trying to count. They climbed down and estimated between twenty-five and forty thousand Berbers were on the march. They couldn't possibly keep up with the Legion's pace but might send their cavalry forward.

The scouts realized that their unit chasing the second group of raiders, who ran off with the animals, were in the path of this horde. Enemy pathfinders were within miles of them. The scouts leapt into their saddles and beat a hasty retreat. They cut the trail of their infantrymen, and the Centurion recognized the danger. He gave his horse to one scout, who galloped forward to inform the cavalry commander, and sent the second scout back to the Legions. He realized he could lose his cavalry and infantry unit to the major Berber force marching toward him.

The cavalry commander scouting the Berber defenses at the mouth of the valley understood he would soon be trapped by a larger force. He ordered his men back. They met the infantry. Every two foot soldiers grabbed the stirrups on either side of every horse and ran alongside to join the main column.

It was an hour before sunrise. Legionnaires ate a cold breakfast. Men chewed their rations dry, washed them down with sour wine, and put on their armor. Pigeons were sent requesting supplies by sea. The Ninth Legion deployed its six hundred horsemen as a rear guard. The Seventh Legion deployed half its cavalry as flankers on the inland side, the remainder as messengers and guides.

Cahena had no idea about the deployment of the Roman troops; she was concerned with the supplies from the ships and the food available to feed her army. Aksil and his group had signaled by fire arrows that the raid was successful, and the ships would be coming ashore with the supplies for her army. He was unaware that the Roman scouts were observing and reporting his actions. Incredibly outnumbered, both Legion commanders realized there was nothing they could do to recapture the supplies. To turn and fight now would be disastrous.

The weather helped. Dark storm clouds filled the morning sky; they rumbled in from the northwest, blotting out the sun. Two inches of rain fell before noon, and the Maghreb became a swampy morass. The quagmire stopped the Berber army. To catch up to the Romans was impossible, and to reach the coast and supplies was out of the question for now.

It didn't matter, for the ships never arrived. The storm scattered them at sea with the loss of two.

On the other hand, the Romans marched over the road they had built years ago. Their hobnailed sandals sparked on the paving stones. The road was a technical work of art; a trench on either side funneled off the rainwater, and paving-stones cut to fit tightly formed the surface. The Legions set off unhindered by the weather. It took three days for Cahena to drag her forces out of the muddy bog and down to the beach. There they waited a day for the survivors of the storm to finally sail in with supplies. By then the Legions had gained a week's march, and Cahena felt her plan might unravel. One advantage was that along with the supplies brought by Uncle Yeshaya was a present from her uncle Benyamin: ten one-hundred-pound sacks of Kaffa beans from Ethiopia.

When she finally distributed the supplies, she led her people onto the Roman road where traveling was quicker and easier. She gave her foot-soldiers a handful of coffee beans a day. It increased their speed to a hundred and thirty steps a minute. They marched fourteen hours a day, gaining about four hours a day on the legions. Forage for the animals was supplied by villagers who reappeared after the Romans left. The captured herds were driven to the paved road and followed the column.

The rain caused the Maghreb to blossom in a riot of colorful flowers. Rabbits could be seen munching the tender shoots of new grass. The air was washed clean, and the sun warm. Everyone and everything, including the animals, breathed the freshness of spring.

Two hundred miles ahead, Josephus neither enjoyed the weather nor disliked it; he factored it into his plans. Tonight would be his first raid on a cache.

There were ten legionnaires clothed as nomads, living in two tents on the site of the cache. One hundred more were stationed on the beach a mile away. Josephus sent one hundred men to take the cache, with orders to allow the Romans to signal to their men on the beach. Josephus led four hundred men to set an ambush for those Romans who would rush to protect the cache.

It was after midnight, and the sky was clear and full of stars when the attack began. The Romans lit their signal fire, and the camp on the beach came alive. Men saddled and raced their mounts on a well-worn path through the high grass to the cache. Five horses and riders went down from a rope across their path. More piled into the melee of struggling animals and men. From either side of the road, Berber warriors with long spears stabbed and lifted men from their saddles. The fight was brief, bloody and decisive; all the Romans were killed.

Twenty men were sent to check the Roman encampment for anything worth carrying away. Everything else was burned or broken. They found digging tools and carts, and brought them to the site of the cache. In shifts of fifty men, each working twenty minutes non-stop digging, in an hour and a half enough food for ten thousand men and fodder for horses was uncovered.

Josephus turned to the warrior who had questioned about the rockets and said, "Fire two red rockets inland to the northeastern skyline."

"Who are they for?"

"King Gershom's scouts. We will flee toward the Numidians, hoping the Romans follow. If not, we'll leave this stuff for the king and raid another cache."

Linus was present at the meeting of both legion commanders. Neither would relinquish his authority to the other in order to create centralized leadership. Thus far two caches between them and Tangiers had been taken. Three deliveries of supplies were made by the Roman navy. The men were on half rations. The people of the countryside had abandoned their homes and farms; some burnt their fields, others leveled their homes. The Roman army commandeered everything they could from retired legionnaires and their estates, causing unwanted friction.

This meeting was to determine what course of action to take on their final drive toward Tangiers. For once the two legion commanders agreed; they should move ahead as quickly as possible, outdistance the larger force behind them, break through the raiders in front of them, and overcome the unprepared group assembled by General Khalid. They must destroy the Muslim ships in Tangiers, except for those required to take away the survivors of both legions, and then they would sail for Constantinople. Both generals dreamed of returning to the Eastern capital with their mission accomplished, and with an armada of captured enemy ships, leaving the Berber army eating the smoke of a devastated Tangiers.

To accomplish this both commanders agreed they would have to give the Berber Army a bloody nose, and make them pull back long enough that Tangiers could be taken.

Aksil's scouts reported a weakness in the Roman defenses around the camp followers of the Ninth Legion. He questioned his men closely. Assured their observations were correct, he set up the largest raid yet. Fifteen hundred horsemen were tasked with carrying out his plan. On the fourth evening the Roman cavalry went forward to the cache for supplies. They left a skeleton guard force to protect the camp-followers and herds. As twice before, Aksil and his men waited until the cavalry were out of sight and then commenced their raid. As before, they let the civilians flee without harming them. The herds were driven off to the west. The supplies, carts, and wagons went east toward the beach.

From the moment the civilians fled, the Roman army went into action. The entire Seventh Legion turned in mass to its left flank, and double-timed into the grassland of the Maghreb. Over four thousand soldiers ran four miles in full armor. On command, they turned left and by columns formed the famous fighting square. At command they trotted forward.

All six hundred cavalry from the Seventh Legion walked their horses north along the beach waiting for the signal. Six hundred horsemen from the Ninth saddled fresh mounts and waited for their signal. It came in the form of two blue rockets fired by Aksil's scouts. The ships headed for shore as the Berbers carried their plunder down to the beach. The Roman horsemen spurred their mounts and charged. Those cavalrymen from Ninth Legion galloped down the Roman road. Half turned left toward the beach and half turned right toward the mountains following the flattened grass left by the captured herds.

Aksil, on the beach, encouraged his men to work faster. Out of the night he saw one, then two, three of his scouts whipping their lathered horses. Behind them was the Roman cavalry. Their armor gleamed in the flickering torchlight. The Roman horse smashed into the line of men standing on the beach with the supplies waiting to be loaded onto the ships. The Romans ran over, through and on top of them. Aksil attempted to form a defense, but it was useless. His men were scattered; most were on foot and being chased down with javelins, swords and spears. Several men formed up around him and were immediately surrounded. The fight was bitter and unequal as the horsemen threw their javelins into the group. The Legion commander was screaming to take Aksil alive. Aksil parried a thrust and stabbed a legionnaire. He was knocked senseless before he could withdraw his sword. The Legionnaires went about killing the survivors. A shout went up: "Ships heading for shore!"

"Take off your helmets, cover your armor," the commander ordered. Capture as many boats as you can. Ten pieces of gold for each boat."

Yeshaya did not expect any problems. The absence of torch signals happened the second time they did this, and it was alright then. The bow ground into the sandy beach and he was about to jump off when an arrow struck him. He looked shocked at it sticking out of his chest, then fell face first onto the beach. Other boats were caught unaware and boarded. Their crews were slaughtered. Six of the boats had their rowers backwater in time to escape being captured.

The horsemen from the Ninth Legion cut off the escape of those raiders driving the herds east towards the mountain. Seven hundred Berbers formed up to meet the cavalry charge. It didn't come, but out of the dark came the cadenced sound of swords beating on shields as four thousand legionnaires advanced on foot. If the Berbers broke and ran, the cavalry would cut them apart.

The Chieftain raised his sword. "We have Cahena!" he shouted. His men joined him, and they charged the infantry.

The Romans lowered their spears, formed a shield wall and broke the charge. Roman horsemen drove in from behind and finished off the survivors. A few Berbers escaped in the dark, but the rest were killed.

On the beach, Aksil was taken prisoner. He was treated roughly but not cruelly. Under guard he was brought before the legion commanders. They had him served liberal amounts of wine. He thought they wished to loosen his tongue. He was careful what he said. But it was great wine. He drank freely and said little. In fact he was not asked any questions about Cahena or her plans.

Only when he requested to be excused to urinate did the two commanders signal the guards. More men entered. Aksil was stripped naked, and thrown to the floor. He was spread-eagled on his back. One man grabbed his penis another tied a leather thong around the base and pulled it tight. Aksil was dragged out, hands tied, and thrown in a hole used as a latrine.

The pain in his kidneys developed slowly but by mid-morning it was excruciating. Linus the Medicus judged Aksil had at least eight hours to live. He was dragged out of the slime pit and tied upright to a post. Linus made measurements from Aksil's heel to his waist. He then had a man sharpen a wooden stake two inches in circumference two feet longer than his measurements, and he placed the stake two feet into the ground, point side up.

The two legion commanders stood several feet up wind from Aksil. His kidneys felt ready to burst. He writhed in pain. A centurion addressed him, "All you have to do is tell us Cahena's plans, her allies and number of troops. We will release the pressure on your kidneys."

Naked and covered in filth, Aksil spat. That action caused him excruciating pain. He was waiting until the last moment hoping the gods would somehow come to his aid—or if not the gods then Cahena, Josephus, or the Numidians. He could not control the muscles of his body. He retched and shivered.

The centurion pointed. "See that man greasing that stake? You will be placed on that stake. It will be inserted into your arse to a height where you must stand on tip-toes or rupture your innards. Slowly you will tire of standing on your toes, and you will come down feeling the point penetrate your guts. Your kidneys will burst. It will take time for you to die, and believe me, it will be most painful."

Aksil began to sweat so profusely that the filth slipped off his body. He trembled, but cursed the centurion. He was taken by two sturdy legionnaires and, guided by instructions from Linus, placed on the stake. When it entered his rectum he could not help but scream. He felt the point inside him penetrating something. He stood on tip-toes to alleviate the pain. He realized he couldn't maintain that stance long. He said a quick prayer and swallowed his tongue. He began to gag and felt the pain from the stake. "Oh gods, let it be over," he prayed silently.

Linus had witnessed Turkish warriors kill themselves when captured by swallowing their tongues. He rushed to Aksil, pushed back his head, inserted his fingers inside the mouth and pulled the tongue out of the throat. Aksil gasped for air. The pain in his kidneys and rectum caused him to weep. He allowed his knees to buckle and plunged down on the stake. It came up through his body. The point protruded from his throat.

Linus the Medicus was in disfavor. Death of a prisoner was a release from pain and the loss of information: a recordable offense. The Legions continued their march south with a new spring in their step. They had met and wiped out a significant number of pests and destroyed half of the enemy's fleet.

The raiding force's misfortune, loss of ships and crews, had a sobering effect on Cahena and was a shock to the morale of her army. They considered her invincible. They believed in her ability to see the future and affect its outcome. Uncle Yeshaya's body was recovered in the surf. Later Aksil's body was found skewered on the wooden stake. A deep dark depression immobilized Cahena. She either ignored requests for instructions or answered with a noncommittal grunt

Ozeret and Lila believed Cahena's depression was made worse by her pregnancy. The Queen of the Berbers tried to hide from her responsibilities, but there was much for her to do. Three days of isolation spread a feeling of despair among her followers.

It was Ahmed who forced his way into her tent. He insisted Cahena converse with him mentally. Lila and Ozeret were witness to their silent dialogue. Neither heard a word or knew what was said. Cahena and Ahmed sat on the floor knees and foreheads touching for a lengthy period of time. Then Ahmed stood and returned to his herds. Cahena bathed, dressed in fresh clothes and called a meeting of her chiefs. Her first order concerned the fifteen hundred dead Berbers. She buried Aksil and help paint his body. She allowed family members to bury those who died. She ordered her chieftains, "Leave the enemy bodies where they are. Follow the Romans." The carrion birds overhead, jackals, hyenas and wolves on the ground moved in as Cahena's army set out to engage the Legions.

Cahena sent pigeons to Tangiers. "To General Khalid Ibn Al Walid: Bring your troops forward from Tangiers. Block the Roman advance at their last cache before Tangiers. Josephus will reinforce you there. Send messengers to King Gershom. His cavalry is to move ahead and attack the left flank of the Roman column; his heavy infantry can follow. I am a week's distance behind the legions. I will leave my foot-soldiers and advance with cavalry to attack the Roman rear column. Give no quarter. Leave every Roman and every Roman sympathizer dead. —Cahena."

Word spread through the Berber ranks. Men sharpened their weapons, saddled their horses and awaited the Queen's command. With the aid of scouts, Ahmed moved his horse herds onto the Roman road. They were a day's ride ahead of the mounted warriors. Cahena rode side saddle at a steady trot followed by fifteen thousand warriors. She rode for twenty-four hours eating in the saddle. She had to make frequent stops to pass water. Her men cheered her as she squatted by the side of the road. A new life was breathed into the army. The men had a purpose. Destroy the Romans.

Legion scouts could not make out the enemy strategy of running the horse herds ahead of their army. The Roman scouts were too few to attack the more numerous Berber scouts. They observed Berbers galloping to the makeshift corrals on worn out horses, change saddles and get dried beef to eat and water to drink. They mounted fresh animals and continued the pursuit. They had gained two days on the legion, and with fresh mounts would gain another two. The scouts raced back to report.

Scouts from Josephus met with General Walid's scouts, and they combined forces for the attack on the last cache. Josephus moved up all his fifteen hundred men. The Muslim scouts insisted on leading the charge.

The Roman garrison had been reinforced; one hundred men had been brought into the cache. They totaled three hundred infantry and a hundred and fifty cavalry, set up in the standard Roman camp fortification. The trench and pointed wooden stakes encompassed the encampment. Men with short lances were placed in the first two ranks, long lances in the next two. The compound wasn't large but it was compact. The legionnaires were prepared to sell their lives dearly. No quarter would be given or taken.

The commander of Khalid's horsemen

placed his one hundred men in position to attack, and addressed his men: "You have been chosen, and are privileged to serve Allah and His Prophet. Let us pray." They all dismounted, and in full view of the legionnaires knelt in prayer. When finished, they shouted, "Allahu Akbar!" and mounted. The leader saluted Josephus with his sword and said, "We will make a gap in their line. Follow us in."

He trotted in front of his men. They loosened their swords in their scabbards and raised their lances in salute shouting, "Allahu Akbar!" Then they charged the Romans.

The Muslim horses attempted to swerve away from the wall of death, but their riders held the reins tight and the horses' heads straight. The charge ran into the wall of shields, spears, javelins and swords. The impact was audible. Stakes, shields and spears unseated the horsemen. They were struck by volleys of arrows and javelins, but the momentum and weight of the dead horses and riders burst through the Roman ranks. The defense was breached.

In all his years as a legionnaire Josephus never witnessed such a dedicated charge. He now understood General Walid's optimism with his three hundred Muslim warriors. Josephus raised his sword and led the charge into the gap created by the Muslim scouts. Once through the Roman line, his men spread out right and left, attacking the Roman square from inside. The combined Berber and Muslim force outnumbered the Romans ten to one.

It was bloody work, and finished in twenty minutes. Josephus sent messengers to Cahena, General Khalid, and King Gershom that this storage area would be the defensive line against the two reinforced Roman legions approaching from the north. They would hold until Cahena's army caught up from the rear and closed the trap.

Roman scouts were unaware of the Numdian cavalry that had detached itself from the heavy infantry and raced forward to flank the Legions. The barebacked, scantily clothed riders raced forward at unmatched speed.

The two legions marched on, confidant they could break into Tangiers, destroy the Muslim fleet, avoid battle with Cahena's army and escape by sea to Constantinople. They were again supplied by sea. This time they did not share food with the camp followers but had their men carry double rations. Then they received word that the last cache before Tangiers had been taken. Cahena's cavalry had gained two days on them and would gain another two with fresh horses, putting them in striking distance.

Now the Romans were left without a choice; they had to break through. The commanders decided not to set up the nightly defenses but march another five hours a day.

The speed of the oncoming Romans surprised Josephus; the commanders of the legion had violated the first rule in the Roman marching manual. Josephus could not take advantage of this. His men were battle-hardened, but the troops sent by General Walid had never fought a pitched battle before. Only twenty of their veteran horsemen had survived the charge into the Romans defending the cache. He ordered his scouts to harass the oncoming enemy and disrupt their sleep. They reported that the Romans were so tired from marching sixteen hours a day that the Berbers' teasing couldn't wake them. The scouts wanted to attack, but Josephus knew that the legionnaires would fight in their sleep. He and Cahena's army could not afford another defeat, nor could he dismantle his blocking force.

General Khalid rode up in advance of his force, and was briefed by Josephus. He complimented Josephus on his deployment of troops, and agreed that although a night raid on the Roman camp was enticing, his men were untrained in night fighting. He could only depend on his two hundred and twenty cavalry men to stand behind the conscripts from Tangiers and force them to fight until Cahena and King Gershom's forces arrived. He put his men to work building traps and digging ditches as roadblocks to hinder the advancing legions.

Legion scouts reported the last cache had fallen, and formed the pivotal point from the sea for the defensive line across the road to the west. They reported close to five thousand enemy: thirty percent well-disciplined, the rest conscripts pressed into service. The Roman infantry numbered ten thousand infantry plus one thousand cavalry; this included the refugee Roman retirees who had fled their plantations.

These were called Greybeards. They arrived with their own weapons, armor and food, and were formed into their own cohort. Both commanders assigned the Greybeards to the center of the hollow Roman square. The two legion commanders each maintained total independence, and this troubled the legionnaires. Their force was divided and separated by a half mile between columns. They had no doubt they could break through the enemy blockade ahead; the question was whether Cahena's cavalry, behind, would catch up before the battle for the road to Tangiers was over. Roman scouts came in with encouraging news; Cahena's cavalry had worn out themselves and their second set of mounts in the mad dash to catch the legions. It would take two days to recuperate horses and men.

Although confident the legions could easily defeat the ad hoc force blocking their path, the commanders knew their men were also worn out. They ordered a twenty-four hour halt. During this time everything not essential to the upcoming battle was burned or broken. Men were given double rations for their last three meals.

After breakfast on the second day, June thirtieth, when the sun cleared the Atlas Mountains on the left, the legions cornets sounded the call to arms. Drums rolled. The legions' standards were uncovered proclaiming seven hundred years of continual service to the Republic. The commanders addressed their men: "No other unit in the Roman army has ever marched faster, more disciplined, and under harsher conditions, than you. That does not entitle us to victory. We are being followed by a Berber army of over fifty thousand. On foot we outpaced their Cavalry. They also had to rest. In front of us is a makeshift force of five thousand: fifteen hundred experienced Berber warriors, two hundred Muslims lead by their General Khalid Al Walid, and four thousand Muslim conscripts—who a month ago didn't know one end of a sword from another. There is no doubt we will defeat them. The question is, can we break through quickly enough to avoid being caught by the Berber army behind us?

"If you want to be inspired, think of this. If we fail to demolish the force in front of us, our bones will feed the carrion birds you saw feasting on those Berbers we killed the other night. We can succeed. There have been murmurs that the division of our two legions weakens us, but we have a plan. The Seventh legion leads the frontal attack on the roadblock ahead. The Ninth legion moves up as if to reinforce us, but it initiates a flanking movement to their right and the beach. Our captured cache is being used as the anchor in the enemy's defensive line; the Ninth legion will destroy them, then attack those we are fighting, on their left flank. That should cause an enemy rout. We will avoid the pits and traps set for us on the road. We will break through their line strung out toward the beach. Then we are unopposed to Tangiers, and eventually sail to Constantinople. You can lay back on the voyage, drink all the wine aboard, and watch the sailors work their arses off!"

The men of the legions cheered and slammed their spears against their shields in unison chanting, "Tangiers! Tangiers!

Tangiers!"

The drums rolled the cadence, the cornets ripped the clear Mediterranean air, and the legions stepped out on the road to Tangiers.

Two of the most advanced Roman scouts, sent to spy out the best routes into the undefended city of Tangiers, noticed a great cloud of dust rising from the north-east desert. At first they thought it a dust storm coming their way. There was not much danger, as the ground around the great city was more rocks and shale than sand, but they noticed the cloud did not move with the speed of the wind. As they watched, small puffs of dust in appeared in a fan-like pattern ahead of the storm cloud. "Scouts!" they shouted to each other. "Who the hell are they?"

One made loose fists of both his hands, put his hands together and looked through the hole, concentrating his view. "They are half-naked and riding bareback. They have only bows, arrows, and javelins. No shields."

"Numidians! How the hell did they get into this fight?"

"Whose side are they on?"

Both men whipped their mounts and raced back to the legions.

CHAPTER 22

BATTLE FOR TANGIERS

General Khalid ibn Al Walid strode in front of his Muslim troops standing behind their makeshift barricade. He walked the entire length of the conscript line looking each man in the in the eye. "I am speaking to you who have truly taken Allah into your heart, you who believe the Prophet Muhammad is the Messenger of God. You have nothing to fear from these Christian Romans. I pray that I may die in Jihad. To those of us who die, the Messenger of God has promised us a life of heavenly bliss; the deserving will be attended by seventy-two virgins.

"You have heard the story of my breaking nine swords in the battle of Mutah. It is true! Now it could be I had a bad sword-maker. That was not the case. It could be the enemy had a better sword-maker. That also was not the situation. The Prophet blessed me before the battle. He did not bless my sword. With the Prophets blessings and Allah's guidance, I survived and we were victorious. I truly was disappointed; I had hoped to die defending Allah the merciful. This sword I hold before me is the tenth sword. The Prophet blessed it. He has blessed me, and through me he blesses you. You are here. The Prophet often says, 'You are where you are supposed to be.' I believe that. Before today you worked as skilled artisans, not war, but you are here. No one else can replace you. To be an irreplaceable person in the eyes of God is a once in a lifetime opportunity! You may not have the knowledge or experience of skilled warriors, but if you have the heart of a faithful servant of Allah you will succeed on earth and in heaven. Earn those rewards today! The battlefield is my home; I stand with you wearing armor, shield and sword, prepared to serve Islam. Submit to God, and be safe in heaven or on Earth. Be a coward and live an eternity in fear. I want men with me who desire death! Together we will enter Eden as companions for eternity. I am the Sword of Allah! You are the warriors of Islam! Together as Companions of the Prophet Muhammad we meet the enemy. It is time for prayer. Allahu Akbar!"

So impressive was the speech, the fire in the heart of their leader shone in the eyes of his men. Veteran Berber warriors also knelt in prayer.

The Roman centurion saluted the commander of the Seventh legion. "They are praying sir."

"We could run over there and kill them all."

"It's their way of preparing for battle."

"They'll all die anyway."

"Sir, our scouts report on the enemy road-block is confirmed. Two thousand of the enemy are blocking the road, another thousand stretched three hundred yards to our right flank and anchored by another fifteen hundred at the cache. Beyond that is the beach. General Walid is commanding the road-block. He set up a solid defense against a flanking by our cavalry."

"Who commands the cache?"

"The traitor, Josephus."

"That bastard once carried our standard. Cut his balls off and stuff them in his mouth."

"Yes sir."

"The enemy is spread too thin. We outnumber them and can bring more force to bear than they can repel. Sound the cornet. Diamond formation!"

The three columns of Roman soldiers molded themselves into a diamond-shaped formation with the point directed at the road block. The Ninth Legion behind did the same. Drums rolled. "Legionnaires! Short guard! At a walk, forward march."

A monolithic monster came to life. Red battle

cloaks of the Seventh Legion rippled in the morning breeze. The red and gold shields glittered in the sun. Their spears and polished helmets sparkled. The Ninth legion followed a mile behind, silver and gray their battle colors. Battle flags unfurled. The trumpets sounded and drums rolled. The hobnailed boots set the cadence on the cobblestoned road. The sound of the ancient battle song carried over the Maghreb.

The point of the leading formation was a thousand yards from the roadblock. Five hundred horses of the Seventh raced ahead as if to crash into the Muslim spear-wall. The new conscripts shied back but did not run. Two hundred yards from the roadblock the horses divided right and left, launching arrows into the defensive line. Few casualties resulted, but the psychological impact on the conscripts was significant. Another wave of five hundred horsemen from the Ninth Legion charged, and they swerved in mass to the right, launching arrows at the defensive line leading to the Cache. At the same moment they turned right, the Ninth legion performed a perfectly executed right flank movement. The pattern of attack changed from the diamond to the hollow square. They moved at one-hundred-thirty paces a minute, through the sand and sparse grass.

The cache was now three hundred yards, two hundred, and one hundred yards away. The cavalry launched clouds of iron-tipped arrows at Josephus and his Berbers, who took casualties.

Berber bowmen and slingers went into action. The three-foot-long rectangular shields of the Romans, and their body armor, deflected most arrows. At fifty yards the arrows and missiles struck with more accuracy. Men fell on both sides. Others filled their places; there was no shirking on either side. At fifty-foot distance, javelins flew from both sides. From the moment the Ninth Legion made the flanking movement into the hollow square, Josephus knew his men could not stop them. His people were born to the saddle; these legionnaires were forged in the fires of close combat on foot. He ordered a retreat to the horses before the lines collided, hoping some of the inexperienced legionnaires would break ranks and give chase, so his cavalry might have a chance to cut them down.

The Romans held the line and came on like a killing machine, trampling the dead and stabbing the wounded. Many of his men were caught trying to mount and died. He urged his cavalry down to the beach; there he had time to reform. But he heard the cornets sound. The Ninth Legion preformed one of the most difficult maneuvers when engaged with an enemy; they stopped. The entire unit did an about-face and attacked the unprotected enemy line leading from the cache to the road. The inexperienced defenders did not know how to change formations to meet the new threat.

At the same time the Seventh Legion executed a flanking maneuver that changed the diamond formation to the hollow square. They abandoned the frontal attack on the roadblock, and in a pincer movement with the Ninth Legion crushed the three-hundred-yard long defensive line. Now both legions were formed in the famous fighting hollow square, side by side, attacking the roadblock on its weakened flank. They had split the defending force, and outnumbered Khalid ibn Al Walid's two thousand men five to one. The fortifications on this side of the roadblock were minimal.

The two legion commanders sat their horses side by side, and observed the Muslim general trying to form his undisciplined troops into a defensive formation. The task appeared hopeless, but General Walid managed to gather his men. The Romans could not hear from that distance and did not understand the language, but the men he spoke to did. General Walid trotted his horse in front of his men, pulled the reins so his animal pawed the sky and shouted,

"Allahu Akbar!" Then he turned and charged. His horsemen followed him in the charge to the Roman wall of spears, and his foot-soldiers ran after him shouting "God is Great!"

From the beach Josephus saw the suicidal attack. He sighed, "This is as good a time to die as any." He signaled his horsemen, and they charged the rear of the two legions.

With a simple command, the legionaries in the rear of the formations turned in place to face the oncoming horsemen. Josephus' experienced men slipped from the saddles at the last moment, sending their mounts to their deaths on the Roman wall of long spears. They ran forward and fought on foot. Khalid and his two hundred horsemen used the same tactic, but it was the impact of the conscript Muslim foot-soldiers that surprised the Romans and confirmed General Walid's belief in Allah. These men threw themselves like berserks onto the spears and swords of the legionnaires with reckless abandon, shouting, "Allahu Akbar!"

Their fury and religious frenzy overwhelmed the first two ranks of the Seventh Legion and threatened to break through to the center of the hollow square. The Ninth Legion pivoted left and caught the Muslims from behind. It was a slaughter. The warriors of Islam were trapped. The Romans locked shields and to the cadence of their centurions put their left feet forward, then brought up their right. "Push, stab, slash! Push stab, slash! Push, stab, slash!" The ground turned muddy red with Muslim blood.

A ram's horn sounded, joined by another, and another, so many and so loud that most men stopped fighting and looked north. The skyline was filled from the sea to the mountains with twenty thousand of Cahena's horsemen.

First to react was the commander of the Seventh Legion. His cornets and flags signaled his men to break off the attack and reform in the marching square. The commander of the Ninth Legion issued similar orders. The vanquished remnants of General Khalid's army staggered, surprised to find themselves alive. There were only three hundred still on their feet. In comparison the two legions suffered minor losses. The Seventh Legion commander signaled the commander of Ninth to lead the way to Tangiers. He would fight a rear-guard action.

Josephus observed the interchange of signals and modification in formations and from these he reasoned their plan. He looked around at the survivors of his cavalry charge on the Roman infantry, and realized Cahena might do the same. He galloped off to warn against it. As he raced across the Maghreb to her battle standards he saw a large contingent horsemen detach themselves from the Berber main body and form a triple skirmish line.

They started at a walk, then a trot. When they were within two hundred yards of the Seventh Legion they went into a full gallop. They did not swerve aside. Horses and men crashed into the Roman wall of shields. They were killed by long spears, short spears, javelins and arrows. The Roman line bent inward with the impact, but the hollow square formation gave resilience to their line. It took ten minutes of hand-to-hand fighting to push the Berber horsemen back. Legionnaires finished off the wounded animals and men with their short swords.

Josephus reached Cahena as she was about to order another charge, and stopped her. "You need heavy infantry, or we can surround, harass and starve them out. But cavalry against disciplined infantry will not succeed." Reluctantly, she agreed and called her troops back.

Cahena was urgently summoned by Lila and Ozeret to the medical tent; General Walid required her attention. Cahena addressed Josephus: "King Gershom and his Numidians are on their way. Take charge of my army. Kill the Romans."

The General lay stripped of his armor, clothes soaked in blood, his face pale and breathing shallow. Lila raised his eyelids. Cahena saw only the whites. He was unconscious and trembling. Ozeret explained the medications they had administered. "Strip off his clothes," Cahena ordered. "Stop the bleeding."

Mai Li brought salve and bandages. When she looked down at the general's naked body she exclaimed in Chinese. Without looking up from her work Cahena asked, "What did you say?"

"The Death of a Thousand Cuts. It is a Chinese torture. Look at his body! What is not bleeding is covered by scars, from his feet to his face."

Using vinegar and sheep-gut thread, Lila and Ozeret cleansed and then stitched and bandaged the wounds. Mai Li returned with a bowl of beet soup, saying, "This will replace the blood he lost." Lila and Ozeret looked at each other and shrugged. Neither had heard of it before, but the soup was blood red and Cahena's ministrations were not effective.

The two Roman scouts reported to the Ninth Legion of the massive military formations of Numidians approaching from the southeast. The commander, a fatalistic man by nature, said: "Killed by Berbers, Numidians, or Muslims: not much difference. I'll take as many to hell as I can. Prepare the legion for a forced march to Tangiers. Have the Medicus Linus brought to me."

Linus confirmed the commander's recollection of him having saved the sight of King Gershom's son. "I want you to take ten men and ask King Gershom whose side he is on," said the commander. "If on our side, have his army form up with our legions on the approach to Tangiers. If he is against us, use your cure of his son's blindness to convince him otherwise. If that fails, ask him to remain neutral. And if that is unsuccessful, head for Tangiers. Prepare as many boats as possible for our escape. If you can burn the rest, do it."

The two Roman scouts led Linus and his ten men, with the white banner of a messenger, at a ground-eating trot into the sand desert, toward the great oncoming cloud of dust. They observed Numidian scouts. Soon a contingent of fifty horsemen approached. Without a word or sign they formed up on either side and directed the Romans on a more easterly course. As they approached the oncoming dust cloud they saw horsemen. Linus was recognized by his elaborate armor and helmet, and brought forward. He requested in Latin and Greek to meet with King Gershom. He was answered in Latin and gave up his weapons as ordered.

Gershom sat a pure white Arabian stallion, accompanied by his son on a fine coal black mare and surrounded by fifty guards. He asked, "What is it that brings a Roman legionnaire to my camp?"

"I come on behalf of the commanders of the Seventh and Ninth Legions to ascertain the intentions of your Numidian Army."

"We have taken the field to aid Cahena, Queen of the Berbers, in her efforts to consolidate the nomadic tribes of the Maghreb and impose her sovereignty on North Africa."

"Your majesty, you are taking a path of conflict with the Empire in Constantinople. Romans have ruled in Africa for eight hundred years. Hannibal won battles against us over many years. In the end even he capitulated."

"What you say is true. It is also history. Constantinople today is not Rome of the past. The Muslims are pounding on your Christian doors from the east, the Huns, Vandals and Goths from the west, and now the Nomads from the south. You can only run so far north and then you'll have to swim."

"To Rome, war is like breathing. It comes naturally. We are preparing to fight on the sea. Have you ever heard of the word *triremes*?"

"An ancient oar-driven warship powered by about 170 oarsmen. The craft is long and slender, has three tiers of oars and one sail. On the bow is a battering ram to destroy enemy ships."

"These ships are equipped with a secret weapon."

"What does this weapon do?"

"If I knew, your majesty, I would respectfully decline to tell you."

The king was considering torture and intimidation when Linus interrupted and waved to Gershom's son.

"You know my son?"

"I am the medicus who returned his sight."

Gershom looked to the boy. "Yes father," the prince confirmed. "He performed the miracle."

The king looked with awed respect at the emissary. He beckoned his son and watched as Linus examined the boy's eyes.

Gershom thought hard about his predicament and said, "Later you will have time to converse with my son. I am in your debt. I had no idea a Roman performed this miracle. I never rewarded you, and now I must. Your first request would naturally be that I side with your legions. Because of another pledge already given, I cannot do this. The first gift I offer is life, for you and your men. Secondly, I will have of you escorted to Tangiers, where you will be given a ship and crew, stocked with enough supplies for your safe return to Constantinople. Thirdly, I will present you with your weight in gold Roman coins. Please do not request what your superiors ordered. I must fulfill my vow to Cahena and help destroy your legions."

With a wave of his hand Linus was taken away. Fresh mounts were provided him and his men. Surrounded by a thousand scantily clad warriors riding bareback they set out for Tangiers.

Josephus saw no complicated strategy for defeating the legions he had once served. He had no misgivings about planning their demise. For eighteen years he had served, and was paid. He had never made deep friendships. Soldiers employed by Rome didn't live too long; few collected their pensions. His decision was practical; slow the legions down until the Numidians arrived.

He sent flying columns of horsemen to harass both flanks of the Roman fighting squares marching to Tangiers. He commanded a third column to collect the survivors at the cache and disrupt the vanguard. The remainder of the cavalry would harass the rear of the Roman column.

Veteran legionnaires dreaded one command

above all others. The cornets sounded and the centurions shouted, "To the winds, defend!" It meant they were surrounded. Each unit faced a separate point of the compass. They locked shields against the arrows and javelins aimed by enemy horsemen. They were reduced to half steps forward, sideways or backward to maintain the square's forward progress while under attack. The division of the two legions became more pronounced and weakened both formations. The Berber horsemen pressed the rear of both Legions, widening the gap between them.

Josephus moved ahead of the leading Ninth Legion and harassed their forward movement. He began receiving Numidian scouts reporting a large force of their horsemen on the way. They explained King Gershom's plan. Josephus agreed. An hour later the Numidian Cavalry arrived. By use of horns and signal flags they formed a great circle at the front of the Roman column. They raced their horses in close while holding the reins in their teeth, and loosed at least three arrows at each pass. The Roman shields became heavy with arrows and javelins sticking out of them. The men tried to pull them out. Exposed, they fell dead or wounded and their fellows marched over both. The Berber ram's horns blew and Josephus' men pulled back from the flanks. Now it was the Numidians attacking the front and the Berbers attacking the rear.

The Romans managed to close the gap between the two squares. Jospehus' commanders begged him to allow them to continue attacking the flank. The Numidians up front were slowing the Romans enough so King Gershom could bring up his heavy infantry. He wanted the enemy tired when they met at the entrance of Tangiers. "Let them walk all the way."

It was four in the evening when Josephus returned his men to attacking the worn-out legionnaires on the flanks. Once again the legionnaires obeyed the command "To the winds march!" The two hollow squares were not as large, the men lethargic in their response. Directly in front of them at the entrance to Tangiers stood the Numidian heavy infantry. Their armor shone brightly in the sun. Twenty-foot spears in the rear ranks and progressively smaller ones in the front ranks held to form a wall of death. It was the ancient Greek hoplite formation, not as mobile or flexible as the Roman hollow square but equally as deadly when maneuverability was not required. King Gershom had deduced correctly. The Romans, fighting and marching since daybreak, were tired. The legion commanders viewed the

Numidian formations a thousand yards away, Berber horsemen by the thousands to the right on the beach, Numidian horsemen to the left and the desert behind them. Berber horse and infantry had caught up with the legions' rear guard.

The legion commanders conferred and agreed. The Berbers on the beach side were almost entirely cavalry; they were the easiest target, and the water would secure the Roman rear. The cornets sounded and the hollow square was formed. Both legions executed a right flank movement toward the beach. The Numidian drums sounded and they marched forward into the attack.

Josephus and his cavalry on the beach were taken by surprise. He had no time to attack. They were being forced back into the Mediterranean surf. He ordered the rams horn sounded and his men fled north and south along the beach. The Romans set up their fortifications. As tired as they were, they dug shallow trenches in front of their line. There were not enough men to form the Hollow Square. They combined both legions into the Greek hoplite formation, but they did not have the long spears to present a uniform wall of spear points.

The commanders of both legions spoke to their men of the centuries of tradition. They pointed to the eagle standards. "If they fall into the hands of the enemy, let not one of us live to see it happen. I have no doubt we are all going to die. Let us make it a costly for our enemies."

There was no verbal response, but the men clashed their swords on their shields and tightened their armor straps. The commanders broke out the remaining food. They watched as the solid mass of heavily armed Numidian infantry came closer and closer. Their spear points formed a glittering silver wall in the setting sun. The Numidian drums changed their beat to a slower cadence. The solid spear wall struck the Roman line. The collision was audible.

The uniformity of the Numidian spears and the freshness of their men caused many casualties in the Roman front ranks. Dutifully legionnaires moved up to fill the gaps. The Numidians continued grinding forward. The left Roman flank buckled. Centurions pulled and pushed their men to keep the line straight. The rear ranks of Romans were now standing in ankle deep water. They were faced with the heavy Numidian infantry and on both flanks by Berber and Numidian Archers, slingers and javelins in front.

A messenger from King Gershom summoned Cahena, and she left General Walid in the care of Lila and Ozeret. She was led to a bluff overlooking the beach. King Gershom waved his staff-officers back, stepped forward and helped Cahena dismount, asking, "How is General Walid?"

"Slowly recovering. Why did you send for me?"

"To watch the end of the Seventh and Ninth Roman Legions. Combined, they have a history of over sixteen hundred years."

"How did you know exactly where to catch the enemy with your cavalry and place your infantry in position?"

"Your scouts gave me your message."

"I sent no message or scouts."

"At your wedding. The two men who presented you with the knives made from falling stars. They appeared before me and gave me the exact position of your troops, the Muslims, Josephus' force and the two Legions. It was they who suggested I rest my infantry and let the Romans march to us. Look below. It is only a matter of minutes before the legionnaires die by the sword or drown."

A cry went up from the Berbers. "Cahena is here! Cahena is here!" The Berbers became so excited that, mounted and on foot, they charged the Roman ranks. Under the sheer weight of the enemy, the Roman lines collapsed. It was sword against sword. The surf turned red with blood. Dead bodies floated everywhere. Josephus was surprised as he felt a pang of remorse on seeing the honor guard form around the legions' two eagles. That was his post: Guardian of the Eagle. The generals and their guards stood, swords drawn, waiting for the end.

Suddenly a ship's horn sounded, and a craft came headed toward the Romans waist deep guarding the Eagles. On the prow of the boat Josephus recognized Linus, directing his boat to the last Roman holdouts. The first things they put aboard were the two eagle standards, then the men. Both commanders refused to evacuate and helped push the ship off so it caught the wind.

Cahena recognized Linus. She shook with anger. "Kill that bastard!" she ordered.

"Why so angry at one Roman?" King Gershom asked.

"That animal concocted the poison which killed my father. He tortured Aksil to death. I'll have his balls for dinner."

Not today, the king thought. The boat caught the wind and Berber arrows fell harmlessly into the sea. The King said nothing about saving the Roman physician's life. Cahena was furious.

She went down to the beach and ordered a

celebration feast. Wounded horses were slaughtered and dead ones butchered. A cavalry unit was sent to bring back food and wine from the city of Tangiers. More than fifty thousand warriors roamed the shore, kicking dead Roman bodies into the sea.

Cahena called a meeting of her officers. She praised their actions by description and their names from memory. She patted her bulging belly and said she must rest. She rode to the medical tent to find Lila by General Walid's side. "He's sleeping," she said, then pointed to Cahena's belly. "You should be doing the same. The child needs rest."

"It's his first battle. I thought to let him enjoy the festivities. Do you think the general will recover?"

"He has fourteen cuts and stab wounds. Only two are serious: one to his throat, and another from behind may have punctured a lung. We'll find out tomorrow. Your ministration brought him through the crisis."

"In the beginning I thought I lost my healing power. I felt nothing when I put my hands on him. He showed no reaction. It was after he drank the beet soup that I felt the warmth in my hands and his body respond."

"The soup may look like blood, but I doubt it was the cause. You didn't drink the soup."

"It frightened me."

"Were you able to help the wounded after the battle?"

"Yes, but some died."

"Were you still speaking in that strange language?"

"Josephus said I was. Can't remember what I said."

"As long as you helped them. Take a mattress. I'll watch over both of you."

CHAPTER 23

THE SPOILS OF WAR

For two days General Walid remained unconscious. Cahena made a decision about Tangiers; she allowed the Muslim takeover of the city and their new fleet. Of the three hundred Muslim warriors who accompanied General Walid, only twelve were able to mount a horse: not enough to take over a city. King Gershom desired to take control of Tangiers, and it would revert to his kingdom after the Muslims set sail for Constantinople. Scouts reported wealthy Pagan families leaving; they were the anticipated source of funds to pay for the Numidian campaign. Cahena agreed with the King. The Numidian cavalry went after the caravans while the infantry took charge of the city. The shipyards, docks and waterfront remained in the hands of the Muslim work force.

Birds of prey clouded the sky over the body-strewn beach where the final battle had taken place. Schools of sharks tore apart floating corpses. Often a tug-of-war took place between jackals, sharks, and birds over bodies rolling in the red-tinted surf. Carcasses of horses, swelled with putrid gas, burst in the summer sun. Stacks of Roman armor and weapons awaited collection. No prisoners were taken. Amputees died from shock and loss of blood. Stomach wounds were more painful and took longer. It was these men and women Cahena sought out with her soothing powers. She ignored pleas from her chieftains, Josephus, and the Numidians for her attention to matters of governing.

Finally the Numidian King entered the sick tent, where Cahena was using her powers to alleviate the pain of the dying, and he dragged her outside. "You can no longer be a shaman or doctor. You are Queen of North Africa!" Gershom shouted. "Act like it!" He pointed to the birds and the corpses on the beach below. "...Or all this will have been for nothing."

Cahena wept, "I don't know what to do."

The King, cleared his throat, realizing he was dealing with an exceptionally bright girl who was only seventeen years old and pregnant. He sighed. "I wish it were in my power to help you. But I must administer my kingdom and assert my claim over the former Roman-controlled cities. My men must receive their rewards in sacking or extorting from Rabat,

Casablanca, and the cities along the Atlantic coast."

Cahena dried her tears. and put both her hands on the King's shoulders. "You are a good man and friend. I thank you for your support and that of your people. Whatever advice you can give me before you leave will be appreciated."

"You are taller than me by half. You are also younger than me by two thirds. Only time will give you experience. Surround yourself with capable advisors. That is difficult in our tribal societies."

"Why so?"

"By nature, the tribe is governed by the strongman. To maintain his strength he surrounds himself with those who can be manipulated."

"You mean he chooses the weakest."

"He requires men of strength to carry out his orders, but he doesn't want independent thinkers who might someday challenge him."

"You are advising me to select advisors who will tell me the truth, not what I wish to hear."

"You have one of the finest men, with more experience at organizing governments after victories."

"Who is that?"

"General Khalid ibn Al Walid. Ask him to

guide you. He has the experience you require. Josephus thinks of him as a warrior saint. But be careful of his preaching Islam. After witnessing the Muslim display of courage at the roadblock, many of your Berbers and my people are considering conversion to Islam."

"I have no problem with Berbers becoming Muslims, Jews, or remaining Pagans or Christians, as long as they support the Berber monarchy."

"Half of Numidia is Christian, and half Pagan. I would not allow a single Muslim in my kingdom. They can only serve one master."

In Mecca, the Prophet Muhammad consolidated and celebrated his occupation of the Kaaba shrine. He proclaimed it the holiest city in the world. His followers took over Pagan holy sites wherever they dominated; they smashed idols, destroyed altars, and slaughtered anyone in Arabia who did not submit to Islam.

This brought the Messenger of Allah in conflict with the heathen Bedouin tribes, who were led by the Hawazin Tribe. The Prophet's warriors met and defeated these Pagans; they killed or converted all the men and boys. Six thousand women and children were taken as slaves. Twenty-four thousand camels and a huge amount of gold were seized. Surviving Bedouin fled to the walled city of Ta'if. Where they reinforced and prepared the city against the Muslims.

The siege began. The people of Ta'if suffered greatly, but held out until the holy month of Ramadan. The Prophet declared no war during the Holy month. He lifted the siege but promised to return, and his threat was taken seriously. The people of Ta'if sent a delegation to sue for peace. The Prophet listened to their proposals.

"Hear me you sinners," he replied, "You foul worshippers of idols, you who fornicate in prayer. There are two conditions you must accept for me to allow you, your women and children to live. Every man, woman and child must accept Allah as the one and only God, Islam as your religion, and me as the last and greatest Prophet. Secondly, all pagan places of worship will either be torn down, burnt, or converted to mosques."

The Ta'if delegation was roughly pushed outside the tent. Waiting there were four Roman engineered Ballistae and other machines of war for breaking down fortifications. The people of Ta'if capitulated.

Muhammad became sole ruler of Arabia.

The Islamic armies from India, Iraq, and Iran, one hundred thousand strong, were poised to invade Turkey by land. The fleet from Tangiers set about collecting the Muslim fighting men from Ethiopia and Egypt for the attack in the Bosporus Strait on Constantinople.

The handover and evacuation of Tangiers was a smooth affair. The Prophet encouraged his people to entice the Numidians by moral actions and dedication to Islam. From his sick bed General Khalid ibn Al Walid directed the takeover.

He was also ordered by the Prophet to convert Cahena. Mohammad wished the child she carried to be born a Muslim.

It was not to be. He was born a Jew to a Jewish mother. The birth was relatively easy and the child and mother healthy. On the eight day a circumcision was performed by a rabbi, and the child was named Moshe ben Shimi, in honor of her father.

Winter passed quickly for Cahena, who utilized the treasure-chest of ideas and experience she had in the form of Khalid ibn Al Walid. She had Ozeret and Lila pamper him. They purposely exaggerated his wounds so he would remain and advise Cahena to manage her new domain.

He understood the need and social mechanisms for sanitation, law, parceling and working of land to feed the population, and roads to distribute goods and services. His solutions were straightforward; all Berber slaves would be freed, Romans sold into slavery. Utilize those people in authority who had worked for the Romans, including Romans, in their old positions. Village councils would settle local disputes. Tribal councils were available for appeal. Complex issues were brought to the queen's court, and what could not be solved by the former would come before Queen Cahena. All lands owned by the Roman government or Roman pensioners would revert to the queen; they would be worked and supervised by tribal elders for the benefit of the crown. Maintenance of roads, bridges, ports, and local municipalities would be supported by a tithe or once a year to the Queen. Baksheesh, bribes, under-the-table money would not be tolerated: first offenders would lose their right hand, second offenders would lose their lives.

At the end of March, warm winds from the Mediterranean melted the winter snow in the mountains. Grass pushed its way up into patches of tender green shoots. Shepherds moved their flocks up the slopes. The smell of spring reached the tent of Khalid ibn Al Walid.

He dressed himself for the first time in months. With the aid of a walking stick he stepped into the sunlight. Cahena usually brought her son Moshe to him; today he hobbled to her tent and surprised her as she was changing his diaper. He bent to kiss the child's naked tummy when Moshe let go a burst of urine that caught the general in the face. The child giggled. Cahena jumped back grabbed a fresh cloth to dry the General's face. He laughed so hard it became infectious. The child and Cahena joined in. Ozeret hobbled through the entrance, asking, "What is going on?"

The General caught his breath. "My enemies have wanted to piss on my grave. This little shit pissed in my face and laughs at me."

The Prophet gave General Walid a year to recover, in hopes he could convert the Berber queen and her realm to Islam while he helped her administer and govern North Africa. Cahena exaggerated General Walid's wounds so he would continue to direct her in governing, for she disliked the process of administration.

General Walid called her to task on this weakness more than once. She said, "When I realized the crown of the Berbers would be mine I thought, how nice. I have a minister of finance, the army, import and export. What is left for me to do but play with my son, begin a new collection of birds, and enjoy life?"

"What the queen does is clean up the crap

made by these ministers," General Walid said. "And if you don't do it, it won't get done. When it isn't done, you can be certain it'll jump up and bite you in the arse. I received a message for you from the Prophet, peace and blessings of Allah be upon him. The Messenger of Allah congratulates you on the birth of your son. He wishes you and the prince long life, and hopes he follows in the steps of his father Moshe ben Shimi of the lineage from Aaron high priest in the Holy Temple of Jerusalem. Consider teaching your son about Islam, for in doing so you will be learning and open yourself to the one and only God. It will be my honor to send teachers for you and the lad. Allah's blessings be upon you and yours."

"How nice," Cahena murmured, turning back to the baby.

With the onset of spring the Prophet's army of one hundred thousand moved overland from Iraq into Aleppo, in Syria, expecting to be joined by the army of King Leo from Damascus. Together they were to march through Turkey and besiege Emperor Theodosius in Constantinople. However, the Syrian King who converted from Paganism to Christianity to Islam made secret arrangements with the Roman Emperor to reconvert to Christianity and ambush the

Prophet's army. For this act of betrayal King Leo was promised to be the next Emperor of the Byzantine Empire.

This posed a major problem for Muhammad's generals. If they turned to fight and punish King Leo, they would be attacked in the rear by the Romans. If they continued toward Constantinople, they must fight their through hostile territory with King Leo harassing their rear. The Turkish people were ordered by the Romans to burn their crops and drive their livestock ahead of the Muslim army, into the mountains and or to Constantinople.

Faced with the possibility of starvation, Muhammad appealed to the merchants of Islam. They responded with overwhelming generosity. Caravans of food and supplies were sent to Turkey from all over the Islamic world. The outpouring of help was sufficient. The Prophet sent his army forward to Constantinople. He launched the troop ships from Tangiers and fleet of fighting craft from Sicily, to converge on the Roman capital by land and sea. The flotilla from Sicily sailed unhindered through the Bosporus Straits. They joined Muslims in Thrace and blockaded supplies reaching Constantinople from the Mediterranean and Black Seas.

Emperor Theodosius was prepared for the siege. The fortifications of Constantinople were repaired, the massive Theodosian walls reinforced, equipped with catapults and the latest siege weapons. Food was warehoused. Families who could not stockpile three years of supplies were evacuated to distant mountain strongholds.

The Roman fleet of triremes was refitted for war with a secret weapon known as, 'Greek Fire'. The formula remained a closely guarded secret. The volatile mixture, when ignited, reached a temperature of two thousand degrees Fahrenheit. A series of pipes and a pump operated each "squirter" located in the bow to eject the stream of fire for fifty feet. Clay grenades could be launched by hand, or fifteen-pound explosive missiles catapulted four-hundred yards. In addition, the Roman triremes were built as deadly ramming vessels. They had three banks of oars and could propel the craft into an enemy ship, then back-oar, leaving the shattered vessel to sink. The Roman crews were experienced, and their commanders skilled in the art of naval warfare.

They allowed the Muslim fighting ships to enter unopposed into the Marmar Sea and drop anchor in Thrace. Emperor Theodosius paid the Christian Bulgars to attack the Muslims' encampment in Thrace by land. His triremes lay in wait for the troop-ships from Tangiers. The

Muslims sailed into the Aegean Sea oblivious to the danger; they were met by Greek fire and Roman rams.

The Islamic fleet was destroyed. Those who escaped to the Mediterranean Sea were overpowered by their Christian slave crews, or lost in an early winter storm. Of three hundred and forty Muslim ships, only seven survived.

The siege was broken by sea. Muhammad ordered his fighting ships from Thrace to disrupt the supply ships entering Constantinople. They sallied out only to be destroyed by the better trained and equipped Roman fleet.

Syrian King Leo deposed Emperor Theodosius in Constantinople, and set about to destroy the Prophet's land army. The weather helped. The worst winter in memory wreaked havoc on the hundred-thousand-strong Muslim army. Their supply lines were now hundreds of miles longer. Caravans had to travel as much as a thousand miles to reach Turkey, then pass through hundreds of miles of hostile territory to reach the siege-line. Winter clothing was scarce. The inexperience of most troops living in the field resulted in a hygienic catastrophe. There were ten times more casualties from malaria, dysentery, typhus, scurvy, and smallpox than battle-inflicted injuries. Supplies were disrupted on land and eliminated by sea. Strict rationing was instituted.

When the Christians celebrated the birth of Christ behind the stout walls of Constantinople, the Prophet's men were chewing their leather boots and harnesses and eating bark from trees. A combination of Cholera and starvation devastated the Muslim military. The Islamic force ceased to function as a military unit in February of the year 632. It was then that fresh meat appeared openly for sale or barter. Cannibalism was approved by default. Discipline was nonexistent. The Prophet's army of one hundred thousand men disappeared into the ground or slavery.

Muhammad abandoned the conquest of the Eastern Roman Empire.

Cahena's motherly instinct was not strong. She nursed the child as a duty, preferring the lips of a man on her breast and caressing her body. She lamented the time taken from her royal duties to attend baby Moshe. The task of caring for the chubby little one fell to Lila. Having no children of her own, she was overjoyed. Ozeret was sleeping more these days; she lacked the strength to keep up with the child. He crawled like a racing lizard and tried to stand by pulling himself erect then toppling over.

Cahena's time was taken up by the complexities of governing; she now understood and enjoyed the intellectual challenges and stimulation of negotiations with the city elders along the Mediterranean coast. She reorganized and adapted her laws to the former Roman-controlled towns, cities and regional capitols. She placed those who had contributed most to the success of her army to salaried political positions.

It was during this period, on the way to what might be a battle for Carthage, that Ahmed came to her with a young prostitute he wished to marry. As his mother was dead and he had no family, he asked Cahena to represent his family. They had placed their heads together and she walked into his thoughts. She was so joyful she whistled the most beautiful bird calls. It was in his thoughts and tears came to his eyes. It was a glorious melody. He asked Cahena if she could tell if children born to them would be mute. "It is in the hands of God," she said. "There is one condition I ask of you, not as queen but as a friend. May I be the godmother of all your children?"

By thought and gesture he replied, "My mother told me that when I was born I made no sound. She didn't hear a cry. and thought I was dead. When they put me in her arms and I moved, her heart felt as if it would fly out her throat. Whenever times were difficult and people said, 'Poor mother, who has a son who cannot speak,' she always remembered that wonderful feeling. Since her death I have felt you are my mother."

They both smiled and wept for joy.

Ahmed requested a proper Jewish wedding. Since they were now on the outskirts of Tunis, preparing to begin the siege of Carthage, Cahena enlisted the help of the Jews of Djerba Island to perform the ceremony. They responded with heartfelt delight. A ship from the priestly village came to take Ahmed and prepare him for the ceremony; another boat came to collect Yonit, the bride, and her bridesmaids. Cahena and Ozeret selected five cows, a flock of sheep, and one hundred cages of chickens to be ritually slaughtered for the feast. Those were sent on a third boat.

Muslim spies must have informed General Walid. From Mecca, by way of the Port of Jeddah, he sent the finest pure white Arabian mare and stallion with a blessing for 'Long Life.' King Gershom sent a matched pair of the finest racing camels in the Maghreb. Tribal chieftains showered gifts on the mute in honor of his service as Keeper of the Herds, in the battles past and those to come. The waters between Tunis and Djerba reflected the torches of hundreds of boats carrying the guests to the wedding. Josephus used his Pagan troops to guard against a surprise attack from the Roman garrison in Carthage, though he didn't think it probable because the Romans were so understaffed and the Berber army drew new recruits every day.

He was preparing to embark for the wedding when he heard an alarm raised from Post Number One guarding the main Tunis-Carthage Road. He climbed into the saddle and galloped there.

To his amazement, ten Roman officers in full dress regalia had dismounted and awaited him. Each man carried a cage full of pigeons. "A gift for the groom," said the senior centurion. He went to his horse and brought to Josephus the Zaimph of Carthage. The ornate veil adorned with precious and semi-precious stones, and woven threads of gold and silver, was draped over the centurion's arm. "This," he said, "Covered the statue of the Goddess Tanit in the sanctum sanctorum of the Carthaginian Temple. This garment, not the statue, is the city's protection—and is worshipped by the Pagans. We Christians bring this as a gift to your queen. It indicates the surrender of Carthage. We ask that you allow us to evacuate our garrison by ship. The city's treasury will be untouched."

"As will your armory, weapons and food stores not taken for the journey," Josephus said. "No destruction of Roman or private property. Leave everything as is."

"I cannot guarantee what the citizens will do once we leave."

"How long before you can leave?"

"A week."

"The wedding feast will continue for seven days. What if I send a battalion of my troops to return with you now and a battalion every day until you leave. In that way the transition will be orderly, looting and civil disruption kept at a minimum."

"That is acceptable. Do we have an agreement for a peaceful surrender?"

"By any chance do you have any survivors from the Battle for Tangiers?"

"Yes, a shipload arrived with the standards of the Seventh and Ninth Legions."

"Was there among them a Linus the Medicus?"

"He is now the highest ranking officer in Carthage."

"As commander of the Queens army I approve your terms, but Linus must be handed over to me alive."

A heated discussion ensued between the Centurions. Finally the senior officer approached Josephus. "Where and when?"

Josephus arrived in time for the groom to break the glass. His wife uttered the words, "If I forget thee, oh Jerusalem, may my tongue cleave to the roof of my mouth and my right hand forget its wisdom." The celebration began.

Wa Ling and Mai Li organized fireworks. Lila's shamans painted good luck symbols on faces, arms and hands of the guests. The fires of roasting pits were seen fifty miles out to sea and from as far away as the the Atlas Mountains. Josephus asked to be seated next to Cahena. "Who gifted those beautiful pigeons?" she asked.

"The Roman Garrison of Carthage."

"Why?"

"They sued for surrender, on condition they are allowed to take their Eagle and supplies enough to reach Constantinople."

"I will have to bring it to the counsel."

"I already agreed."

"You overstepped your authority. I want to make an example of Carthage. Then other cities up the coast will hesitate to oppose me."

"No city in Africa can do battle with you except Numidia, who are allies, their loyalty proven in battle." He handed her the ornate veil adorned with precious and semi-precious stones, and woven threads of gold and silver, that had covered the statue of the Goddess Tanit in the Carthaginian Temple.

Cahena took the veil. "Rationally, you are correct. Procedurally, you violated the chain of command."

"I had to seize the opportunity." Josephus explained the terms of the treaty while watching Cahena's face. Her eyes softened and the tight line of her lips eased into a slight smile, until he said, "The agreement hinges on their ability to hand over Medicus Linus. They agreed."

Cahena inhaled deeply, grabbed Josephus by his leather jacket, pulled him to her and kissed his forehead. "You are vindicated and forgiven." She nodded to Ahmed and his wife. "The bride and groom are showered with gifts, but none could be as satisfying as the one you have given me. I want the skin of one of those cows they slaughtered for the feast. Have it flayed, dried, scraped and stretched in time for Linus."

The Sheva Brachot Festivities consisted of seven meals and blessings, held day after evening in the larger village of the Priests, and the Israelites every afternoon. Each group attempted to outdo the other. The newly married couple were escorted by celebrants wherever they went. When the seventh festive meal was completed and the rabbis had blessed the couple, Cahena set sail for Carthage and the surrender of that city.

Josephus arranged an honor-guard of Berber horsemen to escort Cahena to the dock, where the ceremony would take place. There were only seven hundred Roman soldiers aboard eighteen ships waiting to weigh anchor. The Berber general who took charge of the city reported to Cahena and Josephus: "The Romans destroyed nothing, and took only that which was agreed upon. The city's treasury is safe and the merchants assured of protection. The tide is about to turn and we must leave. The senior officer will now hand over his sword and the city."

Cahena nodded, the general signaled, and Linus led the ten Centurions behind him to face Cahena. Linus placed his sword on the back of his outstretched hands and presented it to the queen. He smiled as she took the sword. He said, "When we first met, my hawks killed your pigeons. I could never imagine you would defeat two Roman legions."

"And I could not imagine you would be the architect of my father's death."

Linus flinched as though whipped across the face. Cahena nodded to the senior Centurion who barked, "To the rear, march!" The ten

Centurions did an about-face and led the Roman garrison onto the ships heading for Constantinople.

Linus was too stunned to resist the Berbers who pinned his arms. He had no idea what the cow hide spread on the ground at dockside was for until he was thrown upon it. Pieces of wood were placed in the crook of his arms and behind his knees. They were bent over the wood and tied tightly with wet strips of rawhide. He was rolled up tightly, with his hands forced into his armpits and legs under him. He and the skin were then doused with buckets of sea water. The skin was again soaked with water and pulled tighter around him. He was left to bake in the heat of the summer's sun. He was surprised that upon request the guards gave him fresh water to drink. He tried to think why his arms and legs were positioned with wood between them.

After several hours in the sun it became clear. The wet cow hide shrank. It forced his legs and bent arms together over the pieces of wood. The pain was slow and excruciating as the bones bent at first and tore the ligaments. At sundown the bones fractured. The shrinkage stopped but not the pain. He promised himself he would not scream but the pain was continuous. He could not control himself. The rays of the morning sun renewed the drying process. The bones in his arms snapped first. Then his legs broke. At noon the shoulders fractured, and Linus spat blood. He made every effort to swallow his tongue.

When he succeeded, the guard was instructed by Cahena. He calmly reached into Linus' mouth and pulled the tongue out. He took a six-inch wood splinter, stretched out Linus' tongue, and drove the splinter through the tip outside his lips.

When his ribs cracked, Cahena was called as the rest of his body was crushed by the shrinking skin. She took satisfaction in his moans and spasms. He was out of his mind and couldn't understand a word Cahena said, but she spoke anyway. "You stole my father from me. You robbed my son of his grandfather and the Jews of a leader who wished to rebuild the Temple in Jerusalem. It was your poison that killed my father, and your poisonous influence that convinced Selim to murder his own son. You tortured and killed my Aksil. Slowly now, the hide will shrink and squeeze your innards up your throat and out your mouth. I will leave you here for the dogs and carrion birds to feed upon. They will then shit your remains all over this beach."

Cahena retired to the house in which she

had lived before the campaign to Tangiers. Ozeret was curled up on the floor like the familiar bundle of rags. Cahena took a pillow from her own bed to make the woman more comfortable—but the moment she touched her, Cahena's heart shrank. Her surrogate mother was dead.

Cahena took the wrinkled face in her hands, and placed her forehead against that of Ozeret. She entered the long hall of souls without windows or doors, ceilings or floors. There was only one soul fluttering in the distance. Cahena attempted to approach it. The soul tried to reach out but was drawn away by an invisible force. It was Ozeret's soul. It shouted, "Whom have you helped? What have you learned?" Then it was gone. Cahena was left holding the wrinkled face in her hands, looking into the dead eyes of the woman who had raised her.

The Witch of the Maghreb was buried in a grave at the entrance to Carthage. The ceremony was secret, held at midnight by Lila and her fellow shamans. Cahena had a domed building built for the use of Pagans, with the name OZERET—helper—carved on the lintel stone. A large kitchen with a royal guarantee of food for wayfaring strangers was initiated in her name.

With the submission of Carthage under benevolent terms, Hippo Regius, Cirta, Sicca, Utica and all cities along the Mediterranean coast sent delegations to pay homage to the new Queen of North Africa. The island of Malta and the Metropolis of Syracuse in Sicily requested vassal status. The city of Carthage became the de facto capitol of the new Berber Government. Roman rule ended in the Mediterranean Sea at Malta.

CHAPTER 24

A LETTER FROM UNCLE BENYAMIN

"To Cahena, Queen of the Berbers, ruler of Africa: This is your Uncle Benyamin, writing you about important matters which fate has thrust upon your humble servant. Needless to say, I hope this correspondence finds you and your son in good health. I do hope the demands of queenship are not too difficult. How proud your father would be! He adored you. Now you must honor him. Be a good queen and leader of your people. Use the Torah as a rule and guide for your faith and practice of Judaisim.

"The new Emperor Leo, described by your Josephus as a twisted liar who could walk upright under a snake's belly with a turban on, is also a clever statesman. To consolidate his power he succeeded in buying the services of the Bulgars against the Muslims in Thrace. His success encouraged him to solicit the Khazars to obstruct the European hordes attacking

Roman territory. The Khazars are an organized group of Turkish tribes, of mixed religious affiliations: Pagans, Christians, Muslims and Jews, who fielded an army powerful enough to defeat tribes from Russia, Sweden, Germany, and Gaul. Their territory borders India, Persia, China, Russia, and Hungary.

"King Ovadia of the Khazars held an intellectual/moral competition between the three monotheistic religious groups to determine which should become the official state religion of Khazari. The Roman Catholic Church sent a bishop, Muhammad a Caliph, and the Jews put forward a rabbi. The debate took place some twenty years ago in the year 611 and lasted several months. Legend said that at the end of the debate King Ovadia asked each divine one simple question: 'What does your religion forbid?' The Muslim quoted all the injunctions in the Old Testament, plus the statements of Mohammed. The Christian quoted all the injunctions in the Old Testament, plus statements of Jesus and the successive Popes. The rabbi quoted only the Torah. King Ovadia chose Judaism.

"More accurately, the Kingdom of the Khazars had become a refuge for Israelites who fled persecution from the Roman Catholics and Muslims. The exiled Jews flourished in education, thrived in trade and excelled in the Khazarian military. The Army of the Khazars was the most powerful in the region. King Ovadia and his advisors, reacting to common sense and the will of the people, recognized the falsehood of primitive shamanism as barbaric and ill-suited to modern national and political needs. Compared to the three great monotheistic creeds, Paganism lacked the spiritual and legal authority required to guide a great power.

"One of his royal Khazarian advisors said, 'There are three groups who claim they have the truth in their religious practices. Invite them to debate the virtues of their religion; then you can determine which is best for our people.' And so it was that the Prophet sent a caliph, the Pope in Rome sent a bishop, and the Jews put forward a renowned rabbi from Babylon. For months the debate continued in the King's palace. The three spokesmen were eloquent in their presentations and persuasive answering questions of the royal councilors. King Ovadia stepped in, saying, 'Enough. This discussion has gone on too long. Bring the Christian bishop before me.' When his order was carried out he said, 'I have one question for you. Which of the other two religions is closest to the truth of your religion?'

"The Bishop answered, 'Judaism'. When

called, the caliph answered, 'Judaism'. When the rabbi was asked, he said, 'There is only one truth. Either it is or is not the truth. Judaism does not seek converts.'

"'What is it you are hiding?'

"'Not hiding, your highness: trying to protect the gentile. Become a Jew, and you must commit to six hundred and thirteen commandments. A gentile need only adhere to the Seven Laws of Noah.' King Ovadia raised his scepter and said, 'By a vote of two to one, Judaism will be the official state religion of Khazaria!'

"And so it was. Hebrew teachers and rabbis were enticed by wealth and persuaded by honorifics to come from the academies in Iraq, Babylon, Spain and Israel to set up schools and teach the Hebrew alphabet. There being no Khazarian alphabet, Hebrew was used phonetically to represent the Khazarian language. The king and four thousand nobles were converted in a mass ceremony. Talmudists were hired from Babylon and Persia. Jewish rabbinical law ruled the land. Much like you and the Berber Jews, the majority of Khazarian converts worship idols, have not been circumcised and do not adhere to the Sabbath. Most of those who do are the elite class. They study in the new academies of Talmudic learning, their food is kosher, and the Jews of Djerba who will not eat in my house would have no problem breaking bread with these true converts to Judaism.

"I tell you this story because Emperor Leo of Constantinople enlisted the services of the most famous caravan master in the East—yours truly, Benyamin of Toledo. I was directed to meet the King of the Khazars in the city of Tbilisi on the Caspian Sea. That is where I am writing from. I was ordered to offer gold, silver, and territories in the Caucuses rich in minerals and forests, for the Khazars to form a military alliance with the Romans to oppose the Huns, Vandals, and Goths. I was chosen because I am a Jew who is known to use his contacts to learn about Jewish communities, dispersed in various parts of the world, and intervene on their behalf when necessary. The above story was told to me by Rabbi David ben Avraham, son of the rabbi who presented the argument for Judaism. Upon hearing the story I felt great pride in being Jewish. It hasn't always been so. I went to sleep thinking of the great debate and how pleased our Lord must be with the results, but I didn't sleep well. Something kept gnawing at me. It had to do with the story and the study of Talmud and King Ovadia's acceptance of Judaism as the state religion.

"Then it struck me. There is an axiom in the study of Talmud: 'Fifty percent of the answer can be found in a good question.' Certainly the king's question to the three clergymen was good. He knew at least fifty percent of the answer before it was given. He and his councilors had to know that both the Christian and Muslim faiths are based on Judaism's monotheistic values and prophetic guidance. So the King knew the answer before he asked the question. My question was, why did he select Judaism? I rushed to catch David ben Avraham at morning prayers. When I asked, 'Why did King Ovadia go through this whole charade to receive an answer he already knew?' the young man patted my shoulder as if I was his student. 'You are right,' he answered. 'And once again look into the axiom of a good question holding the answer.'

"For a moment I was bewildered. Then I began answering my own questions. 'The king wanted a neutral position with the Islamic and Christian worlds.' The young rabbi confirmed with a nod and smile, and he said, 'The Khazars may be illiterate, but they are extremely clever, ingenious, and manipulative. They coordinated the outcome of the debate before it ever started.'

"'And its purpose?'

"'To remain neutral. Khazaria sits on the North/South, East/West junctions of the Silk

Road and the caravan routes from the middle-east. Whether you are coming or going to Europe, you must pay duty to the most powerful military force in the area. That is the key to the Khazarian economy. Neutrality suits them. In Christianity lay the danger of Khazaria becoming an ecclesiastical vassal of the Pope. In Islam the Khazars would be subject to the Prophet and his Caliphs. Judaism has the Bible and Talmud to guide it; the only power enforcing it is rabbinical interpretation. No Israelite force exists to implement compliance. Because Christianity and Islam are founded in Judaism, the Khazars feel protected against interference of Prophet or Pope. Judaism became an acceptable monotheistic faith. It could not be denied by either of the two most powerful military religions.'

"My dear niece, the sheer genius of this plan and its implementation is worth contemplation. But now your humble servant puts forward a separate plan for your approval. The death of your father was ordered by the Romans. I believe he was betrayed be the three rabbis who knew of his intent to seize Jerusalem and rebuild the Holy Temple. Selim, Chieftain of the Helawi, informed the Romans and Linus gave him the poison. Since your father's plan was known, you may be suspect by the Romans and the Muslims of a similar plan. You have a hundred thousand fighting men. King Gershom commands one hundred thousand and the Khazars another hundred thousand of the best fighting men in the region. I have initiated a whispering campaign about restoring the Holy Temple with the help of the Khazars in the north, the Numidians in the south and you from the center. You would field a battle-tested army of one third of a million strong. Together you could crush the Christians and Muslims. I doubt either would attempt to defend the Holy City against such a force, nor would they form an alliance against you because of their religious differences. Please advise if I should pursue this idea.

"Your humble servant, Uncle Benyamin of Toledo.

"PS. I recall those Sabbath evenings together, and fondly remember our visits to the Chinese for dinner."

The letter reminded Cahena, and she had Mai Li prepare a Chinese meal for her, where she took Josephus, Lila, and her councilors into her confidence. She read Benyamin's letter and asked how to proceed. Not one of them had heard of a Jewish kingdom, But all were in favor of exploring the possibility of attaining a powerful religious ally. Most felt the Berbers were not

Jewish enough for the Khazars.

Yakov, Benyamin's nephew, now a handsome young man and Cahena's lover, took over his father's role as commander of the merchant fleet, liaison between the Port of Carthage, the island of Djerba and consultant on Jewish religious matters. He said, "The Khazars appear to have thought out their position in relation to Christianity and Islam. The leaders of this nation may have converted to Judaism, but their purpose was not to serve God; it is to maintain a neutral position between the two great powers. We should explore the possibilities of an alliance with Khazari, If just to keep the Prophet Muhammad and Emperor Leo aware that there are other Jews prepared to fight."

"And about a campaign to take Jerusalem?" Cahena asked.

"It would unite the Jews of the world," Yaakov answered.

"If Uncle Benyamin's figures are correct," Josephus said, "With a hundred thousand each of Numidians, Khazars, and Berbers we could crush the Romans' and the Muslim forces no matter how many times a day they pray. But you would have to strip the garrisons of every town and city in North Africa. Most of our army acts as civil administrators. To have the queen's government disappear just after its birth is recipe for disaster. You could take Jerusalem but lose Africa."

The discussion continued into the morning, when Cahena proclaimed, "I shall encourage Uncle Benyamin to pursue the idea of combining forces to free Jerusalem. I will submit a formal request to King Ovadia of the Khazars to send a delegation to explore this matter."

"Wouldn't it be swifter if we sent a delegation to Khazari?" A chieftain asked

"You are right, and I am not wrong. Our request will take months to reach the Caucasus. If they decide to consider the proposal, another few months will pass before they arrive. By then, hopefully, our government framework will be in place."

"To conduct such a campaign," Josephus said, "We must start planning now. Our conquest of Jerusalem cannot take longer than four years—for in five years the Muslims Led by General Khalid ibn Al Walid will charge into the Maghreb, prayer book in one hand sword in the other."

In the following days Cahena assigned Ahmed to the horse and camel herds of the potential invasion force. Chieftains were delegated to draw up transportation routes to Jerusalem for the Berber and Numidian armies. Stockpiles of weapons were organized. Food, fodder and supplies required to invade Israel and lay siege to Jerusalem were prepared. Training schedules for the army were implemented. The latter included the Chinese crossbow for new archers. Lila assigned her shamans to gather information regarding Jerusalem, its fortifications and water supplies, possible allies and enemies along the invasion route. Josephus was placed in overall command of the Army. Cahena removed the small stone from her purse and handed it to a messenger. "This is for King Gershom. I respectfully request the Numidian Army join us in the re-conquest of Jerusalem."

Cahena's administrative duties left little time to study the mystic arts, and she was less interested in her child's needs. Lila was only too happy to care for the baby. She often brought him to council meetings.

In one of these meetings Cahena inadvertently revealed her ability to read the litigants' minds before they ever spoke. Lila cautioned her to conceal this skill, as people would hesitate to come before her, and a person's thoughts were not always related to their actions.

A month later, while hearing a case between the city of Zama, suing the Berber government for payment of wheat and livestock requisitioned by the army, she accidentally wandered into the mind of one of the landowners. He was thinking, "Why doesn't the government buy the crops in advance? We would receive money for seed, and they pay the going rate when harvested."

The idea was an epiphany for Cahena. She used it in reply to Uncle Benyamin: "Broach the subject of Jerusalem and restoring the Holy Temple to the King of the Khazars. Request they send a delegation to Carthage where the matter can be discussed." She added a second scroll for Benyamin, in which she detailed the following plan; "On your return from Khazari to Carthage, please go by way of Jerusalem. When you leave our holy city I wish you to map all water sources. When you have gone beyond the Roman outposts on the main caravan trail, inquire the following of landowners along the route:

1—Would they accept payment in advance for seed and fodder, and sell the plantings to the Berber Monarchy at the present rate?

2—On the 36th day of wheat growth (called Flag Leaf), a second payment of 10 % will be made at the rate price.

3—On the 90th day of reaping, a final and complete payment made per bushel at the same price mentioned in article 2.

4—Livestock and crops to be stored for a period of one year, at the landowner's expense.

"Dear Uncle, never reveal our purpose. Claim you are a speculator, purchasing crops in advance of them being sown and livestock yet to be born in expectation the prices will rise. I trust your bargaining skills. If required, I am prepared to pay storage expenses; use it as a negotiating point. You probably already surmised the intention of this plan: to feed the two potential hundred-thousand-man armies of Berbers and Numidians marching to Jerusalem. You may say I put the cart before the camel, but I have enough gold and silver from the Carthage treasury and the tribute flowing in from cities in Africa, Crete, Sicily, Corsica, and Gibraltar.

"Four things can happen. Either there is a good or bad crop. If there is a bad crop, we then must import food. If a good crop, then we can feed this massive army. The following two things depend on either marching on Jerusalem or not. If we three monarchs agree to challenge the Romans in Jerusalem, we have a stable food supply. If our coalition of forces does not materialize, then we control the regional output of agriculture and livestock. We set the price. Even more appealing is your nephew Yaakov's idea of using his ships to sell the grain in Italy and Greece. He says it will bring twice the price abroad.

"My dear Uncle Benyamin, I respect your experience and judgment. Please evaluate my idea in light of your skill and knowledge. I await your advice. Cahena, Queen of the Berbers"

Uncle Benyamin forwarded his approval by rider and pigeon. He started the journey to Jerusalem with a delegation from the King of the Khazars prepared to negotiate a military treaty with the queen of the Berbers.

Cahena tasked Yaakov with using his trading connections with the merchants of Naples to have their cartographers create a large detailed map of the known world.

Cahena was twenty years old, stood six feet three inches tall, weighed one hundred and eighty pounds, and could throw a javelin further than most men. With sword and shield she was invincible, and although she attempted to conceal her power of insight the feathered silver streak of hair confirmed her as a sorceress. Even her most courageous warriors avoided eye contact with those fractured grey irises.

In her duties as final arbiter of the Appeals Court she required two witnesses to affirm claims. This and other laws of verification required in the Torah were implemented for

Jews. For non-Jews who agreed, she used the Berber method of boiling water or a hot sword over the tongue.

Her son was into everything. He took after his grandmother: small in stature, light of skin coloring, with red hair and lots of freckles. Cahena enjoyed him in brief periods between diaper changes and cleaning the mud off of him. Lila enjoyed those tasks, and Cahena left her to it.

Two letters of importance arrived.

The first, dictated by her two Bedouin scouts to a village scribe, read: "To our Queen Cahena of the Berbers. Your humble servants know of the five-year truce you have with the Muslims. The Prophet Muhammad has placed General Walid ibn Al Walid in charge of building an army to invade the Maghreb and convert every Pagan to Islam. It gives the General time to form a large, well-trained, and well-supplied force to accomplish the task.

"There are whispers in the tents of Islam: 'Who will succeed the Prophet?' The reason for this is he has taken ill twice, and was unable to lead the prayers in the Medina Mosque. The scribe tells us the Prophet is now sixty-one years old. In the sermons he preaches, it often sounds as if he knows he will not be with us much longer. It saddens us, for if we were younger men, Islam would sound like a better religion. We Bedouin worship nature, but the Prophet preaches that the laws of nature were imposed by Allah. Nature reacts according to God's rules of creation. No one knows what will happen when the Prophet dies. We certainly do not. —Your servants in the Maghreb."

Cahena and her council discussed at length the repercussions resulting from the death of the Prophet. The two main topics were either a complete collapse of the Islamic religion or a consolidation into an organized religious government, ruled by a figure similar to the Catholic Pope in Constantinople. In either case the Prophet's passing would delay an invasion of the Maghreb.

The second letter was received a month later from Uncle Benyamin:

"Two years ago in 629, Heraclius, Emperor of the Eastern Roman Empire defeated the Sassanid forces at Nineveh—mentioned in the Book of Jonah. He took control of what is called the Fertile Crescent, and that includes Jerusalem. He disregards all religions but Christianity, and immediately ordered construction of the Church of the Holy Sepulcher. The Jews who remain in Jerusalem live on alms from Pagans, Muslims, and Jews from abroad. They are desperately poor. Rarely will you find a Jewish workman, few young men or women, and no children. The old men study and argue. It was from them I learned that a great part of the Roman success was that at the battle of Nineveh, against the Sassanid's Army, they had forty thousand of the fiercest Khazars fighting for them. This was not told to me when King Leo sent me to negotiate, nor when King Ovadia assigned a delegation to meet with you. The Khazars are very clever people. Be wary.

To broach the subject of invading Israel and rebuilding the Holy Temple, I had to be very careful. The majority of Khazari Jews avoid stirring up the Romans. Heraclius the Roman calls himself the King of Kings. He is considered a good administrator and military tactician, and utterly ruthless in his quest to succeed.

"A few Jerusalem Jews accept the idea of rebuilding the Temple, as long as we understand there will be no help from them. The remainder opposes us, and had to be convinced it was against the Torah to report another Jew to the Romans, which would result in our death. This group is awaiting the Messiah; redemption, they say, is in God's hands. They will not cooperate. In my opinion this group of fanatics will probably report me to the authorities. Therefore I leave to contact the landowners as per your request. I hope to see you in three months. —Your humble and very proud servant, Uncle Benyamin."

Ahmed's wife gave birth to a boy. Upon being slapped on the rump, he howled and his father collapsed. Ahmed's son had a voice.

As godmother, Cahena sent over a procession of servants with gifts for the child and his parents. Cahena spent as much time with Ahmed's son as she did with her own, which wasn't that often.

She was dedicated to her work, arising at dawn, worshiping her gods, exercising with Josephus on her daily run, waking up Yaakov for breakfast. He then joined the morning Jewish prayer service and went to his headquarters in the Port of Carthage. He had added five more ships, bringing his fleet to twelve. The wine imports from Naples was still lucrative. His captains plied the Adriatic, Ionian and Mediterranean Seas in search of profit. He commissioned five merchant ships to be built in Syracuse and ten more in Tangiers. He would require thirty additional craft to support land forces marching on Jerusalem. With Josephus' advice he designed the new craft to carry more sail and less cargo, and build for speed to outrun the Roman triremes. The Roman Navy had proved its domination against a more numerous Muslim fleet.

The relationship between Yaakov and Cahena began as a simple love affair; they satisfied each other's physical needs. He was superior in academia, being schooled in Talmud and Torah from the age of three, and later in the Carthage Academy of Mathematics and Science. There he had specialized in cartography. She was a naturally brilliant mind combined with mystical skills which she continued to explore spirituality with Lila, sorceress of the Berbers.

The relationship developed to the point where Yaakov proposed marriage. His condition was that Cahena throw away her idols and learn to keep a ritually correct Jewish home. She exploded and threw him out of her home. They were apart for two weeks when he required her permission to sign a contract with Cyprus for shipping rights to and from their major ports.

He was obliged to enter her home. She was alone. He closed the door behind him and tried to speak. The two only looked at each other, and lust consumed them. They were panting within seconds. Cahena ripped wide her vest and her magnificent breasts broke free. "You once asked me if you could touch these," she whispered.

"And you said, no."

"Now I want you to eat them!"

They rushed to each other. He caressed one breast and kissed the other. She rained kisses on his head. He reached down under her skirt with both hands, coming up her legs and bare thighs. She opened his trousers and took his erection in both hands, panting, "Put this into me. Quick! Hurry! I need it!" He lifted her off the floor, rushed her to a table, and put her on it. She raised her legs and he entered her. They clung to each other. "Push! Push it back and forth! Round and round," she gasped. "Pump! Pump up and down in and out back and forth... Fuck me to death!"

She wet one of his nipples with her tongue and then manipulated it with her fingers while sucking the other nipple. He exploded inside her—and continued stroking. His penis hardened again, and she squeezed the breath from his lungs as she threw back her head and moaned, "Fuck me to death! I want to die fucking! I love it. I need it. Don't stop... Oh! Oh! I'm coming again! Keep that erection... Oh, it's melting. I can feel it getting smaller... Why did you take it out? I wanted to come again."

He shoved her backward, put his head between her thighs and his face into the curly black mound of hair. His tongue darted out, and she shivered. He lapped her until his face was wet, and he pressed deeper and deeper extending his tongue over his teeth. She began weeping with joy. He reached up and massaged her breasts while his tongue worked furiously to bring her to a climax. She spasmed and gasped, "Stop! Stop!" She raised his head from between her thighs and kissed his face, wet with her juices.

She slipped off the table and lifted him to stand up on it. First she took his scrotum in her mouth and began to suck until he moaned in pleasure, and as she sucked harder he moaned in blissful pain. His penis hardened again and stood erect. She took it between her lips and sucked him until he wailed.

"Lie down on this table," she ordered. He did, and she mounted him and slipped his erection into her. Now she controlled the up and down, the in and out, the back and forth. He looked up. Her face glistened with sweat. He fondled her breasts and she moved more quickly. He raised his hips to penetrate deeper, and she quivered. Her body convulsed—then went limp. Her expression went from intense grimace to completely relaxed, and she gently kissed him.

"I love you," she said. "Not the marrying kind

of love, but this good fucking love."

"I think we can go on as we were," he admitted.

"It's the best way."

CHAPTER 25

THE PASSING OF THE PROPHET

From Muhammed's sermon in Medina, people understood the Prophet foresaw his death. He said: "There is a slave among the slaves of Allah, the One God, to whom God has offered the choice between this world and that which is with Him, and the slave has chosen that which is with God. Beware of Satan, for the safety of your religion. He has lost all hope that he will ever be able to lead you astray in great things, so beware of following him in small things. People, just as you regard this month, this day, this city as Sacred, so regard the life and property of every Muslim as a sacred trust. Return the goods entrusted to you to their rightful owners. Hurt no one so that no one may hurt you. Remember that you will indeed meet your Lord, and that He will indeed reckon your deeds. Allah has forbidden you to take usury; therefore all interest obligation shall henceforth be waived. Your capital, however, is yours to keep. You will neither inflict nor suffer any inequity. Allah has judged that there shall be no interest...

"O People, it is true that you have certain rights with regard to your women, but they also have rights over you. Remember that you have taken them as your wives only under Allah's trust and with His permission. If they abide by your right, then to them belongs the right to be fed and clothed in kindness. Do treat your women well and be kind to them, for they are your partners and committed helpers—and it is your right that they do not make friends with any one of whom you do not approve, as well as never to be unchaste.

"Remember, one day you will appear before Allah and answer your deeds. So beware, do not stray from the path of righteousness after I am gone. All mankind is from Adam and Eve, an Arab has no superiority over a non-Arab nor a non-Arab has any superiority over an Arab; also a white has no superiority over black, nor does a black have any superiority over white except by piety and good action. Learn that every Muslim is a brother to every Muslim and that the Muslims constitute one brotherhood. O People, listen to me in earnest, worship Allah, say your five daily prayers, fast during the month of Ramadan, and give your wealth in charity. Perform *Hajj* if you can afford to."

What the Muslims took from this was that the Prophet foresaw his death coming soon.

In February 632, the Prophet traveled from Medina to perform the Hajj in Mecca. He was accompanied by all his wives. Thousands of followers escorted the Prophet. He stopped in Miquat, a small city in the province of Mecca, where he taught people the manners of wearing a pure white garment as a pilgrim. He made the ritual bath and then put on the white robe for the Hajj; his *Ihram* was two pieces of Yemeni white cotton. He did his noon prayers in the mosque of Shajara. The next day, Muhammad and his companions arrived at the Masjid al-Harem. They entered from the gate of Dar al-Salam, went to the Kaaba and touched the black stone. Then Muhammad proceeded to Circumambulation of the Kaaba, finally once again touched the Kaaba, kissed it, and cried long near it. Then he did two ritual performances of prayer behind the Station of Abraham. His companions watched avidly and memorized all that he did.

After his prayers he drank from the Zamzam well, prayed, and then went to Mounts Al-Safa and Al-Marwah, and said that he would begin walking back and forth between them. When he arrived there, he turned toward the Kaaba and prayed, and trotted part of the way. When he arrived at Mount Al-Marwah, he stopped and prayed. His companions followed.

On the eighth sunset of his *Dhu al-Hijjah*, Muhammad left for Mina and stayed there for a night. Then he rode his camel, *al Qaswa'*, till he reached Mount Arafat. As he ascended the mountain, he was surrounded by thousands of pilgrims chanting Talbiyah and Takbir. By Muhammad's order, a tent was erected for him on the east side of Mount Arafat at a place called Namirah. He rested until the sun passed the zenith, then he rode his camel until he reached the valley of Uranah. On the 9th day he delivered his Farewell Sermon, concerning different social rights of Muslims, and led the Zuhr and Asr prayer. Then he moved to the plain of Arafat, stayed there and spent the afternoon in supplication.

At sunset, Muhammad rode towards Muzdalifa. There he did his Maghrib and Isha prayers, then rested. At dawn he prayed and supplicated before Allah. Later, he went towards Mina and Jamrah of Aqaba and threw seven pebbles at it. He then sacrificed sixty-three camels—the number of years of his life. He gave Ali thirty-seven camels from a herd to sacrifice. They ate little of the meat, and gave the rest for charity. By his order, a barber shaved his head. He then went back to Mecca, circumambulated the Kaaba again and did the Zuhr midday prayer in Masjid al-Harem. He then came to the well of Zamzam and drank its water, and returned to Mina on the same day and spent the 11th, 12th and 13th days there, where he did the Stoning of the Devil, and then exited Mina.

On his way back to Medina, Muhammad stopped at Ghadir Khumm to convey the message to the pilgrims before they dispersed. He gave a long sermon on a rostrum of camel saddles. At one point he asked his followers whether he, Muhammad, had more authority over the believers than they had over themselves; the crowd's answer was a loud positive. Then he took Ali by the hand and declared: "Whomever's master I am, this Ali is also his master."

The Prophet then announced his imminent death, and charged the believers to remain attached to the Qur'anic teachings. His caravan left for Medina, and arrived on 24th of Dhu al-Hijjah, the last days of the holy month.

The Prophet spent his waning hours with his youngest wife, A'isha. His illness intensified, and he asked Abu Bakr to lead the prayers. He felt better, went to the Mosque with the assistance of 'Ali and Fadl ibn 'Abbas, and when Abu

Bakr retreated from leading the prayers to allow the Prophet to return to his place, the Prophet indicated for him to continue and stood for prayer by his side. Following morning prayers, Abu Bakr visited him and upon seeing his situation slightly improved, returned to his home. However, the Prophet's condition deteriorated suddenly.

A'isha said that before Prophet Muhammad passed away he said softly, "There is no god but God. How difficult it is to surrender the soul!"—and passed away in her arms, whispering the words, "To the Highest Abode." It was Monday, the 8th of June, 632.

The Prophet's death caused infinite sorrow for the Muslims. Some claimed he was not dead. Receiving the news, Abu Bakr came directly to the Prophet's side, raised the veil covering his face and kissed the Prophet saying, "O God's Messenger! You were beautiful while alive and are beautiful in your death." Then going to the Prophet's mosque, he declared, "Oh people, if any among you worshipped Muhammad, then let them know that Muhammad is dead, but whosoever worshipped Allah, God is alive and will never die." Then he recited a Qur'anic verse: "Muhammad is but a Messenger, and Messengers passed away before him. If then he dies or is killed, will you turn back on your heels? Whoever turns back on his heels can in no way harm Allah, but God will reward the thankful ones."

The Prophet's body was washed on Tuesday, by Ali with the help of the sons of the Prophet's uncle, and was kept in the room he had died in. The funeral prayer was not performed in congregation; first the men, and then the women, and then children came into the room where the Prophet's body lay—in groups as large as were possible—and performed the funeral prayer individually. His body was placed in a grave in accordance with a hadith related by Abu Bakr.

Prophet Muhammed left behind a modest inheritance. At his passing, he had under his ownership a white mule, some weapons, and a certain amount of land. He had ordered that the income from these lands be used for his family, with the rest to be handed over to the public treasury. As for Muhammad's spiritual legacy, it was very great and valuable both for his community and, he expected, for all humanity for all times. As he had stated in his Farewell Sermon, he left behind the Qur'an and the Sunna: a verbally transmitted record of his teachings, deeds and sayings. The religion and civilization of Islam crystallized around these two key sources.

Ali, Muhammed's son-in-law and cousin, reported that Muhammed's penis was erect after his death, as a sign of the Prophet's virility.

The Ihram clothing of white cotton worn by the prophet during the Hajj became his shroud.

Cahena in Carthage and Yaakov in the port had little time for each other; both were occupied by decisions and assessments in trade, taxes, crops, land holdings and tribal disputes. In addition, they conferred with Josephus on his deployment and buildup of the army while entertaining foreign delegations bent on economic, military, and social alliances.

It was early in September when Josephus held the door open to Cahena's reception room. Two little ragged sunburned Bedouin scouts shuffled in. Both bowed. Cahena rushed over, scooped them up in her arms and hugged and kissed their balding heads. "I was pitying myself for not enjoying life, and you two bring sunlight and flowers where darkness ruled. You both could use a bath, some Italian wine, and two beautiful girls to scrub your backs. Then we'll have dinner, and you can tell me what's happening in the world. Josephus, take care of these rascals. I have another delegation to meet. You, Lila, Ahmed and his family, join us."

Dinner was served late, as both scouts fell

asleep in the arms of the girls while in the tub. They were hardly recognizable, dressed in the finest brocade jackets, silk pantaloons and jewel-encrusted turbans. The two ate mightily, holding meat and bread in one hand, chicken and vegetables in their mouths, and guzzling a large goblet of wine from Naples.

"Where have you two been?" Cahena asked.

"To Arabia, and all those places in between."

"And do they talk about the Berbers and our defeat of the Romans?"

"Not outside of the Maghreb. Your name and deeds are unknown to the ordinary people."

"What do they speak of?"

"The death of the Prophet. It consumes the thoughts and actions of everyone—Muslim, Pagan or whatever. It must have been a miserable mood similar to this when God struck down the first-born of Egypt."

"What are the effects on the people?"

"Depressing on non-Muslims as well as keepers of the faith. Some rushed to convert to Islam, while many Muslims ran to the shamans for direction."

"Who will succeed Muhammed as leader of Islam?" Cahena asked.

"That's the problem. None of Muhammed's sons lived to adulthood. The Prophet did not say who should rule. The elders of Muhammad's inner circle put forward candidates, and voted Abu Bakr to succeed Muhammad as Caliph. They call themselves Sunni, or Lawful ones. Opposing them is Ali, the Prophet's first cousin also a member of the inner circle. He claims the Caliphate by virtue of lineage. His group call themselves Shia, Supporters of Ali."

"Did they fight?" Josephus asked.

"Not yet. Ali accepted temporary rule by Abu Bakr."

"I would have rather seen them fight each other."

"Ali did not have enough troops. In addition, General Walid is building a force on your southern border to attack you in four years. The two groups, Shia and Sunni, agreed to carry out the wishes of the Prophet and convert all Africa to Islam. Their defeat at Constantinople and loss of so many men and ships delays their entrance into Europe. They vow to try again."

"Tell me about General Walid," Cahena said.

"He was one of the candidates for Caliph, but they needed his services in the army."

"What of his army?" Josephus asked.

"The General is committed to Muhammad's orders. He will not move against your Berbers for the five years. He is patient, meticulous, and determined to build a force strong enough to conquer the Maghreb and make it part of the

Bakr Caliphate."

Lila said, "We've been told that after the Prophet's death many Muslims renounced their faith."

"True. And some of them were in General Walid's army. He recommended to the Caliphate that since Christians and Jews believe in one God they be offered an alternative to death or conversion; they be required to pay *Jizya*—a tax on inferiors called *Dhimmis*. In addition, Muslims would be exempt from most taxes. Most who had renounced Islam reconsidered because of this tax law. Whatever loss in numbers was to Islam was made up for in new converts. They also receive tax benefits."

"I always knew the General was clever,' Josephus said.

"He's practical," the Bedou said. "When conquered, we Pagans have no problem accepting Islam. In secret, we still honor our own gods in addition to theirs. Christians and Jews refused. The Muslims killed so many that there were few left to till the fields or become slaves. The Caliphate established the Inferiority Tax, *Jizya,* to give a place for the non-Muslim. They can now live, as long as they pay."

"We had it all wrong," Lila said. "We thought either Islam would disappear or establish a figure like the Roman Pope. Now we have two religious bodies, Shias and Sunnis, to face."

"Hopefully they will fight each other," Josephus said.

"We may wish what we will, but must prepare for General Walid's invasion," Cahena concluded.

"And the taking of Jerusalem," Josephus added.

A heavy cloud cover obscured the snowcapped peaks of the Atlas Mountains. The lower slopes and the plains leading to Carthage were awash in winter rain. The only passable way was the Roman road. Uncle Benyamin forged ahead of his mile-long caravan to meet Cahena. He stood in the doorway of her reception room wearing a rain-soaked buffalo cape and round fur Kaftan dripping water.

"You look five feet tall and five feet wide," Cahena said. "Drop your wet clothes. The slave will take them." She leaned down to embrace him. "How is your family? How are you? Where are the Khazars?"

"Ho! You've grown a foot taller, and you still have more questions than I have answers. We lost my youngest daughter to malaria. Everyone else is fine. I now have six grandchildren. The trip was the longest I ever made, and profitable. As for the Khazari delegation, they are in the center of the caravan, and will arrive tomorrow. I could use a dentist."

"All the Romans are gone."

"Good. No Roman dentist."

"They were the best."

"Do you know how the Romans clean their teeth? They get up in the morning, piss in a jug, then take a mouthful and rub it into their gums and teeth."

"That's disgusting."

"Some blacksmiths pull teeth with their bare hands."

"Let me ask my Chinese slave. He's our pharmacist."

"Does he cook?"

"I never thought to ask. I'm certain his wife does." Cahena sent for the two.

Wa Ling examined Benyamin, and his wife Mai Li translated. "Your teeth are very dirty. Don't you clean them?"

"No. Do you clean yours?"

"Of course."

"These two don't talk like slaves. How do you clean teeth?"

"Every Chinese child learns to pluck a twig from a tree, chew one end to make a small brush, and force it between your teeth to push out the food. My husband says you have a very bad cavity. A tooth on the lower jaw must come out; it is infected. He will put on medication to stop the infection, give you opium to reduce the pain, and wrap a thin thread around the tooth."

"Is he going to pull it out with the thread?"

"No. He will return later tonight and push the thread further down into the gum. And again tomorrow morning. By the afternoon he should be able to loosen the tooth with his fingers and remove it."

Benyamin's chest heaved in a monumental sigh. "Let's get on with it."

Wa Ling discouraged his wife from cooking food for the patient until three days after the extraction. She then made roast duck, a dish called drunken chicken, lamb and fried rice. The meal finished with dried lychee nuts and Jasmine tea.

Cahena, Yaakov, Benyamin and his family and the Khazari delegation were invited for the Sabbath on the island of Djerba. Only after the Sabbath could business be discussed. Early Sunday morning, Benyamin met with Cahena in her rooms in the Carthage Citadel. He gave a brief history of the Khazars and their conversion to Judaism. "They study Talmud and Torah, and made phonetic Hebrew the written and spoken Indo/Turkish dialect. It is the elite class who studies, prays, eats kosher, and puts on phylacteries every morning. As dedicated as the aristocrats appear to be, their conversion was commanded by King, Ovadia. It is a royal edict, not a subjective yearning of the soul."

Josephus joined them. "Why Judaism?" he asked.

"In my letter I explained the Khazars are put off by the absolute power of the Pope and Prophet, or now the Caliph. Judaism has no mandated leader or army to enforce Torah or Talmudic compliance. The Khazars see themselves as maintaining a balance between east and west. Their neutrality is backed by a large, professional military. It guarantees their position to collect taxes from caravans traveling in either direction, and from all ports in the Caspian and Black Seas. It also makes it impossible for either the Romans or Muslims to fight them. They would join the other side and wipe out the invader."

"Will they join us in the retaking of Jerusalem?"

"No."

"Then why did they come all this way to deny our request?"

"No, is my opinion. The Khazars may not have a written history, but they know who they are and what they want. They are skilled negotiators. Their mountainous geography provides them with an easy landscape to defend. They are satisfied where they are."

"Do they have many forts?" Josephus asked.

"No, they do not require them. The mountains are as high as twenty thousand feet. They have plateaus above the six-thousand-foot mark that can supply them with grain, vegetables, and fodder for their animals. They have a joke about identifying a Khazar; his one leg is shorter than the other, because from birth he is standing on the side of a mountain. The weather also protects them. Above the six-thousand-foot level the average temperature is twenty-one degrees. In some places, it goes down to minus forty in winter. At lower elevations the rain is so prolific nobody has measured it. In the south, leading to the Black Sea, there falls only four inches of rain a year—not on the coast but in the mountains. The Khazars have dams to divert or stop the flow of water down the slopes to any invading army."

"You saw all this?" Cahena asked.

"Most of it was told to me. King Ovadia displayed his power, wealth, and in doing so possibly his strategy for declining your invitation to conquer Jerusalem."

"But Uncle Benyamin, you said they have not made a commitment one way or the other."

"I've been with them for a year, studied with them, and am giving you my opinion based on their history. They negotiate, stall, make more negotiation and rarely go to war, except when paid in gold or threatened by invasion."

"What do you suggest?' Josephus asked.

"Beat them at their own game. Stall. Hold feasts, games, hunting, boat rides. Let them ask for the meeting to discuss cooperation on taking Jerusalem."

Two weeks after arrival in Carthage, the Khazars requested a conference with the queen to discuss Jerusalem.

Josephus had a large contour map of sand built on the floor. It represented the southern approach to Jerusalem by land and sea from Algeria. He too had used the two weeks to impress the Khazars with the military night of the Berbers, and the contingent of Numidian Light Cavalry which represented a second army of one hundred thousand trained soldiers. The delegation from the Caucasus politely acknowledged the power Cahena wielded, but were non-committal when pressed to obligate themselves.

"It's like trying to hold a wet eel," Josephus said. "They are flopping all over the place."

"I believe your Uncle Benyamin is correct," Lila added. "They have their own priorities and Jerusalem is not one of them. Uncle Benyamin pointed out they would be making an enemy of the Romans in Constantinople who occupy Jerusalem, and the Muslims. And for what? Their people are not committed to your one God. Only the aristocrats are."

"How do you suggest I handle the situation?" Cahena asked.

"Don't antagonize them," Yaakov said.

"Agreed! Josephus added. "I've got enough on my plate between the Romans and the Muslims."

"I thought we ran the Romans out of Africa," Lila said.

"We did, but we never touched their navy. They can float a thousand triremes and more troop ships. If they chose, they'd be here in two weeks." He turned to Yaakov. "How many ships have you?"

"A hundred, mostly merchant ships. Our sailors are not fighters. They would run."

"So we will close this negotiation in an amicable way," Cahena said. "The conquest of Jerusalem must wait. We prepare to meet General Khalid ibn Al Walid in the battle for the Maghreb."

The council members were leaving. "Uncle Benyamin!" Cahena called after him. "I would like a word with you." She dismissed everyone and said, "Your silence this evening was deafening."

"What was on my mind had nothing to do with the discussion."

"What is it?"

"That life plays cruel tricks. Your father used to say, 'Man plans and God laughs.' He planned for you to become Queen of the Berbers, but he wanted a Jewish Queen and the restoration of Jerusalem."

"But you heard the discussion. We cannot depend on the Khazars as allies."

"Why?"

"You said yourself; they have different goals than ours."

"Why are they different?"

"Because they are not committed to Judaism."

Tears welled up in Benyamin's eyes and streaked his ruddy cheeks. "And you, dear Queen of the Berbers who worship idols along with the Blessed One, if you consider yourself more Jewish than they, you are wrong. You were born a Jew and chose otherwise. The Khazars were born otherwise and chose to paint themselves Jewish."

"Is that what this is about? My Jewishness?"

"No, it is about my brother's son, who is living in sin with my best friend's daughter. Your father had such plans for you, and Yaakov's father for him. He is a special boy. Since birth he was marked to lead the Jewish people. He can quote passages in the Bible or Talmud and put them into clear language that astounds our Rabbis."

"Your nephew and I are old enough and intelligent enough to know what it is we want in life."

"Sexual immorality is unacceptable."

"Would you accept it if we were married?"

"No. You would first have to smash your Pagan idols and renounce the Berber sorceress."

"Lila acts as a moral guide; through her I can glimpse the future."

"If God wanted you to know what will happen he would reveal it to you."

"He gave me healing powers and the ability to read peoples thoughts."

"Oh, how I prayed for those healing powers when my youngest daughter was dying."

"You would accept my healing, but not my marriage to your nephew?"

"I am only a man, and am fallible. You may be queen, strong physically and command thousands, but you are only a woman. As queen, in the eyes of God you are held to a higher standard. Your sexual relationship with Yaakov is sinful. It is the way Pagans worship their gods."

"Benyamin, you have overstepped your relations with the queen."

"That may be, but..."

"Get out! Out! Quickly!" she shouted. "Leave before I say something I might regret."

"My uncle spoke to you about our relationship?"

Cahena nodded.

"He is right," Yaakov said.

"Does that make me wrong?" Cahena demanded

"It makes both of us wrong."

"How so? Sex is natural, and what is natural is beautiful."

"That's a Pagan concept. In Judaism we control nature. The laws of nature given by God are immutable. Man's use of nature can be beautiful or ugly. We have free choice, nature does not."

"So I choose to have sex with you. What is wrong with that? Don't you enjoy me?""

"So much so that I have broken my vows to God. I no longer pray three times a day. I should be married and have children by now."

"Why does it have to be like that?"

"I demanded that same question of my uncle," he said, "You and I are the product of two-thousand five-hundred years of inbreeding. If we wish to marry, so be it, but to do what you are doing is sinful. Pagans fornicate as a sign of piety and reverence to their gods. The Khazars saw the results. They selected a monotheistic religion in which sex, marriage, and family are sacrosanct. The Greeks and Romans went through the immoral sexual stage, until their Empires crumbled under the weight of intellectually inferior Pagan tribes whose family loyalty predominated. My uncle is prepared to make arrangements for me to marry."

"Who?"

"Yonit, daughter of the chief Rabbinical Priest in Djerba."

"Did you agree?"

"I want to marry you."

"That's not possible."

"Why?

"I may break the laws of Jewish sanctity, but I am not a liar. I loved Aksil of the Chawia Berbers. When you hold me in your arms, it is him I am loving."

"Oh!"

"Don't look so dejected. It is the way I cope with his death. I will never marry, but I do require sex. I am driven."

"I know."

"What will you do about Yonit?"

"Marry her. Fulfill my obligations to Judaism,

family, and the future of my people."

"They are also my people."

"My dear, beautiful Cahena, please do not stray too far among the Pagans, or you may lose your people."

What will be our relations?"

"As your counselor." Yaakov bowed and backed out of the tent.

CHAPTER 26

ISLAMIC RIVALRIES

Messages from Arabia sent by Numidian spies flew into Carthage two thousand miles away.

"Abu Bakr, Muhammad's successor, antagonized a large group of Islamic leaders and insulted other tribes. He heard of a meeting being held by the Ansar clan to elect their own Caliph. Without invitation, he barged in and said to all: 'All the good that you have said about yourselves is deserved, but the Arabs will recognize authority only in my clan of Quraysh, we being the best of the Arabs in blood and country.' Muhammad, the Messenger of God, had not been dead an hour yet when Abu Bakr, in arrogance and Ignorance, claimed before the Ansar that the Quraysh, the tribe to which he belonged, was better than and superior to the Ansar. In blood, morals and country!

"Muhammad never said that the tribe of Quraysh was superior to anyone, or that it had any superiority at all. In fact, the Quraysh clan were the most die-hard of all the idolaters in

Arabia. They clutched their idols, and they fought against Muhammad and Islam, for twenty years. The Ansar, on the other hand, accepted Islam spontaneously and voluntarily. They were still in shock from the Prophet's death. The superiority of the Quraysh which Abu Bakr flaunted was meant to reinforce his claim to Caliphate.

"According to the Prophet's teaching, superiority is judged not by blood and country but by piety. If the Ansar objected, the creed of Islam demanded they declare war against the militarily stronger and more numerous Quraysh. They accepted Abu Bakr as Caliph, but many plan to oppose the new Caliph. Abu Bakr's claim of the superiority is the first symptom of paganism in Islam! Abu Bakr was later informed that the Banu Saeda clan was proposing their own candidate for Caliph. It threatened to split Islam into rival factions. Abu Bakr rushed to offer the same arguments, but it was the army and threat of General Khalid ibn Al Walid that carried the day for the new Caliph, not his piety. Dear Queen Cahena of the Berbers, we led you to believe General Walid was with his troops on your southern border. This was wrong. He found a man who looked and acted like him. The General secretly led a large detachment of his best fighters to Arabia. Abu Bakr ordered him to do so. The new Caliph anticipated that the Prophet's death would cause problems amongst the newly converted, and he was right. Many recanted Islam. The first battle took place in Zafar. A tribal woman chieftain named Salma claimed to be the Prophet's successor. General Walid killed her and seven hundred of her warriors.

"The Battle of Naqra took place in October 633 between rebel armies and Khalid ibn Al-Walid's force. The rebels said they submitted to Muhammad as the prophet of God, but owed nothing to Abu Bakr. Some followed either Tulayha or Musaylima or Sajjah, all of whom claimed to be prophets. All over the Islamic world Prophets appear, claiming to speak for Allah. General Walid put down these rebellions. He did so with one simple rule: swear allegiance to Caliph Abu Bakr, and servitude to Allah, or die. The battles are called the Wars of Apostasy."

Josephus reported to Cahena that he originally thought the wars would distract and weaken General Walid's army. However they appeared to strengthen it. His troops were exposed to actual combat in the field, and they became used to winning.

There remained a year and a half before the

invasion by General Walid's army. Cahena gave birth to a second son. The father was unknown, as she had several lovers. The child, named Aksil, was circumcised and lovingly cared for by Lila.

Yaakov married Yonit. It became the largest wedding feast on the island of Djerba. After the week-long festivities, he set out with his wife in a caravan along the route traveled by Uncle Benyamin to collect the stored grain and herds of livestock his uncle had negotiated. The yield was so abundant it fed the growing Berber army in the Maghreb. Enough remained to be sold in local markets, and there was still more for export to Italy and Greece. Yaakov renewed contracts with the landowners for the coming year. On his return he performed a circumcision ceremony for his newborn son. He named him Yeshia, after his father. Uncle Benyamin was godfather. Yaakov now commanded a fleet of fifty merchant ships and ten Greek fighting craft. Another twenty were ordered from Syracuse.

Josephus pleaded with Cahena and Lila to use their talent of astral travel to learn of General Walid's strategy for the invasion of the Maghreb. He pointed out that the Army of Islam was already larger than the Berber and Numidian armies combined. The two women declined, stating that the General was nowhere near his army; he was away chasing renegade Muslims. This was true, and his absence lead to a lack of discipline among the non-Arabian contingents.

A charismatic young Persian amir, imbued with the fire of a new convert to Islam, wished to show his dedication to his new faith. Meticulous in planning, he pursued strategic friendships with clan and tribal leaders. Armah ibn Abjar was son of a Persian king and the commander of the largest the contingent in the Prophet's Army; he built a large tent for worship and an even larger one for hosting his many guests. His manners were impeccable. The food prepared by the finest chefs always more than sufficient. He was generous with gifts, never indicating in any way how he might be repaid—until after the Ramadan feast of the year 633. He invited chiefs of tribes, heads of clans and influential religious leaders. Prostitution being outlawed by the Prophet, Armah resorted to the legal fiction of concubines. Sexual slavery of the harem was not considered prostitution, and he had the largest harem in camp. Every guest had one woman, and those with more voracious appetites, two. The meal completed, the women worked their magic and everyone was in a relaxed state of undress.

The young amir was built like a Greek god, prepared to address his guests. His curly jet black hair and oiled black beard framed clear blue Persian eyes and a powerful nose over sensitive lips. He stood six feet four inches tall, and addressed his guests in the cultured language of ancient Persian poets. His voice resounded like a wooden wind instrument.

"Brothers of Islam," he announced, "We have lost our beloved Prophet, may his name be forever blessed. The hour is late. Our work is done. Our feast is over. This speech will be our last. The night is dark, and people search for guidance in this world of cruelty, death, and starvation. They know not the word of Allah. They grope through the moral abyss, crying out for a rule and guide to govern their faith and actions. Islam will lead them through the valley and from the shadow of death. They shall fear no evil, for we shall bring Allah to them. They seek Allah and know it not. It is incumbent on us to share with them the teachings of the Messenger of God. It is our responsibility. To avoid it is to betray Islam. This duty falls on our shoulders and weighs heavily on my conscience. General Walid is away doing exactly what the Prophet requested: bringing the Pagans to Allah. You and I have a moral obligation, an ethical duty, to lead the Pagan Berbers and infidel Numidians from the darkness into the light."

The men stretched out on the ornate carpets, pushed their women aside, and sat upright. Their eyes gleamed. Sweat stood out on their brows. "Allah be praised," they chanted. "Allah be praised! When do we set out on this jihad?" they demanded.

"I have been planning for months. That bitch of a sorceress, Cahena, will never expect us to move without General Walid."

"What about the Numidians?"

"We will leave so quickly they can only follow. We use Hannibal's tactic; catch the Berbers by surprise, then turn and face the Numidians."

"King Gershom can field a hundred thousand Numidians."

"Not in one day. He will also be taken by surprise. It will take a month before he can gather his forces and march on us."

"What will General Walid say?"

"He is busy fighting the Iraqi Pagans and Christian forces. They combined to fight him at the battles of Saniyy, Walaja, Ullais and Hira. He is occupied hunting them down. The Prophet Muhammed is dead, but his legacy lives on. What can General Walid say? Will he chastise us for implementing the Prophet's commands?

He will look on us with favor. How can he reject the purity of our purpose when we present him with a million converts to Islam? Will he complain? Allahu Akbar! Am I right, brothers?"

The tent quivered with the roaring chant of approval. It was the cue for one of the prince's officers to continue, "General Walid will be forced to break off chasing the apostates and return to help us. He will catch the Numidians from behind, and then we will have them in a vice. Either they convert or die. Allahu Akbar! Allahu Akbar! Allahu Akbar!"

The fire in the prince's heart caught the dry tinder of dedication and emotions of his satiated guests. The Islamic jihad for the Maghreb was born. Twenty thousand warriors, inspired by Prince Armah and encouraged at prayer by the Mullahs, set off to capture Tangiers.

Prince Armah planned to attack Josephus' smaller force into protecting the city and the ships being built. He commanded two Berber regiments, eight thousand men on a training exercise in the field. Most had been in tribal skirmishes, but never a large scale defense of a city, never against an enemy trained to operate on a large battlefield.

Josephus learned of the prince's plan from spies. He told his pigeon handlers to put hot pepper up the backside of the birds so they would fly faster. Cahena informed him of the impossibility of her troops reaching him in time. She sent pigeons to King Gershom requesting he send his light cavalry forward to harass the Prince's force and slow them until his heavy infantry could catch up. Upon learning of this last message, Josephus wrote the following to King Gershom: "Beware Khalid ibn Al Walid. He may break off his War of Apostates and close on you from behind. Our shaman spies say they expect him to do just that."

Josephus sent another message to Carthage addressed to Yaakov: "Off-load all your ships in port and fill them with the best infantry units available. Stack them asshole to bellybutton. The defense of the Maghreb depends on it. Fire three green rockets when you arrive off Tangiers. If you see two blue and one yellow rocket, it is safe to land. If not, you may tell the queen we died with sword in hand."

The Persian Prince mounted on a giant coal-black Arabian stallion. He led his cavalry and camel corps on lightening raids against Berber and Numidian outposts while his infantry marched for Tangiers. The raids were so swift and well executed that word of the advancing Muslims was often after the fact.

Josephus reached the eastern road to Tangiers and set his defensive position between two hills that flanked the valley road. On top of these hills he stationed his best fighting men. They dug fortifications exactly as the legions did for defensive position: a trench with the dirt piled up behind it, and sharpened stakes driven into the ground facing the enemy. In the center of the circle on both hills stood the reserve force and final redoubt, containing water, food, and weapons. His men dug trenches down the slopes to the valley floor, protecting the road to Tangiers. They built and dug traps, and camouflaged nooses and trip ropes for enemy horse and men. He positioned his archers, armed with the new crossbows, across the road behind a phalanx of spearmen, javelin throwers, and slingers. He remained with them; they were the most inexperienced, and would be required to maneuver under enemy pressure. They dug trenches across the road, and created obstacles for horses. The few cavalry were sent to poison the wells on the approach to Tangiers.

They had not traveled ten miles when they were ambushed by the prince's scouts. Outnumbered, they withdrew and returned with the news. The defenders on the road to Tangiers worked with renewed energy, born of the knowledge that they were about to face an enemy more numerous and experienced.

It took a full week for the prince to bring up the main body of his infantry. Discipline on the march was lax. The late night and early morning prayers were not well attended. The Prince's attempts to institute discipline met with indifference by tribal leaders. They were enjoying themselves winning minor battles at insignificant outposts, then returning to their women in camp. Too late the prince realized his mistake of taking his harem on the march.

When informed of the insubordination of the Persian Prince Armah, General Walid lost his composure. He ranted, raved, and sliced his tent to ribbons with the sword presented to him by the Prophet. He was incoherent after a second messenger informed him that the Numidians were moving behind the prince's force to support the Berbers. The third message caused the veins in his forehead to pulsate until his aides thought they would burst. It was from Prince Armah. In unconciliatory terms he required the general come in behind the Numidians, and proceeded to tell the veteran of a hundred battles how to do it. The General called for his waterpipe to calm him down. It was half an hour before he issued commands for his army to mount up and ride to the rescue of the Persian prince.

In Carthage Yaakov unloaded twenty-three

ships and filled them with four thousand of his best heavy infantry. The chief of the Corsican pirates happened to be selling his loot in Djerba; Yakov hired him and his five ships to lead the expedition. He would be paid double if he arrived in seven days at Tangiers. The Corsican captain conferred with his chief pilot, and they plotted a one-thousand-mile course along the Mediterranean coast at an average speed of six knots per hour. "With stable winds over our fantail, we might just make it," the pirate said. "We cast off now."

Cahena stood on the quarter-deck of the lead vessel. The wind was favorable and the sea calm. They sailed down the Mediterranean coast, picking up more men and ships from garrisons and cities along the way. Cahena released pigeons asking Josephus if her fleet could land on the beach rather than in the port, to save time. If so, she asked that lookouts fire three golden rockets at the place he wanted her to land.

There developed two fleets: the one led by the pirate captain, Cahena, and Yaakov, which plowed on without pause, and the collection of boats and fighting men mustered in the Berber-occupied cities along the coast—which were strung out in a line following, with all sheets to the wind.

On the eastern approach to Tangiers, Prince Armah had trouble bivouacking his troops. His twenty thousand men more than doubled the two Berber regiments, and his scouts reported that the enemy fortifications between the two hills were still being dug. The Prince knew that the time for attack was now, but the tribal warriors bedded down for their afternoon prayer and nap. He couldn't muster a force large enough to win a quick victory. He commanded the largest group of Persian heavy horse and light infantry, and had them stand inspection. Then, as if on formal parade, he marched them down the valley to within sixty yards of the enemy trenches. It was an impressive cohort of veteran Persian fighters who faced the enemy. Their burnished armor gleamed in the midday sun, and their ranks of carefully groomed horses and riders with metal shields reflected the light into the defenders' eyes.

"Why do you think they are showing off?" Josephus asked aloud.

A chief replied, "According to Julius Caesar, power perceived is power achieved."

"I always felt power concealed is more potent when revealed. Don't show them shit!"

"They are sending a delegation forward."

Josephus selected five chieftains and a flag-bearer to meet the Muslims. They returned and informed Josephus that his men would remain unharmed and able to keep their weapons if they surrendered to Prince Armah and professed adherence to Allah and Islam. Josephus sent them back, asking if paying a subservient tax would be accepted as a sign of inferiority. His own chieftains balked at this; they were prepared to die fighting. "I too am prepared to die in battle rather than surrender," Josephus told them, "But I am in no hurry to do so. Let's see how long we can stall them."

In the afternoon the Prince's patience wore thin, but it was time for prayer and his officers wished to rest in the heat of the day. He informed the Berber delegation, "Surrender by morning or die."

At six in the morning the call to prayer sounded. The Muslim army dressed for war and knelt facing Mecca to ask God's blessings. Josephus rested his men, ordered double rations for breakfast, dried meat, bread, and filled water-skins for every man. He waited until the enemy was almost formed up on the valley floor before he addressed his men: "Time is on our side. Presently the enemy outnumbers us, but that doesn't mean they win. It means you have more targets. We await the Numidians closing in from behind the enemy, and there is a fleet of reinforcements on its way led by,

Cahena."

The mention of her name caused a ripple of excitement through the defenders, then a cheer: "We have Cahena! We have Cahena! We have Cahena!"

"Not yet!" Josephus bellowed. "You must hold out long enough for her to arrive. Then all we have to do is wait for the Numidians and slaughter these Muslim invaders of the Maghreb. Remember what you were taught in your field training; a solid infantry formation will always defeat a cavalry charge. Stand strong! If, as sometimes happens, riders break into your ranks, do not panic. Move to the left-hand side of the horseman. It will negate the full use of his sword arm. Secondly, you can more easily bring down the horse, and the man will follow. Then kill him. I never want to see a man-on-man combat; always two or three engage one man. Kill him, and move on to find another. Prince Armah has ordered his men to kill you, so you might as well fight—because if you run, *I* will kill you." Josephus raised his fist and led his army cheering, "All you have to do is hold, and we will have Cahena!"

The chanting of the Berber army sent a ripple of movement through the Muslim cavalry lining up behind the Prince. His coal-black steed, the largest horse on the field, seating the tallest man, pranced as if on show. "You sons of Allah," the prince shouted, "Followers of the Prophet Mohammed, we offered the infidels the teachings of the Messenger of God—and they spat in our faces. We attempted to show them the light—and they threatened to sew us into the bodies of pigs and bury us alive. How shall we deal with such evil?"

"Death! Death! Death!" chanted the Persians.

The Prince trotted his horse out in front of the cavalry. Three ranks of five hundred horsemen straightened their lines. Behind them formed another three ranks, and another, and another. The prince pulled hard on the reins, and the gigantic black stallion reared up, his forelegs pawing the sky. "At a walk, forward!" the prince roared. He swung his horse around and led the formation into the mouth of the valley.

Rams horns sounded for the infantry, archers, slingers and light cavalry to follow. They moved to within four hundred yards of the Berber defense line, and the prince kneed his horse into a light dance-step, and then a trot. The cavalry followed.

At three hundred yards he spurred his steed into a run. At two hundred yards he stood in his stirrups, waved his scimitar, dug his spurs into the flanks of his mighty steed and charged, shouting, "Allahu Akbar!"

On the floor of the valley Josephus walked behind his line of spearmen, his voice calm and even. "Hold steady men. Hold steady. I guarantee you, at one hundred feet from your spear points the big bastard on that black horse will turn, and so will all who follow. Keep your wall of spears steady, and a tight asshole. Archers! Slingers! Fire! Javelins, prepare to launch... Launch!"

The arrows and stones brought down several horses, which in turn tripped up several more. The ground was shaking beneath his feet, and Josephus wondered if he was wrong and the prince would smash his cavalry into the phalanx of spears. Just when he thought the charge would strike his lines, the black stallion slid on its haunches, forefeet pawing the wall of spears. The foam from the animal's mouth spattered the front line of spearmen. It was a wonderful display of horsemanship. The cavalry followed, turning right and left, and fired arrows into the Berber lines.

Josephus pulled up his pantaloons thinking he had almost shit himself. More impressive were his men; most had never faced a cavalry charge. Only a few bolted, and were cut down as ordered.

He had little time for reflection, as rocks, arrows and javelins rained down on his men. The enemy infantry was marching. He had withheld firing his crossbows at maximum range against the cavalry charge, so as to catch the infantry in a hail of arrows. Modifications suggested by Wa Ling had increased the crossbow range; they could penetrate leather armor at one-hundred-and-fifty yards, metal armor at fifty yards.

The Muslim infantry came within forty yards when he signaled his crossbowmen and slingers to launch. Some enemy went down, but the line did not halt. Josephus ordered javelins hurled. He used the Roman pylon: a wicked point on a thin pliable shaft and heavier butt. If it didn't strike a body it more often embedded itself in a shield. The impact and heavier butt caused the point to remain in the shield and the weight of the butt bent the shaft. The pylon could not be thrown back, and it rendered the shield useless.

Josephus signaled, and his crossbowmen climbed the dirt escarpments behind the trenches and fired down into the oncoming enemy. The Muslims never faltered. They marched into the Berber phalanx of spears without hesitation. The Berber line sagged in the middle. Josephus ordered a reserve force into the sagging line. They pushed the line straight, stepping over dead and wounded, friend and foe. Gaps opened in the Berber defensive line. From his magnificent stallion the prince directed his horsemen to enter the gaps and rout the Berber infantry. The defensive trench filled with bodies. It was only Josephus' direction of the crossbowmen that kept his line from splitting open in the middle of the valley floor.

The prince was determined to break through. He sent his cavalry part way up both hills in an attempt to break through and come in from behind. It was hard fought, no quarter given or expected. Several Muslims on horseback broke through and caused a minor panic in the defensive line. The chieftains in charge eliminated them. The line was straightened and reinforced. Prince Armah appeared to be everywhere on the battlefield. He directed, encouraged, berated and wielded his great curved scimitar with deadly skill.

When the sun reached its meridian the Muslim ram's horns were echoed by the Berbers. The fighting ceased. Wounded were either carried off or slain, depending who found them. Burial parties were formed by Prince Armah. The dead would be laid to rest in a mass grave nearby.

Jews and Christians among Josephus' men

buried their dead. Directed by shamans, Pagans scoured the area for firewood and cremated the remains of their fallen, the ashes to be distributed to their tribes and scattered near their homes. Both sides worked through the afternoon into the evening.

Relieved when the prince rested his men, Josephus called a meeting of his chiefs. "I think we put up a harder fight than the Muslims expected," he said. "They fought well, but it wasn't enough."

"If they come at us like that again," one of his chieftains worried, "it will be more than enough. They may have lost more men than we did, but they have twice as many as we do."

"And they are not afraid to die," another gloomed.

"Promise me seventy-two virgins, all the money I want, more wine than I can drink and I'm ready to die," a third chieftain said.

"And I'm ready to kill you," a woman chieftain snapped. "Now shut up and let's hear how we're all going to die."

Josephus rubbed his forehead and said, "From the beginning we knew we couldn't beat them alone. If Cahena or King Gershom's light cavalry arrive in time, we have a chance. I expect the attack will resume tomorrow at dawn. Our objective will be to hold the line across the valley floor until noon. After that it's too hot to continue fighting. I will explain to individual commanders what I want to do if they break through the center."

In the middle of the second watch after midnight, Josephus was awakened. "Rocket signals from our ships," his aide reported.
"Have you answered them?"
"Not yet."
"Fire three gold rockets from the inlet closest to the battlefield."
He shoved the messenger out, and in a moment was hopping around on one leg trying to pull on his leather trousers. Once dressed, he mounted a horse and flogged him all the way to the beach.
Cahena's boat was first to slide into the soft white sand. Shield in hand, she leapt from the bow and greeted Josephus, "Are we in time?"
"How many did you bring?"
"Two thousand heavy infantry."
"Not enough to make a long term difference, but it might set them off balance."
"How do you want to use us?"
"I need you to bolster my men's morale. Have your ships stand off three miles from shore. We'll keep your men hidden as long as possible behind the dunes. When we show

them, let's see how this Persian prince reacts. I am playing for time and the arrival of the Numidians."

Josephus kept the arrival of the ships from his men until they woke; there would be little time for them to rest this coming day. Word spread like wildfire that Cahena and reinforcement had landed. The mood in the camp changed; there were chants, songs and cheers. When the Muslims laid out their prayer rugs and called "Allahu Akbar!" the Berber response was, "We have Cahena! We have Cahena!"

She appeared in full armor in the center of the valley, and their chant of, "We have Cahena drowned out the more numerous enemy.

The prince, astride his magnificent stallion paraded in front of his men in a slow walk, ignoring the Berber missiles aimed at him. Believing the range of the crossbow was eighty yards at most, he sent his archers forward. He signaled his cavalry and on both flanks they trotted forward to protect the archers.

Josephus held his archers in check and explained to Cahena their range was a hundred and fifty yards. Two volleys of arrows rained down on the Berbers before Josephus gave the signal. The crossbowmen were confident, and caught the enemy on foot and horse in their return volleys. Animals and men were killed and wounded before they fled the deadly and unexpected hail of arrows.

As the Muslim cavalry and archers scampered out of range the prince brandished his sword above his head and pointed forward. His heavy infantry had arrived and occupied the center, with light infantry in reserve and on the flanks. Drums and ram's horns sounded and they moved to the center of the valley where Cahena and Josephus stood.

Josephus raised his Roman short sword and signaled. A blue rocket streaked into the sky. Imperceptibly at first, then louder and louder, from the beach came a cadenced sound. The sound grew louder still, and the attacking Muslims became aware of it. From the sand dunes first one, then ten, then a hundred, then two thousand Berber infantry in heavy armor appeared on the enemy's unguarded right flank.

The Muslim commanders were disconcerted. The prince immediately ordered his cavalry to screen his right flank and harass the oncoming enemy. He signaled the attack to stop; he had to ascertain if there were even a larger force in the area. The signal to halt was not clear to all units; several marched into the hail of stones, arrows and Berber javelins. These few Muslim units continued against now concentrated fire, and were wiped out. The others milled about, uncertain what to do.

Prince Armah ordered his units to rest, and sent scouts to reconnoiter the new force. By the time they reported and the prince was prepared to address his commanders, it was past midday and the sun too strong to launch an attack.

Cahena's force had bought another day's grace. Josephus incorporated the two thousand from the beach; he brought the heavy infantry units into the center of his line on the valley floor. Their boat trip in cramped conditions had been an ordeal; some were sea-sick, and all were tired. They'd had to sleep standing up or take turns for a space on the deck; the ships were meant for cargo not people. Even with the reinforcements, the enemy still outnumbered them two to one. Cahena busied herself healing the wounded and comforting the dying. Josephus sought Yaakov, and was told he remained with the ships.

Yakov commanded his fleet of empty ships to the port of Tangiers. They arrived in midday, the five pirate ships in the lead. He sent messengers to Josephus and ordered the pirates to round up every man, woman and child onto the boats, which took most of the afternoon into the night. Then he sailed back to the same beach where he had off-loaded the heavy infantry, fired two red rockets and was answered by two blue, which meant Josephus had secured the beach for landing. The Pirates herded the reluctant people ashore and left all the boats on the beach. There the pirate captain and his men beat, threatened, and cajoled the people into ranks on top of the sand dunes facing the Muslim army.

The morning call to prayer caused consternation among the Muslims as they woke up to see another large formation of troops on the beach threatening their right flank. Initial scout reports to the Prince estimated another two thousand troops, but these reports indicated something out of order. The enemy was not very military in their formations. Those in front were armed with a strange assortment of weapons. After his morning prayers the prince ate breakfast in the saddle on his way to the beach. He immediately sensed something strange about the enemy formation.

He rode to within two hundred yards, then closer yet. "Holy camel shit!" he shouted, "Only the front row have weapons." He sent off a messenger with orders to the cavalry and light infantry to attack.

Josephus received a warning message from Yaakov and readied his own plan. He and Cahena watched the prince and his scouts approach what they considered another threat from the sea. They saw the prince go close to the crowd on the beach and watched him dispatch a messenger to his main force. "He will be ordering his cavalry to attack," Cahena said.

"Fire the green rocket!" Josephus ordered.

Before the green trail reached its apex in the clear blue sky the crowd on the beach were fleeing to the safety of the boats. It took time for the Muslim cavalry to saddle-up, mount, form up and make for the beach. The light infantry followed. Josephus had anticipated this, and sent his newly arrived heavy infantry to strike the attacking Muslim cavalry on the flank. This gave Yaakov additional time to put out to sea.

The Muslim cavalry commander was not to be distracted from his target on the beach. He dispatched a hundred horsemen to engage the Berber infantry. It was not enough. They charged bravely into a wall of spears and were slaughtered.

Behind them came a large formation of the Muslim light infantry, intending to out-flank Josephus' heavy infantry. He ordered a withdrawal and supervised their return to the safety behind the trench and stockade. The Muslims cavalry caught a few stragglers, then launched javelins and arrows with little effect at the retreating boats.

The Muslim field commanders were lax in bringing their troops back from the beach, and reluctant in forming up for another attack on the Berbers in the center of the valley. "Our purpose is to divide the Berber camp in two," they argued. "Then we face only half of them at a time in their fortifications atop both hills. Tomorrow is soon enough."

Cahena and Josephus, aware of the Muslim strategy, had no alternative but to await the arrival of King Gershom's Numidians. For Josephus to attempt a rear guard delaying action on the road to Tangiers against such overwhelming odds was suicidal. Yaakov had bought them another day, but it was that evening that the two Bedouin scouts walked into camp leading their camels as if visiting old family friends.

"Queen of the Berbers," they said, bowing, it is with a heavy heart we must inform you of the Numdian light cavalry approach."

"You mean they are here?" Josephus shouted.

"They arrive tonight."

That's great news!" Josephus said.

The two little men shook their heads saying, "They have ridden so hard and so long they are incapable of fighting. The Muslims poisoned the wells and burned the land. The Numidians and their horses are dead on their feet. You will have to feed and care for them."

Cahena attempted to appear unshaken but her voice betrayed her. "Where is the remainder of the Numdian army?"

"Three days behind and facing the same problems."

"Where is General Walid and his troops?"

"He is behind the Numidians."

"We're all dead," Josephus said.

"Not from General Walid," the Bedou scout said. "He is so angry at the Persian prince for violating the Prophet's orders and entering the Maghreb, General Walid will stop at the border."

"Then the prince will have the honor of killing or converting us," Josephus said.

The two Bedouin looked at each other and nodded. One said, "Queen Cahena, when we were being chased by the Goths, you had a dream of rain in the mountains—and then we had that miraculous flood that saved us. People talk around the campfires of your ability to control nature. Could you do it again?"

"I never thought I did it the first time."

"But it happened, and Lila—head of all the Berber shamans—believed it was you."

"But I didn't."

"What chance do your people have without it?"

"None!" Josephus said. "Did Lila ever explain to you how it could be done?"

"She took me on two astral journeys to explore the possibilities. They were unsuccessful."

"I don't believe in witchcraft," Josephus said, "But I have seen you do some amazing things. Won't you try?"

"There are dark clouds gathering in the north," the Bedouin added. "Could you collect them and create a great flood?"

Cahena's hands came up to her forehead and massaged her temples. Tears welled up and streamed down her cheeks.

"My queen," the Bedou asked, "Why do you weep?"

"Because of my brave and loyal friends. I only wish I could do what you ask."

"You could try."

"Yes."

Cahena left the tent and walked to the rear of the camp where the valley widened. She tried to plan an astral journey. The incantations and ritual were correct in her mind, but the feeling was of emptiness. She whistled, hoping to attract some night birds for company, but none appeared. She felt lonely.

Then two sets of footsteps approached. She could not see who made them. She sent her mind out to read the other's thoughts, but met nothing. The footsteps were steady and confident. In the faint glow of starlight she saw four shining orbs seven feet in the air. She froze. Yellow beaks appeared between the two sets of eyes, topped by balding, small, hairless heads.

Cahena laughed so hard she frightened the ostriches. They regained their composure and approached, pecking her clothes and hair. She stepped in between them, put her arms around their necks and walked them back into camp. People were startled, then they laughed at the two awkward birds fawning over their queen. The small heads on long thin necks kept bobbing up and down pecking those who came too close. The incident raised spirits in camp. Cahena passed the tent for the wounded, and Wa Ling took in the sight of the queen flanked by the two large birds. Cahena thought the Chinese pharmacist went crazy; he shouted, and jumped up and down waving his arms. No one understood him until Mai Li translated. "My husband says everything will be well. He is a Feng Shui master."

Cahena spread her hands. "What is that?"

Chinese philosophy. It uses the universal energy called *'Tchi'* to join with the gods. My Queen," she pointed at the ostriches, "you have found good luck."

"In what way?"

"My husband says, if you place a tail-feather under your pillow, you will be inspired to fly to the heavens and seek advice on how to escape our enemies."

The crowd heard the translation and were elated. Someone had a drum, another a tambourine. People began to sing, then dance. Wooden flutes and stringed instruments joined. In a short time the entire camp was celebrating. Cahena gave the two birds over to Ahmed's care, but not before she plucked a tail feather from each.

She summoned two shamans to her tent. They placed the two large feathers on the ground and a pillow on top. She sat on the pillow and directed the shamans to help her attain astral travel. They prepared a small fire and scattered incense. Chanting incantations they walked seven times around the queen. They prepared hashish and khat leaves for her to chew. The trance state came quickly.

Cahena's spirit broke the bonds of her body. She sped up and out the tent's smoke-hole. She directed her travel by thought to the north where the scouts reported dark clouds. Her knowledge of the stars gave her direction. The landscape under her whizzed by at dizzying speed as she sought the dark clouds indicated by the Bedouin scouts, but the sky appeared clear. She had been taught by Lila that even with a scarcity of clouds a storm could be formed, but she must seek special help from the stars. She directed her thoughts to Sirius, the brightest star in the night sky. Linus had taught her the Latin name: *Canis Major,* the Great Dog, and she remembered that Mohammed, therefore all Muslims, hated dogs. There were four dogs depicted in the constellation; they helped Orion the Hunter to pursue Taurus the Bull.

They were Egyptian hunting dogs of the Basenji breed: short-haired, with upright heads and erect ears, weighing twenty-five pounds, as long as they were tall, with a tight-curled tail. Two were red with white scarf-shapes about the neck, and two were black with a similar white scarf. Lila had claimed that these dogs were unusual in several ways; they were bright and independent. When given a command they thought about it, had a habit of wrinkling their brows as they thought, and if it suited them they obeyed. The Basenji didn't bark; it chortled, or some said it sounded like a low type of yodel. When excited, these animals could jump five feet straight up from a four-footed stance and lick their master's nose. Cahena used the incantations taught by Lila to summon the animals.

Just when she thought her summons was unanswered, the four canines appeared in the night sky before her. They allowed her to pet them, but appeared wary. She projected her thoughts to them. "Guardians of the heavens," Cahena said/thought, keeping in mind Lila's suggestion to praise the animals, as they were proud and egotistical, "I have come to respectfully request your assistance. It is a matter of honor, and a problem of life and death for thousands of people who seek to live and worship as they wish—against the Muslims, who despise freedom and dogs."

The dogs replied with a telepathic question, and Cahena answered. "I need your knowledge and skill in gathering enough storm-clouds to cause a flood in the wadi leading to Tangiers."

"For what purpose?"

"To defeat the Muslim army, that has come to convert us and stop us from worshipping you and other gods of the heavens."

The four animals cocked their heads, furrowed their brows, and stared at Cahena. They looked at each other, turned and trotted off into the night sky. Uncertain of what had happened, she decided to count till one hundred, and then she would continue north looking for rain-cloud formations. At the count of seventy she counted more slowly.

At eighty-five, the four dogs burst out of the dark at her feet. They jumped straight up and licked her face. One by one, she caught all four of them in her arms and nuzzled them in joy. They leaped out of her arms and led the flight northeast across the heavens. The snowcapped Atlas Mountains below them were acting as a dam, holding back great snow-clouds. The clouds were absorbing moisture, and when it reach the point of snow it fell. Lightened, the clouds slipped over the great mountain peaks.

The Basenjis ordered Cahena to wait. They soared higher, then spread out and shepherded the clouds, herding the largest black clouds into warmer air. The snow-clouds dropped rain, then a deluge. The dogs positioned the clouds over the snow-covered slopes. The snow melted into rivulets, then streams, and formed rivers that caused avalanches of vast snow-fields.

Down the mountainsides the flood of water, rocks, trees, and soil roared. The maelstrom tore up the earth, filled the gullies and wadis leading to the main wadi to Tangiers. Boulders, rocks and trees tossed in the cataclysmic surge, acted like a massive drill-bit. It took large cliffs apart, and threw great boulders into the air. The noise was deafening. The air in front of the oncoming flood reached hurricane force. The Basenjis returned to Cahena. She petted them, scratched behind their ears, and explained she must return to warn her people. She promised to include them in her prayers.

Cahena had not returned from her trance-like state. Josephus anticipated a long hard day of fighting. With luck, she would return with a miracle. Or possibly the Numidians would arrive prepared to fight. Josephus' men normally ate morning porridge for breakfast; today in addition they were given two rations of meat, one to be eaten now and the other later. He had every man take a handful of coffee beans from the sacks purchased by Uncle Yeshaya, with orders they were to chew some before each attack. Chieftains topped off their water-bags, and sent the remainder and all food-stuffs to the Numidian light cavalry, who had collapsed from fatigue a mile away.

Josephus reviewed the plan of retreat with his officers. If the Muslims split his line in the center of the wadi, which he expected, no one was to turn his back and run. Both groups would make an orderly retreat up the sides of the wadi to the tops, where fortifications of trenches and palisades of sharpened wooden stakes would protect them. In addition he had crossbowmen and slingers behind the palisades, to shoot over the heads of the retreating force into the enemy. Chieftains questioned the division of forces. He knew it was a violation of basic military tactics, but Cahena agreed with him to use Biblical father Jacobs's tactics when meeting his brother Esau: split your forces, and if negotiations fail, one group may survive by fleeing.

Josephus looked in on Cahena. She was still in the trance state.

Reports of the enemy preparing for battle prompted Josephus to gather his officers. He wrapped a white turban around a long spear, and with five mounted companions went out to gain some time. The larger-than-life prince on his gigantic steed rode out alone. He interrupted Josephus's honorific salutation with three words: "Convert or die!"

The Prince waited. Josephus sat in the saddle with his mouth open. The Prince turned his horse and signaled his troops. The Muslim horns sounded the attack. One of Josephus' officers said, "I guess they don't want to talk."

They sprinted back to the Berber lines in the center of the wadi. Behind them marched the Muslim heavy infantry, backed by archers and slingers, flanked by cavalry right and left. The formation moved forward to the beat of war drums and blasts of ram's horns. The Muslims chanted "Allahu Akbar!" and beat their shields with javelins in time to the drums.

Josephus saw his men shifting in ranks, and then they began turning and looking behind him to the rear.

There stood Cahena, larger than life, balancing her six-foot-three frame standing upright on the saddle of her white mare. The Berbers sparked to life. "We have Cahena!" they roared. "We have Cahena!"

It was all Josephus and his officers could do to stop the smaller Berber force from coming out from behind the palisade of sharpened stakes to attack the overwhelming force marching toward them. Slingers and archers from both armies let loose their missiles; neither side was greatly affected.

The Muslim heavy infantry fought their way up to the trench, attempted to infiltrate between the wooden stakes by stabbing and hacking, but they were fighting uphill at a disadvantage. The Berber defense was so fierce that Prince Armah sent in his second cohort of heavy infantry. The weight and number of the second contingent caused the Berber line in the center of the wadi to shudder, and then sag. Josephus used his only reserve force to push the line straight again. The fighting was fierce. Men pressed so close they could not wield their weapons. Often enemies ended up face to face in weird dance of death, wanting to kill each other but physically incapable of doing so.

Suddenly Cahena was at Josephus' side wielding her great broadsword. He roared, "We have Cahena! We have Cahena!" and they both charged into the fray. His men picked up the chant, and proceeded to fight and swing their weapons in rhythm with it. That stopped the crush of the Muslim heavy infantry. Their line shuddered and, imperceptibly at first, step by step, the Muslims began to retreat.

Berber units on the both hillsides, who were not engaged, without orders rushed down to reinforce the center. Josephus realized his flanks were now exposed to the enemy cavalry. Orders given in this melee were impossible to be understood or implemented. He had witnessed this before; the battle was no longer in his hands. He watched the prince for a sign that he saw the weakness of the Berber flanks and would send his cavalry forward, but the prince did not.

Instead, the prince tried to stem the retreat of his infantry. The Berbers had gone mad; they fought with sheer abandon. They hacked, stabbed, and slashed until the Muslim line collapsed and retreated back to their main formation.

Worried, his men would follow, Josephus

was about to order his offices to prevent his men chasing the Muslims—but stopped when seeing them collapse from the extreme exertion of battle. The Muslims sent cavalry to help their exhausted and wounded troops back to safety.

"Offer them a temporary truce to take away and bury their dead," Cahena said. "It will give us more time."

The Muslims accepted the truce to recover their dead, but decided the battle would continue after midday prayers. "We will bury all our dead after we annihilate you," they replied. "The birds and jackals will clean your bones."

Josephus found Cahena tending the wounded. "Did you succeed with the rain in the mountains?" he asked.

"I think so, but I cannot control the timing of when the flood will arrive. The Bedouin scouts claim they will be able to tell about an hour in advance. Can we hold out that long?"

"I doubt it. The men who fought in the center can barely pick up their weapons. I am transferring them to the hilltops and taking fresh troops from there to man the center."

"Good."

"It won't help much. They are the weakest troops. We will lose the center and retreat up both sides of the wadi. Whichever side the prince attacks first, the other side will flee to the safety of the Numidian s main force. I will go up the west side of the wadi and you the east side."

"You are that certain they will break through?"

"Yes."

CHAPTER 27

THE SPOILS OF WAR

Josephus chose the west side of the wadi for it was further away from the approaching Numidian Army. Cahena and her group might have a chance to reach safety. To accomplish this he put the weakest units on his side of the center and the strongest on the east.

The attack came with the full fury of the frustrated Muslims. Their prince led the charge instilling courage in his men and fear in the Berbers. He dismounted and led the vanguard over the trench, between the wooden stakes and into the Berber lines. Cahena's men held the east side of the wadi five minutes longer than Josephus' men.

The enemy followed the path of least resistance; they trampled the Berbers on the west side until they broke and ran up the hill. The Muslim cavalry swooped in with darts, javelins and swords, and the hillside was strewn with Berber dead. Cahena's men made a relatively orderly withdrawal to the palisades atop the eastern hillside. Waiting for her were the two Bedouin scouts. "Your flood is coming," one of them said, 'And it's a large one."

"There isn't a cloud in the sky," Cahena worried.

"Look north."

"I see birds in the bright sun."

"Keep watching."

"More birds. They are rising up in a line."

"They are being flushed out by the oncoming flood. Some of those Condor's nests are over a thousand feet high. You created a Biblical flood. Now what you must do is put the Muslims in its path."

"How long before it reaches here?"

"An hour."

Cahena watched the fighting on the opposite hillside. She saw the Muslim signal flags call their reserves into action on the western slope. "Assemble all the men!" she ordered. She stood facing north. "Josephus and his men purposely lured The Muslims to attack them so we would have a chance to escape. I propose we charge the rear of the enemy attacking Josephus."

"My Queen," A chieftain said, "If we don't run we will die and achieve nothing."

"Look north. See you that line of birds in the sky? Keep watching and you will see more and more birds taking flight. They are flying from an oncoming flood over a thousand feet in height. I propose we charge down into the wadi, attack the Muslim rear until they turn and fight us, then we run back up here and hold them on the lower slopes until the flood hits."

The soldiers were silent until one man shouted, "We have Cahena!" Others took up the cry. It became a wild animal roar. Cahena brandished her sword and led the uncoordinated rush down the hill. They swept by and through the ranks of Muslim light infantry, and down into the valley floor, catching the Muslims unaware.

Their charge sent shockwaves through their ranks of the heavy infantry units. Josephus's men took heart and briefly stopped the Muslim advance. The prince felt a moment of fear that he was being overrun, and stopped the uphill attack.

He had his men turn to face the desperate charge. The overwhelming numbers of Muslims and their ferocity stopped the Berbers and pushed them backward. Cahena appeared to be everywhere at once; she stabbed, hacked, and slashed, inspiring her warriors. From the corner of her eye she saw a cloud of arrows from the eastern fort sail into the Muslim ranks.

There was a collective moan from the enemy. Another cloud of shafts forced the Muslims into a defensive position with their shields up. A third flight of arrows, and Cahena was dragging, throwing, and pulling her men up the hill under the protection of her crossbow-men.

The wind being pushed out of the narrow wadi a mile behind the Muslims ripped into the valley at hurricane speed. The onrushing water and debris swept down the great wadi at eighty miles an hour. It exploded out of the mouth of the wadi at over one thousand feet in height. The initial wave remained that high for one hundred yards and then spread out on the wadi floor.

Muslim tents and equipment were lost in the gigantic surge. The wave collapsed as it was released from the constraints of the wadi walls, but by the time it struck the troops it was still ten feet deep. Those on the wadi floor were swept away. Others, part-way up either hill were tumbled and rolled in the muck and mud.

Cahena attempted to identify her men and joined in pulling them from the quagmire below. The archers who had saved her were firing without stop.

A messenger from a unit of Numidian light cavalry on foot approached, saying, "That food and water you sent invigorated our men to fight, but it was Ahmed with the kaffa beans that got us moving. We tried to give it to our horses, but they didn't like the taste."

The prince sat his stallion amidst the carnage. Men and horses were mired in the mud, and more than a thousand were drowned. It took great effort for men to pull one foot out of the mud and then the other. They lost their sandals and boots. The horses foundered. The animals fell on their sides and couldn't rise. The Numidian archers ceased their attack on the helpless foe. The prince waved a turban and Josephus shouted to him from the hillside. "Surrender or die!"

The Prince threw down his sword. "Surrender!"

Except for three hundred Muslims determined to achieve their heavenly reward, the prince's entire force surrendered. Although battle-weary and splattered with mud, the three hundred martyrs lined up in formation and charged the Berber lines shouting "Allahu Akbar!" It was an audacious display of bravery, but they could not keep formation in the mud. Numidian archers decimated their ranks before Berber javelins were thrown. The remaining few died in jihad by the sword.

"A hard way to get seventy-two virgins," Josephus said.

"What are we going to do with all the prisoners?" Cahena asked.

"Separate those who can pay ransom from those who can't. The redeemed go back to General Khalid ibn Al Walid. The remainder go to King Gershom as slaves. He'll keep some and sell most. All booty will be equally divided."

"Who is going to feed and house the prisoners?"

"We include the cost in their ransom. The longer they stay, the more they pay."

"You've given this some thought."

"It's standard procedure in the legion: a good business, when winning."

The problem of feeding the captives was intensified by the poor condition of the Numidian army. Numidians in Tangiers emptied the markets and picked the fields to supply their people and animals. What was left went to Cahena's army. Yaakov's ships scoured the African coast purchasing food, grain, and fodder as far away as Portugal, Spain, and Corsica. The Muslims supplemented the little food they received by fishing and eating grass.

Every morning Cahena met with Josephus and his military counselors. Problems were discussed and decisions made as breakfast was served. Cahena then met with Yaakov,

Ahmed, Lila, and the supply and logistics officers. She judged serious legal cases, most of which dealt with dereliction of duty during and after the battle, and violations of Josephus' hygienic rules for the encampment. For those a first offense was twenty lashes, a second offense death. Her talent for healing the sick and wounded and comforting the dying, she administered in the evening. Muslim prisoners were used to cremate or bury the dead of both armies. After dinner she met again with Josephus, Yaakov, Ahmed, and Lila to learn what was accomplished and set the agenda for the morning meeting.

She also held a celebration among the Berbers to thank the Star Dogs for the victory. When the Muslims heard of this, they claimed to be offended. Cahena ignored them.

Still, like many of the Berbers, Cahena quietly admired the dedication and courage of the Muslim warriors, especially their prince. He had fought in the forefront of the battle. He had wielded his sword with skill, and had driven his mount into the fiercest part of the fight. His size alone was enough to draw attention. His actions inspired his men. At six foot four inches, he was slightly taller than she was.

She mused and speculated upon what coupling with him would be like. Was he well endowed? She had known big men with small penises. She consciously attempted to dismiss him from her thoughts, but somehow found herself fantasizing.

Two months passed before a partial ransom was received for all the Muslim officers, except the Persians. General Walid wrote that since the prince had defied explicit orders, he would pay for his own men. They made up the majority of redeemable prisoners.

Cahena addressed the prisoners, explained the terms, and said, "No one will force those ransomed to return to the Army of Islam. You may remain with us and practice whatever religion you wish, or live as free men in the Maghreb."

Not one man opted to stay.

Cahena went on, "You Persians will have to wait until we come to terms with your Prince and his father Emperor Kavadh. That will be a minimum of three months considering the distance from here to Teheran."

A Persian approached on his knees, saying, "My Prince humbly requests to address the queen."

"Bring him forward."

Cahena watched as the ranks of Persian nobles parted and revealed the most beautiful man she had ever seen, wearing an open black silk jacket showing a large hairy chest and black pantaloons embroidered with gold filigree, soft golden slippers and a silver silk turban with a large sapphire embedded in its crown. He bowed, stepped closer, knelt and kissed Cahena's shadow on the ground. He placed a necklace of thirty-six perfectly matched pearls with a large blood red ruby pendent on the queen's shadow and stood.

Cahena had never met another man's eyes as she did his. They were a light blue, contrasting with his black curly hair that hung in ringlets onto his broad massive shoulders. Those blue eyes held the hint of a smile. In a tone harsher than she intended, "What is your request?"

"I thank you for accepting our surrender, and realize the supply problem you face in feeding and housing such a large group of prisoners."

"Be brief."

The prince picked up the necklace and handed it to Cahena. "This is a payment on whatever terms you suggest for ransom. I am the oldest son of emperor Kavadh, and heir to the Persian throne. My family dates back twenty-seven generations. On their honor, and that of my father, and mine, I pledge to fulfill all agreements for ransom. Please let my officers leave. Hold me and my cousins. We number forty-three, and represent almost the entire male progeny of our father Emperor Kavadh. In that way you are relieved feeding and housing over one thousand men. It will require six months to communicate and negotiate with Teheran. I and my men also wish to thank you for your comforting our wounded and dying."

"You accept whatever terms I stipulate?"

"I do."

"How do you know your father can afford it?"

"The Persian Empire is over two thousand years old. We expanded as far as China, Russia, and Turkey, while defeating Greece and collecting over five hundred Roman Legion standards. Emperor Justinian is still trying to recapture them. My father is the wealthiest man on earth. On my honor, I swear the ransom will be paid." He bowed.

"You and your men acted courageously and honorably on the field of battle. I will consult my advisors."

"With respect, most honorable Queen of the Berbers, is it true you called down the flood that decimated my troops?"

Cahena ignored the question and he was led off. She held a meeting of all the chiefs and several senior officers from the Numidian army. There were three subjects for discussion: the fate of the Muslim hostages, how best to prepare for General Walid's invasion in two years, and the division of loot. This last was the easiest problem. All loot would be divided equally between the Numidians and the Berbers. A court of nine was to oversee the distribution. The subject of the future war with General Walid was initiated by Cahena. "We have a unique opportunity. We hold the captured elite officer's corps of the Muslim army. They can be a treasure trove of information. How can we best make use of that?"

"If we agree to hold back the Persian Emperor's sons and his forty-three cousins," Josephus said, "I am confident the ransom will be paid. In the meantime we pick their brains about the size, condition, and make-up of their army. What is their invasion strategy for the Maghreb?"

"We can get them drunk," a chieftain suggested.

"They don't drink," Josephus said.

"They have great hashish."

"I see no harm in trying to loosen the officer's tongues," Josephus agreed, "But I doubt General Walid shares his strategy with anyone but Allah himself."

"I agree," Cahena said. "Lila, what are your thoughts about permitting all but the Emperor's sons to return before we receive the ransom?"

"I trust this prince."

"Me too," Josephus said. "It will take a great burden off, our men and our treasury. While all the captives are here, there is little we can do in training our people for mass military formations and movements on the battlefield, for our troops are required to guard and oversee the prisoners. The Muslim army that is coming will be well versed in mass movement strategies. King Gershom's men are trained for lightening quick cavalry strikes. To stop the Muslim army we need a larger heavy infantry contingent. They must be armed and trained."

"The weapons captured from the prince's army should help."

"True," Josephus said, "But the men will require months of training to convert them from farmers and shepherds to warriors."

"Can you do that?" Cahena asked.

"That was my expertise in the Legion."

"What about hiring Roman pensioners to train them?"

"I'll look into it."

Yaakov's ships and those foreign merchantmen he had hired began arriving in Tangiers port. At first one a day, then two, and finally a steady stream of wheat, produce, and livestock grew on the docks of Tangiers and the beaches north of the city. The Muslim officers directed their former soldiers in unloading and preparing the food. Word spread throughout the seven seas that premium prices were being paid to sustain Cahena's army in the Maghreb. Day by day the stores grew in size and the animal herds increased. Ahmed worked with the cameleers and horse wranglers to return their herds to health. Many of the older or disabled animals were slaughtered for food. He sent out buyers along the Mediterranean and Atlantic coasts to purchase additional animals.

King Gershom requested a meeting with Cahena, Josephus, Lila and Ahmed. "There are three subjects I wish to discuss," he said. "First, Ahmed's resupplying us with camels and horses."

"Isn't he doing right by you?" Josephus asked.

"The answer is a hesitant yes."

"Why hesitate?"

"Because he is attempting to save you money by rehabilitating the animals we almost beat to death to arrive in time to support you."

Cahena looked to Ahmed who nodded his agreement.

"My Numidian military is founded on the swiftness of my cavalry. Everything is built around it. We must make a two thousand mile journey to our oasis. Our three-mile-long column's right flank will be exposed to General Walid's forces. I require well mounted cavalry to screen my troops."

"I know General Walid, "Josephus said, "And have complete faith he will not attack,"

"In his two months of recuperation, I too learned to trust the general," Cahena said. "He will abide by our agreement and not invade the Maghreb earlier than expected."

"I do not know the general," King Gershom replied, "And even if I agreed with you, I cannot take the chance he might attack. My men must have better mounts. We are prepared to take the weaker horses and camels and slaughter them for food, but we require healthier mounts to return home in safety."

Cahena looked to Josephus. He lowered his head, thought, then asked, "When do you wish to leave?"

"Yesterday." King Gershom sighed. "The air here is so heavy, and everything is damp."

"We will make every effort to give you the best mounts as soon as possible."

"Ahmed," Cahena said, "Send pigeons to Djerba Island. Yaakov will stop there to see his wife. Tell him to purchase horses and camels. It must be good stock, and as many as he can find. In the meantime, send your wranglers to look over the captured Muslim animals. The king's men will have first choice." She looked at Gershom. "What is your next problem?"

"We will require three-and-a-half months of supplies for the journey home."

"But you made it here in one third the time," Lila said.

"And killed our mounts doing so. We almost killed ourselves. That march will go down in history. Even the Alexander Great never moved so far so fast."

"We have taken note of your sacrifices," Cahena said, "And will do everything to see that you are rewarded. Have your supply people draw up a list of requirements. Ahmed, Josephus, you are responsible for the Numidian supply arrangements. Do your utmost to fulfill them."

King Gershom nodded. "More complicated is the third problem. My men are influenced by the fighting spirit and religious dedication of the Muslims."

"Among the Berbers also," Josephus said. "How has it affected you?"

"It's mostly the Muslim rank and file, not the Persian officers. They begin speaking about Mohammad and his spiritual influence for good. They almost sound like Greeks promoting logic when endorsing Allah the one God. They freely admit the mistakes of Mohammed, unlike the Christian Jesus, who espouses the trinity and calls them one. They also claim Mother Mary a virgin, even though Jesus had six brothers and sisters. Many of my people are Christian and cannot answer these questions."

"Are they influenced by these preachers?" Cahena asked.

"Yes. The most effective are those newly converted. Their emotion catches the hearts and minds of my Numidians."

"Have any converted?" Lila asked.

"A few. But I worry if they continue preaching what will be two years from now."

"Forbid it," Cahena said.

"My people, like yours, are a free people. You don't stop the Muslims speaking to your Berbers."

"And they have the same affect," Josephus said.

"I believe in the one God," Cahena said. "This God is master and ruler over all the other gods. I think Allah is just another name for the same god."

"My concern is how many Numdians will stand to fight General Walid's army in two years. And how many will join him to fight us?"

Lila said, "My shamans' reports are similar. Islam teaches that shamanism is the work of

Satan, and that we are devil worshippers."

"I recommend sharing ideas to combat this religious incursion," Cahena said, "Then adopt the best solution." She knew it was an evasive answer to a growing problem, but she adjourned the meeting.

CHAPTER 28

LOVE, LUST AND LOGISTICS

"Questioning the prince and his cousins is a sham," Josephus said. "They all look for his approval before answering."

"He's physically powerful, and mentally charismatic," Lila commented.

"We've met with them three times," Cahena said. "I have no more knowledge of Persia than I did before."

"I don't trust the prince," Josephus muttered. "He manipulates others."

"That's what royalty does." Cahena asked, "How did he get so many cousins?"

"You know how sex is," Lila chuckled.

"His father the Emperor has over a thousand women in his harem," Josephus said. "If he has forty-three male cousins he probably has as many females."

"How can his father keep up with all those women?" Cahena queried

"Ask the son," Josephus answered.

Prince Armah entered Cahena's tent unescorted. She was attended by Josephus, and Lila. Her question caught the prince off guard.

"My father rarely uses a woman more than once," he explained. "And yes, there are sixty female cousins and twelve more young males in the capital city of Babylon."

"And what does that city look like?" Josephus asked.

Pleased and proud to answer, the prince said, "A traveler coming upon Babylon would see a walled city. The wall is not that high, deep or impressive. Its gates are strong, but of wood and can be breached, but behind it are six more walls each sturdier than the other."

"And what do we find behind those walls?" Josephus asked.

"The Seventh Wonder of the World: the Hanging Gardens of Babylon. This feat of architectural landscaping, once viewed, determines your concept of beauty. There are theaters including schools of dance, music, and art. Strolling musicians, mimes, and clowns perform in the squares. The streets are swept, and the waters of the Euphrates activate hundreds of public fountains. The law courts, archives, and treasury are located in one area, schools for medicine, science, and mathematics in another. There are hospices, courts, and palaces, and then of course the military."

"We just fought," Josephus said. "Aren't you concerned about the information you just revealed?"

"Not at all. There are about a million Berbers in the world, but in the city of Babylon alone we have more than that. Our empire extends from China in the east to Russia in the north, Turkey in the west, and India in the south. You are three thousand miles from my capital city. A Berber threat reminds me of the mosquito who approached the elephant for sex. The elephant nodded her approval, and while the mosquito was performing the act the elephant hiccupped. The mosquito asked, 'Did I hurt you my dear?'"

"Were you Pagan before converting to Islam?" Lila asked.

"A follower of Zoroaster. He was like Moses, Christ and Mohammad. He had a mystical experience with the supreme god, Mazda. He also wrote what god dictated, and thus spoke Zarathustra."

"Are most Persians followers?" Lila asked.

"It has been our religion for over a thousand years."

"What does it preach?"

"A messiah, heaven, hell: freedom of choice and responsibility for choices determines the future. Zoroastrianism is the emphasis on moral choice and duty. Reward and punishment, happiness and grief, all depend on how individuals live their lives. Simply put, good thoughts, good words, and good deeds: *Humata, Hukhta, Hvarshta."*

"It sounds like Judaism, Christianity, and Islam," Lila said. "Why did you become a Muslim?"

"My father became interested in the new prophet from Arabia. I was giving the King a headache looking for wars to fight or wrongs to be righted. To keep me busy and away from court, he sent me to follow the Prophet when he made the Hajj in Mecca. I listened to some of his talks. He spoke well, but was not a gifted orator. Physically, he was an average-looking man. It was his actions that spoke volumes. In the process of performing the Hajj he never faltered, and some of his activities were strenuous for a man his age. The heat bothered younger men. I was personally shamed because I attempted to duplicate him and weakened. I saw in the Prophet's eyes the strength that comes from knowledge of Allah. Yet when I left Mecca I prayed to Zoroaster's god Mazda."

"But that changed?" Lila asked.

"Yes, on the return journey to Babylon. We pitched our tents in the desert and drank a goodly amount of wine. Sleep came easily.

Then I woke. The stars flooded the night sky. My dream was still before me, and the Prophet beckoned me."

"How do you know you were awake?" Lila asked.

"I dug my thumbnail into the palm of my left hand until I drew blood. Believe me, I was awake. I scuffed my bare feet in the sand to be certain I was standing. The Prophet beckoned me for midnight observances. He pointed to a flaming prayer-rug. I pulled back in fear, but he beckoned me with his eyes. I knelt on the fiery rug, but was not burned. I said prayers I was never taught. When I stood to say 'Allahu Akbar', I realized that all those in my caravan were also praying. The Prophet Mohammad was gone but his message remained in our hearts. The first thing we did was to throw out the wine and unclean food. We remained several days, fearing to leave that holy place, but we were eventually forced to move for need of food and water.

"Wherever we went we told the story. Without intending, we became apostles of Islam. We converted many along the way. When I told my father, he ran me out of his chambers. He ordered I be given cold and hot baths until I came to my senses. I converted those guarding me. Meanwhile, my comrades, many who were also princes, converted members of the royal court. My father couldn't stop it. When we heard General Walid was going to make a desperate attempt to stop the Romans from destroying his fleet in Tangiers, we wanted to go. My father sent us off to join him. He was certain we would not arrive in time. He was correct. We did join the Army of Islam and I took the initiative, while the general was away, to conquer one million Berbers."

"And look how it turned out," Josephus said.

"Man plans and God laughs." The prince bowed to Josephus.

"You and your followers must have discussed the different religions," Cahena said. "Why convert?"

"You ask two questions. I and my followers converted because of the mystical experience. Also because in Islam, whether you are black, white or sky-blue makes no difference. Rich, poor, educated or not, we all stand before Allah as equals. Each of us bears responsibility for the way we act. Those who act righteously are rewarded, and evildoers are themselves to blame for their ruin. Now you know why I converted. The question you haven't asked, and is more important, is why do most people submit to Islam?"

"What is the answer?" Lila asked.

"Survival and privileges. Until recently, you converted to Islam or died. They killed so many, they had no one to work the fields, tend the livestock, or keep the canals from silting over. To alleviate the shortage of workers, the Imam's created a legal fiction, called *Dhimmi*. It is the protected status of a persons living under Muslim rule, who pay a subservient tax allowing them to practice their own religion."

Cahena held up her hand for him to stop speaking while she thought. Her vest was open and her movement caused her bare left breast to slip out. She saw the Prince's eyes widen at the sight of the smooth large breast and its purple nipple so erect. She inhaled, and the second breast appeared. The Prince was fascinated. She replied "Then most Muslims convert for practical motives, not authentic religious reasons?"

"Correct."

"If that is true," Josephus said, "Every Muslim is not looking to die in Jihad."

"Correct again, and we true believers despise those who choose Islam as the most convenient course to life."

"Although Islam appears a monotheistic pillar of faith," Lila noted, "Its conversions are based on survival and privileges gained by adopting Islam."

"Yes and no," the prince said. "Many like me were motivated to convert for altruistic reasons. We desire to serve the one God and follow his greatest and last Prophet Mohammed, may his name be forever blessed. Of those who converted to save their lives or gain material advantage, we often find that the repetition of study and prayer results in a true conversion of the heart. They too enter the soul of Islam."

"But there are still enough dissidents to create discontent among General Walid's soldiers?" Josephus asked.

"True."

"How can all Muslims serve two caliphs?" Lila asked.

"That is a problem. Both caliphs claim the right of inheritance from the Prophet Mohammed. Both have substantial tribal followings. Caliph Abu Bakr is by far militarily superior to Caliph Ali. The former call themselves Sunni, and the latter Shias. Being the weaker, Ali has refrained from criticizing Caliph Abu Bakr, but it is only a matter of time before the two groups clash."

"And which side are you on?" Cahena asked.

"Caliph Abu Bakr and General Khalid ibn Al Walid."

Cahena was finding it difficult to suppress

her sexual fantasies about the prince and maintain her questioning. "You are dismissed," she ordered, and the prince backed out of the room.

"That was an abrupt end to a very enlightening discussion," Lila commented.

"I agree," Josephus said. "He was so confidant of being the Persian elephant that he talked about weakness in the Muslim army."

"And that is why I sent him out. If we plan well, he can inform us of other flaws and faults."

"He already has," Josephus said. "The newly recruited Muslims seeking tax benefits, and the Sunni and Shia leadership, creates divisions of loyalty. We can exploit that."

"Equally as important," Lila said, "Is his revelation of the morally and socially corrupt Persian society. Their hedonistic family morals have created a decadent social structure. His story about our Berbers exchanging gold for silver in equal weight was comical."

"That shows our lack of education and sophistication," Cahena replied, "Not Muslim intellectual superiority. I thought his account of the Roman's ransom was better."

"You mean, the Berber asked 1,000 silver coins when he could have received ten thousand—and he answered that he didn't know there was a number greater than a thousand."

"That is the strength of Islam," Cahena said. "They educate their people. To be a practicing Muslim you must learn to read, write and memorize the Koran."

"They only teach the males," Lila pointed out. "Women in Islam have a lower status. It would be impossible to convince Berber women to accept inferiority."

"Muslims don't ask women," Josephus said, "They tell them."

Cahena and her small group planned and framed questions for the prince into the early hours of the morning.

The queen's sleep was restless. She tossed and turned, dreaming of the prince. They were both fully clothed. His eyes were on her bare breasts. She wanted him to touch them, but he lay beside her on his back. Then his hand reached out and touched hers. She climaxed and reached out for the prince, but the bed was empty. She touched and manipulated the tips of her breast, then touched her vulva, inserted her finger, masturbated, and slept.

Because of bandits and civil unrest in the Mediterranean cities of Russadir, Cartenna and Saldae, Cahena was called away for three months. She returned to Carthage with a need to learn more about her enemies from the

Persian prince, and a burning between her thighs she felt only he could satisfy.

She held the first meeting with Lila, Josephus, and her senior chieftains. "The ransom offer from the Emperor of Persia for the ranking officers is the weight of each man in silver," Cahena said. "For each of the princes, their weight in gold."

Josephus stood and picked up a tray of food. "Where are you going?" Lila asked.

"To fatten our hostages." He held up a roasted chicken. "The weight of this in gold can buy a lot of supplies."

"Oh, sit down," Cahena said. "I wish Yaakov were here to calculate how much the ransom will be worth."

"He's busy making babies and buying ships," Josephus chuckled. "He also earned a large profit from those fields your Uncle Benyamin invested in for our attack on Jerusalem."

"That plan is set aside. The Khazars returned home without making an alliance."

"Your uncle Benyamin warned they would not support an attack on Jerusalem, as it would antagonize the Romans and the Muslims."

"The elite of the Khazars," Lila said, "Adopted Judaism not from religious conviction. They desire to remain neutral between the Muslims and the Romans. Jerusalem has less meaning for them than it does for us Pagans."

"We must concern ourselves with the upcoming invasion of General Walid and his army." Cahena noted.

"And I do not think it a good idea for you to meet alone with Prince Amar," Josephus said.

"What are your objections?"

"Last night you adopted him into the tribe."

"You were put off by the ceremony. It is common for Berber women to have men or boys suckle their breasts as a sign they are being adopted into the family."

"I thought you were a Jewess?"

"I'm both."

"As a Christian I find the ritual difficult to accept. You and he were enjoying it. And his hand was massaging between your thighs."

Cahena recognized the jealousy in Josephus' objection, but understood and said. "You may all leave. I wish to question the prince on my own."

"May I have a word in private?" Lila asked.

Cahena dismissed the others.

"I agree with Josephus. The prince is far too sophisticated and worldly. Do not meet with him alone."

"If that is all you have to say, leave now. I have the needs of a woman."

"There is something else we must discuss:

your children."

"Again? Accept that I'm not a good mother. Neither the Emperor of Persia or other kings and queens are good parents. They leave the raising of the child to someone they respect and can trust. That is you."

"You are correct, and I am not wrong. The children know you are their mother. They respect me as their guardian."

"Rightly so. They are princes. They should have a male attend them also."

"In a way, they have; the Persian prince has taken an interest in them. While you were away he played with them almost every day."

"Do the children enjoy him?"

"Of course. He made them wooden swords and brings them sweets. He's now teaching the oldest to wield a bow and arrow."

"That's a good thing."

"He's is getting too personal. Don't sleep with him."

"You overstep your bounds."

"And you are relying on a man who only four months ago attempted to wipe out your people."

Cahena massaged her forehead and ordered, "When you leave, send the prince in, alone."

He was clothed in sky-blue pantaloons and vest

open from the waist, showing his massive hairy chest. His beard was immaculately trimmed, and ebony-black hair spread over his broad shoulders in ringlets. He knelt before Cahena and kissed her shadow. "Come," she said patting the pillows by her side. "Sit close. I wish to question you." She was already reading his mind, and he was thinking of her naked. He was caressing her with his muscular body, hands, lips, and tongue and she shivered. His dark eyes met hers, and for an instant they remained so. He crept on all fours onto the pillows by her side and asked, "Was your trip successful?"

"Boring. Administration is like being a Caravansary owner. You indicate where to put their camels, graze their livestock, and maintain peace between feuding tribes."

"You are queen. Tell them and they'll do it."

"I would rather have them understand my rulings and agree."

"A waste of time and energy. Tell them! You will gain more respect. People want to be told what, where, and how to act. In that way they are not responsible."

"I am influenced by my father. He usually had a consensus to whatever policy before he entered a meeting."

"Your father was chieftain. You are queen of more than a million people, and as many square miles of territory. You cannot afford to consider individual personalities."

He was thinking of suckling her breast, and she desired him to do so. She pulled back her vest and nodded for him to bring his head forward. His lips encompassed one nipple. He wet it with his tongue, scraped his teeth lightly over it and went to the other nipple while manipulating the first between thumb and forefinger. He crept closer, and placed his knee between her thighs and rubbed. She moaned. The last thought she read in his mind he said out loud: "I want to fuck your brains out."

She grabbed both his shoulders and kissed him. Their tongues met. Their bodies clung to each other. She gasped, "It's enormous! I never saw a man's penis that large."

"Twelve inches," he said, and stood before her. He reached down and took her hands and placed them on his erection. She closed both her fists on the shaft, and the head still peeked out.

"It looks like a Jewish penis. It doesn't have a hood on."

"My father would only have the best do the circumcision. He hired a Jewish rabbi."

Cahena leaned forward and kissed the head. The prince threw her back on the pillows and spread her legs, saying, "I am going to pound you into the earth! You will be fucked like never before." Cahena watched his penis enter. He kept moving up and down thrusting deeper each time. "Oomph!" She exclaimed, "That's far enough."

"Bullshit! I've fucked smaller women to death. You are large enough, strong enough to take it all. And I am going to penetrate until it comes out your mouth."

Cahena looked up and his eyes rolled to the back of his head. He threw his shoulders back and his hips forward, pounding her into the pillows. The fire that was lit between her thighs became a furnace, and she climaxed. He kept driving into her, and she climaxed again. The third time she reached up and wrapped her arms around his neck crying, "You didn't stop. You didn't stop!"—and she felt him explode inside her. She was wet and sticky, but he kept gyrating up and down. Some times he manipulated his penis with his hand, making it go round and round, up and down in and out. She climaxed again and her arms loosened and she fell back gasping. He withdrew, panting. She moaned, "Put it back in."

"It is beginning to wilt."

"How can we make it stand up again?"

"Pet it, massage it, kiss it."

Using a wrestling grip, Cahena reached up

and flipped him onto his back among the pillows. She took up the limp penis, saying, "You poor little one-eyed snowsnake. You worked so hard making me happy that you're all tired out. She stroked the penis, then kissed it, then sucked on it, and used her tongue up and down its length. Slowly it began to swell and stiffen. He moaned, "Oh! Oh! Yes. Easy. Oh, you're killing me! If you want my cock inside you, climb up on me and sit on it."

"I never did that before."

"Now you control the depth, the rhythm and your own climax."

"It is going in even deeper..." She reached down and manipulated his nipples and he rammed his hips up and into her. They rolled over with him on top, then she on top. When they finished, they were on the carpeted floor locked together in a lovers' embrace, where they lay panting into each other faces. "I never experienced anything like that," Cahena said.

"There is much more to teach you."

"And where did you learn?"

"My father's harem. From the age of nine, I helped pleasure his wives. They taught me. Do you know what the Kama Sutra is?"

"No."

"The ancient Hindu sex manual. The harem girls helped me improve on some of the positions. The one you experienced when you sat atop me is called the Horse Rider."

"I enjoyed that."

"There are ninety-nine other positions."

Several things changed in Cahena's life. She spent most of every day and night with the prince. Her sexual appetite was so great he introduced her to the khat leaf. Both chewed the leaf daily. Soon she could no longer read his or other people's minds. She rarely visited the sick, and only adjudicated when Josephus insisted. He constantly harassed her regarding her blatant sexual activities with the Persian. Annoyed by his attitude, she placed him in charge of the Berbers going to the Imilchil Plateau for the yearly festivities.

Jews throughout the Maghreb and beyond were informed that Cahena, Queen of the Berbers, would host the High Holidays on the island of Djerba. Yaakov was put in charge, and arranged for a fleet of fifty ships to transport the worshippers from Carthage to the island. He also set up tents, water, cooking schedules, toilet facilities, and corrals for the animals.

Fewer people attended the High Holiday services than expected. The largest group of absentees was the conservatives who rejected women as Rabbis or teachers, next were those who considered themselves more Berber than Jewish, and finally those Jews who desired to enjoy the festivities of the annual Berber meeting rather than the strict adherence to Jewish law on Djerba Island. The Ceremonies for Rosh Hashanah and Yom Kippur went smoothly. Yaakov's logistics were well managed, and there being fewer people, easily organized. Prince Armah questioned why the queen and he were separated during the religious ceremonies and yet Cahena took no part in them.

"The Djerba Jews adhere to the strictest definition of the Torah. Women are separated from men, and no matter their rank do not participate with them or lead in prayer."

"Like Muslims," the prince noted.

Another modification in Cahena's daily schedule was the prince's insistence she spend more time with her sons, while the Prince taught both boys the use of the sword and the older the bow and arrow. He presented each of them with a pony. Now and then he casually mentioned something about Islam and the Prophet Mohammad. They enjoyed his heroic stories of General Khalid ibn Al Walid.

On one such occasion Yaakov overheard the prince extolling the virtue of The Sword of Islam. He rushed the bigger man, caught him off guard and knocked him to the ground. Cahena signaled her guards who pinned Yaakov's arms and dragged him before her.

"You attacked my guest," she accused.

"He is your prisoner. He's promoting Islam to your children. You'd best be rid of him and his fellow princes, for they too are preaching Islam among our people."

"The children should have knowledge of all religions."

"When they are older. They do not know enough about Judaism. You are the Cahena, Queen of the Berbers and Jews. The Chief Rabbis will be here soon. What if they learned the prince is teaching Islam to your children?"

"And what if they learned I pray to Pagan gods? Do you know that three of those five illustrious rabbis were instrumental in my father's death?"

'Your Uncle Benyamin will be here for the celebration of Rosh Hashanah. He will have more to say on this subject."

"You may be correct about the hostages. Prince Armah suggested that, since the silver and gold to be paid for them is already on its way, we rid ourselves of the forty-two other princes and retain the Emperor's oldest son and heir to the throne"

"Good riddance to bad rubbish," Yaakov

growled.

"Release him!" Cahena ordered the guards. "See to your duties, and do not set foot in Carthage until after the High Holidays."

The prince dusted off his clothes and approached Cahena. "Are you hurt?" she asked.

"More amused, by the size of him. He took me off my feet. I could swat him like a fly."

"He is rather small."

"But very intense. What did he mean, that you are the Cahena to the Jewish people?"

"Cahena is a bastardization of the word Cohen in Hebrew. Cohen refers to a priest related to Aaron, the high priest of the Holy Temple in Jerusalem and brother of Moses. 'Cahena' means Priestess. I have a secret name."

"Why secret?"

"According to my foster mother, known as the Witch of the Maghreb, my enemies could use it to harm me."

"What is it?"

"Can you keep a secret?"

"Of course."

"So can I."

They both laughed, and he asked. "What did three rabbis have to do with your father's death?"

"They revealed to my future father-in-law my father's intention to organize the Berbers,

Tuaregs, Bedouin, and Jews under my rule as Queen, to attack Jerusalem and rebuild the Holy Temple. My father in-law was a mean old bastard. He poisoned my father and his own son, then used an ancient clause in Hebrew law to claim me as his bride."

"What did you do?"

"I married him, became queen, and killed him on our wedding night."

"How did his tribe react?"

"I was queen, my tribe and allies outnumbered them, and we were prepared. They weren't."

"What about the three rabbis? Are they coming to Djerba?"

"They will not reach the island. Lost at sea will be their epitaph."

"You finalize your solutions."

"Keep that in mind if you ever think of betraying me or my people."

The festivities for Rosh Hashanah went well. The somber mood of repentance during the twenty-four hour fast of Yom Kippur was replaced when Cahena hosted everyone at breaking the fast. The visitors took ship home, and the people of Djerba set about building flimsy shacks called Succoth. They were framed of bamboo, walls of cloth decorated with symbols of the temple and Rabbinical sayings. Roofs of palm leaves and grain stalks were placed so the stars could still be seen from inside. Cahena explained to the prince, "Mosaic law dictates we remember our forty years in the desert by dwelling seven days in Succoth. Christians call it the Feast of Tabernacles."

"Will we be sleeping outside?"

"If you'd like to."

"I could teach you the Huntsman's position."

"At the beginning, I enjoyed learning the Kama Sutra positions. Lately, though, I feel like a cordbraider. Some of these positions are very athletic and unsatisfying."

"Good you told me. It is my sworn duty to love you to distraction."

"That's why I sent Josephus away and Yaakov to remain in Djerba. Although Lila is pleased I spend more time with my sons, she too complains you take too much of my time."

"There are other methods taught to me by the harem girls. It is time you were introduced to hemp flower and opium mixed with wine."

"What does this do?"

"When chewed, it releases energy into your body, much as your man Ahmed did for the Numidians with the kaffa beans. When the leaf is chewed with wine, it becomes a wonderful aphrodisiac. There is a legend that 'God said to the people:

> "'Guard the leaves with much love and when
> you feel the sting of pain in your heart,
> hunger in your body,
> and darkness in your mind...
> Take them to your mouth and softly, draw up
> its juice which is part of me....."
> You will find love for your pain
> food for your body and light for your mind
> Further more, watch the leaves dance with the wind
> and you will find answers to your queries.'"

"Lately queries to my unconscious mind go unanswered. My healing powers have also eroded. Possibly the flowers will help."

"In the sukkah?"

"Of course."

"Did you mean it when you said you might free my fellow princes?"

"If you swear to me the ransom will be paid."

"Your carrier pigeons have already confirmed the treasure caravan is on its way. It must be heavily guarded. Send a larger force to guard my brothers, meet the Emperor's caravan and trade prisoners for wealth. It will also give you the advantage of spreading the wealth to your communities on the return journey. You can repair roads, bridges, and increase water supplies for your army next spring when General Walid and his army invade the Maghreb."

"Aren't you betraying Islam by advising me in such a manner?"

The prince stood. He paced back and forth. He started to speak, stopped and continued pacing. He stood in front of her, looked down and said, "I am a traitor to Islam. I cannot deny Allah, I will not, but General Walid..." He pointed down at Cahena and said, "May God forgive me, but I believe I am in love with you."

CHAPTER 29

THE LETTER

Cahena accepted the prince's suggestion, and set in motion the release of prisoners with a large armed escort. Pigeons were sent to arrange a rendezvous of the two caravans. The prince wrote two letters, the first to his father, the second letter entrusted to his closest brother—with instructions not to return to Babylon, but personally deliver the letter to General Khalid ibn Al Walid, saying to him, "Allahu Akbar".

After the holidays, Uncle Benyamin appeared before Cahena, saying, "There is discontent among some of the tribes."

"Why is that?"

"Of late you have not made your presence felt, and because Josephus is away. They require his strong hand. You also allow unarmed Muslims to preach throughout the Maghreb."

"We Jews in Africa are only a fraction of the population. Most are Pagans. They want to be entertained."

"Then teach them Judaism. Every morning I thank the Almighty for making me a Jew. You could convert tens of thousands."

"Except for three requirements: circumcision, no work on the Sabbath, the prohibition and preparation of certain foods. The Muslim preachers are usually illiterates. The people will see through them."

"You are inviting the fox into the hen house."

"Then we shall be wearing fox tail caps. But that is not why you are here. According to Yaakov you've come to scold me about my public disregard of Judaic law, the public desecration of the Sabbath, the Pagan idols in my home and the company I keep."

"Did you order the disappearance of the three rabbis associated with the Helawi tribe?"

"I would have been well within my rights. They caused my father's death."

"A court of law should determine the crime and penalty. Their sin was revealing your father's plans for the invasion of Jerusalem to Selim. He ordered the death of your father. You killed him without trial."

"And I'd do it again." Cahena stood to her full height towering over her adopted uncle. "Only this time it would be more painful. Be careful what you say in the court of the Berber

Queen. I want no more whining from you or your nephew about my Judaism, my actions or personal involvement with Prince Armah."

"Yaakov is one hundred percent correct. He is trying to protect the future of Israel. You are the product of more than two thousand years of inbreeding. Have you no shame that your children learn about Islam from your Persian lover?"

"Silence! I am the law in Africa."

"And I am the law in my caravan. I am going back on the trail."

"Remain quiet while doing so."

Cahena and the prince often left Carthage for excursions into nature. She returned to her passion of sketching birds on Chinese paper. These drawings and her observations were organized by scholars at Carthage Academy into catalogues for study.

She no longer visited the ill and injured. Her power to heal was gone. Her own son was wounded by a splinter from a wooden sword, and she could not relieve his pain. The white feather of her hair was now indistinct. Rumors circulated that Cahena had lost her powers. To even hint at it caused a tirade and banishment from her court. Not even Lila mentioned it.

Josephus returned from the yearly gathering

of Berbers with disturbing news. Muslim missionaries were preaching throughout Africa. Josephus was outraged to find Prince Armah at Cahena's side as her advisor. She thwarted his efforts to dislodge the prince from this position. Josephus busied himself with organizing, training, and supplying the soldiers. Distribution of food and clothing were given to Yaakov. He also took responsibility for the fleet of fifty ships plying the seven seas. These he put under the command of a Sicilian pirate captain named Roberto. Ahmed was responsible the armies livestock; he moved the large herds slowly up the mountain slopes to graze on the new grass of spring. Lila's Shamans were helpful with information from the tribes. Not so from General Walid's army; shamans were banned from Muslim camps, cities, and villages, by order of General Walid. Reports from the Shamans confirmed Josephus' description of the influence of the Islamic preachers amongst the Pagan and Christian tribes.

After a meeting with her counselors, Cahena questioned the prince. "You were unusually quiet during discussions concerning the Islamic preachers."

"I am conflicted between my love for you and my duty to Allah."

"Can it be resolved?"

"I've thought long and hard on this problem."

"Share your thoughts with me."

"The only solution I can envision is the avoidance of war."

"That appears impossible."

"There may be a way?"

"Explain."

"The solution is so drastic I hesitate to speak of it."

"The future of both our peoples could depend upon it. Certainly our future does."

"The tactic is not new. It would involve great sacrifice on your part."

"According to our spies General Walid has over a hundred thousand troops, all Muslims. They will have been training for five years. I will field almost two hundred thousand. Ours are not as well trained, and are made up of different tribes. The sacrifices on both sides will be terrible. But we will win."

"To avoid this war you must take away what the enemy desires. What does an invading army want?"

"To defeat us, then control the land and its wealth."

"Maghreb is wealthy in its people, its agriculture, forests and mining the Atlas Mountains. You can't move the mountains, but you can move or destroy the grain fields and forests.

"You are speaking of a scorched earth strategy."

"I am." Prince Armah waited for Cahena to digest the proposal rather than lead her to his desired conclusion. She closed her eyes and attempted to contact a spirit guide but to no avail. The only one of her closest advisors in camp was Lila, who was far from being a military strategist. Cahena thought of the campaign against the Romans and how her people along the Christian army's route of march destroyed their crops, abandoned and even burnt their villages, so the Romans found nothing to loot and were forced to be supplied by sea. "What naval force does General Walid control?" she asked.

"None. He hires ships for transportation of men and materials."

"And Yaakov commands over fifty ships, one-third of them fighting vessels. They could destroy any supply fleet General Walid sent."

"It won't be necessary. The General also has spies, and will know of your naval power. Since the Muslim fleet was destroyed by the Romans in Constantinople, they haven't a rowboat to fish from. It would take them another five years to build a fleet large enough to defeat yours. The General promised he would invade this coming spring."

"And you believe he would abandon his plan if...?"

"If there is nothing for him to conquer or gain but a burnt out landscape and a protracted, indecisive war that drains his treasury. He will petition the Caliph to end it."

"I know the general. He is not concerned about money. He gave his word he would invade the Maghreb."

"The Caliph is concerned about the expense of expanding the Caliphate. It is his money the general is spending. You asked me for my opinion. Your people living in the plains can take refuge with the mountain Berbers. Yaakov and his uncle will transport supplies from those farms he hired on the invasion route to Jerusalem. Your pigeons will maintain communications with your Tuaregs and Bedouin in the desert. Then you have King Gershom and his Numidians."

"I included them in the two hundred thousand."

"Yes, but they will be positioned on the right flank of General Walid's army. He will have to respect their ability for swift attacks. That is another reason for the general not to engage in a war where there is nothing to gain."

"I must think on this," Cahena said. "Let us chew khat leaves."

The Queen of the Berbers met with her chieftains. She consulted with tribal leaders regarding the scorched-earth approach to avoiding war. The details of the plan were too complicated to explain in brief messages flown back and forth to Josephus and Yaakov. She referred to a scorched-earth policy similar to that used against the two Roman legions. Each agreed with the plan.

The only advisor vehemently against was Lila. "They aren't coming for your money or your land," she argued. "The Muslims are coming for your soul."

Cahena ignored her protest and proclaimed throughout the Maghreb, "Sow every inch of your land, right up to your doorstep. Store that which you require until next spring. Prepare to send your surplus to the mountains for the following spring, and then plant nothing. We hope to leave a desolate place for the Muslims invaders to occupy and thereby avoid a bloody and costly war."

To most people the following spring seemed far away, and with some grumbling they continued to live as they had for generations. Several of the larger cities sent delegations to question the supply of food to be sent into the mountains. They listened to Cahena explain the storing of excess food this year, and food to be brought from the properties leased on the way to Jerusalem to supplement the supplies. There were some protests from those with fixed places of businesses required to destroy their buildings. Cahena assured them she had enough ransom money to help them rebuild bigger and better than before. An agreement was reached; the queen appointed administrators to assess property to be refunded by the treasury. The prince was helpful in organizing and implementing this plan.

Josephus often slept in the saddle. He implemented military training schedules for the residence cities and towns along the Mediterranean coast to the Port of Tripoli. There he met with Yaakov and Roberto, the pirate captain of the Berber fleet. They had just commandeered five Roman grain ships from Alexandria headed to Europe. During a discussion of this new policy of organized withdrawal before the Islamic army, the pirate captain guaranteed the delivery of food, supplies, and men by sea. "I control the Mediterranean coast on the left flank of the attacking Islamic army," he said, and volunteered to put raiding parties ashore to harass the Muslims.

"That's the first promising news I've had in weeks," Josephus said. "I'm up to my eyeballs in land feuds and blood vengeance generations old."

"You've got to keep the feuding tribes separate," Yaakov said.

"I know. But then how do I train them in mass troop movements?"

"Cut off a few heads," The pirate suggested.

"Won't help," Yakov answered. "If blood was spilled it must be avenged. Even the Muslims cannot stop vengeance killings; it's too deeply ingrained. First separate them, then place them in training with distant tribes."

"I don't have enough time," Josephus said.

"There is no alternative," Yaakov sighed. "This problem has been with us since Cain killed Abel. I have faith in you."

"I wish Cahena felt the same."

"The prince?"

Josephus nodded, and Yaakov asked the pirate to leave. "What are your problems with the queen?"

"Her inner circle of advisors consists of the prince and sometimes Lila. She calls in the chieftains when they grumble, but she decides—and her thoughts are influenced by this Persian lover."

"Do you know about the khat leaves?"

"Everyone knows. Her actions are disgusting."

"Don't tell her that."

"She anticipated my big Calabrese mouth, and sent me out here."

"Me too. My uncle is also persona-non-grata at court."

"Where did he go?"

"First to see if the plantations he rented are living up to their promises. Then he will visit Jerusalem, and from there to Constantinople and the Khazars along the Black Sea."

"How long will he be gone?"

"Two to four years. It depends upon whether he can find suitable grooms for his two daughters in Jerusalem."

"With his wealth he should have his pick."

"They are mostly the old toothless Jews come to the Holy Land to die."

"If we defeat the Muslim army it will take us two years to organize and march on Jerusalem."

"That is the first time you've expressed doubt of our success."

"Cahena brought me back from the doorstep of death. She appears to have lost the magic or spirit guides that allowed her to read minds, cure people, and travel in dream flights. I blame the Persian prince."

"My uncle and I agree, but there is nothing to be done. Cahena dismisses anyone who disagrees with her."

"But she listens to her Muslim advisor. He must be inserting Islamic teaching into his lovemaking."

"You think that is what makes him such a good lover?"

"No, it's the khat leaves. They chew them most of the day."

"As an aphrodisiac?"

"Of course."

"How do you know?"

"I too have spies. Best we end this conversation; the queen has more spies than me."

Three months later, his camel on the verge of collapse, a weary Persian prince arrived in General Khalid ibn Al Walid's camp. It took him a full day of pleading, a bath, and change of clothes, before he was granted an audience. He delivered the prince's letter into the general's hand, who waved the message in his face. "If your father were not Emperor, I would hang you and your older brother by the balls."

"Sir, we are devoted disciples of the Prophet, and followers of Allah."

"You are shit for brains. I left explicit orders not to enter the Maghreb. Prince Armah chose to ignore them. He was trapped and defeated."

"He did so in an attempt to gain your favor

and Allah's blessings by conquering and converting the infidels. The Witch of the Maghreb defeated us with sorcery. She commanded a flood..."

"I've heard all the bullshit stories. If you weren't there you would not have been crushed. Your father had to pay a pretty price to ransom you and your brothers."

"Only the prince remains in captivity."

"My spies say he is enjoying himself with Queen Cahena." He flourished the letter. "What does this say?"

"I was not privy to its contents, but was instructed to say: 'In the name of the prince, Allahu Akbar'."

"Then Prince Armah did not want you to know what is written. Get out of my sight and go eat something; you look as if you've been in a famine, and I look as if I caused it." The prince bowed again and exited. General broke the seal and read:

"There is no God but Allah and Muhammad is the messenger of Allah. I wish to be accepted as your humble servant, and beg forgiveness for those actions I took in contradiction to your orders. Please do not cast blame on my followers; I convinced them it was with the Blessings of Allah and approval of the Prophet that I envisioned bringing a million converts to Islam.

I was wrong. If you would accept my sword once again in your service, place me where it is considered most dangerous so I may serve Allah, the Prophet, and you. About my actions after the battle:

"The moment I was outmaneuvered, I thought to take my own life. My stupidity in disobeying your orders and my honor required that. Then I met Cahena. She told me much about you and your recuperation from your wounds in the battle outside of Tangiers with the Christians from Constantinople. I think you will agree that Cahena is very intelligent, quick to learn, but unsophisticated about life's intrigues and complexities at court. She is especially naive about cultured, erotic sex. I may not be a military genius, but I am learned in the art of sex. From the age of nine my father's concubines instructed me. I too am quick to learn, and intelligent. I could feel Cahena looking at me when we were brought into her presence. She was first attracted by my height, which is six feet four inches—one inch taller than she. I contrived to dress in the most subtly provocative clothes to attract her attention. This was effective. She has no husband, but a voracious sexual appetite. I satisfied that, and then instructed her in Kama Sutra. I worked my way closer through her two sons. She holds little affection for either, and did not object when I taught them with wooden swords or told them stories of the exploits of General Khalid ibn Al Walid. I later injected tales of Mohammed the Messenger of God. I was challenged at court for doing so, but Cahena defended me. She exiled the challenger, and in addition to becoming her lover I replaced the banished advisor. Initially I contemplated assassinating the queen or dying in the attempt. It is true we were defeated by her magic; she admitted to me that she was capable of astral travel, and under the ideal circumstances controls the weather—which she did to defeat me. I am now a senior advisor in the queen's court. I maintain the option of assassinating her or reporting to you what her plans are to combat your invasion this coming spring. I am your faithful servant. The following information should be helpful.

"The Berber army is commanded by General Josephus, who is as dedicated to the queen as we are to the Prophet. A veteran from the Roman Army, he served in Spain and throughout the Maghreb. He too is intelligent, unsophisticated, and drives his men hard. He says he has met you. His spies put your army at one hundred thousand. With the Numidian Army, Josephus expects to field two hundred thousand. I question his expectations. Berber spies return with tales of Islamic preachers among the Numidians and tribes of the Maghreb, making converts. The senior shaman in North Africa failed to convince Cahena that this is a serious problem. Her name is Lila, and she is the surrogate mother of Cahena's two boys. I agree with the shaman and suggest you consider sending more unarmed preachers to the Pagan tribes. The enemies' loss is our gain. Every convert to Islam is worth two soldiers.

"Josephus and the tribal chieftains see your strategic weakness as a lack of sea power. I concur. The disaster wreaked by the Roman Navy on the Islamic fleet at Constantinople was catastrophic. In a land war you require the ability to supply and communicate with your army by sea, especially if a scorched-earth policy is initiated against you. Consider the following; my father the Emperor of Persia has often found it more convenient to buy off adversaries than subdue them. Pirates by definition are not interested in religion or crops, other than those they can steal. They are assassins of the seas, and for sale to the highest bidder. Consider the benefits to be achieved by outbidding the Berbers for the services of the Pirates. A fleet of fifty cargo ships laden with supplies can be bought for your army instead of hers, also enough fighting craft to blockade eastern

Mediterranean ports. The pirates will demand payment in advance. You, on the other hand, must have iron-clad guarantees. I do not know what you can hold over the pirates to make them comply. If the Caliphate cannot provide the money you require, I sent a letter to my father asking him to extend any credit you may need."

As he continued to read of the leased plantations on the route to Jerusalem, and the Khazars rejection of a military alliance, the general began to formulate a plan to defeat the Berber Queen. He summoned his spy master, and together they reread the letter and agreed that the most pressing issue was that of the pirates. The general drafted a letter to the Caliphate, requesting funds enabling him to bribe the pirates of Sicily. He explained in detail the commercial, military, and proselyting benefits derived from such a venture. The general was not on the best terms with the caliph, and he anticipated an ambiguous reply from the Caliphate.

The spy master suggested, "We offer the pirates two safe ports in the Mediterranean, three more along Africa's Atlantic coast, and two each in the remaining Seven Seas in addition to gold. The Island of Djerba would remain the major clearing house for all pirated goods."

"During my recuperation in Carthage," the general said, "I visited Djerba. They are very religious Jews, and will support Cahena."

"My spies indicate the Jews have problems with the Queen's personal behavior. She antagonized the rabbis by flouting religious laws. She worships idols. It is whispered she is responsible for the disappearance of three rabbis. Her romance with a Muslim draws criticism."

"So you confirm the prince's wooing the queen of the Jews?"

"I was contemplating how to break the news when you summoned me." The spy master pointed to the letter. "This information is worth a wagon-load of gold. Those same rabbis on Djerba are also businessmen. If their island becomes the clearing house for stolen goods in the middle-east, they will profit beyond their wildest expectations. The key element is the Berber courier pigeon network, which is in Djerba. Destroy her communications, and you have the advantage."

General Walid contemplated his options. The spy master remained silent as the old veteran made a list of possible actions and projected results. An hour passed before the general looked up and said, "Enlist every Muslim who hunts with falcons. Pair them with our people who fly pigeons. The objective of the falcons will be to bring down every pigeon that flies. If it is one of ours, send the message on with another bird. Before you do that, prepare the fastest riders on the finest mounts to take a letters to the caliph in Arabia and emperor in Babylon. The riders will remain at the posts along the way to carry the replies. How long will it take?"

"Three-thousand-five-hundred miles to Babylon, ten days: two-thousand-one-hundred miles to Mecca, six days. A total of twenty-four riders and almost two hundred horses"

"If they can make the return journey in the same amount of time, there will be a gold coin for every rider and each station manager."

The spy master stood, slammed his fist over his heart, bowed and said, "So it is ordered: so it is done."

"Before you leave, what is the greatest vulnerability of the Sicilian pirates?"

Now the General waited while the master spy thought. He tugged his goatee several times and replied, "Family. I spent several years in Sicily. They may pray to the Christian God, but when it comes to right or wrong, family always wins. If you are thinking of capturing their leaders' families and holding them to guarantee his cooperation, the idea is workable."

"Could you arrange to gather up families of prominent pirate captains?"

"I will do it."

"One more question. What is my greatest vulnerability?"

"Your predictability. What you say, you do."

"You mean I talk too much?"

The spy Master remained silent and bowed.

"Thank you." The General picked up his quill and contemplated Josephus' preparations for war. The more he thought about the prince's letter and his colleague's assessment of his own weakness the clearer became the plan to defeat the Berber Queen.

CHAPTER 30

PREPARATION FOR WAR

"You cannot enter the Maghreb armed," the spy master told a tent full of agents. "This is the agreement we made with the Berbers for her help in defeating the Romans outside of Tangiers. In the spring we invade. Your tasks are threefold. First, each of you find and enlist a Muslim falconer and a person who has trained pigeons. The falconer will down any and all messenger birds. If it is ours, the pigeon man will send on the message to a central post I will designate. Your second task is to report military movements of the Berber army by your pigeon-man. Not the least important is for you to support our mullahs who are preaching Islam to the Christians and Pagans. You will do this by mingling with the crowd when the preachers talk and encourage those around you. You have the privilege of being the advance guard of the Army of Islam preparing to conquer North Africa. Allahu Akbar!"

"Allahu Akbar! Allahu Akbar! Allahu Akbar!"

the men chanted.

Before the spy master left camp he sent five men on a special mission to safeguard the Persian prince in Carthage. He parted from General Walid with a contingent of fifty assassins. In the port of Tangiers the hired killers straggled unobtrusively aboard several ships bound for Corsica and then Sicily. They weighed anchor on the morning tide.

General Walid knew the Emperor Heraclius had defeated the Prince's father, Emperor of Babylon, at the Battle of Nineveh. The Roman Christians from Constantinople claimed to have recaptured the true cross on which Jesus was crucified; Heraclius was now in Jerusalem supervising the building of a Church to house the holy artifact. General Walid wrote to him: "Most illustrious Emperor, although we have been on opposite sides of the battlefield I respect your position and military ability. You recently defeated the Babylonian Army at the Battle of Nineveh. This allowed you to recapture Jerusalem. You reclaimed the true cross upon which your prophet Jesus died. Furthermore you are building a church to house that holy relic. You are in danger. Cahena, Queen of the Berbers and ruler of the Maghreb, is about to implement a plan of her father's to oust you from the holy city and rebuild the sacred Jewish temple. Benyamin of Toledo, Caravan Master from Spain and adopted Uncle of Cahena, has bought up the crops and future livestock for three years in advance to supply Cahena's Army on their way to Jerusalem. They have already harvested one crop. Another will be ready in the fall unless you capture or destroy it. The third crop will go to feed the Berber army in their war against me and the Army of Islam. Now you know why your enemy relays such vital information. I wish you to confiscate or destroy their future food supply. Everyone believes I am predictable; therefore I will not invade this spring. Cahena will have an Army of two hundred thousand; that is three times your Army. She must feed, house, and clothe them. If she is not in confrontation with Islam she must turn her attention to Jerusalem. Otherwise her vast army will denude the land like a plague of locusts. You have already surmised my intention; she is planning a scorched-earth policy against me. Without much effort it is possible to starve her army into submission and lead to her downfall."

Emperor Heraclius was meticulous in authenticating the contents of General Walid's message before he replied. Having confirmed the purchase of crops by Benyamin, the caravan master, and that a plan did exist for the Berbers to conquer Jerusalem, he replied to the general's query:

"Respected General of the army of Islam, the Sword of Allah, your reputation precedes you. My officers compare your tactical brilliance in battle with that of Hannibal. Your information has proved correct and most timely. I have taken action. Benyamin, the Caravan Master from Toledo, was assassinated in Constantinople this past summer. My troops are in the process of confiscating this fall's grain, produce and livestock purchased by him. It will feed my army this winter. The following spring when you prepare to enter the Maghreb we will burn or confiscate those same fields to deprive the Berber army of supplies. I now share with you intelligence garnered from our spy network. There is a large group of Berber Jews who may not support Queen Cahena in the battle against you. These are the more religious Jewish tribes who walked out of the yearly meeting because of some religious ruling regarding women Rabbis. They have not attended or cooperated with Cahena in religious matters. The Queen appears distracted by a love affair with a Persian prince who is heir to the Babylonian throne. It is whispered she has lost her so-called mystical powers. Her scorched-earth policy has met with opposition amongst the lowland Berber farmers along the Mediterranean coast. I believe this information is payment in kind for that which you shared with me.

"Emperor Heraclius, ruler of the Eastern Roman Catholic Empire."

The North African winter in the year 636 was ideal for growing. There was sufficient rain and sun, temperature along the coast never went below fifty degrees, and the fertile soil awaited the seeds of spring. None were sown. By order of Cahena, towns and cities of the Maghreb were evacuated in preparation for the invasion of the Islamic Army. Houses, barns, all buildings were put to the torch. The fields were picked clean and torched. The people moved up the slopes of the Atlas Mountains to seek refuge with the hill tribes. A pall of thick dark smoke diffused the sun's rays over the coastal plains for a thousand miles. Josephus and Yaakov attempted to disperse the people evenly, reducing the burden of hosting the uninvited guests. Grain and dried fruit were dispersed, and firewood deposited along the route into the foothills. Josephus was vigilant regarding hygiene and clean water sources. He and Yaakov created three reservoirs to accommodate the two hundred and fifty thousand people from the plains. Water from the spring snow-melt and occasional rain was plentiful, but that would change with the onset of summer and temperatures of over a hundred degrees. Smoke from burning villages, cities, and fields turned day into night. Fires up and down the coast lit the night sky.

Rumors of the invading Islamic army flew faster than the pigeons, but no enemy appeared. Lila's shamans either fled the Muslim areas or were executed. Without their spy network, Josephus and Yaakov felt blinded. From King Gershom's Numidian spies they learned of a secret meeting of the caliph Abu Bakr in Mecca regarding a sensitive request from General Khalid ibn Al Walid. King Gershom wrote to Cahena:

"The desert, which is a barrier to most, serves us as our protection. No army on earth could sustain themselves without our water sources. These I have heavily guarded. If the wells are overrun, they will be poisoned. We are safe from the Islamic army, but have no defense against their Mullahs; they enter unarmed and preach in the name of Allah and his Prophet Muhammad. Many of my people have taken them to their bosom. This has weakened my spy system. Summer is approaching and General Walid's spring invasion has not taken place. In June I thought he was preparing to attack; instead it was an exercise of mass troop movements. I sense something awry, but could not fathom it. Our pigeon messenger service has been interrupted. We have had to double and treble the number of birds carrying the same message to assure its arrival. Inform General Josephus that fifteen thousand of my men have converted to Islam and will not take up arms against their Islamic brothers. I will have eighty-five thousand men to support you rather than one hundred thousand. My son sends his best regards. He will ride at my side in his first campaign."

Cahena handed the message to Prince Amra and asked his assessment. "I would make every effort to learn the reason for Caliph Abu Bakr's secret meeting. It may have something to do with the delay of General Walid's invasion of the Maghreb."

"Josephus has questioned your loyalty. You remain Muslim but help me plan to defeat the Muslim army."

"You are in conflict with Caliph Abu Bakr. I believe he is a usurper who took by force the inheritance of the Prophet Mohammad. It rightfully belongs to Caliph Ali, and one day I will help rectify that."

"Not if General Walid has his way. Did you read the postscript?"

"Yes. It is only right the general wants to plant my head on a stake. I disobeyed him. It is one more reason for me to remain with you."

"I thought it was my charm that keeps you here."

"That too. And your sweet ass, lovely breasts and honeyed lips."

"Why do you say I have a sweet ass?"

Your face is heart shaped, as is the cleavage of your bosom, and your fine rounded thighs forms a heart shape. When viewed from behind your backside forms the shape of a heart, and I'd like to bite it."

"You are not hobbled. Let's see if you have the strength to overpower me."

He untied his silk jacket, kicked off his slippers and dropped his pantaloons. Standing naked before her he moved from side to side so his phallus swung back and forth. He cupped both hands before him, and Cahena poured sweet oil into them. She stood naked as he anointed her with the oil, and then she covered his hairy body until it glistened. They embraced. He bent her arm behind her but she easily slipped out of the grip and tripped him so he fell onto a leopard skin. Their arms and legs intertwined and they slid in and out of wrestling grips. She sucked his breast and stroked his hardened penis until he released his grip and lay back. They pleasured each other for an hour, then chewed khat leaves and returned to lovemaking with renewed vigor.

The five men sent by General Walid drifted into Carthage unnoticed. One, a former bodyguard for the prince, arranged a secret meeting with the heir to the Babylonian empire. They agreed upon an escape plan if required, and a method of smuggling messages fifteen hundred miles to General Walid on the Atlantic coast of Africa. The prince gradually inserted four of these men into his household staff; the other became his personal bodyguard.

It was a rainy wind-swept day when two old men on worn-out camels plodded up the Roman road into Carthage. At the southern city gate they demanded to be taken to Cahena. The commander of the guard recognized them, and brought the two Bedouin scouts to Josephus.

He and Yaakov were discussing the problems of maintaining such a large armed force in wait for the delayed invasion of the Muslims. They greeted the scouts and tried to order food and wine, but the two men insisted on telling their story. Shortly after they began, Josephus ran to the door and grabbed the first guard he saw.

"Notify the Commander of the Guard to imprison Prince Armah!" he snapped.

The guard, who was one of the prince's spies, ran to deliver the message. The moment he was out of sight, he sought the prince, who was teaching Cahena's sons with wooden swords. The bodyguard whispered in his ear. The prince excused himself from Lila, and went off with the guard. The other four men joined them at the corral, where they mounted six of the fastest camels in the herd and left Carthage in the rain.

Josephus and Yaakov hurried to meet Cahena in her reception room, with the two Bedouin in tow. Each of the bedraggled men had a piece of cold chicken in one hand and a large slab of laffa bread in the other. They bowed. Cahena came off her throne and embraced both men at the same time, lifting them high off the floor. "What brings you two scoundrels out in this weather?" She put them down. "It's been two years since we last met. What news have you brought?"

"Bad news."

Cahena stepped back to sit on her throne. "Tell it so we can all hear."

"My queen you are betrayed. There was a

meeting of Caliph Abu Bakr's Supreme Council in Mecca."

"We heard, but could not find out what was discussed."

"A request for funds by General Walid to bribe the pirate captains that command your fleet."

"It's a smart tactic but I doubt there is enough money in the Caliphate's treasury."

"The Emperor of Babylon will stand good for what is lacking."

"Impossible! I hold his firstborn son and heir to the Babylonian throne."

"It was Prince Armah who suggested the plan."

Cahena leapt off the throne. The two Bedouin fell to their knees trembling. Cahena towered over them. "Proof! Where is your proof!"

"Why didn't you send a pigeon?" Yaakov asked.

"They cannot read nor write," Josephus said. "It would have been too dangerous to dictate it to a scribe."

"How did you come by this information?" Cahena demanded.

"All Arabs are brothers," the scout answered. "The winter nights are long and there is nothing to do but keep warm by the fire and talk. What we told you is what we heard."

"How do you know it is true?"

"Other things prove it."

"Such as?"

"The disruption of your pigeons. General Walid pays a coin for each pigeon that is brought down, and five coins for every Berber pigeon. He has recruited falconers to disrupt your messenger service."

"They have succeeded," Cahena said, "But that is not proof."

"Have you heard about the caravan master?"

"My Uncle Benyamin?"

"He is dead, assassinated by the Romans on recommendation from General Walid. The crops you paid for in advance were either confiscated or destroyed by the legions. This was Prince Armah's idea. May we ask a question?"

She nodded dumbly.

"Whose idea was it to burn the crops and prevent the spring sowing?"

No one in the room moved until Cahena said, "The prince! Why?"

"Rumors abound that General Walid did not attack this spring because the Prince believes your scorched-earth policy, loss of the crops and lack of a fleet to deliver food will cause starvation in your army."

"I want proof!" Cahena shouted. Her face flushed and saliva bubbled at the corner of her lips. She pointed to Josephus. "Bring the prince here immediately." Josephus grabbed the first guard he saw and sent him with orders to bring the prince, under heavy guard, to Cahena's reception room.

It took a half an hour before the guard returned, with the commander of the guard who knew nothing about a prisoner, much less the Prince of Babylon. Inquiries were made. A guard at the southern gate reported a group of six unidentified men traveling south four hours earlier.

When Cahena was informed of the prince's flight, she lost her composure. She screamed, wept, and threw things at those in the room. She struck Lila, knocking her to the floor. A handmaid was felled by a blow to the head with a pitcher of wine. The blood and wine mixed on the tile floor. Cahena went to strike one of the guards, slipped in the bloody wine and fell. She slapped away Josephus' helpful hand and ordered everyone from the room. She could be heard crying, wailing, and cursing into the early hours of morning.

Twenty miles from Carthage the prince led his group off the Roman road, angling into the flat agricultural land, on the shorter route to Rabat in Morocco. There was enough food gleaned from the burnt fields and purchased from farmers avoiding Cahena's scorched-earth policy to sustain the group. Their camels were well chosen, as they loped on through the rain and sleet. They avoided towns where pigeons might have alerted the Berbers of their escape.

The spy master of the Islamic Army left the convoy of ships sailing into the Roman-dominated Mediterranean, entered the Tyrrhenian Sea and cruised up the west coast of Italy to the island of Corsica. It was a haven for a vicious band of Italian pirates. Few in number, they were feared throughout the Seven Seas.

The spy master hired sixty pirates, five for each of his twelve two-man teams. They boarded ship, sailed down the coast of Italy around the Heel of the Boot and into Sicily's main port. They off-loaded wheat and bargained for casks of rich red wine to be sold in Carthage, while the spy master met with agents who had preceded him to Sicily. They handed him a list of the fifteen pirates in the employ of the Berber Queen. Twelve families were chosen, and carriages rented for the abductions.

On the evening of March 12[th,] 634 CE at eight o'clock, twelve families were captured, bound, gagged, and hustled into covered wagons headed for the port. In each home was left a silver coin, a stiletto, and a carrier pigeon tucked into a stocking with a note that read, 'Choose'.

The spy master left the office of the senior representative of Sicily's Lawyers Guild with simple demands: "All pirate captains serving in the Berber fleet will deliver their cargo and ships to a port of my choosing. Comply, and by the beard of the Prophet, I promise to pay for the ships and fifty percent more than the market price of its cargo. You will be reunited with your families and given safe passage home. By Allah I swear it. I also do so swear to cut the throats of every infidel hostage if you do not submit. Furthermore, those families not taken hostage will be hunted down by General Khalid ibn Al Walid if they do not comply. So it is ordered. So it is done. Allahu Akbar!"

The operation was carried out with such stealth and speed that the kidnappers hoisted anchor on the midnight tide and sailed for Corsica. The hostages were housed in a large stone fortified villa outside Ajaccio, the regional capital. The kidnappers formed an outer perimeter guard around the villa and a tighter-knit one closer in. Lookouts were posted to identify every ship entering the port and ascertain if Sicilian pirates were aboard.

In late April, the negotiations completed, pirate ships surrendered in the ports of Tangiers, Corsica, and Rabat. Families were reunited; payment was made for the delivery of fifty-two ships and their cargo. Transportation by ship was arranged for the hostages to return to Sicily.

Prior to the hostage's departure from Corsica, a pigeon flew in with a message from the Muslim spy master for his agents. "Kill all the Sicilian pirates and hostages. Drop the bodies on the incoming tide at the port of Sicily from whence they came. Those above the age of fifteen who fail to accept Islam must die. The younger ones and any prepared to convert will be brought to Mecca for indoctrination into the True Faith."

A month earlier, the spy master had bypassed General Walid and sent a request to directly to the Caliph in Mecca requesting authority to kill the hostages and pirates. He argued, "They are infidels, kafirs, who reject the one true God and the truth of Islam. I did give my word to return the captives and the pirate captains to Sicily; I did not say they would be alive. Although this may be considered a lie of omission, we are dealing with infidels. According to the laws of Taqiyya, as taught by the Prophet Mohammad, we are permitted to lie to idol worshippers. These Sicilian pirates are staunch Catholics; they bow down to sculptures of wood, stone, and plaster. I turn to the Caliph and his council for a ruling. Is it permitted to offer them a choice of accepting Islam or death? I had promised to bring them and the hostages home; I never said they would be alive."

After consultation with the Islamic court in Mecca the Caliph sent the following reply:

"Muslims should generally be truthful to each other.

"Does Islam permit Muslims to lie? There are several forms of lying to nonbelievers that are permitted under certain circumstances, the preeminent being Taqiyya. These circumstances are typically those that advance the cause of Islam—in some cases by gaining the trust of non-believers in order to draw out their vulnerability and defeat them.

"Quran (3:28)—This verse tells Muslims not to take those outside the faith as friends, unless it is to 'guard themselves' against danger, meaning that there are times when a Muslim may appear friendly to non-Muslims, even though they should not feel friendly.

"Quran (16:106)—Establishes that there are circumstances that can 'compel' a Muslim to tell a lie.

"Quran (9:3)—'...Allah and His Messenger are free from liability to the idolaters...'

"Quran (66:2)—'Allah has ordained for you the dissolution of your oaths to idolaters.'

"Quran (2:225)—'Allah will not call you to account for thoughtlessness in your oaths, but for the intention in your hearts'."

"The concept of lying to a pirate is a inconsistency in terms. Those who pursue the idolator's way of life are not worthy of respect. The question arises with their families and children under the age of fifteen. If nonpirate male and or female adults are prepared to accept Islam and learn the teachings of the Prophet, their lives should be spared. The younger ones will be separated from their families and converted. Taqiyya is an Islamic judicial term whose changeable meaning relates to when a Muslim is allowed, under Sharia law, to lie.

"Your situation certainly warrants a mendacious approach to the truth.

"You have my permission to proceed as planned based on the above references.

"Caliph Abu Bakr, Mecca"

Chapter 31

PREPARATIONS FOR BATTLE

After five years of preparation by the Berbers for the promised invasion of General Khalid ibn Al Walid and the Army of Islam, Josephus had his forces in strategic positions throughout the Maghreb. The scorched earth policy was grudgingly put into effect by the villages and towns, and although some cities and tribes refused and Josephus had to discipline them, the effect was dramatic. The burning fields and houses sent a heavy pall of smoke over the entire Mediterranean coastline for months.

The expected Islamic invasion did not take place. Small Muslim raiding and scouting parties harassed the Berber forces by land and sea. Manned by Muslim captains and crews, the former pirate ships blockaded Berber seaports. Food from the farms along the route to Jerusalem was unavailable. The Romans either took or destroyed the farms and produce. Muslim falconers disrupted the Berber pigeon communication system. But the Islamic army did not invade. It remained in winter quarters through the spring, summer, and winter of the sixth year. Food for the Berber army was in short supply. Provisions, materials, and reinforcements poured into The Muslim camp, donated by zealous converts to the new religion and encouraged by tax breaks.

Berber mountain tribes, used to living in tents and off the land, fared better than their cousins from the lowlands taking refuge in the mountains. An unhealthy tension developed between the two groups. Josephus was often required to send troops to separate them. At the same time he had to integrate the disputing factions into military units that could coordinate their movements in combat. He worked himself into a state of exhaustion. Cahena tended to him while Yaakov attempted to take over his duties, in addition to supplying the Berber people to avoid starvation. He was unsuited for the task. Tribal and religious disputes erupted.

Desertions took place. The first to desert were the three Helaway tribes. Their departure was followed by the conservative Jewish tribes. Others felt the destruction of their homes, fields and businesses were unnecessary measures weakening the Berber nation. Cahena isolated herself. Her appearances in public were brief, and orchestrated by Lila to encourage the people to withstand the harsh winter, lack of food, fuel, and the rains of March. Lila exposed her shamans recklessly to obtain information about the Islamic army and when it would invade.

At the same time she attended Cahena, who was in a deep state of depression. The Queen failed to understand how she could have been duped by the Persian prince. It was Lila who finally explained it to her: "Your sexual desires and self-gratification were more important than your children, your people, or your future. The scorched earth policy of the prince might work against the Romans and Barbarians, whose objectives are to destroy, loot and control. To the Muslims these objectives are secondary. They want our souls. I attempted to tell you this on several occasions, but you would not listen."

Cahena broke down in uncontrollable sobs. She sat on the floor with her knees pulled up and buried her chin in them and wept. "What am I to do? Who can I turn to? What will become of us if General Walid invades now?"

"I believe you can expect it. He is a wily old fox. Can you confide in Gershom, King of the Numidians?"

"Were I to tell him the state of my people and condition of my army, he might withdraw his support. If he knew Josephus is bedridden,

King Gershom might withhold his troops. We are facing defeat on the battlefield."

"Then we must resurrect Josephus."

"It could kill him."

"He was born a professional soldier. His duty is to serve until, and including, his death. Give him some of those khat leaves you chew. I'll make a potion that will keep him moving."

"Can you give me some of that too?"

"Only if you try to help yourself. You look as if you lost a wrestling match with a bear. I will prepare a bath and then a sweat tent for you. I'll send a girl to comb your hair. She will lay out proper clothes."

"Where are my sons?"

"I'll bring them to you."

Prince Armah arrived at the Muslim base camp outside of Tangiers. He had traveled seven months from Carthage, using back trails and smugglers' routes to avoid detection. Two of his men died of exhaustion; a third was killed by bandits.

He was dragged unceremoniously before General Khalid ibn Al Walid. The prince attempted to stand erect to his full height of six feet four inches, but his guards kicked him behind the knees and he collapsed on all fours before the general. Unbeknown to the prince, the Grand Vizier of Persia, sent by the Emperor to ascertain his son's safety, was standing with the general's counselors. He was in agreement with the treatment of his Prince for disobeying the general's orders.

"Prince or not, you are on trial for your life," General Walid said. "You disrupted a well calculated plan to defeat and convert the nomadic tribes of Africa. This was my assignment from the Prophet himself."

The Prince's clothes hung loosely on his thin shoulders as he looked up from the floor. He had lost forty pounds, and his voice rasped. "Like a child, I sought to gain your admiration by conquering the infidel and converting them to Islam while you were away."

"And you were defeated."

"By witchcraft. The Cahena controlled the weather."

"How can you know that?"

"Cahena told me."

"Why would she do that?"

"I was her lover."

"How did that come about?"

"Like most of the Berber people she was unsophisticated, especially in affairs of the heart. On the other hand, I was taught from childhood by the most desirous females in the Empire how to manipulate women."

"And you did so with her?"

"I did. When the ransom demands were made, I decided that my betrayal of your orders could only be redeemed by an act of interference so great that it would win your approval and reduce my punishment. I decided to remain and work my way into her confidence. My being heir to the Persian throne, and my height, would draw her attention. It was easier than I contemplated. Initially I thought to escape after a couple of months, and return to you with information about the Berber Army, its size, makeup, and location. But I was taken into the Cahena's confidence, and eventually became her closest advisor."

"Closer than General Josephus?"

"Yes."

"Did you have to foreswear Islam?"

"Never. In fact, I taught her two sons the True Faith. Jews and Pagans have little interest in converting people. That is how I was able to persuade them to use the scorched earth policy against you. The Berbers think of you as they do of the Vandals, Huns, or Romans. They believe you seek wealth and power, when our goal is really the expansion of Islam. Already the Jewish religious Berbers have withdrawn their men from her army. They do not represent a large contingent, but there is discontent with the scorched-earth policy amongst the farming Berbers of the coastal plains. There are fuel and food shortages. Soon even the mountain Berbers, Tuaregs, and Bedouin will have to come down from the mountains to eat. They will have to force you to fight them, or they must disband and flee."

"And you accomplished all this with love?"

"Passion! And a good amount of khat leaves."

"You can't imagine how often I thought of causing you excruciating pain. Even now, after hearing your well-intentioned actions, it gives me a degree of satisfaction to see you on your knees. Help him up," the general ordered. "In the letter you sent by messenger you asked to be placed in the forefront of the upcoming battle with the Berbers."

"Yes, General. I wish to serve Allah and you in the most dangerous place, so that I may display my commitment to Islam and my respect for you."

"You have been traveling for the better part of a year, therefore you are unaware Caliph Bakr died of natural causes. He's been replaced by Caliph Umar ibn Al-Khattab. I am not one of his favorite generals, having supported Ali and the Shias for the Caliphate against the first Caliph. Umar is suspicious of me, so the most dangerous place for you will be at my side to protect me from assassination."

"Thank you, my General."

With a flick of his hand the general dismissed the prince. One of his councilors whispered, "I thought you would be more severe."

"What I want and what is best for Islam are in conflict. The prince will eventually replace his father. When the son sits on the throne as a Muslim, Islam will supplant Zoroastrianism as the state religion. The Persian Empire stretches from India through the middle-east, Turkey, and the Caucasus, all the way to the Russian border. Islam will become the largest religion in the world, and I will have fulfilled my promise to the Prophet. Islam will be poised on the doorstep of Europe and the end of Christianity. I must keep the prince safe."

Josephus appeared before Cahena. He looked older. The flesh of his forearms hung loose where it had been taut over muscle, sinews and veins. Worry lines creased his weather-beaten face. But his dark eyes were bright and clear, his stance aggressive.

"My general," said Cahena, 'Are you prepared to lead the Berbers and Nomadic peoples of Africa against the army of Islam?"

"I am, my Queen. While recuperating, I have

been kept abreast of events."

"What is your assessment of our army compared to General Walid's Muslims?"

"We are *huskedivised*."

"What?"

"In the legion it means we are two pounds of shit in a one-pound sack."

"That's not good?"

"We have more men than officers to lead them."

"Josephus, my brother, you were correct with your warnings about the Persian prince. You and Yaakov cautioned me more than once."

"It must be the loneliest place in the world to occupy a throne without a helpmate."

"That does not excuse my actions."

"My Queen, there is a saying in the legion: "Only important people can make big mistakes. Foolish ones make them twice."

"Where is Yaakov?"

"On his way from Greece, with three shiploads of much needed provisions. He will have to run the Muslim naval blockade to unload in Carthage."

"We desperately require that food."

"I have arranged an alternative landing site. He will signal with rockets; I will then secure the beach where we defeated the Romans, and he'll land there. If you will order the army down from the mountains, we can distribute the food."

"That means we must fight."

If we do not fight now we will lose most of our army to desertion and or starvation."

"So you know about the desertions and withdrawals of the Jewish tribes?"

"And King Gershom's Numidians."

"Many of his people converted to Islam and refuse to fight fellow Muslims. He will send an army of only seventy-five thousand warriors to support us."

"I know the story of the King's promise to redeem the stone. One thing takes precedence over his oath: his son's succession to the throne. The King abides under the Sword of Damocles."

"How so?"

"If he honors his word to you, the Muslims converts he leaves behind will take over. General Walid would be a fool not to order it."

"What do you suggest?"

"I respect King Gershom as a great, wise, and straightforward leader, but his choice is between family and friend, the future and the present."

"You believe he will fail to support me?"

"Can you take one of your astral journeys to observe?"

"I no longer have those powers. Even my ability to heal, reduce pain and communicate with the birds is lost. Lila might take me on that journey. She did so the first time."

"Send messengers ahead to confirm King Gershom's alliance. Have it delivered on a specific date and time, so you may observe the reaction."

"It will take two months to reach him."

"That is about all the time we have if Yaakov arrives safely with the provisions."

Cahena sent messengers to Numidia and ordered her army down from the mountains. Josephus deployed them south of Carthage. There were ninety thousand, waiting for Yakov's supplies.

On the fourth of March 636 C.E. multi-colored rockets lit up the night sky over the Mediterranean Sea. They were answered by rockets fired from beaches far south of Cartena. The Muslim ships blockading raced south to intercept, but Yaakov sailed north and reached the same place where his father was killed by the Romans. He beached four large craft crammed with food and livestock.

"Where did you find this fourth ship?" Josephus asked.

"We liberated it from Naples harbor under

cover of darkness. It was one of mine that the Muslims took. It contains enough wheat to feed an army."

"That's who is waiting for it. There are ten thousand men starving in Carthage and another ninety thousand camped south of Carthage. What are those lights far out to sea."

"The Muslim fleet. They realized your rockets from shore deceived them."

"Is there any way you can escape?"

"No."

"That may also serve my purpose."

"How?"

"Rip the boats apart."

"For what?"

"Firewood. We've stripped the forests from the mid-slopes of the Atlas Mountains down through the Maghreb to the sea."

"My crews will be in tears."

"Better than eating cold food and shivering in the rain. A warm fire and hot food can do a lot of good."

"When will the war begin?"

"Within six weeks."

"Do you or Cahena have any tricks up your sleeves?"

"We were getting ready to eat our sleeves when you showed up. We haven't got enough food to do anything but attack or run. If we run they'll hunt us through the scrub and thorn. Maneuvering an army this size in its present condition is impossible." Josephus pointed to the sea. "The enemy has us blocked in the west with ships. Their army opposes us in the south. The east is a wasted landscape; our troops lived off the land for a year. The only way open to retreat is the north. If we retreat, half our army will desert. They can live if they become Muslims."

"Why wouldn't they all desert?"

"The other half is too loyal."

"When their lives are at stake they will smarten up quickly."

"Our only option is to attack, defeat General Walid, and take his stores."

"Are the Numidians with us?"

"Cahena and Lila are about to find out."

A pigeon arrived, informing Cahena when her message would be delivered to King Gershom. Lila's senior shamans prepared a special tent near the Carthage beach for the astral journey. Cahena and Lila bathed, sweated in a Turkish bath, and submerged themselves in the cold Mediterranean waters. Wrapped in heavy furs, they entered the ritual tent. Guards were posted in a circle one hundred yards from the tent. The shamans prepared the ritual fire with the correct number of rocks surrounding it and two skins of black leopards facing each other on either side of the fire. "What is the cauldron of boiling water for?" Cahena asked.

Lila did not answer, but had her assistants bring in a camel saddle bag. Before dismissing them she cautioned, "Under no condition is anyone to enter this tent or in any way disturb the queen." Lila unpacked the saddle bag, brought out various pans and a pestle, several leather pouches, a jug of strong smelling vinegar and one of white wine.

"Are we going to picnic along the way?" Cahena remarked

"I am going to change your hair color."

"Whatever for?"

"To boost the morale of your followers. Since you lost that white streak in your hair that people called the Witches Feather, people say you lost your powers."

"Sadly enough, they are right."

"No matter how much I tried to keep it secret, the entire army knows we are about to take this mystical journey. When you step out of this tent again your hair will be white as the driven snow."

"So they'll think my powers have returned."

"Exactly."

"That's deceitful."

"What do you think shamanism is? You recognized it the first night you challenged my shaman at the festival on the Imilchil Plains. Most of the charms we give and rituals performed have no real value. Yet from these harmless antics we get fifty percent cures. It's in the people's minds, and that's what we must return to your Army. They must believe in you so they may fight for themselves."

Cahena's shoulders slumped, her long black hair hung down in front of her face and she wept. "I can't ask my people to retreat. It would be a disaster. They'd be slaughtered along the roads, in the fields, and on the beaches. They must fight. It is our only chance."

"Wet your hair with hot water from the cauldron." Lila brought two bars of lye soap and a pan of wood ash. She and Cahena worked the combination into the hair and scalp. Lila waited until Cahena complained of it burning her scalp, then she poured cool water over Cahena's head, washing out the potent mixture. While Cahena dried her hair, Lila mixed honey and white wine which Cahena applied. Using the pestle, Lila ground celandine roots, olive-madder, oil of cumin seed, and saffron into a paste. This was applied too, and Cahena's hair wrapped into a large cone on top of her head.

The two women sat on opposite sides of the

fire on the leopard skins, and held hands. Eventually their foreheads met, and they journeyed upward out the tent smoke-hole into the starlit night. There was nothing for Cahena to do but observe. They flew over the campfires of her army, and the outposts. The heavens were filled with stars, and a three-quarter moon reflected a path on the sea's surface. It was a pleasant journey to a crucial destination.

Fires of the Islamic army outposts appeared two hundred miles from Tangiers. It meant General Walid had already invaded the Maghreb. Lila turned eastward over the foothills of the Atlas Mountains to the great Sahara desert and the Oasis of King Gershom. The string of green oases radiated like five emeralds in the white sand below. The royal oasis was lit by pine-nut torches leading to the king's pavilion. The enormous tent was filled with tribal chieftains. Talk amongst the guests was in hushed whispers. Men and women caressed their swords and spears for reassurance. King Gershom strode to the throne with his son at his side. The people touched their foreheads to the ground and sang a stirring song of greetings to his Majesty and Prince Ishmael. Warriors beat their shields with spears. Gershom sat on the throne his son on the floor at his right side. Cahena and Lila floated above viewing the scene.

The King pointed the horsehair scepter at his grey-bearded master of ceremonies, who announced, "In deference to the Muslim contingent from the army, the King has granted this audience to discuss Numidian participation in the war against General Khalid ibn Al Walid and the army of Islam. Those who wish to speak, come forward on bended knees."

Three men dressed in pure white robes of the Haj went down on all fours and crept closer to the king. He motioned them to stand and ordered, "State your case."

"Your Majesty, you are taking our people to war against the Islamic army when a goodly number of our people are now Muslims. Many more are considering conversion. Islam makes a mockery of Paganism, Christianity and Judaism. They are false religions."

"Stop!" Gershom said. "I thought it was made clear to you. This audience is for one purpose: to discuss going to war. I will not countenance a diatribe on the aspects of Islam."

"I beg the King's pardon. It is our belief in Allah and his Prophet Mohammad that brings us before you. We who accepted Islam love you. Your people who have converted feel tainted because we cannot support you in a war against our fellow Muslims."

"Your argument might be acceptable but that Muslims do fight Muslims. Is it not so between the Sunni and Shias, in Mecca and Medina?"

"The latter are not orthodox enough for the former, so they kill each other."

"Then why can't you kill Muslims?"

"Caliph Umar forbids it."

"What is it you want from your King?"

"Sire, we ask that you withhold our army's support from the Berbers. Cahena must surrender."

"Surrender, die, or convert. The latter is what you really desire. A Muslim world."

"It is inevitable."

"It is not as long as I am king."

"Your Majesty, your obligation to the Jewish Queen of the Berbers was given because she helped save your son's sight. Yes?"

"And I will keep my pledge."

"What if your son was to release you from that oath?"

Shocked, the king turned to look down at Ishmael sitting at his side. For the first time he looked at him with the eyes of a king and not a father. Ishmael was a strapping seventeen-year-old who returned his gaze without flinching and nodded for his father to accept the offer. Betrayed by friends and family, Gershom stood.

He clenched his teeth and the muscles in his jaw danced. His eyes widened until they fairly popped from his head. He pointed down at his son. "Seize him!"

Ishmael stood, waved the master of ceremonies aside and signaled two spearmen. They stepped forward and threw their weapons with such force that King Gershom was pinned to his throne with a spear through each breast. He slumped in the throne and his head fell forward onto his chest. The master of ceremonies stepped forward, removed the crown and intoned, "The King is dead." He stood in front of Ishmael, who bowed his head and received the crown. "Long live the King! Long live the King! Long live Ishmael, King of Numidia!"

The two astral voyagers watched as bedlam reigned in the king's tent. Fights ensued, knives were drawn by supporters of the dead king, and were met with swords by the more prepared Muslims. The Christians fled. Many packed their belongings and headed into the desert for the nearest Christian enclave.

Tears clouded the Cahena's sight. The beloved son had betrayed his father. For what? The boy would be controlled by stronger, wiser men. The Berber people required a miracle Cahena could no longer provide. She motioned to Lila and they began the return journey.

CHAPTER 32

WAR

On the return astral journey Lila insisted they make an ostentatious entry to the Carthage fortress. In the tent she undid Cahena's hair, and it was bleached pure white. Lila helped the Queen suit up in her burnished armor, and ordered a contingent of criers to precede them to Carthage. Drummers and trumpeters marched before them. The affect was lightening-like; the people took the color of her hair as a sign the Queen's mystical powers had returned. They cheered until they could no longer speak. In the Carthage fortress, Lila had the Queen sealed off from interruptions as she required rest. Thousands gathered outside the fortress chanting and singing songs of praise to their queen. Lila arranged for Josephus and Yaakov to be secreted in dressed as servants.

The two men spoke over one another. "What happened to your hair? Did you learn what King Gershom will do? How many troops will he send? Do you know when the invasion will begin?"

Lila explained the whiteness of Cahena's hair. Cahena answered, "The trip was successful. What we learned disheartening."

She explained, and Josephus erupted, "That ungrateful little bastard! He kills his own father, whose only goal in life was to give him the crown and secure a long stable reign for the cross-eyed little shit."

"Considering our plan of battle is given to General Walid," the queen said. "Do we have time to change it, or must we surrender?"

"Surrender is out of the question for Pagans and Christians, unless they convert." Yaakov said. "Jews with money can pay the subservient tax. Others must run or die."

"I would not attempt a retreat," Josephus said. "Our army is not disciplined enough."

"What is there to do?" Cahena asked.

"We have two choices," Yakov answered. "Attack or defend."

"Both appear destined to fail," Lila said.

"My Queen," Josephus said, "Your father once said, 'Every problem presents an opportunity'. You two ladies rest. Yaakov and I will search for that opportunity."

Josephus brought in his scouts and officers to the horse-training gallery. There he had cartloads of sand delivered. With the help of these men he built a contour map on the floor. It took in the Maghreb from Tangiers in the south to Carthage in the north, and from the Mediterranean Sea to the Atlas Mountains. He and Yaakov called in the two Bedouin scouts who critiqued the work. The sun had risen when the project was completed. Josephus sent everyone but Yaakov and the two old scouts to breakfast. The four ate while overlooking the mountains, valleys, rivers, and trails laid out before them on the training room floor. The Berber camps were represented by chips of wood, the Muslim forces by camel turds. "The turds are larger and more numerous." Yakov said.

"That's a fact," Josephus said. "We can't underestimate."

"What are you thinking?"

"Divide our forces."

"That violates every rule from Julius Cesar and Hannibal to the lowliest of officers."

"That is why it may work. General Walid and I met when he was recuperating. He knows of my life in the legion; he will never expect me to do that."

"What can you gain?"

"Surprise, momentum, and victory in the opening battle."

"How?"

Josephus took an olive branch switch and pointed at the contour map. "Cahena will take one third of our infantry to the west."

"The prince knows that is the plan. So will General Walid."

"We planned to take all our troops there, hold the enemy at bay and wait for the Numidians to attack them from the rear."

"That's not going to happen."

"But General Walid doesn't know we know the Numidians betrayed us. Therefore he will bring all his might to bear on the high ground."

"Where will the other two thirds of our army be?"

"Following me. We will hug the cliffs along the beaches of the Mediterranean until we are in position to attack the Muslim left flank. We must surprise them, and hit them so hard we roll that flank up into the main army and create a panic."

"And if they don't?"

"Our ass is glass. They'll break us."

Yaakov studied the contour map and reviewed the proposed tactics. "The first part of your plan requires Cahena to lead a third of our forces sixty miles over burnt-out fields with no roads."

"They will have to do it within forty-eight hours from now to convince General Walid. If he doesn't divert his troops, we are lost."

"Can Cahena get our men to march that far and that fast?"

"She must."

Josephus scribbled a message to Ahmed, using five pigeons to carry the same copied note. Those who wrote thought it was coded: "Prepare horses, camels for battle. All livestock distributed as food. Send the tails of three pure white horses, and the largest white stallion you can find, to me."

Josephus and Yaakov explained their plan to Cahena. She walked around the contour map asking questions. "You are using me as bait to draw the main body of the Muslims to the high ground, so you can attack their unprotected flank."

"It is the only way I can manipulate even a temporary numerical superiority," Josephus answered. "You should be able to stave off their initial assaults long enough for me to collapse the Muslim left flank. At the first sign of panic amongst the Muslims, you must attack with everything you have."

"If this fails, is there a secondary plan?"

Yaakov and Josephus looked at each other, but it was the Bedouin scouts who answered. "My Queen, if this does not succeed there will be no more problems."

"You mean, we'll all be dead?"

The four men nodded.

"When should I lead my force to the high ground?"

"Yesterday," Josephus said. "Have your mounted warriors drag shrubs behind to raise a cloud of dust. It will indicate a larger size force than you have. Have each man light a cooking fire. Muslim scouts must think it is our main force. I will lead the remainder of our army to out-flank the Silver Fox."

"Are you referring to General Walid?" Cahena asked.

"His men call him that. He's survived a hundred battles, and if you and Lila had not nursed him back to health, we wouldn't be in the predicament."

"My father, Moshe ben Shimi, had a saying, 'Man plans and God laughs'." Cahena reached out and gathered the four men into her embrace saying in Hebrew, "May it be Your will, our God and God of our fathers, that You lead us to victory. Direct our footsteps to triumph, and help us reach our desired goals. May you rescue us from every ambush, attack, and the plans of our enemy. May You bless our handiwork and grant us grace, kindness, and victory over the Army of Islam. Blessed are You, oh Lord who listens to prayers."

Cahena signaled the two scouts to accompany her. "I have alerted the men, and ask you to lead us on the quickest route to the high ground. What do you think of our chance to succeed in the upcoming battle?"

The two little men looked at each other. One began to weep. The other said, "My little Cahena, it was we who brought the Witch of the Maghreb to the camp of your father, Moshe ben Shimi. Her child was bound to die, and you were needed to live."

"How could you know that?"

"You are not the only one granted special powers. Our entire lives have been spent under the stars, and we learned to read them."

"Then tell me, will the Berber army be victorious?"

"My Queen, we have on occasion lied for you, but never to you." He lowered his head and stared at the floor.

"If disaster awaits, I must protect my sons."

Without raising his head the older man mumbled, "Then do so."

Cahena embraced both men and pressed their faces into her bosom and whispered instructions.

Outside, shouting and sounds of an army readying to march filled the air. It was daylight. Men and animals lined the road leading to the mountains. The two scouts led several heavily laden draught camels.

Like a lethargic sleeping dragon the Berber army came to life. A third of it followed Cahena east to the high ground.

At the Numidian king's oasis Ishmael attempted to appear confidant, but he felt small on the large wood carved throne encrusted with precious gems. Without a spoken word, he slipped into a pattern of accepting the Master of Ceremonies' lead to agree, reject, or postpone a judgment. The most important decsion in his short career as monarch was now before him: to allow those converted Numidians to join the Islamic army against the Berbers. The argument had been made that he was not bound by his father's vows. He could disavow his alliance with Cahena.

"My sovereign," the Master of Ceremonies whispered, "To keep these Muslim zealots among us endangers you and our people. They are fired up with religious fervor. They wish to participate in jihad. Keeping them here will lead to trouble. They will force conversion on our Christians and Pagans. Many nonMuslims are fleeing to their brethren further in the desert. Give these newly made Muslims an opportunity to take out their passion on the Berbers; they will return calmer and more amenable."

Ishmael, the youngest King of Numidia, nodded his approval.

Forty thousand Numidian converts started the long journey to Tangiers. It was an emotional decision, made and implemented in haste. If not for the intervention of Islamic Army scouts, spies, and guides, this Holy Army would have died on route of starvation and thirst. These emissaries of General Walid brought a semblance of order to the enthusiastic horde of converts inspired by Mohammad and blessed by Allah. The scouts convinced the Numidians that they had plenty of time to reach Tangiers before the battle took place—which was untrue—but along the way they could conquer and convert those towns, villages, and cities who had not evacuated. As Muslims, the new converts would be obligated to supply the Holy Army with food, water, and quarters. Many men along the way would be inspired to join the campaign. They could earn a place in heaven if killed, or wealth from looting, tax reductions, and privileges in the expanding Muslim Caliphate if they lived.

Josephus employed his best scouts to lead fifty thousand Berbers out of camp, down to the shores of the Mediterranean, where they hugged the cliffs to avoid being seen. The scouting parties on the bluffs above the beach swept it clean of enemy and shepherds.

Josephus' orders were simple: "If you engage a force you can overcome, kill them. Anyone not of our Army dies. In the case of a larger force, form a rotating screen retreating to the north. Keep them from seeing the main body of our army under the cliffs. We must arrive on the left flank of the Muslims unobserved. When the Muslims attack Cahena's position, we charge them with everything we have."

Out to sea, first one fire and then another and another was seen by the Berbers along the beach. No one had an explanation until two merchant ships sailed directly into the beach, grounding their hulls in the sand. Immediately men abandoned the ships and attempted to flee, but the Muslim crews were surrounded by Berber warriors. Yaakov questioned them and reported to Josephus. Twenty-two Muslim ships carrying light infantry units were to be landed and attack us from the rear, but they had been intercepted by a squadron of seven Roman triremes. It appeared to have been a chance encounter. The Muslims were defeated.

Yaakov learned how the Romans had attacked. Ramming and using Greek Fire, they had destroyed the entire Muslim fleet except for these two craft. "They are supply ships, and ran for shore," he reported. "What do we do with the crews?"

"Kill them," Josephus ordered, "Distribute what food they have, and set a skeleton crew to refloat the ships and guard them."

"Where do you want me?"

"With the boats."

"But I can fight!"

"You're an intellectual, not a fighter. You may have to perform a far more important task."

"What is that?"

"Every legion has a historian. If my plan does not succeed, you must promise to tell the story of the Free People and how the Berbers lost their independence."

"I will feel like a traitor."

"What I am asking you to do is make others understand. Tell them the story about Moshe ben Shimi and his daughter, the Cahena."

"What if you triumph?"

"Then you will have another chapter to add."

"I cannot stay behind!"

"Tomorrow thousands will die. Time will pass, and no one will know why. Your intellect was not meant to be splattered over an unknown battlefield. Those on both sides are not fighting for wealth, power or land. It isn't often men fight for what they believe in. I beg you; do not let our sacrifice be in vain."

The Roman warrior and the rabbinical student embraced.

General Khalid ibn Al Walid received a briefing from his commander of scouts. "The Cahena is leading her entire force to the high ground as the prince predicted. She is pushing them very hard."

"When will she arrive?"

"She can't maintain this pace. We are picking off stragglers. Her men will be exhausted. If they are able to continue, they will arrive in two days."

"Then I'll attack as soon as she takes up her position. Are you certain Cahena is there?"

"Absolutely. Her hair is pure white. The Pagans believe she has regained her mystical powers."

"That could be dangerous. I sense something awry. Did you see Josephus?"

"No, but he doesn't stand out as Cahena does."

"He wouldn't allow her to run her troops into the ground on the eve of a battle." The scouts remained silent and the General said, "Send a reconnaissance party to our left flank on the beach. I want no surprises."

"There is no one left in the Berber camp. We can count cooking fires. They are all on the road to the high ground."

"Make it a small unit, to satisfy me."

"Ibrahim ibn Salah," the chief scout ordered. "Send him and ten mounted men to the beach. When he returns, I want his left foot wet to the knee."

"Why so?"

"To be certain he covered the beach below the cliffs."

Ibrahim ibn Salah was restricted to his tent for smirking at a senior officer. This assignment, although the worst a devote Muslim could be given, he considered a blessing; it allowed him outside. He cursed the officer who had disciplined him as he lined up his men; they were a group of malcontents, sloppy in their morning prayers and slow to obey commands. At least they knew how to mount a horse. Whether they could remain seated was another question.

He checked their weapons, water bags, food, and fodder. Instead of riding at the front, he rode in the rear of the column to be certain no one disappeared. They were a group of slackers, and did not mind missing the glories of battle with the Pagans. They moved at a leisurely pace across burnt-out fields, through the patches of grass, and onto the sandy beach. They walked their horses slowly, talking, joking, and speculating on when the battle would take place.

In front of them they saw a shepherd holding a staff—then another, and another appeared. There were no sheep or goats. "See who they are," Ibrahim ordered.

The soldier replied, "Those aren't staffs; they are spears."

Ibrahim looked up to the cliffs and saw several armed horsemen above, and on the beach behind him twenty more. Outnumbered, with little confidence in his men, he called out a greeting, "Allahu Akbar," hoping they were Muslims.

The riders behind him kept coming, their swords drawn. Ibrahim unbuckled his sword and threw it to the ground. He signaled his men who did the same. The Berbers motioned the Muslims to dismount and pick up their swords. "Use them to dig your graves," the Berber leader ordered.

Some of the Muslims began to weep and wail. Ibrahim cuffed them into silence and said, "We are newly converted Muslims. We only did it to remain alive and take possession of land when this war is over. I am prepared to become Pagan again, and I am certain my men will do the same."

"You are all going to die. Whether it's as a Pagan or Muslim doesn't matter to me."

"Why the hell should we dig our own graves?"

'Because I promise you a relatively painless death if you do." The scout signaled his spearmen. They selected a Muslim, tied a strong rope to each of his ankles, and handed each rope to a horseman. They spurred their animals in opposite directions until the man split in half and parts of his bloody body were dragged through the sand.

"I can make your deaths slower and more painful," the scout said. "Dig."

Ahmed was informed by Berber scouts; he could not deliver his massive herd of horses and camels to Josephus. The Muslim army occupied everything between him and the Berbers on the beach. He had a vast herd of several thousand animals corralled in a wadi on the high ground east of the two confronting armies. He was able to look down on what would become the battlefield. Muslim scouts had been trailing him for days. There were too many animals for them to capture. They watched and reported on Ahmed's movements. He decided that, if he were going to die, he would set the animals free and attempt to escape with his family in the confusion. He had his herders settle the animals down for the night where there was water and enough grass for them. He and his wife prepared two pack camels, and four more to carry his children if they had to escape. He sent two of his herders to inform Cahena.

Cahena maintained the pace of the long column until the marchers began dropping like flies. She halted and ordered everyone to light their own cooking fire. Food was eaten and the troops thought they were settled for the night.

After two hours sleep she rode to the head of the column and relived the two old Bedouin scouts of their pack camels. She undid the burlap bags and ordered the march to resume. Everyone who passed, on both sides of the road filled, their pockets with kaffa beans and chewed them for energy. The stimulant increased their pace. There was even joking and singing in the ranks. She was now certain to arrive at the position selected by Josephus in good time.

Cahena withheld the news about Ahmed and the animal herd from her chieftains. The mounts were of no use in the heights, and Ahmed certainly couldn't reach Josephus. She discussed it with Lila, and both women devised a plan which they sent to Ahmed with his messengers.

By the time Cahena and her force arrived at the designated hill, the effects of the caffeine had worn off. Her men and officers collapsed in place.

Muslim scouts reported this to General Walid. He immediately changed orders to his cavalry and heavy infantry, to cease setting up camp and mount an attack on the enemy's high ground. At first there was confusion in the Muslim ranks, but soon the officers brought order and began forming cohorts and regiments into attack formations.

They were observed by Berber scouts who reported to Cahena and Ahmed. The mute Master of Herds promptly implemented Cahena's plan. First he had the camels driven through the horses to the front in the high-walled wadi, then he had his herders tie bundles of dry brush to the horse's tails.

He observed the enemy below take the field and move into battle formation; the Muslim infantry came first, followed by the cavalry and rank upon rank of archers. The infantry halted, and the formation's right flank stretched across the mouth of wadi—where the Berber herds were hidden. On command, the infantry opened ranks to allow the cavalry to pass through and mount the first attack on the heights. It was a hastily made and ill-conceived plan by an overzealous commander.

His cavalry never reached the Berber lines; they foundered and slid backwards on the steep shale slope. In desperation, the horsemen dismounted to attack on foot. The Berber archers and warriors able to fight were led by Cahena, and they easily repelled the cavalrymen on foot. The enemy withdrew from the slopes, and the infantry prepared to assault.

From above the Wadi overlooking the battlefield, Ahmed signaled. His men lit the bundles of brush tied to the horses' tails. The panicked animals burst into the main herd, driving the camels and other horses ahead of them. The fear-crazed animals with burning brush tied to their tails ran into, over, and through anything in their way. The hooves of seven thousand stampeding animals sounded like thunder. The earth shook.

They burst from the mouth of the wadi into the flank of the Muslim heavy infantry. Men drew their weapons to no avail. Those who stood their ground were trampled. Some saved themselves by grabbing the mane of a horse and were dragged out of the maelstrom. Dead and wounded animals and men were scattered in every direction for a mile.

General Walid held his head in both hands, and moaned. "I never commanded men more dedicated, nor more stupid. Allah, give me patience with these novices who wish to earn a place in heaven."

He set about clearing the battlefield of the dead and wounded soldiers and animals. Camels and horses were butchered, and cooking fires lit. It took well into the night before the task was completed. General Walid called a meeting of his senior officers, who pleaded with him to attack the Berber positions. "The Pagan army is exhausted from the long march," argued his men.

"I don't want to give Cahena another victory when they didn't deserve the first," said Walid.

"They'll believe she really has mystical powers. We have thirty thousand more men than she. Our troops have been training for years and dedicated to Allah. I couldn't lose this fight if I went blind, deaf and dumb. Most of her Jews abandoned her, the Numdians betrayed her, and the scorched-earth policy antagonized many Pagan tribes. She can't win! Have you heard from that patrol I ordered to the Mediterranean shore?"

"No news is good news," the Senior Scout answered.

The general grunted, and gave assignments for a late morning assault against the Berbers. The cavalry he placed on the left flank, with orders to capture or kill fleeing enemy. The light infantry would lead the archers and slingers into battle. "Engage the enemy until the heavy infantry arrives to break through the defenders," he ordered. "The light infantry and archers will slip to the right and left flanks, and surround the enemy. You have one question to potential prisoners. 'Convert or die?' Conversions will take place in camp conducted by our Imams. No ransoming of prisoners, no matter how wealthy or important. Only the Cahena: I want her alive. She saved my life. If she accepts Allah, I will save hers."

"General," a commander ventured, "We could earn great wealth for our cause by ransoming these Pagan chieftains."

"First rule: never leave a potential enemy in your rear. The message must go in advance of our army: capitulate and convert. The more we slaughter now, the less we must fight in the rest of Africa. The caliph has ordered me to lead this army through North Africa, into Libya, then Algeria, and pacify all of Egypt. Killing today will avoid future battles, save lives, and garner more converts tomorrow."

General Khalid ibn Al Walid had one more

meeting before he would sleep. The commander of the defeated Muslim force entered the tent. "General," he said, bowing, "I am to blame for the blunder and today's catastrophe."

"What is your excuse?"

"Stupidity. I deserve to be sentenced to death."

"Yes."

"I have fought at your side on numerous occasions. I committed an unpardonable blunder, but you know I am loyal to Allah, Mohammed, and you."

The general waved impatiently for the man to continue.

"In view of my service, permit me to die in jihad so I might reap the rewards of a shahid, a martyr in the service of Allah."

The general considered. "All that you have spoken is true; many good Muslims died because of your mistake. You should have secured your right flank. Your previous actions in the name of Allah have earned you the right to choose your place in the attack formation. Have you thought how you will explain to your men already in heaven?"

The Commander shook his head and replied, "No, but Allah is all merciful."

As was his custom, the general slept in his armor the night before a battle. His sleep was deep and untroubled. He awoke to the Muezzin's call to Morning Prayer. He ate a breakfast of cheese, hot bread, figs, olives, and tea. He buckled on his sword presented him by the Prophet and went out to inspect his troops.

The messengers from Ahmed to Josephus informed him of the stampede in the opening battle for the Maghreb. Josephus was pleased by the success, but had to revise his plan of attack. The messengers also witnessed the morning Muslim formation for attack. Josephus especially questioned their reports that the Muslim cavalry could not be used in the attack and was protecting the left flank of General Walid's army. "My infantry will scatter them," he said.

The messengers handed over a large saddle-bag from Ahmed. It contained the tails of three white horses. They also informed Josephus that a large white stallion was tethered outside.

"Bring in Musa," Josephus ordered

"The one they called Tiny?"

"Yes. And fetch someone who knows how to sew."

A six-foot-tall Berber entered Josephus' tent. "Now you will learn why I had you transferred to my personal guard," Josephus said. He held up the three white horses tails and said, "These will be sewn as a wig for you. You will wear clothes and armor exactly like Cahena. It will inspire our men. I will instruct you."

Pleased by his scouts' reports of the Muslim left flank being guarded by their cavalry, Josephus placed his most skilled fighters opposite them. He had trained his men for more than a year how to take advantage of mounted enemy, but even this advantage did not allay his fears of defeat. The enemy numbered thirty-thousand more men; they had trained together for five years, and were led by a military genius. Josephus re-examined his plans and could not improve on any aspect, which troubled him. He reviewed again, and listened to the reports of his scouts as General Walid set in motion a second attack on Cahena's position.

Forty thousand Berbers lay in the sand at the base of the bluffs, and waited. Cahena, with only thirty thousand fighters, had her chieftains utilize every aspect of the terrain to enhance her defenses. They worked loose boulders to create landslides, made piles of rocks to be hurled, and sharpened stakes angled into the earth. She expected the Muslim light infantry to initiate the battle, and Josephus told her to hold a force of ten thousand in reserve. His message read:

"The light infantry will slip to your right and left flanks, trying to surround you. Their place in the front line will be taken by the heavy infantry supported by archers and slingers. Your reserve force must stop the flanking movement. You must hold the line until the heavy infantry retreats. They will be sent against you a second time, and again you must hold. Tomorrow, when they attack again, use every man in the front line. When you are fully committed I will charge their left flank. The moment you see the effect of my attack on those facing you, charge downhill with all your forces. Pull those units in from protecting the flanks and meet me in the middle of the battlefield."

Cahena accepted Josephus' directions, but she also had instructions from another source.

During her sleep she was visited by a spirit. It took Cahena on a journey over a battlefield strewn with dead bodies. They were mostly Berbers, and those who walked the battlefield in victory were Muslims. She saw her own body face down in the mud, her head severed and left arm missing. Her sons stared at her body, then looked at each other, then to Cahena. She attempted to reassure them but they could not hear her. She panicked and woke herself shouting for them to run, then realized they had no place to go. Lila entered the tent and attempted to comfort her. Cahena asked for the senior shaman of the Berbers to interpret the dream.

"You do not require mystical powers to interpret the end."

"What of my children? I haven't been a good mother. They don't deserve to suffer because of me." Lila did not answer. The two women sat in silence for some time. Cahena said, "I must go out to the troops. The attack will begin soon. Send in the two old scouts; I have a special task for them."

Cahena mounted her white stallion in full armor, and when she appeared to the troops they roared, "We have Cahena!" The chant resounded from the heights into the valley where the enemy infantry had formed. Trumpets sounded below, and the Muslims roared back, "Allahu Akbar! Allahu Akbar!"

Whistles shrieked, drums boomed, and the Muslim light infantry marched forward shoulder to shoulder. They started up the incline in good order, but as the slope became steeper men's feet slipped and slid on the loose shale. Officers attempted to keep the cadence in time with the drums, but the lines wavered as men slipped and staggered. They slowed but did not stop until the first hail of stones rained down on them. They faltered again when large boulders were loosed from above and landslides tore through their ranks. They reformed while under attack and drove hard up the slope. Some crawled on all fours to close with the enemy. Men covered themselves with shields to deflect the arrows and stones, and died moaning, "Allahu Akbar!" A few reached the Berber lines but were easily dispatched.

General Khalid ibn Al Walid watched with pride as his men never faltered in the attack. His only regret was that he could not lead and die with them. He gave the signal for the light infantry to break off the attack, divide their forces and slide to the right and left flanks. The heavy infantry, with their long black-and-gold oblong shields and sixteen foot spears stepped out in formation up the slopes. They were followed by archers and slingers. On the steeper part of the slope the commanders ordered, "Half-step march!"

There was less slipping, but slower progress. Once within range of the Berber missiles the Muslim infantry commanders ordered, "Turtle formation!" The forward, right and left flank soldiers kept their shields straight up. Those behind raised their shields overhead. Enemy arrows, rocks and missiles smashed harmlessly on the shields, but the slope steepened. Men began to slip and slide. The commanders issued another order, and while under cover of the turtle the troopers bent over on all fours, putting their helmets in the backsides of the men in front, and continued crawling up the slope. Cahena ordered a flight javelins to no avail. Slowly but surely, the deadly turtle crept forward. She moved her long spearmen into the front ranks in preparation for the clash. She had prepared a number of large boulders she ordered cut loose. They crushed those in the packed enemy ranks but therest kept coming shouting, "Allahu Akbar!"

"They were answered by, "We have Cahena!" The Berbers had the advantage of the high ground, and when the turtle lowered its shields they unleashed their fury. Muslim bodies piled up one on the other. They had to climb over their own dead and wounded to reach the Berbers, where more of them died. They never faltered until General Walid sounded the recall trumpets. He personally greeted each unit and praised their courage and skill. "We will go at them again tomorrow until the Barbers no longer exist. Allahu Akbar!"

Cahena received word that Josephus would wait no longer. Tomorrow when the Muslims attacked he would strike their left flank. It would be the final battle.

At midnight the two Bedouin scouts entered

Cahena's tent. She asked, "What did he say?"

"He thanks you for allowing him to repay your kindness in nursing him back to health. The general is not a married man, so he cannot adopt your sons. His brother will."

"Is his brother a good man?"

"General Walid says, he is not a warrior but a recognized Muslim scholar teaching in Mecca. He brought the general into Islam, and was a student of the Prophet himself. The boys will be raised as Muslims."

"They have been introduced to that religion. I am only glad my father is not here to witness this."

"We knew your father as an understanding man. He would want his grandsons to live."

"His Jewish name will die with me."

"His bloodline will continue through your sons."

"They will be Muslims."

"It seems to us, you both worship the same God under different names."

"But with different purposes."

Cahena gathered the two little men in her arms and said, "I owe you so much. What can I do for you?"

"We have two of your swiftest camels and your love. Nothing more is needed. We will disappear after we deliver the children and

Lila."

"Where will the exchange take place?"

"There is a sacred tree to the right of the battlefield. Even the Muslims wouldn't violate their oath under this Pagan shrine."

"When do you leave?"

"Now."

"I will prepare the children." Cahena went to their tent and woke each one with a kiss. "Your uncles are going to take you on a special nighttime trip," she said. "You will see all the stars and meet one of the greatest generals who ever lived. Your mother loves you, and may the God of Israel bless and protect you."

The two scouts rode double with the children, and Lila followed on her own camel. They sauntered out of camp down the eastern slopes like shadows using the clouds masking the sky to pass through the Muslim lines without being challenged. They arrived at a gnarled olive tree believed to be fifteen hundred years old. From its branches fluttered thousands of strips of cloth representing prayers. The children had fallen asleep and were transferred with Lila to Muslim horses. Nothing was said. The two Bedouin disappeared into the night.

Cahena awoke with an empty feeling in her heart. It was for her two boys. Never before had she missed them, or thought about their future.

The Islamic army had an overwhelming superiority in numbers and training. She considered surrender, but her Christian, Pagan, and Jewish warriors expressed their desire to die in combat rather than to bow before the Muslims. In every battle it was always the will to win that triumphed, not just the numbers of the enemy. Her men were rested, and ready. Josephus' surprise attack on the Muslims left flank had a chance of success. Victory was possible.

For the first time in years Cahena performed her morning prayers in Hebrew. She went outside with her white hair unbound and flowing behind her. She mounted her stallion and rode from one end of the front line to the other, greeting soldiers by name. The troops roared, "We have Cahena!"

From below, the great Muslim Army of more than a hundred thousand men arose from their prayer rugs and chanted, "Allahu Akbar! Allahu Akbar!" Then they chanted, "Dihya, you die this morning! Dihya, you die this morning!"

The prince had revealed the secret name of Cahena, and it was bad luck to be said aloud. General Walid had his men chant it as they lined up in battle formation. Cahena was the only one shocked by this; her men had no idea what it meant. She broke into a cold sweat and knew she was going to die. The worst of it was that everything she had hoped for, a Free Berber country, the liberating of Jerusalem, and secure borders for the Maghreb, would not happen. Anger welled up in her stomach, enveloped her heart, and she gave the order for an all-out attack. She dismounted to lead the charge wielding her great sword and shield. The Berber Army leapt out of their shallow trenches and with the downhill momentum pushed the front ranks of the Muslim heavy infantry aside. They barreled downhill until they reached the eleventh rank that stood their ground, and then it was shield to shield, sword against sword, and battle axes hacking away at each other.

During the night Josephus had secreted his entire army of forty thousand men up on the bluffs, in position to attack the Muslim left flank. He watched as the enemy heavy infantry valiantly crawled up the slopes. They were initially stopped, regained their coordination—and that was when he saw Cahena attack. She was supposed to wait for him to initiate the assault on the flank.

He watched as the Berbers broke through the enemy ranks until they ran out of strength. The discipline of the Muslims was better than Josephus had expected. He was left with no alternative. He gave the signal.

Ram's horns blew, whistles shrieked, and the Berber army arose from the grass and marched into the attack.

"I knew something was wrong!" General Walid shouted. "Signal the cavalry to engage the Berbers on the left flank! Signal the infantry units from the twentieth rank to face left and be prepared to defend! That Roman bastard split his forces."

The General ordered his reserve archers and slingers to attack the unprotected Berber right flank, and this master-stroke doomed the Pagans. Their archers and slinger were in the center, and could not respond to the missiles raining down on their flank. On the other side of the Berber formation their infantry dispersed the Muslim cavalry with ease, but it slowed forward progress and gave the Muslims time to strengthen their lines and organize a defense. They stood strong and stopped the Berber attack.

Josephus led the attack astride an old war horse. He signaled behind him. Suddenly the rear ranks parted and Cahena appeared in full armor astride a large white stallion. Her white hair flowed behind as she galloped down the entire length of the formation. The troops roared. "We have Cahena!"

Tiny rode in front of the army brandishing a

long sword and shield. He reined his horse in and up on its hind legs, forelegs pawing the air. He pointed his sword forward and led the army into the attack at a walk. Forty thousand men stepped forward to join their queen. Tiny nudged his horse, and the momentum picked up. The men trotted to get ahead of the Cahena as they charged the Muslim flank.

General Walid was taken aback to see a second Cahena appear on his left flank, and realized one of them was false. "That damned Roman is clever. He is desperate to have split his forces."

But he realized the danger, and immediately set about reorganizing and moving troops from his right and left flanks. He ordered a division of heavy infantry from the rear to strike the flank of the attackers. Through clever manipulation of his forces and courageous fighting, Khalid managed to split the attacking Berber formation in half. He sent in his cavalry to cut down the broken enemy units. The General signaled a cohort of heavy infantry to pass through his archers and attack Josephus' right flank.

The timing was perfect, and the Berbers unprepared. The Muslim heavy infantry cut a swath through the Berber ranks and confusion ensued. Commanders lost control of their units. It was mass of individual fights. General Walid sent a second cohort into the attack. They took control and crushed the Berbers into the sand.

Further up the hill, Cahena's force was surrounded. She was covered with mud and blood. A group formed around her and they fought valiantly, but they fell one after the other. Cahena chewed coffee beans and wielded her great sword and shield with the strength of a lioness. Wherever she fought, men fell like mown wheat—but after an hour off continuous fighting her sword strokes and her step slowed. The men around her were cut down. The enemy climbed over Berber bodies to get at her. She was struck from behind by a battle ax. Her left arm went numb and the shield fell from her hand. A Muslim warrior in front of her saw the opening and rammed his spear through her stomach and out her back. Her pure white hair was red with blood from a head wound.

The surviving Berbers surrounded her body, shouting, "We have Cahena!"—and fought to the last. Their bodies covered hers. In their fury, Muslim warriors hacked and chopped all the Berber bodies into pieces, Cahena's body included.

She was never identified.

Other Berbers dropped their weapons from exhaustion. In six hours of battle, forty-five thousand warriors died from both sides. Those

Berbers who lived, converted to Islam. Cahena was brought before General Walid, only to reveal himself as a male Berber warrior. Tiny chose death rather than conversion.

Josephus had no reserves to assist his men being slaughtered by the combination of Muslim heavy infantry and cavalry working in perfect coordination. They were followed by a division of light infantry, who swept the field. Josephus gathered those commanders still with him, saying: "You may run, convert, or fight with me. Be certain, if you choose the latter you will die." He took out his whetstone and ran it up and down the edges of his short sword.

His senior officer struck Josephus behind the neck, knocking him unconscious. He and three junior officers tied his hands and legs and carried him to the beach where Yaakov, who had disobeyed orders, waited with the two ships. He took aboard many survivors before fire arrows made it impossible to remain, and then set course for the island of Djerba.

Cahena *Warrior Queen*

Dihya (Cahena) memorial in Khenchela, Algeria

Stories abound about Cahena's death. Most prevalent is that she died in battle. Others claim she took poison to avoid being tempted to convert to Islam. One story by Ibn Khaldun marks her death in 703 AD. She would have been 127 years old. It is accepted by all scholars that Cahena passed into the historical realm of myth, legend and fable. Many Berbers who today remain Pagans worship her among other gods. Some modern day freedom movements in Algeria and Morocco use her as an inspiring symbol of freedom.

Her sons Bagay and Khanchla, (their Muslim names) were converted and raised by General Walid's brother. Rather than become scholars, they followed their mother. They developed into military leaders of the Berber-Muslim Army invading Iberia. They entered Spain in 712 CE and conquered it by 735 CE.

The story of Cahena is taught in North African schools as a legend. If you were to speak seriously about her exploits, most modern Berbers would consider you unusually naïve. She did exist. She was a Jewess and a powerful Queen of the Berbers, Bedouin and Tuaregs. She defeated Roman Legions, held the Muslim army at bay for five years, and did succumb to the love of a sophisticated Persian prince. His burnt earth policy is deemed the cause of her demise. Her father's dream of rebuilding the Holy Temple in Jerusalem was never fulfilled. However, starting in 1948 CE almost one million Jews migrated from North Africa to Israel. They and their descendants believe the Temple will be rebuilt.

General Khalid ibn Al Walid, the Sword of Allah, led the Muslim armies to victory in Iran, Iraq, Syria and Lebanon. He never lost a war. He is studied in most modern war colleges as one of the greatest Generals who ever lived. Islamic scholars claim because he became a devout Muslim; western scholars pay little attention to his genius. The end of his military career came about because of religious politics, something the General never discussed.

The Fourth Caliph was convinced the General was a supporter of the Shiite faction of Islam, and discharged him from the army. His only wish was to die in a Holy War. He changed his name, disguised himself and served as a common soldier in the ranks for two years before being exposed. He was again discharged and died a natural death in bed. It is said there was hardly an inch of skin of his body that was not scarred. To this day storytellers in coffee houses of the mid-east tell of the exploits of Khalid ibn Al Walid. He captured Jerusalem from the Romans and in the year 637 CE. The Caliph allowed Jews to return to their Holy City, but very few took advantage of the opportunity.

Josephus left the island of Djerba vowing to assassinate Babylonian Prince Armah. Something he never accomplished. He died dead drunk in the streets of Sicily.

Prince Armah did not inherit the Babylonian throne. His father was murdered by the King's brother. The uncle became emperor and lost his Empire in war to General Walid. Islam became the official religion from present day Afghanistan in the east to Greece in the south and Belarus in the north.

Lila, Cahena's senior shaman, disappeared after Cahena's sons were adopted.

Ahmed and his family escaped. They converted to Islam, He fathered four more children and had a total of four boys and three girls. Two brothers who own a car dealership in the city of Tunis claim to be descendants of the mute cameleer.

Yaakov went on to be a scholar. He was invited by the Jewish community to teach in Cordova, Spain. His family lived there until 1492 when Queen Isabella confiscated Jewish properties to finance Columbus' voyage, and expelled the Jews. Yaakov's family settled in Holland, where he took on the surname of that country as his. Four hundred and fifty years later, his descendants were turned over to the Nazis by their Dutch neighbors. Only one survived, and recently passed away in Bnei Brak, Israel.

A few Jews remain in Djerba. Most returned to Israel after 1948. Many live in Safed, where I was privileged to teach their children for twenty years and was inspired to write the story of Cahena.

Abu Abak the storyteller is a fictional character based on the life of Ar-Rabī' bin Abī 'l-Huqayq (Arabic: الحقيق يبأ نب عيبرلا) a Jewish poet of the Banu al-Nadir in Medina. His poems and prose are heard in present day coffee houses and studied in Islamic Universities.

The hospice built by Cahena for Ozeret the Witch of the Maghreb no longer exits. It became a watering point for Rommel's troops and later Montgomery's British army in the Second World War battle for the African desert.

The Prophet Mohammad set in motion one of the greatest religious movements in the history of mankind. The influence of Islam is so vast and intrinsically involved in the evolution of mankind it requires a life time of study to understand. It is continuing to evolve and inspire people to this day.

The first caliph died of natural causes. The following three were assassinated. The Sunni (orthodox) Muslims was and remains the largest faction in Islam. They comprise ninety percent of present day Muslims. Shiites make up only eight percent and other groups compose the one billion Muslims in the world today. They equal the number of Christians. The concept of *Dar al-Islam* and Dar al-harb, (the world of Islam and the World of War) continues as part of Sharia Law. Adherents believe there can be no peace between Islam and non-believers. Cessation of fighting is only a strategic truce.

Caliph Umar ibn al-Khattab in 638 permitted Jews to return to Jerusalem after 568 years of Roman rule. Some believe he was assassinated for doing so.

Below is the list of battles fought by Islamic armies in the following sixty-three years.

BATTLES OF ISLAM TO THE YEAR 700 CE

637: Conquest of Syria, Conquest of Jerusalem, Battle of Jalula.

638: Conquest of Jazirah.

639: Conquest of Khuzistan. Advance into Egypt. Plague of Emmaus.

640: Battle of Babylon in Egypt.

641: Conquest of Alexandria in Egypt.

642: Battle of Nihawand; Conquest of Egypt.

643: Conquest of Azarbaijan and Tabaristan (Mazandaran).

644: Conquest of Fars, Kerman, Sistan, Mekran and Kharan. Assassination of Umar. Uthman ibn Affan becomes the caliph.

644: 5 November—Assassination of Umar, second caliph of Islam. buried in the house of Aisha in Medina.

646: Campaigns in Khurasan, Armenia and Asia Minor.

647: Campaigns in North Africa. Conquest of the island of Cyprus.

648: Campaigns against the Byzantines.

650: First conflict between Arabs and Turks. Khazars defeated an Arab force led by Abd ar-Rahman ibn Rabiah outside the Khazari town of Balanjar.

652: Disaffection against the rule of Uthman.

655: Naval battle of the Masts against the Byzantines.

656: 17 June — Assassination of Uthman, the third Caliph of Islam. Ali ibn Abi Talib becomes the fourth caliph.

656: 10 December— Battle of the Camel.

657: Ali shifts the capital from Medina to Kufa.

Battle of Siffin.

658: Battle of Nahrawan.

659: Conquest of Egypt by Muawiyah I.

660: Ali recaptures Hijaz and Yemen from Muawiyah. Muawiyah I declares himself as the caliph at Damascus.

661: 29 January— Ali ibn Abi Talib, fourth Caliph, is assassinated by Kharijites. buried in Najaf, Iraq.

662: Kharijites' revolts.

666: Muawia bin Hudeij raids Sicily.[4] Abdu'l-Rahman ibn Abu Bakr,[5][6] Muhammad ibn Maslamah and Ramlah bint Abi Sufyan dies.

669: Hasan ibn Ali, the second imam of the Shiites is poisoned and killed. Husayn ibn Ali becomes Imam of Ali ibn Abi Talib's followers.

View of the Mosque of Uqba founded in 670 by Uqba bin Nafe, Kairouan, Tunisia.670: Advance in North Africa. Uqba bin Nafe founds the town of Kairouan in Tunisia.[7] Conquest of Kabul.

672: Capture of the island of Rhodes. Campaigns in Khurasan.

674: The Muslims cross the Oxus. Bukhara becomes a vassal state.

676: Muhammad al-Baqir, the fifth imam of the Shiites is born.

677: Occupation of Samarkand and Tirmiz. Siege of Constantinople.

680: 28 April— Death of Muawiyah. Yazid I

becomes caliph.

680: 10 October— Battle of Karbala and Husayn bin Ali is killed along with his companions. Ali ibn Husayn becomes Imam of Ali ibn Abi Talib's followers.

682: North Africa Uqba bin Nafe marches to the Atlantic, is ambushed and killed at Biskra. The Muslims evacuate Kairouan and withdraw to Burqa.

683: 11 November— Death of Yazid I. Muawiya II becomes caliph.

684: June— Muawiya II abdicated.

684: Abd Allah ibn Zubayr declares himself as the caliph at Mecca. Marwan I becomes the caliph at Damascus. Battle of Marj Rahit.

685: Death of Marwan I. Abd al-Malik becomes the caliph at Damascus. Battle of 'Ayn al-Warda.

686: Al-Mukhtar declares himself as the caliph at Kufa.

687: Battle of Kufa between the forces of Mukhtar and Abd Allah ibn Zubayr. Mukhtar killed.

691: Battle of Maskin. Kufa falls to Abd al-Malik.

692: October— The fall of Mecca. Death of ibn Zubayr. Abdul Malik becomes the sole caliph.

695: Kharijites' revolts in Jazira and Ahwaz. Battle of the Karun. The Muslims once again withdraw to Barqa. The Muslims advance in Transoxiana and occupy Kish.

www.ingramcontent.com/pod-product-compliance
Lightning Source LLC
Chambersburg PA
CBHW050146130526
44591CB00033B/695